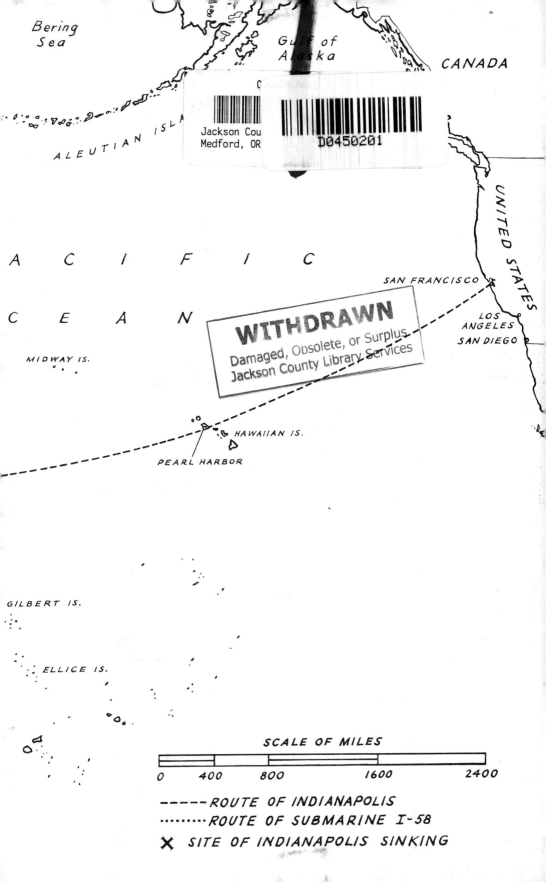

Bering
Sea

Gulf of
Alaska

CANADA

ALEUTIAN ISLA

P A C I F I C

O C E A N

UNITED STATES

SAN FRANCISCO

LOS
ANGELES

SAN DIEGO

MIDWAY IS.

HAWAIIAN IS.

PEARL HARBOR

GILBERT IS.

ELLICE IS.

SCALE OF MILES

| 0 | 400 | 800 | 1600 | 2400 |

------ ROUTE OF INDIANAPOLIS

·········· ROUTE OF SUBMARINE I-58

✗ SITE OF INDIANAPOLIS SINKING

ALSO BY DAN KURZMAN

A Killing Wind: Inside Union Carbide and the Bhopal Catastrophe

Day of the Bomb: Countdown to Hiroshima

Ben-Gurion: Prophet of Fire

Miracle of November: Madrid's Epic Stand 1936

The Bravest Battle: The 28 Days of the Warsaw Ghetto Uprising

The Race for Rome

Genesis 1948: The First Arab-Israeli War

Santo Domingo: Revolt of the Damned

Subversion of the Innocents

Kishi and Japan: The Search for the Sun

The Sinking of

the USS *Indianapolis*

FATAL VOYAGE

DAN KURZMAN

NEW YORK   *Atheneum*   1990

Atheneum
Macmillan Publishing Company
866 Third Avenue, New York, N.Y. 10022
Collier Macmillan Canada, Inc.

Library of Congress Cataloging-in-Publication Data
Kurzman, Dan.
Fatal voyage : the sinking of the USS Indianapolis / Dan Kurzman.
p.   cm.
Includes bibliographical references.
ISBN 0-689-12007-9
1. Indianapolis (Cruiser)   2. World War, 1939–1945—Naval operations, American.   3. Shipwrecks—Pacific Ocean.   I. Title.
D774.I5K87   1990
940.54′5973—dc20   89-77074
CIP

Macmillan books are available at special discounts for bulk purchases for sales promotions, premiums, fund-raising, or educational use. For details, contact:

Special Sales Director
Macmillan Publishing Company
866 Third Avenue
New York, N.Y. 10022

10 9 8 7 6 5 4 3 2

Designed by Jack Meserole

PRINTED IN THE UNITED STATES OF AMERICA

For my dear wife, FLORENCE—

who illuminates my life

as the moon does the sea

CONTENTS

ACKNOWLEDGMENTS

I am especially grateful to my wife and collaborator, Florence, for her invaluable assistance on this book. She helped to edit it with her usual professional excellence, rewriting passages and inspiring some of the narrative.

I also wish to thank Thomas Stewart and Evan Oppenheimer, my editors at Atheneum, for their fine editorial suggestions; Mitch Douglas, my agent at ICM for his support and encouragement; Kinji Kawamura, director of the Japan Press Center in Tokyo, and his assistant, Seiichi Soeda, for their unstinting help in arranging interviews with former members of the *I-58* submarine crew; Yoko Okabe, Manami Shimizu, and Yuko Yamaoka for their skillful interpreting and translating; and Richard Deane Taylor for his excellent map of the Pacific Ocean area.

Others deserving of my thanks include Lieutenant Colonel Peter Badger, Anita M. Coley, Captain Nick De Carlo, and Lieutenant William Van Blarcum of the Office of the Judge Advocate General, Department of the Navy; Captain Patricia Gormley of the Office of the Naval Inspector General; Mike Walker and Kathy Lloyd of the Naval Historical Center; Janice Beattie, Paula Murphy, and John Vajde of the Navy Department Library; and David R. Kepley of the National Archives.

Among those kind enough to grant me interviews were:

Ensign Donald J. Blum—officer, *Indianapolis*
Yeoman Second Class Victor R. Buckett—sailor, *Indianapolis*
Captain John P. Cady—defense counsel for Captain McVay
Seaman First Class Grover Carver—sailor, *Indianapolis*
Seaman Adolfo Celaya—sailor, *Indianapolis*
Lieutenant Commander W. Graham Claytor—commander,
  Cecil J. Doyle
Gunner Earl R. Duxbury—member, Lieutenant Marks' crew
Radioman Robert G. France—member, Lieutenant Marks'
  crew
Major Robert R. Furman—custodian, atomic bomb
Betty Gray Gibson—wife of Lieutenant Stuart Gibson
Lieutenant Wilbur C. Gwinn—Ventura pilot
Commander Mochitsura Hashimoto—skipper, *I-58*
Yeoman Second Class Otha A. Havins—sailor, *Indianapolis*
Lieutenant Commander Lewis L. Haynes—medical officer,
  Indianapolis
Edward Hidalgo—assistant to Navy Secretary James Forrestal
Ernest J. King, Jr.—son of Fleet Admiral King
Gordon Linke—stepson of Captain McVay
Jocelyn Linke—wife of Gordon Linke
Lieutenant R. Adrian Marks—seaplane pilot
Private First Class Giles G. McCoy—Marine, *Indianapolis*
Lieutenant Charles B. McKissick—officer, *Indianapolis*
Betsy McVay—wife of Kimo McVay
Charles B. McVay IV—Captain McVay's elder son
Kimo Wilder McVay—Captain McVay's younger son
Kinau Wilder McVay—Captain McVay's first wife
Katherine D. Moore—widow of Lieutenant Commander
  K. C. Moore
Master-at-Arms Eugene Morgan—sailor, *Indianapolis*
Captain Oliver F. Naquin—surface operations officer, Guam
Florence Regosia—Captain McVay's maid
Lieutenant Richard B. Redmayne—chief engineer, *Indianapolis*
Admiral Harry Sanders—Captain McVay's superior
Chief Donald H. Shown—sailor, *Indianapolis*

Winthrop Smith, Jr.—stepson of Captain McVay
E. Seward Stevens—lawyer of Vivian Smith McVay
John Sullivan, Jr.—son of court-martial judge
Lieutenant Hirokoto Tanaka—navigator, *I-58*
Lieutenant Toshio Tanaka—chief torpedo officer, *I-58*
Ensign Harlan M. Twible—officer, *Indianapolis*
Private First Class Paul R. Uffelman—Marine, *Indianapolis*
John P. Williams—cousin of Lieutenant Stuart Gibson

FATAL VOYAGE

I

The Victor and the Vanquished

THE TWO MEN furtively exchanged glances across the bare, whitewashed courtroom in the Washington Navy Yard, intrigued, it seemed, by the irony reflected in each other's eyes.

Captain Charles Butler McVay III, a strikingly handsome man with slightly pouting lips, dark, dramatically arched eyebrows, a stubborn chin, and graying hair, sat ramrod-straight in his chair, resplendent in his blue naval officer's uniform. His chest was ablaze with battle ribbons, one of them signifying the Silver Star, which he had won for displaying courage under fire.

Now, in December 1945, the forty-six-year-old skipper was under fire again, and his cool manner once more attested to his courage. But no medals would be won in this battle, and not even victory could remove the taint of the catastrophe that had befallen his men. About five months earlier, on July 17, McVay's heavy cruiser, the USS *Indianapolis*, sailed from San Francisco for the Pacific island of Tinian and, after unloading there the vital parts of the atomic bomb that would destroy Hiroshima, headed toward the Philippine Islands. En route it was sunk by a Japanese submarine, and only 316 out of 1196 men aboard survived—after floundering for five days in the shark-infested waters of the Pacific Ocean, most of them supported only by life preservers. It was the worst sea disaster in American naval history.

McVay, one of the survivors, was being court-martialed for "suffering a vessel to be hazarded through negligence" (failing to steer a zigzag course), and "culpable inefficiency in the performance of duty" (failing to make sure his crew abandoned ship in time). He was the first captain ever to be tried by the U.S. Navy for losing his ship in battle, and his pain was all the greater since his family was steeped in naval tradition.

And now, the final humiliation. There, sitting uneasily as a witness at the prosecution's table was Mochitsura Hashimoto, the thirty-six-year-old commander of the Japanese submarine *I-58*, which had sunk the *Indianapolis*. Hashimoto's close-cropped hair covered a square-shaped head that broadened into expansive jaws, and his sizable pointed nose overlooked tightly clamped lips. His short, stocky physique was draped in an unpressed civilian blue suit and an ill-fitting frayed white shirt with the collar sloppily turned up.

The contrasting images of McVay and Hashimoto lent a rather startling touch to the irony of the occasion. While McVay appeared elegant and calm, Hashimoto looked rumpled and anxious. One personified World War II's victor, the other, its vanquished—except that the victor, in this bizarre courtroom context, was at the mercy of the vanquished.

This extraordinary confrontation brutally symbolized McVay's ordeal. The *Indianapolis* tragedy and its aftermath had transformed the skipper into a troubled, introspective figure his old friends could hardly recognize. He had always been a happy man who lived life to the fullest, never taking it too seriously, forever humming "Pennies from Heaven" or some other cheerful tune, telling jokes to his comrades over a dry martini and, at least until his second marriage, living up to his nickname, "Rabbit," which he had richly earned at Annapolis. He was constantly in search of feminine company, not a difficult pursuit since his charm, good looks, and athletic build (he had competed in swimming, tennis, and soccer at school) attracted some of the world's most beautiful women, including movie star Signe Hasso, who shared his cabin on a voyage from the Philippines to San Francisco.

Another stunning conquest was the heiress Kinau Wilder, the great-granddaughter of Dr. Gerrit Parmele Judd, the first missionary to settle in Hawaii, which at that time was a Polynesian kingdom. In 1831, three years after his arrival, his wife, a descendant of a Pilgrim who came over on the *Mayflower*, gave birth to a girl, the first white child to be born in Hawaii.

According to legend, Queen Kinau, a six-foot, four-hundred-pound giant, "kidnapped" the child and refused to give her back to her parents. "God will punish you!" Judd warned the heathen queen, and he proceeded to perform a "miracle" to impress her; he turned his Bible upside down and pretended to read it, though in fact he knew the passages by heart. Stunned, the queen cried, "It is a sign from heaven," and she handed the baby back to her father. But the child, she demanded, must take her name, Kinau.

"I am sorry," said Judd, "but I cannot give this Christian child a heathen name."

Thereupon, the queen agreed to be baptized and the child was given her name, breaking an ancient taboo that no commoner could bear the given name of royalty. Together with this honor, the queen gave her "adopted" daughter a choice piece of the Crown Lands at Waikiki, where the family would live for generations in a beautiful mansion known as Kinau Hale, or the House of Kinau. Judd himself eventually became prime minister of the kingdom and helped to modernize it, enjoying the rights of royalty and preserving these rights for his descendants.

Born in 1902, his great-granddaughter, who also bore the royal first name, was blessed with a vivacious, irrepressible personality and a genteel beauty reminiscent of actress Bette Davis. She had large, mischievous eyes and an engaging smile. Kinau Wilder lived like a princess—and suffered like one, under the domination of an overbearing and overprotective mother. Determined to escape from her palatial prison, she saw Charles McVay as just the white knight to whisk her to freedom.

Kinau first glimpsed him in 1923 at a party in San Francisco's Fairmont Hotel and immediately told her girl friend: "Hands off! That's the man I am going to marry!" Later that evening, at another party, they met and danced, and four days afterward Ensign McVay, who had graduated from Annapolis three years earlier, proposed marriage. They were wed in a lavish "royal" ceremony at Kinau Hale under a flowering kamani tree, with the bride wearing a ten-foot-long lei of white ginger blossoms looped around her neck and festooned on her arm.

But the blossoms soon faded. On their modestly budgeted honeymoon, tailored to McVay's Navy income, Kinau, who was accustomed to a legion of servants and had never cooked before, dropped a lobster into a pot of boiling water and nearly fainted when the creature vaulted out. She thereupon hired a chef and never cooked for her husband again. It grew clear who would pay the bills, a fact the proud young officer accepted reluctantly.

When McVay was posted to Washington in 1925, he, Kinau, and an infant son were greeted at the train station by the ensign's father, Admiral Charles B. McVay II.

"Son," announced the admiral, "we've bought a house and you will live with us and help pay for it."

Kinau, who had only recently sprung loose from her mother's clutches, grew pale, but the son acquiesced. From the time he was born in Ephrata, Pennsylvania, in 1898, the younger McVay would almost never defy the admiral, who had himself been born into a Navy-oriented family. Charles B. McVay I, who had been president of the Pittsburgh Trust Company, made large donations to the Naval Academy and was rewarded with honorary membership in the class of 1890.

Charles II had arranged for his son to attend Yates Academy, then asked President Woodrow Wilson to give him an appointment to Annapolis in 1916. The young man must one day match his own record. In the Spanish-American War, the father had shared the glory of victory as an ensign; in World War I he had commanded the *Saratoga*, the *New Jersey*, and the *Oklahoma*; and after that war he had headed the Washington Navy Yard (where his son would be tried), the Bureau of Ordnance, and finally the U.S. Asiatic Fleet. Yes, his son would be an admiral like himself. No questions asked.

Charles III feared his father, but he loved him, too, if in the impersonal way a nonobservant believer might love God; in any case, as much as a son could love a father who cast an awesome shadow he could not escape. The elder McVay had not always been tyrannical, not before he had hardened himself to the point he considered necessary to reach the military pinnacle. Yet Charles III never really knew the more loving and sentimental father because the elder man, like the son he would mold, was seldom home. In fact, when the son was born, the father, a young ensign serving somewhere on the high seas, didn't even know about it until days later. When he found out, he wrote to his wife Edith in a manner he would almost certainly frown upon as gushy nonsense in later years:

> I long to see you both . . . I was looking at your picture before going to bed, as I always do, and was hoping that the boy would look like his mother. . . . I am happy and proud and very much in love with my wife. . . . I believe I will be afraid of you—you have been through so much, and can look down upon poor me from your high position of mother. . . .

Now, almost fifty years later, the admiral was rather less humble. Indeed, he utterly terrified his wife and frequently, with his tongue lashings, drove her from the dinner table weeping. And though he apparently still viewed motherhood as a "high position," he no longer considered the mother someone to "be afraid of," or even to respect.

"Daughter," he admonished Kinau, "don't forget, you are nothing but the baby's mother in my house."

Kinau wouldn't forget. Life became unbearable for her, even more lonely and repressive than it had been in her Waikiki palace, especially with her husband often at sea; and her mother-in-law could offer her little support. Eventually, Kinau persuaded her spouse to challenge his father and move to an apartment of their own. The admiral was furious. How dare his son override his orders! Who would help pay the mortgage now? He would hardly speak with Kinau after this. She was a bad influence.

Kinau tried to recover her self-esteem in the social whirl of Washington and Honolulu, a whirl too dizzying and sophisticated for McVay, who preferred more intimate get-togethers with drinking friends. He would often sit alone and sip dry martinis all evening, then dine in silence and go to bed. Nor did he appreciate the classical music Kinau loved, any more than she could abide his jazz tastes. Then one day she returned home and found him in bed with another woman.

"I adored Charlie," Kinau would say, "but I realized I did not love him. He was a kind man, but he was insensitive."

They were divorced in 1936.

McVay's "insensitivity" extended to his two sons, Charles IV, known as Quarto, and Kimo. Away from home most of the time, he grew distant from them and seldom took an interest in their schoolwork or other activities. Having experienced the cruelty of the martinet when he himself was a youth, he demanded little of his sons, carrying his detachment almost to the point of apathy, though he encouraged them to continue the family naval tradition.

Like the captain, Charles IV had striven to please the "old man," even while blaming him in part for his miserable, lonely childhood. Rarely did he see his father, and he didn't see his mother very often either, for she was usually out socializing. Even his English nanny cared mainly for his younger brother and virtually ignored him, except when she scolded him for misbehaving. Charles grew morose and bitter, and began lying to his family and stealing from school lockers.

"If they thought I was bad," he would say, "I felt that I might as well be bad." He finally dropped out of high school.

His father had wanted Quarto to enter the Naval Academy, but since the youth lacked the academic credits and suffered, in any case, from a serious eye defect, he urged him to enlist in the Navy. The boy's grandfather saw to it that the Navy accepted him, calling the naval recruiting station personally.

"This is Admiral McVay," he barked to the duty officer. "My grandson is coming down to enlist. He's 1-A. Understand me, young man? He's 1-A!"

The duty officer understood—and young Charles thus joined the Navy as an enlisted man and, without telling his father, faked his way through training by wearing contact lenses. Perhaps for the first time, to the captain's joy, three living generations of a single family were in the Navy simultaneously. But one day Charles was accidentally struck in the eye with a rifle butt and couldn't wear contacts for a while. The masquerade was over and he had to resign. McVay was even more despondent than his son.

But aside from this bitter disappointment, which stemmed more from respect for family tradition than from concern for his son's welfare, the captain hardly noticed or seemed to care about the boy. He was too wrapped up in his efforts to win the approval of his own father, who he knew would never be content until he became an admiral. Meanwhile, Kimo, who might have filled in for his brother, joined the Army, adding to the captain's chagrin.

"Father," Charles IV would say, "discharged his obligations to his sons. He went by the book. But he could never get himself to say he loved us."

In fact, McVay was greatly embarrassed when Kimo, on returning from a trip, was so happy to see his father that he grabbed him and kissed him on the mouth. One didn't behave like that with a Navy man!

It had been difficult for McVay to love an individual, perhaps because his father had taught him that love was an undisciplined emotion not becoming a future admiral. Or that there just wasn't enough room in a real sailor's soul for more love than he could lavish on the Navy.

But he finally found enough room when, one evening in 1943, he stopped off at the Chevy Chase Club on the outskirts of Washington, where he was then based, and met Louise Claytor. This time there was no whirlwind romance leading to a grandiose wedding under a kamani tree. He courted her with all due decorum for a year before they married.

Louise, who at forty-four had never been married, could not have contrasted more sharply with Kinau, McVay's first wife, though, as the daughter of a prominent Washington physician, she, too, had been raised in affluent surroundings. For one thing, Louise, unlike Kinau, was no raving beauty, though her plain face, especially her bright, intelligent eyes, radiated a warmth and gentleness that captivated people. She had simple tastes and felt somewhat ill at ease at the social affairs that were so much a part of Kinau's life. She enjoyed fishing and hunting, as McVay did, and she was an impeccable house-keeper with little need for servants.

More important, Louise practically worshiped Captain McVay. She bathed him, emptied his ashtray every time he flicked ashes into it, cooked his favorite meals, showed great respect for his father, satisfied his every whim. Her dedication proved the magic answer to his bent toward infidelity, and he found an intimate kind of re-lationship that he had never known before.

And now, as the war dragged on, winning meant more than defeating the enemy and earning the rank of admiral. It meant coming home to an idyllic life with his beloved Louise.

II

The Secret Weapon

AFTER YEARS of war at sea, Lieutenant Commander Lewis L. Haynes, chief physician on the *Indianapolis*, longed to set foot on Connecticut soil. And, in early April 1945, he would have the chance, for the ship had been badly damaged at Okinawa when a kamikaze plane smashed into it and was limping back to Mare Island, near San Francisco, for repairs. But when Lieutenant T. M. Conway, the Catholic chaplain aboard, asked him what he planned to do on his leave, the doctor dejectedly replied: "I don't know. I can't afford to go to Connecticut to see my family or to have them come to Mare Island."

That night Father Conway visited Haynes' quarters and dropped a wad of bills on the table.

"Doc," he said, "now you can go home."

No, he couldn't accept the money, Haynes protested.

But the priest insisted. After all, weren't they good friends? Lew even sang the hymns at the Protestant services that Conway, the only chaplain aboard, conducted every Sunday. And they had been through many battles together, one man soothing the soul, the other healing the flesh. What was a few dollars to friends?

Haynes finally took the money, promising to repay the priest as soon as he returned—a promise he would meticulously keep. He spent three weeks with his wife and two young sons at home in

Fairfield, Connecticut, fishing with the boys and dreaming of the time when he could hang up his shingle and, he hoped, earn a decent living as a surgeon. He had joined the Navy on graduating from Northwestern Medical School because he couldn't afford to live on the meager salary he would earn during his internship. Now, six years later, with many expenses at home, the thirty-three-year-old doctor was still almost penniless.

But Haynes was reluctant to accept aid from anyone; he was accustomed only to giving aid. From 1939 to 1941, in pre–Pearl Harbor days, he treated men on three destroyers that escorted British convoys across the Atlantic. When the United States entered the war, he served aboard the battleship *New Mexico*, which fought at Midway, and in spring 1944, he joined the *Indianapolis* crew in Saipan, treating the wounded there and, later, in Okinawa. Slender and soft-voiced, with a gentle countenance featuring, incongruously, it seemed, a rather intimidating chin, the doctor blended compassion with tenacity.

Haynes would never regret his decision to enlist in the Navy. He had learned how to heal wounds under the most terrible conditions, and worked with people he would always love—men like Father Conway, who considered the whole crew his flock, and Commander Stanley W. Lipski, the gunnery officer, one of the finest officers aboard and a warm human being with whom Haynes happily shared many drunken hours. He liked Captain McVay, too. The skipper, he felt, was a snob who preferred martinis to good old-fashioned booze, but he was a fair, understanding man, a man with class.

The captain, for his part, respected and liked Haynes, and probably wouldn't have traded him for any doctor in the fleet, but he was a bit concerned about what he considered the man's tendency toward indiscretion, however innocently displayed. Haynes, he would say after the war, was often "kidded . . . in the wardroom, and then he would take it as a fact and it would be all over the ship."

But Haynes seldom spoke of his personal plans. And when he did, who could believe that he would ever leave the Navy, or that the Navy would ever leave him?

.   .   .

While Dr. Haynes was ready to leave the sea forever, another veteran, Lieutenant Richard Redmayne, felt the sea was where he belonged. A tall, slim man with a trigger temper that sometimes punctuated his conviviality, Redmayne had learned that his superior was to be transferred and that he, as the man's assistant, would shortly take over as chief engineer of the *Indianapolis*. At twenty-six, he was only a lieutenant, but he was being promoted to the rank of lieutenant commander—and since the job was normally held by a full commander, he could expect a second promotion soon afterward. He would make the Navy his career.

Nor did Redmayne believe he faced any further serious danger. Virtually the whole Japanese fleet had been sunk, and the war, he felt, was already won. Besides, ever since Pearl Harbor, luck had been with him. On the morning of December 7, 1941, he was asleep aboard his seaplane tender after spending a memorable Saturday night in town with his girl, Trude, when he felt someone shaking him. Dreaming it was Trude, he opened his eyes and glared at the chief petty officer. An enlisted man had no business touching an officer.

"What the hell are you doing?" Redmayne barked.

"The Japs are attacking!"

"You're drunk!"

"No, sir, I'm not."

Redmayne ran out on deck in time to see one of his men shoot down an enemy plane about two hundred yards away—just before it could get into position to drop a bomb on his ship.

In February 1945, Redmayne joined the *Indianapolis* crew in Saipan, and was shortly at Iwo Jima sweating in the engine room, expecting a boiler to burst every time the screech of an enemy shell overhead drowned out the moan of the ship's engines. And at Okinawa he thought he was a goner when the kamikaze plane struck the deck. But he survived, as did the ship, thanks in part to his role in patching up the damage. Having thus struggled through five years of war, Redmayne felt he was indestructible.

The lieutenant, who had been a Merchant Marine officer before switching to the Navy on the eve of the war, had good reason for refusing even to consider death: Not only was his career blossoming, but he had married Trude in 1942. He was now the father of two children, and was in a position to give them a life far more rewarding than the hard years he had spent in Massachusetts under the wing of his own father, a chauffeur of limited means.

As the *Indianapolis* prepared to leave Mare Island, Redmayne, whose family had moved into his Quonset hut, frantically made last-minute repairs on the ship's damaged turbines and reduction gears. Once he became chief engineer, he was confident, no hole any Japanese missile could make in this ship would be able to stop his engines.

Captain McVay was chagrined. It was Sunday, July 16, and he had received orders only four days earlier that the *Indianapolis* must sail from Mare Island today—even though he didn't feel the ship was ready. Where was it to go? The orders didn't say. McVay, being a by-the-book Navy man, didn't question his superiors, but he was concerned. All the damage inflicted on the *Indianapolis* at Okinawa had, in the three months in port, been repaired, but the renovated ship with its new instruments and fresh complement of personnel— some 30 officers and 250 enlisted men, many inexperienced—had not been fully tested yet. The crew was in dire need of a refresher course, which it was scheduled to take in San Diego. Furthermore, the ship had completed only a one-day "shakedown" cruise, though the normal testing cruise lasted three or four days. And the skipper wanted to make sure that his vessel was in perfect shape and his men superbly trained and familiarized with their duties before they sailed.

McVay's troubled feeling was apparently tinged with a personal concern. The hasty departure would cheat him of a little more time with Louise, who was staying with him in a Quonset hut near the port. He had finally found the woman he knew he would never want to leave. And now he would be leaving her abruptly—possibly never to return. By the summer of 1945, American forces had captured Okinawa, Iwo Jima, Saipan, and other key island stepping stones to Japan, and an initial invasion of the southern Japanese island of Kyushu was scheduled for November. There would surely be many weeks of bloody battle, since the Japanese had sworn to defend their homeland to the last man.

But it was impossible for Admiral William R. Purnell and Navy Captain William S. Parsons to postpone McVay's mission. In fact, they had called McVay to naval headquarters in San Francisco to give him his final orders. The *Indianapolis* was to carry to Tinian the vital parts of a secret weapon that could end the war swiftly.

Did the two officers inform McVay that the secret weapon was an atomic bomb? Some experts believe that since he didn't *have* to know, he would not have been told. But long after the war, McVay would claim that he *was* told. He was given a sealed letter with the information, he would tell his stepson, Gordon Linke, and he read it when the ship had left San Francisco. In any event, Purnell and Parsons made it clear to McVay that his mission was of extraordinary importance. Parsons, tall and distinguished-looking, was especially eloquent, for he was, in a sense, the father of the bomb. Under Brigadier General Leslie Groves, who headed the Manhattan Project, code name for the atomic bomb program, Parsons was the chief engineer. He would command the mission of the *Enola Gay*, the B-29 that would drop the first bomb on Japan, though the Air Force would make sure that Colonel Paul Tibbets, the pilot, got the recognition.

McVay would have to move his ship later that day to Hunter's Point Navy Yard in San Francisco, where the secret cargo would be carried aboard. While it was in his care, he would have to guard it with his life. In the event the *Indianapolis* was sunk, he was to reserve a lifeboat for the cargo even if this meant some men had to be left to drown. However, since the ship would be tracked constantly— while the weapon parts were aboard—help would arrive almost immediately if something happened to it.

The vessel would sail full speed in the morning for Tinian, stopping only in Pearl Harbor to refuel and discharge military passengers. (From Tinian, McVay was apparently not told, the *Enola Gay* would take off on its historic mission.) The *Indianapolis* would not be given a destroyer escort to Tinian, since speed was of the essence and an escort could not move as fast as a cruiser. In any event, there had been no sign of Japanese submarine activity in the area between San Francisco and Tinian; Japan was too busy trying to protect waters closer to home.

Despite his misgivings about the rush, McVay was happy to be able to play such an important role in the war. He wanted to think that his ship was chosen for the job because he had proved to be an exceptional commander. And Washington did appreciate him. He had already served with distinction as Chief of the Joint Intelligence Committee of the Combined Chiefs of Staff, and there was even talk that he might one day be chosen Navy Chief of Operations. His combat record was excellent. In addition to the Solomon Islands campaign (in which his role as executive officer of the cruiser USS *Cleveland* had earned him the Silver Star), he had taken part in many battles, including the landings in North Africa and Iwo Jima and the assault on Okinawa, where he had skillfully saved the *Indianapolis* after the kamikaze attack.

McVay was especially proud of his success in turning the *Indianapolis* into what he regarded as one of the most efficiently run ships in the Navy. After taking command in November 1944, he held regular emergency drills and raised the sagging morale of the officers. At first, McVay would say, they "were afraid to come to the bridge" to talk with him, and they "looked to me to make every decision for them. I . . . told them that I was up there to help them in an emergency. . . . When they themselves felt they could not handle the situation, they . . . should feel free to call upon me at any time."

And McVay pointed out that discipline was no problem on his ship; fewer than six men would fail to sail with him to Tinian, and only two were arrested for misbehavior while ashore—"a better record than any other ship in the fleet." In fact, he had had "many an officer . . . come to me and tell me that he had never seen such a change in a ship in so short [a] period of time."

Even more important to Captain McVay was the knowledge that his father was proud of him. He did not let this knowledge cloud his sense of realism, however—he was a damn good Navy man, yes, but he knew he was not in his father's class. He lacked the old man's iron toughness, and some of his men, he apparently realized, even thought he was a bit too soft for a skipper, too nice a guy. At the same time, he was too aloof to command the kind of reverence accorded the elder man.

True, many of the father's officers loathed the admiral, but his enlisted men worshiped him—even if they did so, in the view of some members of the admiral's own family, because they didn't know him. On the other hand, while almost all of the son's shipmates, officers and men, liked and respected their skipper, and many would eventually love him, their feelings were not sparked by gut emotion. And that was the essential difference.

The ship, in any event, was not chosen for its skipper, but for its availability and capability. It was very swift, and even though older and (with its peculiar swayback profile) less sleek than other cruisers, it was now fitted with the most modern equipment, including new radar, radio, and fire-control systems. The ship also had an enviable history of service and survival.

Commissioned in 1932, the *Indianapolis* was the first major naval vessel to be built after the London Naval Conference of 1930 at which cruisers, among other combat ships, were limited in tonnage and size of guns. It had fought with distinction in the waters south of New Britain, at New Guinea, and in the Aleutians, the Gilberts, the Western Carolines, the Marianas, and the Marshalls, in addition to Okinawa. Furthermore, the *Indianapolis* had spacious living quarters, apparently one key reason why Admiral Raymond A. Spruance, Commander of the Fifth Fleet, chose the *Indianapolis* as his flagship, his headquarters at sea. Spruance was so enamored with this ship that he selected it even though, due to its easily floodable design, he felt it could not "sustain even one torpedo."

Given both his and the ship's past successes, McVay, even while recognizing his limitations, was certain that he would carry out his new mission flawlessly. And he could, after all, test the fresh equipment and train the men while it was being carried out. Besides, the crew would surely be given a refresher course somewhere in the Pacific before it was sent into combat again.

Actually, wasn't his mission designed to end the war in days? Japan probably wouldn't have to be invaded after all. And his men would most likely never be called upon to exhibit their nautical skills. Regardless, he thought, his green sailors had learned enough to help him get to Tinian without too much trouble.

• • •

Among McVay's green sailors was Ensign Donald J. Blum, one of twenty newly commissioned officers who would make their naval debuts aboard the *Indianapolis*. Blum felt lucky to have struggled through midshipmen's school; though he had a degree in mechanical engineering from a civilian technical institute and top marks in navigation and mathematics in a naval school, a learning difficulty had kept him from excelling in other subjects, including Morse code.

Thus, Blum, a gunnery officer whose main function was to direct the aiming of the 44-mm antiaircraft guns, was "apprehensive" as he joined the crew of the *Indianapolis* while it was being overhauled. His limited knowledge showed. Instead of giving orders to the enlisted men, he sometimes had to ask for their advice. He had, after all, never fired a real gun except in simulation. And occasionally he even forgot the rules of rank. Once, as he was about to engage in some carpentry work aboard ship, he suddenly heard the loudspeaker blast: "Ensign Blum, put down that hammer!" Only enlisted men were to work with their hands.

Nor was Blum sure how his fellow officers, particularly the veterans, would accept him. He was, he mistakenly thought, the only Jew aboard, and he was well acquainted with anti-Semitism. Though he regarded himself as an agnostic, maybe even an atheist, and his family was so assimilated that it belonged to the Community Church, he couldn't forget that he was a Jew: People kept reminding him. Even in Scarsdale, the wealthy suburb of New York City where his well-to-do family lived, he was banned from a local country club and was asked to leave when he once dared set foot in it. And he was not consoled by the assurances of his family's minister that "Jesus Christ himself couldn't get in there." Blum also remembered that his roommate at Columbia University's Midshipmen's School ignored him because he was a Jew and would not visit his home. The new ensign thus treaded gingerly amid the crew. An excellent poker player, he decided that to avoid making enemies unnecessarily he would never win big.

One shipmate whom Blum could feel perfectly at ease with was

a friend he had known since their grammar school days together—
Thomas D'Arcy Brophy, Jr. Brophy had been commissioned an
ensign about the same time as Blum at another midshipmen's school,
and he was serving on his first ship, too. But this redheaded young
officer, brilliant and good-looking, was not, like his old schoolmate,
lacking in confidence. After all, had not an admiral presented him
with a sword to reward him for his record in naval school? The touch
of arrogance that some people perceived in him was a trait he apparently inherited from his father, a highly successful advertising
executive.

Still, Brophy's charm never failed to win admirers, and in Blum
he aroused a nostalgic feeling for home. Here was someone with
whom he could enjoy his liberties. Mare Island didn't exactly vibrate
with excitement, but it was rumored that the ship would be an-
choring in Hawaii, and Blum, whose piercing, rather playful eyes
lured the ladies, could envision the hula girls beckoning.

The night before the *Indianapolis* was to leave Mare Island, Blum
wanted to go ashore with his comrade for one last fling, but they
weren't allowed off the ship. Well, they could wait until Pearl Harbor. Besides, though it was against the rules, Blum had smuggled
three bottles of whiskey aboard and hidden them in his sleeping
compartment. This might turn out to be a pleasant voyage after all.

Nothing about this voyage could be pleasant to Yeoman Otha
Alton Havins. Pearl Harbor! His beloved elder brother had died there
on the battleship *Arizona* on that day of infamy. Havins was incon-
solable. Though he was a religious man and had considered entering
the ministry, he now began to have doubts. His family had already
suffered enough, almost starving during the Depression on their little
Texas farm. He resolved to take matters into his own hands.

Vowing revenge, Havins quit school a few months later and, at
seventeen, joined the Navy. His parents were anguished, but he tried
to convince them that lightning would not strike twice in the same
family. In March 1943, he clambered aboard the *Indianapolis*, his
boyish face still taut with grief and remembrance.

Though Yeoman Havins served mainly as a clerk, he saw his share of fighting. At Okinawa, as the kamikaze plane dove toward the ship, he thought for a moment that he would be joining his brother. But he survived, and felt especially lucky when he found that the room he had left just before the explosion had flooded after it, killing almost every occupant.

Havins didn't know if his narrow escape was a sign or not, but he decided not to leave matters to fate. On arriving in Mare island, he asked to be transferred to a home base. After three years of brutal combat his passion for revenge had dissipated. So many men had died—on both sides. Was the answer to personal tragedy revenge, or a commitment to future peace? Besides, he was exhausted; he longed to return home for a while to comfort his grieving mother and make sure that his girl friend, Billie, would never send him a "Dear Otha" letter.

Havins had met the young woman in his hometown of Shafter, California, where his family had moved from Texas some years earlier. On their second date, he asked her to marry him. No, she replied, she did not intend to end up as a war widow. He persisted, proposing again and again, and each time the answer was the same. So he had no choice; he *had* to survive.

Even though he was told that orders for a transfer would come through shortly, he soon learned that the *Indianapolis* was about to sail off into the Pacific—before the orders could be finalized. Billie seemed to be weakening, yet he wouldn't be able to propose to her even one more time since he couldn't get off the ship.

"Don't worry," his educational officer said consolingly. "You'll get your transfer in Pearl Harbor and then you can come back."

But Havins worried. Pearl Harbor, after all, was the symbol of his family's ill fortune.

Captain McVay stood on the bridge of the *Indianapolis* in the warm darkness of night and, with suppressed enthusiasm, addressed his senior officers. The ship, which had moved to Hunter's Point the previous day, would shortly head out to sea again—as soon as a secret cargo had been hauled aboard. He couldn't tell them what its mission was but said that "every hour we save will shorten the war by that much."

The crew had been awakened about 3 A.M. and ordered to report to their stations, and among the sleepy, disgruntled sailors was Adolfo Celaya, a seventeen-year-old fireman who had fought with the *Indianapolis* since November 1944. Like Donald Blum, Celaya didn't feel entirely comfortable on board. A bronze-skinned man of mixed Mexican and Spanish blood, he found himself, to a large extent, isolated from most of the crew.

Still, Celaya wasn't too disturbed; he was accustomed to such separation. His hometown of Florence, Arizona, near Tucson, had a population 70 percent Mexican and 30 percent white, and while he had never felt discriminated against, he had never set foot in the house of a white family. The best friends Celaya ever had, he felt, were the animals on the small cattle ranch his family had owned. Sadly, it had lost the ranch in the Depression when Adolfo was a young boy. Shortly after that, his parents separated and he lived with his father, who got a job operating a steam shovel and then a bus.

Unable to adjust to urban life, Celaya dropped out of high school and joined the Navy. During the days at sea, he pondered his future and thought that after the war he might study to become a physical education instructor. Tall and powerfully built, he had been the best basketball player in Florence. Maybe he would even qualify as a professional, and if he made enough money, he could get himself a ranch and buy back his horse and his cows. . . .

But this was no time for dreaming. Something unusual was happening. Celaya had never seen a naval shipyard so deserted, with no other ship in sight and no one on the dock. In the total silence, it seemed that the world had come to a stop. Suddenly, two Army trucks roared out of the night and lurched to a halt alongside the ship; one carried a large wooden crate about fifteen feet long, and the other, two small canisters about three feet high and two feet in diameter. Several men rushed down the gangplank and tied ropes around the crate, which was then lifted by a huge crane onto the hangar deck; from there it was carried into the hangar.

At the same time, the canisters, which weighed about two hundred pounds apiece, were attached to crowbars, and two muscular sailors lifted each burden to their shoulders and stumbled up the gangplank coolie-style, depositing one of them in the captain's cabin and the other in a nearby room on the main deck. Trailing right behind were a Marine guard and two Army officers, who, it seemed to the crew, were simply bumming a ride. In the cabins, shipfitters welded the canisters to the deck.

Few crew members actually took much notice of the canisters, though some wondered how something so small could weigh so much. There was more curiosity about the enormous crate. Celaya guessed that it contained new furniture for the captain, who, Celaya noticed, seemed to be a man who liked nice things. Celaya had an underlying distrust of people with power. Hadn't they taken away his father's ranch with his horse and cows? Didn't they give the best jobs to white people? He himself never expected to be promoted in the Navy.

Others guessed the crate was full of radar devices, sophisticated radio equipment, even whiskey or mattresses for the officers. Bets were taken, but this was one wager no one would win. None of the sailors could have guessed that the crate was loaded with the detonating mechanism of a bomb that could blow up a city, that the canisters contained the fuel for the bomb, a subcritical quantity of uranium 235, about half the amount available in the United States. (The other half would be sent to Tinian by air.)

Well, the furniture, the booze, or whatever it was that was so important was aboard. Now the crew wanted to know when the ship would be leaving. Rumors that the first stop would be Hawaii had hardened into fact, and many men, especially Donald Blum and Tom Brophy, were impatient to taste the exotic delights of Polynesia. What was the captain waiting for?

He was waiting for a signal, which (he may not have known) would come from the Alamogordo Desert in New Mexico, where the uranium bomb was being tested that morning in Operation Trinity. If the test failed and there was no explosion, there would be no reason to send the secret cargo across the ocean. But it did not fail.

Early that morning of July 16, a Marine rushed into Dr. Haynes' cabin and, as medical officer for Admiral Spruance's staff and the only member available, Haynes signed for a radio message to the staff from Admiral King: "INDIANAPOLIS UNDER ORDERS OF COMMANDER-IN-CHIEF AND MUST NOT BE DIVERTED FROM ITS MISSION FOR ANY REASON."

Haynes was stunned by the implications. Under orders of the President himself! What the hell *was* the ship hauling? Booze was now eliminated since Harry S Truman was not a drinking man. The only whiskey aboard, it seemed, belonged to artful smugglers like Donald Blum. Some of the other men may have wished they had been as resourceful—especially since a sudden ominous rumor was sweeping the ship: Three fortune tellers, it was said, had predicted that the vessel was embarking on a journey that would end in disaster.

At 8 A.M., the *Indianapolis* cast off and glided through the Golden Gate toward a new dawn.

III

The Heavenly Mission

THAT SAME DAY, another craft, the submarine *I-58*, cast off from Kure Harbor, twelve miles southeast of Hiroshima, but it wouldn't sail toward a new dawn; Commander Hashimoto knew that only darkness lay ahead for Japan. Still, he now had a chance to make the sun shine for the Emperor, if only for a fleeting moment. Maybe his submarine would score a kill.

I-58 was one of six submarines gathered in a flotilla called the "Taimon Group" that was setting out on a hunt for American prey. This offensive mission signified a desperate shift from the previous policy of using submarines almost exclusively to reconnoiter and supply troops stranded on bypassed islands. The submarines' new directive was intended to help delay an American invasion of Japan.

But Hashimoto had no illusions. American forces had seized almost every blood-stained island leading to Japan, and now an invasion and a final suicide battle were inevitable—unless the unthinkable happened: surrender. Hashimoto felt uneasy thinking the unthinkable—was he being disloyal to the Emperor?—but deep in his heart he saw no other solution and was already beginning to rationalize it. In the limitless stretch of eternity, after all, one lost war was a temporary setback, merely a prod toward greater future glory.

Hashimoto, however, found it harder to rationalize his own failures. As a submarine officer during the strike at Pearl Harbor, he had dispatched one of six midget submarines armed with torpedoes, but, like the others, it did no damage and failed to return. As a commander operating in the Marshall Islands, he had sighted six enemy destroyers, but was forbidden to attack because his mission was to deliver food to starving troops on isolated islands. At Guam, he had sought to blow up an aircraft carrier, but found that it had already left the scene. At Iwo Jima, he had sighted a large warship, but couldn't attack because his batteries needed recharging. At Okinawa, he had sat for seven days waiting for the fog to lift so he could launch torpedoes, but in vain. Hashimoto was crushed. After five years of war, he had failed to score a single confirmed kill.

Now his submarine slowly slid away from the dock once more, with a tattered banner attached to the mast proclaiming an old Imperial slogan, LAW ABOVE REASON, HEAVEN ABOVE LAW. About a score of military people stood on the dock wanly waving while several motley figures blared a cacophony of martial strains. Hashimoto recalled his departure the previous November. Crowds roared their blessings; cameras clicked; crammed motorboats churned alongside, their occupants chanting in unison the names of the departing heroes; human torpedo pilots sat in their craft with white scarves dashingly wrapped around their heads and shiny swords held aloft.

But Kure, essentially a naval base, had since become a shell of a town, a bombed-out rubble, and not many people were in the mood to cheer amid the horrible realities of this war. Even Hashimoto's own house had been partially destroyed, though his wife and three children had miraculously escaped unharmed and were living with friends. His dear, gentle wife, Nobuko. He had married her in 1937, when the future looked as golden as a Japanese summer landscape. The daughter of a well-off Osaka businessman, she had been brought up in fine surroundings, but now she and the children did not even have a home. The commander tried to drive his family's plight from his mind. Nothing must distract him from his present mission.

Hashimoto had dreamed of fighting for the Emperor since he was a youth. Upon graduating from Kyoto's superior Third High

School in 1927, he decided to apply for admission to the Naval Academy. Though this was a time when few Japanese remembered past Imperial triumphs, Hashimoto basked in the glory of the Meiji Restoration, which, in 1867, restored the Emperor to power and triggered the modernization of Japan, permitting the country to win its great naval victory over Russia in 1905. This was the spirit that had made Japan great—and the spirit that drove Hashimoto. Yes, he would try to join the Navy, even though it had grown weaker and less prestigious than ever after the 1922 Washington Naval Treaty that limited world naval armament.

There was one obstacle, however—his father. The head priest in a Shinto temple in Kyoto, the spiritual center of Japan, he wanted his son to become a priest, too. The youth was the descendant of an unbroken line of priests dating from before the 1867 Restoration, when Kyoto had been the capital of the country. After he died, the father made it clear, one of his five sons would have to replace him and carry on the family tradition, conducting services and taking care of the temple and its grounds, which the Hashimotos owned. An elder son had already joined the Army, and Mochitsura seemed the best candidate for priesthood as he was apparently more compassionate and more understanding of Shinto teachings than his siblings. Besides, as the youngest son, he had the least to say about his own future.

But young Hashimoto resisted. He firmly believed in Shinto (the Way of the Gods), an ancient Japanese religion that originally called for the worship of nature, but ultimately, of the nation's heavenly conception. The Emperor, descendant of the gods, was divine—infallible and unchallengeable. However, the youth argued, he could more actively serve his god as a warrior than as a priest. Besides, he had no desire to live the ascetic, secluded life of a cleric. And in any case, he pointed out, the government subsidy for Shinto priests was very slim, barely enough for the Hashimoto family of eleven to subsist on. His naval pay would add greatly to the earnings of the family.

But his father was unyielding. Let the other sons contribute. This one owed it to his ancestors to become a priest.

Mochitsura found himself trapped between two conflicting obligations. Within the traditional Japanese social order, overseen by the Emperor, every individual was fixed in his place according to his class, occupation, family position, age, and sex, and held there by a complicated network of interlocking obligations. Throughout his life he had to constantly repay the Emperor for his goodness (a debt called *chu*) and his parents for theirs (a debt called *ko*). These exalted creditors were owed absolute obedience and devotion.

Now Hashimoto was faced with the choice of repaying either *ko* to his parents or *chu* to the Emperor. He had to shirk one obligation in order to fulfill the other. Agonizing as this choice was, the Emperor, of course, came first, for though the young man loved and respected his parents, they were only mortals while the Emperor was descended from the gods. Hashimoto politely told his father that this one time he must disobey him. And the elder man, his distress somewhat eased, paradoxically, by this demonstration of the boy's devotion to the Emperor, finally bestowed his blessing upon him. Even so, he was not much happier about his son's decision to join the Navy than Captain McVay was about *his* son's failure to stay in the Navy.

Hashimoto eagerly enrolled in the Naval Academy on the island of Eta Jima off Hiroshima, and graduated in 1931. After several years of sailing on everything from a destroyer to a subchaser, he was sent to the Navy's torpedo and submarine schools to learn how to fight underwater as well. Finally, in 1941, he climbed aboard a submarine as torpedo officer. The timing was ideal. His submarine, along with four others, glided stealthily across the Pacific; shortly before midnight on December 6, it slid to a halt, as the pounding of the engines gave way to the pounding of drums and cymbals from a radio jazz concert on Hawaii's neon-lit Waikiki Beach.

At dawn, each craft launched a midget submarine toward the U.S. Fleet anchored at Pearl Harbor, while Japanese planes zoomed off carriers and swooped down to hammer from the sky. The damage wreaked was catastrophic, but the midgets did not sail away with any of the honors. None of these two-man submarines sank a ship with their torpedoes, or returned as they were supposed to, and the mother subs slunk back to Japan, humiliated amid the general merriment of victory.

Hashimoto would never fully recover from this enormous loss of face at one of the greatest moments in Japanese history, taking the failure personally. For, as torpedo officer, he had launched the midget even though it had had a last-minute engine problem. And Japan's submarine fleet would never recover either. It had been expected to play a role at Pearl Harbor and in future battles equivalent to that of the Air Force, but who could depend now on this "blundering" naval arm? It would never again receive top priority in strategic planning, nor would it be at the front of the line when money and equipment were handed out. It was not wisely employed.

In the first months of the war, when the Japanese Navy was constantly on the attack, Hashimoto and other submarine commanders were ordered to torpedo enemy ships regardless of risk or tactical logic, rather than strike at enemy communication lines as the American submarines did. This archaic strategy brought some deceptive early victories, but the submarine fleet suffered such heavy losses that it ultimately could do little more than supply troops stranded on isolated islands—though these troops would have been better off retreating so that they could fight elsewhere. Hashimoto was exasperated. The admirals and generals were conducting a war with the heroic but inflexibly simplistic tactics of their samurai forebears, without any detailed operational planning and with scant regard for scientific methods.

The High Command, it grew clear to Hashimoto, had completely underestimated the strength of the American submarine force. It had expected to conquer most of Asia before the Americans could rally from Pearl Harbor and other initial defeats, but it hadn't counted on either the American spirit or the well-equipped, flexibly used American submarine. As for the Japanese submarine, even when it *was* used intelligently, it lacked the modern equipment needed to fulfill its mission properly. Controls were complicated and inadequate; engine vibration was excessive; living conditions were overcrowded;

and sanitation was poor. Morale, naturally, was at rock bottom. Hadn't his forefathers vowed to learn from the West how to beat the West?

Hashimoto's spirits were somewhat rejuvenated in mid-1944 when he was given the task of fitting out and commanding a huge new submarine, *I-58*, that, along with other submarines of the same class, was expected to sap America's growing naval power. But he remained skeptical, especially after the admiral in command of the submarine fleet ruled that surface radar sets installed in these vessels be removed because they were "useless." Useless?! Hashimoto was stunned. After many knocks on many doors and a flurry of bows, he finally managed to have the order rescinded—to the astonishment of his colleagues, most of whom would not dare to question the wisdom of their superiors.

I-58, about 355 feet long, with a beam of 30 feet, was larger than any of the American submarines, and had a very swift surface speed of 17 knots. It could simultaneously fire six Model 95 torpedoes, which were able to reach the remarkable speed of 48 knots and had a range of nearly five miles, making it deadlier than America's best. These missiles were a submarine-carried version of the Long Lance, Model 93, used by surface ships, which had sunk or badly wounded dozens of American vessels. Once his precious radar found the enemy, Hashimoto hoped, these 30-foot-long, oxygen-driven torpedoes would almost certainly hit home—if his superiors didn't interfere.

But before Hashimoto could finish fitting out his craft, Japan's losses on land and sea began escalating dramatically, and the fall of Saipan profoundly shook the High Command. Its desperation gave birth to the suicide fighter—the kamikaze pilot who would crash into American warships from above, and his underseas counterpart, the kaiten ("human torpedo"), who would strike from below. The concept of the kaiten was not new; it had been conceived shortly after Pearl Harbor, when the midget submarines that Hashimoto helped direct failed to damage the American fleet. Since the pilots didn't return to the mother submarine anyway, why not put them into torpedoes, wish them well, and send them on a one-way trip to heaven?

The Japanese militarists carefully pondered the idea. No, they decided at first, it was not really necessary to send men on death missions. But now, with the whole nation on the brink of extinction, there seemed little objection to volunteers committing suicide for the Emperor and his godly ancestors. Perhaps to soothe the conscience of the Navy, an ejection mechanism was built into the torpedo. But which volunteer would use it and cheat himself of everlasting glory? Which one would choose to suffer so horrendous a loss of face? Anyway, it was too late to leave Japan's destiny up to the Model 95 torpedo. This missile had to backed up by the human torpedo. Appropriately, the literal translation of "kaiten" was "sky change"; so overwhelming would the effect of the kaitens be on the course of the war that even the heavens would move.

Hashimoto was appalled by this strategy; it only underscored Japan's catastrophic situation. It symbolized the kind of thinking that should have ended when the samurai exchanged their swords for guns. Science could not be fought with heroic gimmickry. Besides, why should certain people be chosen to die so that others might live?

But Hashimoto, reluctant though he was, obeyed orders. He picked up four human torpedoes at their training base on the island of Otsushima off Kure, and in early January 1945 groomed them for an attack on ships anchored at Guam. As the first one was about to crawl into the torpedo compartment—which had installed in it a seat, a periscope, and controls—Hashimoto could not be silent.

"I regret," he said, "that you shall die in an attempt to save the rest of us."

The kaiten stared at his commander scornfully and replied: "Do not say such a thing. It's that kind of attitude that has created difficulties in this war. You must survive so that you can launch more kaitens."

Hashimoto was deeply moved, and apparently felt a slight sense of shame and guilt. Perhaps he was too pragmatic after all, especially for the son of a Shinto priest. While he had repaid almost none of his own debt to the Emperor yet, this young man was offering his life. At the same time, Hashimoto tried to ease his sorrow for the boy (and his guilt for feeling sorrow) with a certain fatalism. Had not the High Command ordered the Army and Navy to fight until every man was dead? Sooner or later, he and all his crew would be joining the kaitens anyway.

Yes, he would send kaitens out if he had to. After all, their weapon *was* more reliable against more distant targets than the unmanned torpedo. But he preferred the unmanned kind. Not because he would be saving a human life, of course, but because it was a better torpedo (though it could hit targets only at relatively short ranges). The fifty-four-foot-long kaiten's torpedo, while larger, was not really very good. Even though a man was in it, this warhead-nosed coffin often missed its target and sometimes had to be redirected many times before it scored a hit—or was itself hit. Why, he asked himself, didn't the Navy improve it so the kaiten could die more efficiently?

Hashimoto thus rationalized sparing use of his kaitens. He would save them if he could, however determined they were to die.

While Hashimoto struggled to suppress his sorrow over the inevitable fate of the kaitens, his second-in-command, Captain Toshio Tanaka, had no such problem. He was in charge of the torpedoes, iron and human, and launching either one was simply a task like any other. After all, the kaitens were volunteers; they knew what they were doing.

Tanaka liked and admired his sacrificial comrades, but he didn't show a hint of sadness before they set out for paradise. He especially enjoyed himself at a farewell party held for them before they attacked the ships at Guam. The honored guests and members of the crew nibbled at eel and savored sake sent by the Emperor himself, while jokes brought laughter that mingled with belches of gastronomical satisfaction. A wonderful time was had by all—though Hashimoto's merriment was not altogether convincing. Tanaka then told the kaitens to do their best and sent them on their heavenly journey with a glittering smile that revealed two long cuspids.

Tanaka envied the kaitens in a way, for they would die killing many more of the enemy. It wasn't just a matter of winning a war or even of surviving it, but of getting even. The Americans had bombed almost every Japanese city into dust, and his own home in

Kure lay in ruins. They had even machine-gunned, he had heard, simple Japanese fishermen off the coast of Japan. Barbarians! He wanted a chance to machine-gun a shipload of them. The kaitens, at least, could now take a measure of revenge, and not simply in an impersonal way from afar. Their blood would stain the enemy's ship; their bones would linger over its grave.

Tanaka had often been driven by a desire to "get even" with foes, a trait that, curiously, helped propel him up the ranks. As a middle school student in a southern Japanese town, he took an examination to qualify for entry into high school, but failed. To prove to himself that he was, in fact, superior to those who had passed— and, equally important, to take revenge on those who had failed him and cause them to lose face—he decided to take the Naval Academy entrance examination. He studiously pored over books for a year and passed this test, which normally only high school graduates took.

But Tanaka's troubles were not over. As a younger student at the academy, he was brutally beaten by the older ones for every minor breach of discipline. He hated the system—until he himself became a senior student with beating privileges. When he graduated, he was well prepared to deal with the enemy; and he didn't need litanies about the Emperor to inspire his passion for blood.

Tanaka was, like Hashimoto, an ultranationalist, but his nationalism was less mystical and more aggressive than the commander's. He, too, would die for the Emperor, but he thought of the Sovereign more as a symbol of Japan than as a descendant of the gods. There was, however, little friction between the two men. Tanaka, at twenty-seven, regarded Hashimoto, nine years his senior, as a kind of big brother. He remembered him from his days in submarine school, where Hashimoto had served as an instructor. The commander was a man to be admired—smart, tough, yet fair. And though he didn't smoke and almost never drank, even those who viewed such vices as manly trademarks held him in high esteem. Hashimoto, like his American counterpart, Captain McVay, rarely had to scold his men; they obeyed him because they respected him.

Tanaka was proud indeed to serve under a commander of such sterling character. He hoped, though, that Hashimoto wouldn't let "character" prevent him from taking vengeance on the survivors of any ship *I-58* might sink. And this hope burned especially bright as the submarine, serenaded by a tinny blare of farewell, floated out of Kure Harbor to hunt quarry in the waters beyond—perhaps for the last time.

Tanaka was realistic enough to recognize that Japan had been defeated and rational enough to recognize that it would be foolish to fight to the last man. But he thirsted for at least a taste of retribution before Japan surrendered. All those lost cities. Only a few remained intact—neighboring Hiroshima, for one. He stood on deck and gazed at Kure's receding skyline, with its half-demolished buildings that poked into the heavens like crippled fingers.

Which city would be next? he bitterly wondered.

IV

Toward the Dawn

MARINE PRIVATE FIRST CLASS GILES McCOY hated standing guard, even when he could sit. And now on the morning of July 16, at about the time *I-58* was setting out on its hunt, he sat atop the huge crate that had been hoisted aboard the *Indianapolis* and welded to the hanger deck just before dawn. Dressed in starched khakis by order of his punctilious Marine commander, he sweated in the summer heat as he toyed with his .45-caliber pistol. The hangar was like an oven despite the coy breeze wafting through the open door.

McCoy had been disgruntled even before drawing guard duty. He hadn't had a chance to say good-bye to his mother, his sister, and his girl friend before the ship pulled out—after they had come all the way from his hometown of St. Louis to see him. When he complained to the ship's executive officer, Commander Joseph A. Flynn, the commander simply replied: "What about me? My wife expects me home for dinner tonight!"

McCoy was not pacified. This was no way to treat a Marine— especially one with a pretty good battle record. He had volunteered for the corps at age eighteen, feeling that he was especially qualified. His wiry physique and powerful chin, which lent an iron-willed expression to his thin, oblong face, suggested the toughness one expected in a Marine. He had been a star athlete in high school, playing shortstop on the baseball team and dreaming of a contract with the St. Louis Browns. He also loved to hunt and was good with a gun.

He first served with a Marine unit that stormed the beaches of Palau in the Marshall Islands. Then, aboard the *Indianapolis*, he fired on Tokyo in support of a carrier task force. Later, in prelanding battles, he helped to shell Iwo Jima and shoot down six aircraft around Okinawa—before the shock came.

McCoy would never forget the moment when he looked up and saw a dark speck bursting through the clouds over Okinawa. The dot grew larger and larger—a kamikaze plane was heading directly toward him!

"Set condition one in antiaircraft battery!" a panicky voice cried over the loudspeaker.

McCoy helped turn a 5-inch gun toward the target but it was too late. Like some heavenly dragon, it rocketed down, closer, closer. Someone screamed, "He's gonna hit!" and McCoy threw himself on his belly as the plane, with a terrifying blast, smashed into the main deck of the ship about twenty feet away from him. A bomb released by the pilot seconds before the crash bored through the vessel and exploded under it, killing nine men in the mess hall and wounding many others. Though a piece of the plane lodged in a box of shells next to McCoy, he somehow survived intact.

After all he'd been through, McCoy thought he shouldn't be treated so shabbily. What could be in the box that was of such world-shaking importance that he couldn't even kiss his mother and his girl friend good-bye? What an unjust war!

McCoy was a member of an around-the-clock thirty-nine-man Marine guard keeping watch over the mysterious containers earmarked for Tinian. The crate was roped off and the hangar was off-limits for everyone except Captain McVay, Commander Flynn, and the two artillery officers who had come aboard with the freight.

Artillery officers? Few crew members really believed it. No artillery officers could know so little about artillery. Actually, one of them, Major Robert R. Furman, was an engineer, and the other, Captain James F. Nolan, a radiologist. When Donald Blum asked them what kind of gun they fired, Nolan tried to demonstrate the size by cupping his hands, and Furman talked about his 75-mm guns—which he had learned to use in the horse-drawn artillery of bygone days. What kind of recoil mechanisms did they use? Well, it was hard to say. . . . Others wondered why Nolan would every so often disappear during the showing of a film and then return after some minutes. He was always seasick, but he couldn't be *that* sick. The truth was that Nolan would go to the captain's cabin and the stateroom he shared with Furman, where the uranium was kept, to check on a possible radiation danger.

General Groves had ordered the two men to watch over the atomic bomb components until the ship docked at Tinian, and so they had disguised themselves as artillery officers. Furman had organized ALSOS, a secret military and scientific group that had sought out German scientists and documents that related to the atomic bomb. Nolan engaged in radiological research at Los Alamos, where the American bomb had been built. They had escorted the truck carrying the cargo from Los Alamos to Albuquerque in a convoy crammed with security men, then flown with it to Hamilton Field near San Francisco, and finally driven with it in another convoy to Hunter's Point.

Aboard the *Indianapolis*, these "artillery officers" became part of the puzzle intriguing the crew. Who were they and what was their connection to the giant crate and the "buckets"? Why had a life raft been tied to a bulkhead near their cabin? Why did they rush to check on the canisters when a couple of minor fires broke out on the ship?

Captain McVay himself, when he wasn't pressing the engine room to move ever faster, seemed to join in the game. The secret cargo, he suggested to the two men, pertained to bacteriological warfare. They were mute in response. Since McVay would later claim he knew the truth, he may have been unsure if the "artillery officers" did, and wanted to test their knowledge. He made the same suggestion to Dr. Haynes, perhaps seeking to throw him off the track. Haynes, after all, was a doctor familiar with radiation and might have surmised what the contents were. Of course, McVay may simply have been as confused and curious as the rest of his crew.

While the captain was proud to be part of a mission that could end the war quickly, he had other reasons to be proud, too. In just a few days aboard, he had held damage control, abandon ship, and other emergency drills, as well as battle exercises, and despite the large number of military passengers wandering around the ship and getting in the way of the crew, his men, especially the many new recruits, had greatly improved their combat efficiency. Once they had their refresher course—apparently in Guam—there would be no enemy submarine the ship couldn't handle.

As the vessel rounded Diamond Head in Hawaii, McVay learned it had broken the speed record from San Francisco, averaging about 29.5 knots in completing the journey of more than two thousand miles in 74.5 hours. The ship slid into Pearl Harbor, which had been cleared of every other large craft, and docked for refueling and re-supply amid jubilance over news of the speed record—and the prospect of celebrating in a whirl of swishing grass skirts.

But except for military passengers, nobody without orders could leave the ship, came word from McVay, who feared some men might have gleaned too much information about the contents of the secret cargo. Not even the sick or injured could debark. Dr. Haynes vigorously protested to Commander Flynn, arguing that there was no reason to keep aboard a patient like Marine Private First Class Robert Frank Redd, who had broken some bones in his foot when he dropped an ammunition can on it. Redd himself wanted to remain aboard, good Marine that he was, but the foot was in a cast and he could hardly walk. "Sorry, captain's orders" was the reply.

Among other disappointed crew members were Ensigns Blum and Brophy, who had dreamt all the way across the ocean of at least one memorable night. Blum, on his first time out to sea, was especially agitated. He saw nothing unusual about the mission because he had nothing to judge it against. So there *was* some well-guarded freight. Probably gun parts. So his ship *was* the only one in the harbor. Were there normally more ships? So there *was* no waiting in line for fuel. Maybe it was just naval efficiency. And those two artillerymen—there were a lot of unqualified men in the Army. Blum wasn't even sure whether it was normal to keep a crew from spending a few hours ashore in a place like Hawaii. If it was, he could hardly imagine a more insensitive attitude toward men who simply wished to face death with a smile on their lips.

Another sailor who wanted to get off was Otha Alton Havins. The educational officer had promised that he could debark at Pearl Harbor and return to the States, but his transfer orders still hadn't come through. Have patience, the officer said, assuring Havins that he would be getting off somewhere in the Pacific.

Not every member of the crew was eager to debark. Lieutenant Redmayne was satisfied to watch his superior in the engine room jump ashore—to another job. That left Redmayne the chief engineer of the *Indianapolis*, a goal he had long cherished. And Captain McVay was sending a message to the Bureau of Personnel requesting that he be promoted to lieutenant commander. Not bad, even if he was stepping into a full commander's shoes. He had already made an excellent start—helping to set the speed record. But for all his euphoria, Redmayne felt a bit sorry for his old boss. Shore duty! It was rather humiliating. Still, he couldn't regret too much that the man's bad luck was his own good luck.

After about six hours in port, the *Indianapolis* raised anchor and headed toward Tinian. Since the ship was ahead of schedule, McVay ordered Redmayne to lower the speed to about 24 knots. This pace would presumably still be fast enough to cheat any submarine of what would be the most important torpedo strike ever scored.

Fully aware of the special role in history the *Indianapolis* was playing under his command, McVay, it seemed to his officers, was as tense as he was exhilarated. He would stand for hours on the bridge, high above Turret 2, as if searching for some hidden danger lurking behind every wave. If he didn't complete this mission, history would blame him for prolonging the war and causing an untold number of unnecessary casualties. He appeared to be counting the moments until the *Indianapolis* reached Tinian, mentally measuring the distance as it gradually contracted. At night, between glances at the charts and dials, he would stare into the black void as if entranced by some vision meant only for his eyes. It was no doubt a rosy vision. The precious cargo he was carrying apparently held the key to a swift peace—and a swift return home to Louise.

On the warm, clear morning of July 26, Captain McVay was on the bridge again, but this time he appeared neither tense nor introspective. He was wreathed in a youthful smile that his men had come to know but had rarely seen on the five-thousand-mile trip from San Francisco. As the ship approached Tinian, he gazed contentedly at the palm-dotted island with its giant B-29 airfields. The *Indianapolis* had finally reached its destination.

The ship slipped into the small harbor and dropped anchor offshore, while crew members, among them Donald Blum, crowded against the railing on the main deck. Blum still wasn't sure whether things were normal or not. His ship was being greeted by a swarm of small boats carrying generals, admirals, and other high-ranking officers, as well as squads of heavily armed Marines. Was this a typical island welcome?

The brass climbed aboard and checked the canisters and the crate that had served as a seat for Giles McCoy. When seamen had lowered the containers into two separate landing craft manned by Marines, the two "artillery officers," Furman and Nolan, jumped aboard the one with the canisters, and the boats immediately sped off to shore, followed by the brass.

Captain McVay's voice then trumpeted over the loudspeaker: "You have done a great job. The material you have brought over, I believe, will shorten the war."

Cheers pierced the tropical air; it was time to celebrate. There had to be some women under those coconut trees, the men figured. But they would never find out; though they no longer carried the secret cargo, they were still forbidden to leave the ship, which would take on fuel and then weigh anchor. Where was it going? Only the commanders knew, but the scuttlebutt was that it would participate in an invasion of Formosa.

Blum was devastated. Betrayed once more. He had been saving

his whiskey for a night of bliss, a night, it seemed, that might never materialize, especially with deadly battle just ahead.

Shortly before sailing, McVay knew the route he would take to battle. Admiral Chester W. Nimitz, Commander in Chief, Pacific Fleet (CINCPAC), based in Pearl Harbor, issued him orders to sail to Guam, where Nimitz had his advance headquarters, and then to the Philippine island of Leyte. Here his men would train for ten days with Rear Admiral Lynde D. McCormick's Task Group 95.7 and then join Vice Admiral Jesse B. Oldendorf's Task Force 95, which would play a major role in the projected invasion of Japan. Both McCormick and Oldendorf were sent copies of the orders. And to ensure that all others concerned with the voyage could keep track of the vessel, copies were also sent to Admiral Spruance, Vice Admiral George Murray, Commander of the Marianas, and the port directors in Tinian and Guam.

McVay was disappointed. He wanted his men to have refresher training in Guam before heading into a zone more vulnerable to enemy attack. Still, as the *Indianapolis* weighed anchor for the overnight trip to Guam, he was confident that, when he arrived on the morning of July 27, the local CINCPAC commander would agree to change the training site to Guam.

V

The Merchants of Tranquility

BOUT THE TIME the *Indianapolis* nuzzled into Guam's Apra Harbor, the submarine *I-58* nosed onto the route from Guam to Leyte and slowly followed it westward. Commander Hashimoto was glum. His mission was to attack enemy vessels off the east coast of the Philippine Islands, where American forces were building up an invasion fleet. At the same time, sister submarines of the Taimon Group were to cruise in other buildup areas in the region. One of them, *I-53*, which had sailed from Kure shortly before *I-58*, swerved off to patrol the zone east of Okinawa.

Normally, Hashimoto's boat would carry enough fuel to permit him to stay out for about three months at a time. But fuel was now so scarce that he had merely one month's supply. So rather than cruise leisurely around the sea looking for enemy ships, he would have to follow the most direct routes to the various Pacific crossroads and wait there for prey to happen by.

So far, Hashimoto's luck had not changed, and the war, it seemed, might end before he could chalk up even one certain kill for the Emperor. Yet there was no one to blame for his ill fortune, except perhaps some angry gods. His crew had done a fine job. There was no more skilled a torpedo officer than Toshio Tanaka, his second-in-command. Nor was there a better navigator, or at least a more

41

enthusiastic one, than Lieutenant Hirokoto Tanaka (no relation to Toshio). Though only twenty-one, Hirokoto, an elfish little man with a ready, optimistic smile, was a seasoned sailor. He had been aboard the aircraft carrier *Unyo* when an American submarine torpedoed it in January 1944, killing thirty men and wounding about sixty. Then, after serving on the aircraft carrier *Kaiyo*, he went to submarine school and was assigned to *I-58*, which he helped to construct.

Despite his youth, Hirokoto was endowed with greater self-confidence than perhaps any other man aboard. He was convinced that the Americans would invade Japan and ultimately defeat it, but only after every Japanese defended the land with swords, spears, and sticks. They would fight to the last man, woman, and child . . . actually, not quite the last man. *He* expected to survive, no matter what happened to the rest of the population. Hirokoto Tanaka was too clever a fighter to die.

As the navigation officer, Hirokoto felt he knew exactly where and how to fight. He had as intimate a knowledge of the Pacific Ocean as he had of Tokyo, his hometown, and, after studying intelligence reports, he was as familiar with the routes that American ships traveled as the Americans themselves were. Mapping out a detailed plan that would take *I-58* to each route and crossroads in turn, he was positive that, this time, his submarine would score at least one hit.

Hashimoto was less cocksure; he feared, most of all, an attack by enemy submarines. At least *I-58*, unlike his previous boats, was equipped with air and surface radar, which would warn him of an approaching vessel. But in a cat-and-mouse game, the enemy would have the advantage. The United States could afford to lose a submarine; Japan could not, and therefore could take fewer chances.

After leaving Kure, Hashimoto's submarine had sped along, zigzagging at high speed, finally sailing into the Saipan-Okinawa route. There was the usual ceremonial farewell dinner for the kaitens, who were, like their predecessors, eager to die. The sea was calm under a bright moon; conditions seemed ideal for a hit. Except for one thing—no enemy ships sailed by.

Hirokoto Tanaka was undaunted. There were other routes, he pointed out, tracing alternative ones on his navigation map. And on July 22, *I-58* was cruising down the Okinawa-Guam route, with the moon even fuller and brighter. Once more the kaitens were toasted and success seemed assured. But again the horizon remained un-blemished. When the moon began to fade, Hashimoto, apparently worried about the angry gods, went to pray at the ship's shrine. Just one prize for the Emperor, please!—before the fuel ran out. Then *I-58* headed for the Guam-Leyte route for what might be his last chance to achieve the divine goal that had eluded him since the war began.

Hashimoto perhaps would have been more confident if he had known that three days earlier, on July 24, *I-53* had sunk a ship—with the cooperation of the ship itself. The submarine had fired a human torpedo toward the destroyer *Underhill*, which was escorting a convoy of fifteen smaller ships from Okinawa to Leyte, and the destroyer commander, on sighting the periscope, mistook the missile for a midget submarine and rammed it. The resulting explosion cut the ship in two, killing 119 men. Ships in the convoy saved 109 others—men who probably would have died as well if the *Underhill* had been traveling alone.

Commodore James B. Carter, Admiral Nimitz's assistant chief of staff for operations, was adamant. The *Indianapolis* must leave for Leyte no later than the next morning, July 28, he told Captain McVay at advance CINCPAC headquarters in Guam. He wanted McVay to "get out there as soon as possible." Only in Leyte could his men take the refresher course they had missed getting in San Diego. Admiral Spruance wanted his flagship back, and there was no time to lose.

But McVay pressed his case. The crew, especially the recruits, needed refresher training without delay, he made clear, even though they had had some aboard ship. Why couldn't his men remain in Guam to take the course? It was risky to send green personnel into a danger zone without such training. He would later say: "I made the remark that at the rate I was going, my refresher course would probably be conducted in Tokyo Bay. They [obviously Carter] said, 'No, we will send you to Leyte to get your training. We no longer give such training here in Guam.' "

Carter gave no information about security conditions en route, nor, apparently, did McVay ask for any. After all, the port director and the routing officer would give him such data routinely before he left. And Carter's stress on the need for a hasty departure surely made it evident that the ship would be facing no great threat on the trip.

Actually, Carter was privy to information that McVay vitally required if he was to take the basic precautions for a reasonably safe voyage—information that might even have justified canceling the trip, or at least changing the normal routing for the journey. He knew that there were about four Japanese submarines cruising in the general region between Japan, the Marianas, the Palau group, and the Philippines; that these submarines, unlike those in the past, had been sent out to attack enemy ships, not simply to deliver supplies to stranded Japanese soldiers; and that one of these submarines had been cruising within a few miles of the *Underhill* on the day that ship was sunk—though this information had been so secret that even the captain of the endangered vessel was never informed of the threat. The commodore also knew that Hashimoto's *I-58* posed a similar danger to the *Indianapolis* as it headed toward Leyte.

Carter was so well versed in Navy secrets because they were funneled to CINCPAC via the Washington pipeline from Captain William R. Smedberg II, assistant chief of naval intelligence. The information would reach Captain E. T. Layton, CINCPAC combat intelligence officer, who would relay it to the commodore. Carter's casual attitude toward the menace seemed to mirror that of his immediate superior, Vice Admiral Charles H. McMorris, Nimitz' Chief of Staff, who would later explain:

"I do not know now the degree of accuracy of that information, nor would I have been very much disturbed if I had known it. . . . Any passage [in that area] would necessarily be a certain degree of hazard; but the fact that a submarine had sunk a vessel along a particular route would not be a deterrent toward the routing of other vessels passing that way some days later."

But while Carter may have taken a cue from his boss, he was less frank. When asked later why he didn't inform McVay of the danger, he replied:

"The question of which route he would take wasn't yet determined. As a matter of fact, the question of whether or not he would go to Leyte was not decided until the last minute. The *Indianapolis* was slated to become the flagship, Commander, Fifth Fleet—and there was some reason to feel it desirable to retain her in Guam in order that she might be available for Admiral Spruance when he became ready to go aboard."

Why didn't Carter tell McVay of this uncertainty instead of ordering him to leave for Leyte "as soon as possible"? Carter's statement was especially puzzling in light of what Spruance would have to say. McVay lunched with Spruance and his staff in the officers' mess right after his talk with Carter, and the admiral neither questioned his departure for Leyte nor said he should depart without delay.

Oddly, Spruance, like Carter, failed to mention to McVay the four reported submarines in the region or the sinking of the *Underhill*. Had CINCPAC leaders neglected to pass this vital information on to Spruance, even though his own flagship was about to churn through these dangerous waters? Or did the admiral have this information but feel, as McMorris and Carter did, that it was not important enough (and apparently too secret anyway) to pass on to McVay?

Only one naval official appears to have taken the intelligence seriously. Captain Samuel Clay Anderson, Pacific Fleet operations officer for the Chief of Naval Operations in Washington, was frightened when he learned of the *Underhill*'s fate. He drafted a dispatch to Admiral Nimitz recommending that, because of the submarine menace, CINCPAC change the current routes in the Western Pacific. But the message was stopped by Anderson's superior, Admiral R.S. Edwards, vice chief of naval operations. The matter, he implied, would be considered by a higher authority—presumably Fleet Admiral Ernest J. King, Navy Chief of Operations. The message, however, apparently never reached Nimitz.

As with the *Underhill*, skepticism alone did not keep the information about the submarine threat from reaching the man who needed most to know. Ironically, its security classification—ultrasecret—also did. Only a few department heads and intelligence chiefs were considered trustworthy enough to be informed. Thus, the data went from Commodore Carter in CINCPAC to Captain Oliver F. Naquin, surface operations officer of the Marianas Command, which was subordinate to CINCPAC. Naquin locked it in his filing cabinet and left it there. He did not even pass it on to his superior, Vice Admiral Murray.

Since Naquin plotted friendly and enemy ship movements in the Marianas region, he had to know every scrap of information that might help to safeguard American vessels in the area. Normally, his data would be seen by the intelligence department of the Guam Naval Base, then by the base's port director and his routing officer, who would give the information to ship commanders. Reports stamped "Ultrasecret," though, seldom left Naquin's office.

Actually, Naquin was authorized to pass along even these reports if necessary—but without details that could compromise the source. He was, however, a very cautious man, and so paranoid about security that he seemed prepared to jeopardize the safety of a particular ship in order to maintain the integrity of the system. In any case, Naquin was often unsure of his information. Too many people had cried wolf too often.

"We were continually receiving reports of submarine sightings throughout the Pacific at all times," he would later say, "but the general conclusion to be drawn, in view of the fact that we had so extremely few sinkings out there, was that these merchant skippers [who gave most of the sightings] were just reporting things that were not actually there."

So what effect did the information on the four enemy submarines and the sinking of the *Underhill* have on the operations of his office?

"It had no effect," Naquin would reply.

When Captain McVay stopped in at the Naval Operating Base shortly after lunch to hash over the details of his journey with the port director, he was welcomed into a den of tranquility. Greeting him in the Quonset hut was Lieutenant Joseph Waldron, the port director's routing officer. He would be getting a thorough briefing that would leave few questions unanswered, Waldron assured the visitor. The routing officer then called in two members of his staff to brief McVay.

There was no mention of the four submarines possibly lying in wait near the route McVay was to follow, nor of what happened to the *Underhill*. Since Naquin hadn't informed them, they knew nothing of the threat. Indeed, they spoke of the trip as if it would amount to little more than a pleasure cruise.

When did he wish to leave? one of the men asked, apparently unaware that Commodore Carter had ordered him to depart in the morning.

McVay was baffled but put at ease. If there were any danger, they would be *telling* him when to leave, not asking him when he *wanted* to leave.

About nine in the morning would be fine.

What speed did he contemplate?

McVay was further tranquilized. Submarines on the prowl? Doubtful. Otherwise, they would have surely *advised* a speed, a higher one than the 16 knots normally allowed a ship in these oil-short days.

He would like to enter Leyte Gulf at sunrise so his men could engage in gunnery practice before landing. If his ship steamed along at a leisurely pace of 15.7 knots, it would get in at dawn, Tuesday, August 1.

Which route should he take? McVay wanted to know.

The direct one, the so-called "Peddie" route. No sense going the roundabout way and losing a lot of time.

Even more reassurance. Would they be telling him to use a route they considered dangerous?

Nothing was said about a possible destroyer escort for the *Indianapolis*, but this omission did not greatly disturb McVay, who viewed it as further confirming the absence of real danger. While the *Indianapolis*, like most other cruisers, had no underwater sound gear, it did have surface and air search radars. Besides, an escort would slow up the ship, perhaps making it *more* vulnerable to an enemy attack. And he seldom traveled with an escort anyway. Smaller craft were furnished escorts, but it was commonly thought that cruisers could take care of themselves. In any case, with so many vessels preparing for an invasion of Japan, there was a shortage of escort ships.

Still, McVay remarked, he would prefer to sail in company with another ship if it happened to be going his way—mainly because he could use the other vessel as a simulated enemy craft in training exercises en route.

Waldron was sympathetic. He didn't know of any such vessel, but called Naquin to see if he did. Naquin's assistant answered. No escort would be necessary, the man replied, and he hung up.

Waldron, who had routed about five thousand ships so far in the war, expected this answer—though all he had asked for was a ship that might be going to Leyte anyway. (Actually, three vessels were making the trip within the next two days.) McVay did not press the matter. Too bad about losing a chance to conduct more exercises, but nothing he was told made him feel that he really needed another vessel to accompany him for protection.

When McVay asked for "general information" about possible dangers, one of the men replied that "there was nothing out of the ordinary in the area." McVay "imagined they meant the usual reports of mines, rather indefinite reports of sighting of periscopes, or possible contacts which were not verified." In other words, "nothing to be on guard for, out of the ordinary."

The captain felt so confident that he let his navigator, Commander John Janney, pick up the final departure documents later and deal with any minor unanswered questions.

VI

An Ordinary Cruise

WHILE Captain McVay hurried back to his ship that evening of July 27 to finish taking on supplies and fuel for the journey ahead, Commander Hashimoto was slowly making his way westward along the Guam-Leyte route toward the crossroads with the Palau-Okinawa route. It had been another discouraging day. His limited supply of fuel was gradually evaporating and not a ship had been spotted. Then, at about dawn the next morning, there was more bad news. An enemy aircraft showed up on the radar, and there was enough light for the pilot to see the boat, which had been gliding on the surface during the night.

"Dive!" Hashimoto cried, and the submarine plunged into the depths. A close call. The gods were with him this time. After a number of hours under water, the commander brought the submarine up to periscope depth. He peered through the scope and scanned the pencil-line horizon, which divided a clear sky from an ocean sparkling under the afternoon sun. Suddenly, he stopped turning the instrument. There in the distance, bobbing toward him, was a three-masted ship. A large tanker!

"At last we were face to face with the elusive enemy!" he would later exclaim.

As Hashimoto continued to gaze at this magnificent target, an escort ship loomed into view—a destroyer. This "made the situation less simple." The destroyer might seek out his submarine when he attacked the tanker, and he couldn't afford to disperse his power—conventional and manned torpedoes—trying to sink both ships. He would go after the tanker.

But then Hashimoto found that his hydrophones were not functioning properly, and there was no way for him to move within torpedo range of the tanker if these sound instruments couldn't tell him exactly where the destroyer was. He would have to sacrifice his kaitens, who, Hashimoto hoped, could find their way to the target from a greater distance.

"Kaitens prepare for action!" he cried over the telephone to Toshio Tanaka, his torpedo officer. Tanaka passed on the order to the kaitens. "All tubes to the ready!"

Then: "Numbers 1 and 2 kaitens—stand by!"

Hashimoto gave the enemy course and speed and ordered Number 1 to start his engines, but they wouldn't work. The commander anxiously looked through his periscope once more and, in near-desperation, ordered Number 2 to start his engines. They worked! Launch! Tanaka released the last securing band and the kaiten, crying "Three cheers for the Emperor!" sprang loose toward his target. When no explosion could be heard after ten minutes, Number 1, who finally had a torpedo with working engines, was also launched. He headed for oblivion, shouting, "Thank you all for taking such good care of us."

The seconds passed, then the minutes—fifteen, thirty, forty-five . . . and still no explosion. Not another failure! Then, about fifty minutes after Number 2 had streaked off—a great blast. And ten minutes later, a second one. The tanker finally vanished from the periscope mirror. Had it been sunk—or had it escaped, perhaps after the destroyer blew up the kaitens? Hashimoto would have been more optimistic if he had heard the explosions earlier, before the enemy could sight the periscopes and strike. When he surfaced to investigate, a squall obscured everything. Now he might never know if he had finally scored a kill.

Hashimoto knelt in his shrine to pray for the happiness of the departed kaitens in a future existence. Had they died fruitlessly? He hoped he wouldn't have to use his remaining four. Then, amid scampering rats that were also hungering for a decent meal, he sat down for a dinner of onions, the only fresh vegetable left, and canned sweet potatoes. They had the taste, appropriate to the moment, of sand and ashes.

The *Indianapolis* had pulled out of Apra Harbor at about 9 A.M., July 28, and cruised toward Leyte in overcast weather that seemed to match the spirits of many of the men. Once more, they had been "cheated" out of shore leave. Ensign Blum finally set foot on land —but only to supervise the loading of supplies! They let him touch the ground but not a girl or a glass in town, teasing him, making him feel more deprived than ever. The Navy was clearly out to wreck his morale.

And Yeoman Havins was no happier. He didn't even make it down the gangplank. Had his orders for a transfer come through yet? he asked the educational officer once again. No time to check, was the answer. He should wait until the next island. Havins began to wonder if that island might be Kyushu, Japan!

The rather somber mood only began to lighten some time after the ship got underway, when Captain McVay declared a "ropeyarn Sunday"; this meant that, except for some routine duties, there would be no drills or work on board. Dr. Haynes was one of the few who worked anyway. After helping Father Conway conduct Protestant services, as usual on Sundays, he had the whole crew line up in the mess hall for cholera shots. None of *his* men was going to die of cholera in China, Formosa, or some other disease-ridden oriental hellhole. More gripes—at last a day off, and Doc had to interrupt them in the middle of a craps game, a bull session, a nap. Couldn't even finish a letter home. Doc was okay, but he worried too much about people.

After standing constant four-hour watches and training continuously from the time the ship left San Francisco, the men were exhausted and irritable. They badly needed a breathing spell, and this voyage seemed like it might fill the bill since strict battle rules weren't necessary on this run. There had been no serious hint of any submarine activity in the area. At least this is what Navigator Janney told McVay after he had read the intelligence report that accompanied the ship's orders picked up in Guam. (Copies of the orders had been sent, of course, to the same commands that were earlier informed of the ship's anticipated voyage to Leyte, and they would certainly keep track of the ship.) The intelligence brief contained nothing out of the ordinary:

On July 22, shortly after midnight, a submarine had been reported surfacing about seventy miles south of the Peddie route. But that was several days earlier.

On July 25, an unknown ship reported sighting a possible periscope over ninety miles north of Peddie. But intelligence files were clogged with false periscope reports.

Also on July 25, sound contact was reported that could have indicated a submarine. But the contact was described as "doubtful."

The same old contacts, Janney told McVay. Like so many they had seen in the past. Nothing to worry about. And McVay didn't worry. As he would say later: "The knowledge which I possessed indicated to me that there was little possibility of surface, air, or subsurface attack, in fact, no possibility."

At the Sunday dinner for department heads, Janney even joked about the "submarine menace" to his colleagues, who included Commander Flynn, Dr. Haynes, and Lieutenant Redmayne (Captain McVay had his own mess). The atmosphere couldn't be more cheerful as they dined in the wardroom on steak and strawberries (the enlisted men made do with cold cuts and syrup-smothered ice cream). There was, Janney said with a smile, a Japanese submarine in the area. He had overheard a radio conversation between two ships and several planes that Sunday afternoon. One of the craft, the merchant ship *Wild Hunter*, had reported the day before that it had sighted a periscope about 170 miles ahead of the *Indianapolis*. When the ship had seen the periscope a second time and fired on it, the Marianas Command, which had jurisdiction over the area, sent out a hunter-killer group—the destroyer *Albert T. Harris* and some planes—to search for it. Last he had heard, this group was still looking for the enemy submarine (though it would call off the search that evening).

"We'll pass that sub sometime during the night," Janney said to the amusement of the other officers. The ocean, it would seem, was dotted with Japanese periscopes! In any case, someone said humorously, their ship's "destroyer escort" would take care of *that* submarine.

This was obviously nothing serious, or the Marianas Command would have diverted the *Indianapolis* to another route. No use bothering Captain McVay with such nonsense. Somehow the war seemed all but over, especially since the captain had told them they had delivered a decisive weapon to Tinian. They would go through the motions of training and preparing for an invasion of Formosa or Japan, but such action wasn't likely now. Anyway, after their ship had managed to survive almost five years of war, it was hard to get ruffled over a vague submarine threat at this moment of near-victory.

Drawing even less attention than Janney's report was another that was received that night in the radio room: About three hundred miles to the south, two torpedoes had missed a merchant ship. The communications watch officer on duty broke down the code and shrugged. It seemed like just another submarine report. No sense disturbing the captain.

Equally reluctant to disturb McVay was Lieutenant Charles B. McKissick, who was an officer of the deck that evening from 6 to 8 P.M. A tall, dark-haired man with a gleaming smile and a physique hardened on the football field, McKissick had fought as a gunnery officer from one island to the other for more than twenty months and was sensitive to the slightest possibility of an enemy threat.

But when he climbed to the bridge to look through a file of radio messages and found one that seemed rather unusual, he wasn't greatly impressed. It stated that there "was some sort of anti-submarine patrol that had reported contact" about two hundred miles south of the *Indianapolis'* position. Nothing urgent, it seemed. The contact (apparently referring to the destroyer *Harris* expedition) had been made too far away to spell danger. So McKissick did not bother to check where the patrol was on his navigational chart.

When he was about to leave his post, however, he did ask his relief whether he agreed with his own estimate of a possible threat. How far away did he think the patrol activity was "in relation to our position and course"? McKissick's estimate was probably accurate, came the reply. Any submarine that distant could hardly reach the *Indianapolis* before the ship reached its destination.

Like Commander Janney, McKissick did not inform Captain McVay of the submarine report, and Janney himself apparently did not know his ship had been officially notified of it; in his dinner revelation, he had quoted only the intrapatrol conversations on which he had eavesdropped.

Yet, though McKissick may have been misled by the low-key nature of the dispatch, he would, if he had sensed any real danger, have certainly reacted with a violently protective instinct, one that would apply not only to the crew but to the ship itself. For to the lieutenant, the *Indianapolis* was not just an inanimate jumble of iron and steel, but a cherished object with a heart and soul. A swaybacked monster? Nonsense! Why "it was one of the prettiest ships" he had "ever seen . . . of any class . . . that had come down in recent years." Could one ever find a more beautiful clipper bow?

McKissick was proud of his ship indeed. No sailors had seen "more action in more places in the Pacific than those who were fortunate to serve aboard the *Indianapolis*." His love and respect for the cruiser "almost defied description," he would say. And that was one reason why he didn't mind serving as deck officer. For him, there was no greater pleasure than presiding over the ship after dark, when the silence of the sea was broken only by the slap of white-tipped waves against the slender ironsides, the steady moan of distant engines, the occasional cry of glee from someone who had rolled a double seven, the subdued chatter of men reminiscing about their sweethearts, the rhythmic creak of decks wet with the ocean spray.

It was the ideal time to think about home in Midland, Texas, where he was born in 1917 into a minister's family; about those ambitious days at Texas Christian University and the Southern College of Optometry in Memphis, Tennessee, from which he graduated in 1942; about his doting parents, his five sisters, and three brothers. All tree were in the service, but he was the luckiest: He was on the *Indianapolis*. In fact, he had been with the ship almost since he had joined the Navy as an ensign in 1943. Yes, he loved being out on deck at night; it was the best time to think and dream, especially when the moon and the stars bathed the sea in a twinkling brilliance that seemed almost sacred. On this particular Sunday night, though, the sea was dark and rough.

At about 7:30 P.M., Captain McVay came to the bridge to give McKissick his orders for the night. The two men scanned the semi-dark sky; the cloud cover was heavy, but occasionally thinned out enough to let the half-moon shine through in bright flashes. In general, they noted, visibility was very poor. Earlier, when it had been better, the ship had zigzagged in accordance with the fleet rule that in fair weather all warships sailing in possibly dangerous waters must zigzag, since they would presumably stand a better chance of evading enemy torpedoes this way. McVay knew the rule, but he also knew that ship commanders used their discretion in deciding if and when to zigzag, and that some commanders thought zigzagging was futile. In fact, his instructions issued in Guam specifically gave him discretion in this matter.

Zigzagging after dark, he decided, wasn't necessary, for even if Guam's intelligence was wrong, he couldn't imagine any submarine being able to zero in on his ship in such overcast weather. When the moon did emerge, it was only for a quick peek—not enough time for the enemy to take action. Moreover, the ship at night was moving at about 17 knots, fast enough to leave a submarine behind. Zigzagging would only slow the ship down and increase its vulnerability. So McVay gave the order: Cease zigzagging after dark! Of course, McKissick and the other officers knew the standing order that if the weather changed while the captain was asleep, they were free to make the appropriate decision about a zigzag course even before consulting him.

McKissick didn't protest the decision. He had enormous confidence in the captain, and if this man felt there was no need to zigzag, it was not for McKissick to second-guess him. Anyway, the weather *was* bad, despite the teasing flashes of moonlight.

At 8 P.M., McKissick passed on his orders to the officer who relieved him, then went to the wardroom to watch an old movie. When it was over, he made his way to Bunk Room JJ (which was located two decks below at the water line), removed his clothes, and crawled into his bunk at about 10:30 P.M.; he was too exhausted to read a pamphlet someone had put on the bed entitled *Survival on Land and Sea*. It had been a relaxing day of prayer and play, the kind of day when McKissick felt in perfect communion with his beloved ship. Only the moon dappling upon the sea, it seemed, was missing—though who could tell if later that night it might sneak from behind the clouds and show itself a little more brazenly.

At about the time Lieutenant McKissick went to bed, Captain McVay strode to the bridge to take a last look at weather conditions before he also turned in. He had been reminiscing about old times with a classmate from Annapolis, Captain Edwin M. Crouch, whom he had met in Guam and invited on the journey to Leyte. Crouch, a director in the Bureau of Ordnance in Washington, had been planning to go to Leyte anyway; why fly when he could enjoy a pleasant cruise?

Now, on the bridge, McVay gazed into a "confused sea, with long swells, long deep swells, light wind, and a dark night. It was apparently overcast. . . . The visibility was well below average." He entered the chart house with his navigator, Commander Janney, and examined first the chart with its little red indicator lights, then his night orders, reviewing some of the points with Janney to make sure he understood them.

There wasn't much to review. The orders specified the required speed, course, and other routine data, and stated that the captain should be informed (through the voice tube leading to his cabin) of any changes in the weather or signs of possible danger.

McVay thus saw no reason to sift through the message file personally, the file that would have informed him, as it had McKissick, that a submarine had been sighted farther along the Peddie route and had been hunted for two days by an American hunter-killer team. And he could never have guessed that the man he was now talking to—Commander Janney—had overheard the ships involved exchanging information about the patrol operation and, in fact, had repeated the report he had whimsically made at dinner to the watch officers who had come to the bridge after McKissick left. Captain McVay now seemed to be the only top officer on the ship who *didn't* know about it. When, after the war, Dr. Haynes mentioned the dinner conversation to him, the captain would exclaim to naval investigators with a sense of shock, hurt, and disbelief:

> The navigator would not discuss with the doctor the contents of dispatches or things of that nature, because they had been warned many times that general bits of information were never to be discussed in the wardroom where they could be made light of, where they could be misunderstood or misinterpreted. . . . Had [Janney done such a thing], I am sure the Executive Officer, or somebody else, would have told me.

But neither the executive officer, Commander Flynn, nor anybody else did. So Captain McVay, deprived of the ultrasecret reports in Guam and now of this latest information, signed the night orders after about fifteen minutes on the bridge and retired to his emergency cabin nearby—he had given his main cabin to Captain Crouch—confidently expecting a good night's sleep. By the time he lay naked on his bed and closed his eyes at about 11 P.M., the moon had slid once more from behind the clouds.

At precisely this time, Commander Hashimoto awakened from his evening nap, quickly dressed, and mounted the conning tower of *I-58*, possibly the mysterious boat being sought by the hunter-killer team.

"Night action stations!" he cried. And the submarine suddenly sprang to life. Because of the overcast weather, the dimly lit craft had dozed for several hours, the sealed-in silence broken only by the hum of the air-conditioning system, the sounds of the hydrophones and rudder, and the squealing of rats that were still running rampant in the kitchen. About two-thirds of the crew had been sleeping naked sprawled on torpedoes, rice sacks, shelves—anywhere but in their bunks, which were stuffy despite the air conditioning.

When the crew, in response to the voice booming over the intercom system, had scrambled into their uniforms and rushed to their battle stations, Hashimoto ordered his officers to steer the craft toward the surface and raise the night periscope to a point just over it. He peered through the tube and found that the visibility, which had been zero before his nap, was much better now; he could almost see the horizon. The moon hovered brightly in the eastern sky, though clouds drifted threateningly nearby.

At last, reasonably clear weather again—clear enough, at least in one direction, for a submerged attack. He had just prayed at the shrine and felt renewed confidence. Now if only some ship would stray past before the moon vanished into hiding again. He raised the periscope gradually and turned it slowly from side to side two or three times. Nothing but water and sky. This was near the intersection of the Guam-Leyte and Palau-Okinawa routes, which should, it seemed, be seething with enemy ships. Hashimoto refused to give up; he would surface and continue the search with his powerful binoculars. Certainly, there must be one enemy vessel out there he could deliver to the Imperial Palace while the moon still smiled in the darkness.

Lieutenant Redmayne was happy to perform his new duty, which gave him even greater authority than before. Since leaving Pearl Harbor, he had been in charge of the engine room, and his promotion to lieutenant commander would come through shortly. Now he would undertake an additional task: supervising the night watch.

Redmayne would advise the officer of the deck on how he should carry out the captain's orders, and would be responsible, while the captain slept, for the safety of the ship. In a sense, he would serve as the acting skipper—a most prestigious position. But since he was inexperienced in this job, he was merely an apprentice on the night of July 29 when he reported to the bridge for the 8-P.M.-to-midnight watch.

Redmayne's mentor was Commander Lipski, the most experienced supervisor of the watch, who set standards of excellence that Redmayne knew would be hard to match. Lipski, a genial man of thirty-four, was generally considered one of the most brilliant sailors on the ship. A former naval attaché in Helsinki, Finland, and an expert in the Russian language, he was just the kind of officer naval intelligence valued most. But Lipski insisted on seeing combat and managed to break away from Washington and join the *Indianapolis* in 1943.

In any case, Redmayne felt it was better to be out on deck at night than in the steaming interior of this aging ship. So stifling was it below, especially in these summer days, that many men wouldn't, or couldn't, sleep there. Thus, Redmayne had to step over scores of half-naked sailors sprawled on blankets and mattresses that covered the decks from railing to railing. And those who remained below could survive only because the ship used Condition Yoke Modified. "Yoke" meant that all the doors below were to be sealed shut to assure the vessel's watertight integrity; if water leaked into the hull, it would be contained by the closed doors.

"Modified" permitted enough doors to remain open to keep the crew from virtually suffocating. Captain McVay saw this as a pragmatic compromise. It placed the ship in a bit more jeopardy, but kept morale high enough so the men would be able to deal effectively with any possible trouble. One had to be realistic. Of course, the condition would revert to "Yoke *Unmodified*," as the captain would explain, if a "threat from enemy attack might be expected"—an expectation that didn't exist that night.

Another officer on the 8-P.M.-to-midnight shift that night was ambitious, redheaded Ensign Harlan Twible, who stood watch in sky aft, supervising men on duty at several gun mounts. His partner was Lieutenant Leland Jack Clinton, who had come off a PT boat.

As Twible would say: "He was not too conversant with modern armor, . . . and I more or less had the running of the sky aft unit."

Twible was not unhappy about this responsibility. For, like Redmayne, he was, at twenty-three, a man who relished authority. An Annapolis graduate, he also respected authority—especially if his superior officer was an Annapolis man, too. He would never forget how Captain McVay greeted him when he first came aboard, the last officer to join the crew: "You're Naval Academy and we expect a lot from you." Twible had replied, "Ay, ay, sir," and he was determined to give a lot—despite his chagrin at being assigned to the *Indianapolis*. His demeanor, unsmiling, supremely self-assured, reflected a will to succeed at any task, to carry out any order. Still, he was perturbed.

Twible had wanted to be either a flyer or a submariner. And here he was assigned to an old, unglamorous cruiser, a different ship, it seemed, from the one that Lieutenant McKissick so cherished. It was, in fact, one of the last ships in the world he would have chosen. Though he was convinced that nothing could kill him, he felt strangely uncomfortable on this vessel, which, he would say, "had an aura about it." It had barely survived the kamikaze attack at Okinawa, and somehow he sensed, as the three fortunetellers had warned in San Francisco, that its future would be bleak. He even wrote his brother, a Navy medical student, about his foreboding—though he assured his sibling that he personally would survive.

This confidence was not mere bravado. Twible was a deeply religious man who had become "aware of God's part in this world" during the Depression, when family disaster had seemed neverending. After losing all his meager savings, his father, a woolen mill worker in Gilbertville, Massachusetts, who had immigrated from Ireland, lay ill for several years, while Harlan himself almost died from a ruptured appendix. Despite it all, his parents sent him and his two brothers to college, and finally Harlan received an appointment to Annapolis. God had come through—even tossing in a bonus when Twible met Alice Southworth and then married her in June 1945, shortly before leaving San Francisco.

If God instilled in Twible a sense of justice, the young ensign was given a chance to exhibit this quality as soon as the ship sailed through the Golden Gate; Captain McVay appointed him prosecutor in court-martial cases to be tried aboard ship. Twible went easy on the first defendant, who had made a girl pregnant while absent without leave but agreed to marry her by proxy. Surely God would have shown such compassion. But in another AWOL case, Twible was tougher; he saw to it that the man was sentenced to several days in the brig on bread and water. God could be angry, too.

Was it perhaps because Twible felt close to the Almighty that he sensed the ship had an "aura"? Did he hear what others had heard only from fortunetellers? Twible would later think so. After all, when the 8 P.M.-to-midnight watch was ending, why did he choose to remain at his post while his partner descended into the bowels of the ship to awaken their relief—never to be seen again?

While Ensign Twible looked to God to protect his ship, Commander Hashimoto looked to the gods to help him sink such a ship. And shortly after 11 P.M. on July 29, he would surface and start searching for one, perhaps for the last time, given the submarine's dwindling fuel supply.

"Stand by, type-13 radar—stand by, type-22 radar," he cried. The radar operator raised the receivers above the surface to search for aircraft and surface craft. When all seemed clear, Hashimoto ordered, "Action stations!" and alarm bells rang, calling crew members to their battle stations. "Surface!" Then: "Blow main ballast!" High-pressure air suddenly burst into the main tanks, expelling the water, and the submarine I-58 broke the foamy surface like a great whale leaping from the depths.

Hashimoto again swept the horizon with his night periscope; but though visibility was now fairly good for about ten thousand meters in the direction of the moon (if very poor in other directions), no shadow of a ship marred the calm beauty of the ocean landscape. He ordered the yeoman of signals to open the conning tower hatch and climb out to the bridge, and the yeoman, obeying, was followed by Hirokoto Tanaka, the navigator. According to Hirokoto's carefully gathered intelligence, ships regularly passed this way, since it was near the crossroads of the Okinawa-Palau and Guam-Leyte routes. He hadn't picked the right spot up to now; it wasn't his fault that the ocean was so large. Yet he felt driven to find a target before returning home so that he wouldn't lose face in the eyes of Commander Hashimoto and the crew.

Hirokoto gazed through his binoculars, scanning the ocean systematically to the horizon. The moon hung in the black sky as if painted on it, suspiciously eyeing, it seemed, the barely perceptible cloud banks that hovered nearby. Nothing . . . nothing . . . but then his eyes lingered on the moonrays as they gently pricked the ocean. What was that tiny shadow? . . . An enemy vessel? He shouted: "Bearing red nine-zero degrees, a possible enemy ship!"

When Hirokoto had sent the yeoman to Hashimoto to have him confirm the sighting, the commander immediately rushed to the bridge and gazed in the same direction through his own binoculars. . . . Yes, a dark spot on the horizon. Was this, finally, the gift he would present to the Emperor?

"Dive!" Hashimoto ordered. And the commander, followed by the others, scrambled down the ladder and resumed watching the black shape through the periscope. He must not lose sight of this sacred target, whatever it was. When the submarine had reached a depth of seventeen to nineteen yards, he cried, "Ship in sight! All tubes to the ready!" And he added, "Kaitens stand by!"

The four remaining kaitens, like racehorses in their starting stalls, could hardly wait to be loosed. One of them even called Hashimoto on the phone; Hirokoto Tanaka answered while the commander stood by his side listening.

"Please send us," the kaiten pleaded. "Do not deprive us of this opportunity!"

Hashimoto whispered to his navigator: "Don't commit yourself." Who knew what the situation would require? For now, he decided, he would use only his conventional torpedoes. He would not waste lives needlessly, even if the kaitens were impatient to blast their way to heaven. Yet, should the ship change course or the regular torpedoes miss it, he might have to send them after all.

Meanwhile, the whole crew was "agog"—a ship for them to sink! And Torpedo Officer Toshio Tanaka, who had to make sure the submarine remained level so the torpedoes could be launched, was euphoric. He felt himself to be the ultimate samurai, about to avenge all the "barbaric" acts that America had ever committed against Japan. (His previous targets, he had to agree, may have escaped.)

Hashimoto kept his eyes pressed to the periscope as the dark shape gradually took the form of a ship. He soon realized it was coming directly toward the submarine, and his joy was suddenly tinged with fear. Had the ship seen his own craft? Was it a destroyer planning to launch a depth charge? In any case, if it passed directly overhead, it would be difficult to hit with a torpedo.

The commander glanced at his watch—11:09 P.M. "Six torpedoes will be fired!" he ordered in a raspy voice he hoped would not betray his apprehension. When the ship approached within fifteen hundred yards of the submarine—in less than an hour, he calculated—he would fire from all tubes in one salvo, fanwise. One of the torpedoes might hit, but in case none did, he would use his kaitens. He ordered Number 6 to get into his torpedo and Number 5 to stand by.

The shape had become triangular and was gradually expanding. If he could only see the height of the mast, he might better estimate the range. Otherwise, one of his officers would have to estimate it by listening to the sound of the propeller, a rather unreliable method since American ships often operated with more than one propeller. And if he could determine the class of the ship, he could judge the speed by counting the engine revolutions with the hydrophones. If not, he would have to assess the speed with his naked eye—another unreliable method.

Finally, the ship changed direction slightly and two masts came into view. Hashimoto sighed with relief; the vessel wouldn't pass over the submarine after all. It was a good thing it had "zigged" a little. The masthead, he could now determine, was about ninety feet. It was surely a battleship or a large cruiser, he decided after consulting with Hirokoto Tanaka. Probably an *Idaho*-class battleship, they agreed.

"We've got her!" Hashimoto thought. What a prize!

.   .   .

At about 11:45 P.M. aboard the *Indianapolis*, Ensign Blum, awakened by Lieutenant Clinton, Harlan Twible's partner on watch, wriggled into his uniform and groggily made his way to the wardroom. He grabbed a sandwich from the pantry, then climbed to sky aft to relieve Twible.

Blum was one of some two hundred men who reported for duty on the midnight-to-4 A.M. watch. They would now serve under the new supervisor of the watch, Lieutenant Commander Kyle C. Moore (known as "Casey" because of his initials), a former newspaperman and photographer from Knoxville, Tennessee; Moore was the ship's damage control officer and, like Lipski, one of the best and best-liked officers aboard. His officer of the deck would be Lieutenant John I. Orr, who understood better than most of the crew the importance of an alert watch; his previous ship, the USS *Cooper*, had been sunk.

Blum put on his sound-powered headphones and, munching on his sandwich, called to his men in the gun mounts he supervised: Did they see anything to fire at?

Not a thing. Quiet night.

Blum gazed at the dark, slightly choppy sea. It was the kind of night he and his buddy, Tom Brophy, should be spending in an exotic hideaway smelling the flower in some island beauty's long flowing hair.

Yes, a quiet night. Nothing to report.

Meanwhile, Giles McCoy stood leaning against a bunk in a sleeping compartment three decks below in the fantail, barely able to keep awake. So damned stuffy, he thought. The Navy men stood watch on deck where they could breathe fresh air, smell the sea, listen to the waves dash against the hull—and search for the enemy. But where did they put a Marine like himself? Down below where there was almost no air to breathe, and the only smell was of sweat, the only sound, of snoring. Worse, his only duty was to watch the brig, situated at one end of the compartment and partitioned off by a metal latticework wall.

At least if he were on deck, he might catch sight of a torpedo heading his way. What a waste of a good Marine to make him guard a couple of nice guys who had gotten drunk and gone AWOL in San Francisco—guys whom Twible, in his search for justice, had demanded be punished and put on a bread-and-water diet. McCoy was glad to see, however, that, in addition to the bread and water, his prisoners were being fed all kinds of goodies by their buddies in the bakery. Of course, he happened to be looking elsewhere when they came with these delicacies. It didn't bother him that the men he was guarding were, in fact, eating better than their guard.

But what he wouldn't give for a cool ocean breeze, to feel the spray on his face. Anything to keep him from falling asleep in this stifling dungeon. If he dozed now, he wondered if anything could wake him up.

Though Commander Hashimoto was exhilarated when he realized the size of his target, he kept a calm demeanor. Experience had taught him that it was difficult to sink or even hit a ship, especially one this fast. He estimated that this "battleship" was moving at about 20 knots—and it could change course at any moment. After so many disappointments in the war, he wouldn't let himself be too optimistic, even though conditions for success could hardly be more favorable; even though, as Navigator Hirokoto Tanaka would say, "this was a textbook situation."

Adding to Hashimoto's anxiety were the kaitens, who would not stop pleading for the chance to die.

"Why can't we be launched?" they cried over and over again. Hashimoto wanted to please them, but he couldn't. How could he explain to them that he didn't want them to die needlessly? After all, he, too, wanted to pay his debt to the Emperor; if he failed, he would be condemned to a life of disgrace. Should the kaitens live through no fault of their own, they would still be honored in life, as they would be in death. If he could accept his fate, they should accept theirs—even life.

As the moment of glory neared, Hashimoto kept gazing through the periscope in the electric silence, undisturbed even by the kaitens. He altered the setting of the director to green 60 degrees, range 1500 yards, then set the depth of the torpedoes at 6 yards and their speed at 42 knots, with each being fired at two-second intervals fanwise. He then began the approach for firing and, finally, in a loud voice cried: "Stand by—fire!"

The commander returned to the periscope and, with pounding heart, waited for the torpedoes to strike the ship. He could see almost nothing now, for the moon had just retreated behind a cloud. Thank the gods that the missiles had been launched in the nick of time, when the moon was still bright. His signalman, standing beside him, stared at his watch. Five seconds . . . ten seconds . . . thirty seconds. . . . The torpedoes, with no kaitens to steer an indirect course, had to hit within a minute—unless they missed. The ship, now an obscure shadow, was still moving in front of the submarine. Forty-five seconds . . . fifty . . . fifty-one . . .

Hashimoto shook with emotion as a column of water suddenly towered over the ship on the starboard side by the forward turret, than another by the after turret, then still another near Turret 2, which seemed to envelop the whole ship. Surging through the spray of the spent geysers were flashes of glowing red flame.

"A hit! A hit!" Hashimoto shouted, more in relief than in elation. Almost simultaneously, Hirokoto Tanaka, peering through another periscope, cried the same words. Hadn't he assured the commander that they would catch a big fish in these waters? And the several enlisted men present "danced round with joy," then, at Hirokoto's invitation, rushed to his periscope to take turns watching their dream become a reality.

VII

Revenge of the Samurai

APTAIN MCVAY'S DREAM suddenly came to an end. The first explosion flung him out of his bunk, and the second bounced him around on the shuddering deck. Like most of the men aboard, he did not hear a third explosion, perhaps because it was virtually simultaneous with the second blast, or because Hashimoto and Hirokoto Tanaka had erred in thinking they saw a third one.

"My God!" the dazed captain thought. "We've been hit by another kamikaze!"

He vividly recalled the horror of that moment when the kamikaze had struck the ship off Okinawa and nearly sunk it. But as he gradually came to his senses, he realized there was little chance that an enemy plane would be flying nearby—the ship was too far from Japan. Perhaps it had hit a mine? Also unlikely. He knew of many vessels that had struck mines but none that had even been shaken up by them. The ship must have been torpedoed. But why hadn't he been warned of any enemy submarines in this area?

McVay picked himself up and, without clothes, groped his way in the dark through clouds of acrid smoke to the bridge, where he found Lieutenant Orr, the officer of the deck.

Any reports on what happened? the captain asked.

"No sir," Orr replied. "I've lost all communications. I've tried to stop the engines. I don't know whether the order has ever gotten through to the engine room."

McVay agreed that the engines should be stopped since the vessel was listing slightly and might be drawing water. Orr had tried "in every way" to contact the engine room, but all electrical and sound-powered forms of communication were out—the engine-control-room telegraph, telephone, loudspeaker system, MG circuits. And a messenger Orr had sent there had not reported back yet.

McVay then turned to Commander Janney, who was also on the bridge. Go to Radio Central (Radio 1), he ordered Janney, to make sure a distress message got out. He should report that "we [have] been torpedoed, what our latitude and longitude [is], that we [are] sinking rapidly and [need] immediate assistance."

Yet, though McVay was worried, he was not alarmed. He was simply taking all precautions. He gazed from the bridge, hoping to find some clue as to what had happened, and to assess the damage. But with the air a smoky haze and the moon again blacked out, he "could see nothing"; unable to "make out anybody on deck"—or even on the bridge—he had to ask people their names.

Where was Casey Moore, his supervisor of the deck? As the damage control officer, he would know something about the situation. Unable to find him, McVay headed back to his cabin to put on his clothes and was about to enter when Moore came running up to him breathlessly. He had just come from below and what he had seen—the fires, the chaos, the dead and wounded—was horrifying.

"We're badly damaged," he gasped. "We're going down rapidly." The compartments up forward were flooding swiftly, and he couldn't close the watertight doors since nobody would help him.

"Do you wish to abandon ship?" Moore asked anxiously.

McVay was stunned. The situation couldn't be that bad. "No," he said. The ship had only about a three-degree list. They had "been through a hit before" and "were able to control it quite easily," and they could do it again. He was "not at all perturbed." So far as he knew, the ship was "not damaged aft at all." He should go back, he ordered Moore, and try to find as many men as he could to help him close the doors.

Moore slouched away, deeply disturbed, it seemed, by his conversation with McVay, obviously feeling that there was little time to save lives. The captain entered his cabin, hurriedly dressed, then rushed back to the bridge. Abandoning ship at this point was unthinkable to him; no responsible skipper would give such an order until all hope for saving his ship was gone. He feared, however, that the main engine control room had not gotten the message to stop the engines. There was always the danger of scooping in too much water if the damage was sizable, as Casey thought it was.

The fate of the ship, it seemed, could depend on what Chief Engineer Redmayne was instructing his men to do—if, in fact, he was in the engine room.

Redmayne wasn't. After being relieved on watch, he had descended from the bridge to the main deck and had stopped off in the wardroom to grab a ham sandwich, then climbed up another ladder to the forecastle deck to visit the head (toilet). As he stood up and began buckling his belt, the first torpedo hit just forward of the head, shaking him severely, followed by the second just below it. Almost immediately, he heard the crackling of flames right outside the door. Redmayne was in shock.

"Holy Jesus!" he cried. Trapped! Was his blossoming career to end ignominiously in the head? Cautiously, he opened the door, and as he closed his eyes to protect them from the smoke, he tripped and screamed in agony as his left hand touched the red-hot metal deck. A sheet of fire had seconds before swept through the passageway, turning the deck into a steaming grill.

Redmayne scrambled to his feet and climbed down a ladder to the main deck through a screen of white smoke illuminated by the reflected firelight. He had to get back to the after, or main, engine control room, even though it was situated under the water line deep in the entrails of the ship and was an extremely dangerous place to be if a sinking seemed imminent. But Redmayne did not think the ship would sink, nor, as chief engineer, did he intend to shirk his duty. He reached the main deck and, stepping over scattered equipment, cots, and displaced furniture, threaded his way through the port hangar and climbed down to the after engine room.

"What have you heard from the bridge?" he asked the officer on watch there.

"Nothing," came the reply. "We're unable to communicate with the bridge."

Redmayne almost despaired. What did the captain want him to do? Should the ship plow ahead? Should it stop? If he made the wrong decision, it could mean the death of the *Indianapolis*—and Dick Redmayne. He found that because the forward engine room, which supplied power for the forward part of the ship, was no longer generating any, only two of the vessel's four engines were still operating, and the pressure on one of them was falling rapidly. The water pressure was down, probably because of ruptured mains, and the inclinometer showed the ship to be listing at more than twelve degrees starboard.

Redmayne wavered. If he stopped the single engine that still worked properly, would he be creating a still better target for the submarine that might have already struck the ship? And if the ship was taking water, would he be hastening its demise by driving ahead? He finally reached a decision. Since no word had come down from the bridge, he would simply follow the captain's last instructions: Keep the ship moving. Redmayne thus ordered his men to work the remaining good engine to the limit, and pump the oil from the starboard tanks to the port tanks in an effort to correct the list.

But the lieutenant was growing ever more alarmed. He had always been self-confident, always certain he could master any situation. But now he had doubts, especially when a machinist's mate arrived breathless with a terrifying story about how he had narrowly escaped from the steaming ruins of the forward engine room. Redmayne had to find out what the captain wanted him to do.

"Stay where you are!" he ordered his men, and headed toward the bridge himself, apparently convinced he would be back soon. But as he began climbing, the list suddenly grew, and he could barely make it up the ladder. He wondered now if he would even reach topside. Had his luck finally run out?

Many other men were also caught deep in the belly of the ship, among them Marine Private First Class McCoy, his two prisoners, and the sailors sleeping in the bunks adjacent to the brig, who shared with the prisoners a steamy compartment on the bottom deck under the fantail. The blasts hurled the men from their bunks, lifted the bunks from their bulkhead mountings, and sent the debris crashing down on the stunned victims.

McCoy, buried like the others under a jumble of iron, wood, and bedding, dragged himself out, shaken up but miraculously unhurt. He stumbled around in the total darkness that engulfed the compartment after the dimly lit blue battle lamps had gone out. What had happened? As with Captain McVay, the nightmare of Okinawa suddenly flashed through McCoy's mind. The kamikaze plane was streaking toward him! Not again!

While moans and cries pierced the night, McCoy crawled around until he found a battery-powered lamp and switched it on. He stared incredulously at the terrible chaos, at men sprawled under the crush of bunks, some with just their twisted limbs showing. McCoy's first thought, however, was to set free the prisoners, who were clamoring to get out; in semishock, he tottered to the brig, unlocked the cage, and released the two Mexican youths. Then the three, together with others able to walk, pulled out the trapped victims, lifting the bunks, pushing, prying. McCoy had cursed the oppressive temperature before the explosions; now he sweated in the scorching heat of a ship afire.

Within minutes, the men dug about thirty comrades out of the mountain of tangled wreckage, many with broken limbs and injured backs, and carried them to a ladder that led to the chief petty officers' compartment above. Some able men had already scrambled to relative safety, leaving the rest behind, but most, including McCoy and his prisoners, formed a human chain and passed the wounded up the ladder one by one. However, as the ship tilted more sharply to starboard, men lost their balance and bodies came tumbling down. Then, suddenly, a dreaded warning sounded from above:

"Sorry, but we're going to dog [close] the hatch!"

With water bursting into the ship, the lower compartments had to be made watertight to contain the flow and possibly prevent the vessel from sinking. And every second counted. McCoy, though, while understanding the cruel logic of the chief petty officers above, was appalled. Were he and the others still below to be sealed into this coffin alive?

"No! No!" he cried. "A few more, wait!"

But it seemed hopeless. Those not already evacuated would have to be sacrificed so that the ship might be saved.

In his stateroom on the starboard side of the main deck, Dr. Haynes, a light sleeper, had just awakened and turned toward the porthole over his bunk when suddenly his eyes caught a bright white flash that lit up the night sky. At that moment, the first explosion thrust him from his bed onto the desk next to it. As he struggled to his feet, he thought about that submarine story he had heard at dinner; it didn't seem so funny anymore. The second explosion then rocked the cabin, knocking him down again. His hands sizzled on touching the steaming deck, but he managed to rise once more, only to face a wall of fire shooting from a ruptured diesel fuel oil line that ran through the room.

Wearing only his pajama bottoms, Haynes grabbed his life jacket, skirted the flames, and ran to the door. But as he opened it and stepped into the passageway, an officer in the room across from his cried, "Look out!" The doctor ducked back just in time to elude a tremendous flash of flame that shot through the corridor, though it singed his hair and burned his face. Then he heard a third explosion, and the ship lurched drunkenly to starboard.

Careening toward a ladder that led to the higher open forecastle deck, Haynes found the way barred by another sheet of white fire, and headed instead for the wardroom, two rooms down the corridor, another route to the upper deck. As he entered the wardroom, he felt that he was stepping into a furnace, but this was the only way out. Blindly, he reeled across the room toward another door before falling to the deck and burning his hands again.

He pulled himself up and thrust forward, fumbling in the bitter smoke for the elusive door, but he couldn't find it. Choking, breathless, he stumbled into chairs, lamps, all the accessories of a comfortable clubroom where he had spent many pleasant hours chatting with his buddies, playing cards, watching movies, and listening to gossip at dinner about amusing fantasies like the sighting of an enemy submarine.

Finally, overcome by the fumes, Haynes collapsed in an easy chair with a feeling of intense drowsiness. He knew he was dying, but he experienced an almost euphoric sense of peace and well-being; he couldn't even feel the pain in his scorched hands anymore—hands that might have belonged to a great surgeon.

Lieutenant McKissick, blasted awake in the room directly under Haynes' on the second deck, opened his eyes and found himself flying, it seemed, through some alien constellation as the mirror over his wash basin burst into a thousand flashing stars. A submarine! he immediately guessed—perhaps the one being sought by the hunter-killer team. He lifted himself from the deck and, dressed only in shorts and undershirt, rushed into the passageway. The heat was so intense, though, that he bolted back into his totally dark room, felt around for a flashlight, and, wetting a towel, wrapped it around his head to absorb some of the heat.

Then McKissick strode out again, waded through ankle-deep water, which he realized must be seawater, and hurried up the ladder to the main deck, burning his palms on the steel rungs as he climbed. Dizzy from the lack of oxygen, he felt that he had to breathe in some fresh air soon or he would collapse. He looked aft in the passageway through which Haynes had just staggered and, with sinking heart, found it swirling with smoke and flame. Men were running, screaming, slipping on a deck slick with oil spurting from ruptured pipes. Yet the only way he knew of getting to the forecastle deck without going through a wall of fire was via the wardroom off that corridor—the same route that Dr. Haynes had found blocked. Should he surge into those bitter-smelling clouds, fighting his way through the confused mob?

In the thickening haze, McKissick saw a nearby cabin that was rservedfor Admiral Spruance's staff. A porthole! Air! He rushed into the room but found the porthole window dogged down. With his burnt fingers, he tried desperately to loosen the nut, but in vain. Normally, a wrench was bracketed on the wall for use in an emergency, but now there was none.

McKissick stared out the window at the black sea, barely able to make out the glistening waves waltzing gently in the wind. If he could just break the glass. He had always taken the fresh air he breathed for granted; now he would give anything for just one lungful. How could he live a minute more without it? But, like Dr. Haynes, he was hemmed in by fire, smoke, and glass.

Another sailor who set out for the wardroom was Yeoman Havins. In fact, he was supposed to have reported there for watch before midnight. When someone awakened him in his bunk in the port hangar on the mezzanine he glanced at his wristwatch—after midnight! He was late. As he jumped to the deck and started dressing, the ship suddny shook with the explosions, and he felt a splash of seawater on his face.

Havins found it hard to believe. Although his transfer had been approved and he was simply waiting for the orders to come through, he had, it seemed, been caught in another suicide assault. Didn't God know that he wasn't supposed to be on this ship?

Havins rushed off toward the wardroom, where his job—apropos at this time—was to help control any fires that might break out in the area. But he never got there. As soon as he climbed down to the main deck, he ran into the same fire and confusion that had blocked McKissick's way. Men were splashing around in ankle-deep seawater desperately looking for guidance while flames raged through the corridors.

Suddenly, Havins saw several men emerging from a hatch that opened to a lower deck, their faces and bodies burned black, their skin hanging loosely from arms and legs. He ran over to them and helped pull them through the hatch, then, as they wailed and moaned, he wrapped the first man in a blanket, the only one he could find, and carried him up to the drier port hangar, which had become a dressing station for the wounded. He gazed around at the scenes of human suffering. His brother had died at Pearl Harbor in the first battle of the war. Now it seemed he, together with the rest of the crew, might meet the same fate in one of the last battles—with his transfer orders probably waiting for him in Leyte. He had been told that he could get off the ship somewhere in the Pacific, but in the middle of the ocean?

There wasn't time, however, to ponder the irony. He had to bring in the others—and find Dr. Haynes so he could relieve the agony of these men.

As Dr. Haynes lay slowly dying in the wardroom, a voice suddenly resonated ghostlike through the reddish haze: "My God, I'm fainting!"

Then, as the voice faded, the "ghost" fell across the doctor sprawled in an easy chair. Somehow, the shock renewed Haynes' will to survive. As he pushed the man aside and pulled himself to his feet, he was accosted by other disembodied voices:

"Don't light a match, don't!"

"Open a port! Open a port!"

Of course! Why hadn't he thought of it? He wasn't dead yet. How many dying men were out there? He must live so he could save the others. But then, in despair, he realized that the ports were tightly shut, and that his burnt hands wouldn't be able to open them anyway. But when he had hobbled to the bulkhead and felt around, he found to his joy that one port was open.

Haynes thrust his head through the opening, feeling, after being almost roasted alive, as if he had inserted it into a "deep-freeze cooler." He inhaled deeply, ecstatically, and his head began to clear.

He wanted to help the others in the room, but he knew he would die if he went back and tried to find them. Looking down, he saw a clutter of debris and paper in the agitated water below. Should he jump? He decided not to "because I [would] be sucked in toward the ship again." He was still trapped.

Suddenly, something from above brushed his face—a rope! He pulled on the line, which dangled from a floater net on the forecastle deck above, and found that it held fast. Like a baby squeezing its way into the world, he tortuously wriggled through the porthole and, ignoring the pain that shot through his hands, climbed up the rope inch by agonizing inch to the forecastle deck. Then he stumbled up a ladder to the main deck and into the battle dressing station someone told him had been set up in the port hangar.

Haynes found the chief pharmacist's mate, John Schmueck, hovering over about thirty horribly burned men, who were screaming, crying, begging for relief. But all he found here were a few bandages and a box of morphine capsules. He took a needle and jabbed the worst cases—one after the other, giving renewed life to men who could not live long. Finally, racked with pain himself, his lungs still poisoned from the reddish fumes, he fainted and collapsed on a patient.

When Haynes regained consciousness after about a minute, he sent a man to the sick bay to bring back more medical corpsmen. The messenger soon returned with devastating news: The whole sick bay was flooded. The doctor gasped. How long could the ship stay afloat? These dying men wouldn't survive even an hour in the ocean, with the salt water eating at their wounds, their bandages soaked, and only the sea as their bed. If they didn't drown, the sharks would be drawn by the blood. Still, he had to prolong their lives if he could, for he was a doctor.

Haynes thus sent Schmueck to get some life jackets and went himself to look for some, climbing to the gun deck on the port side. By the light of the moon, which now slid again from behind the clouds, he saw men cutting down sacks of life jackets that hung from a bulkhead and passing them out. Fortunately, there were enough for everybody—at least for those who could get there—since the ship had been mistakenly supplied with a duplicate shipment of them. For once, the doctor felt grateful for a bureaucratic blunder. He grabbed an armful of jackets and made his way back to the makeshift hospital.

With Schmueck's help, Haynes began tying the jackets around the patients—even around the severely burned youth with the folds of skin hanging from his outstretched arms who was screaming, "Don't touch me! Don't touch my arms, Doc! Please don't."

"Oh God," Haynes thought, "let the ship be saved!"

Ensign Blum was still nibbling on his sandwich at his post in sky aft when the first blast threw him to the deck. With a chill, he saw flames shooting from the forward stack and believed that a boiler must have exploded. Then the second blast—apparently another boiler. But the sky control officer nearby was not so sure.

"Fire if you see anything!" he shouted into Blum's sound-powered headphones, the only communications circuit still open.

Blum and the two enlisted men assisting him scoured the ocean, but could see nothing from their relatively high perch except an endless stretch of dark, murmuring emptiness. As the ship began to list, the thought struck Blum that he might have to dive into that infinite void—and, unlike the men he commanded, he didn't have a life jacket. It was regulation to wear it on duty at all times, but who could have imagined that he would really need it, except for an abandon ship drill? So he called over one of his men and sent him below with orders to bring back a jacket.

Blum wasn't really worried, though. After all, how many ships, even when hit, actually went down, especially a big cruiser like this? Granted he still knew little about the Navy, but it simply didn't seem logical that this vessel would sink because of an explosion or two.

When the ship suddenly lurched farther to starboard, however, Blum's rosy optimism wilted. Everything loose on deck started sliding in a massive avalanche of gear and garbage—ammunition cases, sleeping cots, empty cans. Was he asleep and suffering through a bad dream? Or was this real?

Whichever the case, as the slope grew steeper, Blum and his remaining assistant lost their balance and slid in a heap into a corner. Blum hadn't heard any order to abandon ship, but now, as he disentangled himself from the enlisted man, he wondered if there was any alternative. He would call sky control for guidance. But then he realized he couldn't, for in the tumble he had broken his headphones. He alone would have to decide whether and when to jump into the inky unknown.

Marine Private First Class McCoy had almost lost hope that he or the others still sealed in the brig area below would be allowed to escape when the warning voice shouted down from the hatch, "All right, get 'em up fast!"

McCoy and his comrades frantically pushed the wounded still in their hands through the hatch, but then the voice again: "All right, that's it!"

The human chain suddenly burst apart as men in panic leaped up the ladder, with McCoy the last one to hurl himself through the opening. He was dazed, exhausted, horrified. Faint cries rode the waves of heat and smoke swirling from below: "Don't leave us!" "Come back!"

Then the crash of the hatch slamming shut. Then silence.

McCoy was aghast. About fifteen wounded and unconscious men had been locked in their graves.

As soon as Captain McVay returned fully dressed to the bridge from his emergency cabin, Commander Flynn confronted him.

"We are definitely going down," he said, "and I suggest we abandon ship."

If McVay had been stunned by Casey Moore's report, he was now shocked. He had convinced himself that Moore must have exaggerated the situation, that the ship could somehow be saved as it had been at Okinawa. But here was his executive officer, whose opinion he so deeply respected, telling him that the ship should be abandoned. A captain's worst nightmare had become a reality. He would have to give up his ship, and without even being able to put up a fight. No one would believe that he wasn't at fault, even though he hadn't been warned of a submarine danger and had, in fact, been told that there was none.

McVay finally uttered the most difficult words he had ever spoken: "Pass the word to abandon ship!"

"Ay, ay, sir," Flynn replied. And since communication was impossible from the bridge, Lieutenant Orr, who was present, ordered Edward Keyes, boatswain's mate of the watch, to go below and alert all hands to come topside and "stand by to abandon ship." Orr then told the bugler, Donald F. Mack, to stand by to sound that call. Mack never would sound it, for in the ensuing confusion McVay never ordered Orr to have him do it. And when Orr later told Mack it was time to abandon ship, the bugler took the order to mean, he would claim, that he personally should go over the side, whereupon he dropped his bugle and jumped overboard.

Now McVay complained to Orr that he was "unable to determine whether the distress message which I told the navigator [Commander Janney] to check on has ever gotten out." Janney, oddly, had not returned from below, and it was "absolutely essential that someone be notified where we [are]." So McVay would personally go to Radio Central to find out if the message had been sent. He would also check a part of the main deck that some people said had split. Why, he wanted to know, was the ship going down so fast by the head?

"Nobody," he would say later, "had given me any report that we were other than just badly damaged." Nobody had told him that the first forty feet of the bow had been severed, and tons of water were pouring into the ship, all the faster because the vessel was still moving forward.

As McVay was about to leave for Radio Central, Edward Keyes ran up to him and reported on his effort to call those below to topside. He had passed the word aft (without also mentioning that they should "stand by to abandon ship," as he had been ordered), but not forward because he couldn't get past the fire in sick bay and the smoke in Number 1 Mess Hall.

The captain could only comfort himself with thoughts of the kamikaze attack at Okinawa. As soon as the men had sensed disaster, they had all rushed to topside voluntarily. They would do the same now—those who could. He then hurried to his emergency cabin to put on a kapok life preserver before descending to Radio Central to make sure that help would soon be coming.

The euphoria of Commander Hashimoto and his crew at this great moment was tempered with anxiety. So important a ship was probably escorted, and everyone expected to hear a depth charge from an enemy destroyer at any moment. Logically, though, Hashimoto knew this was unlikely, for the target vessel was too close to his submarine and could be further damaged by such a charge.

In fact, when several heavy explosions followed the actual hits, members of the crew began shouting "Depth charge attack!" and the commander had to reassure them that it was simply their target exploding, that no other vessels appeared in his periscope. But he was nevertheless disturbed that the image of the target ship persisted. It hadn't sunk, at least not yet. And now the kaitens renewed their campaign to die heroically.

"Since the enemy won't sink," they cried, "send us!"

Hashimoto, however, still resisted. The ship might sink before the kaitens reached it, and "once launched," as he would later say, "they were gone for good. It seemed a pity to risk wasting them."

When his sound equipment indicated that the stricken vessel was using its underwater detector apparatus, Hashimoto, worried that it was trying to get his submarine's range, ordered his helmsman to dive to a depth of seventy yards, and told Toshio Tanaka to reload for a second salvo of unmanned torpedoes. With deep gratification, Tanaka mounted six more on the launching pad. He felt certain that the ship was mortally wounded, but to make doubly sure he would hit it again, even if it was on the way down. The "barbarians" deserved no mercy.

Hashimoto also thought that the ship was doomed, but if it didn't sink soon—and he couldn't risk waiting too long—he might not be able to capture any survivors. He wanted at least two or three so he might learn just how important his prize was and be able, finally, to confirm to the gods that he had sunk a ship for the Emperor and was worthy of an honored niche in heaven.

As Lieutenant Redmayne precariously climbed from the bottom of his ship after leaving the main engine room, heaven seemed to him no farther away than the navigation bridge at the top. With almost each step upward through a terrifying eternity, the vessel tilted more to starboard, and with almost every new tilt he lost his footing on the steel rungs and had to hang on virtually with one hand, since the other had grown stiff from its burns.

When Redmayne finally reached the deck just below the main one, he found a man in Number 2 Mess Hall who was trying to use a sound-powered phone. Perhaps now he could contact the captain and find out what he should do.

Could he communicate with anybody? Redmayne asked the man.

No, only with the engine room.

The lieutenant frowned. Did he know the condition of the ship forward?

No, the man replied.

The frown hardened. But Redmayne still couldn't believe the ship was going down—until he resumed his climb and the ship lurched again, this time to at least a thirty-degree list. The bridge? Heaven suddenly dropped to the level of the main deck. He had to get above the water line, or, it now appeared, that anticipated promotion wouldn't be worth a damn.

The lieutenant finally scrambled onto the main deck, but in the enclosed section, where he couldn't abandon ship if necessary. The vessel now tilted so steeply that the deck became a steel slide for every object not bolted down. If he slid down himself, he would probably be crushed by the falling equipment. He thus tried to crawl up to the top of the port side, but he kept sliding down, until finally he caught on to an electric welding that protruded from a bulkhead.

The ship at this moment rolled virtually on its side and Redmayne found himself suspended in air, as if from the window of a building. If he fell, he would plummet to a bulkhead halfway across the deck, and would be killed by the fall or drowned by the water that would soon engulf the starboard side of the ship. This was the end, he was sure. Good-bye, Trude . . .

Then, suddenly, he saw four oxygen bottles attached to a nearby bulkhead, which had been vertical but were now almost horizontal. If he could swing from one to the other and reach the last bottle, he would be able to jump to the open part of the deck, and then go over the side.

Redmayne reached for the first bottle with one hand, then, not daring to look down, slowly swung, hand over hand, to the second like a gymnast on the bars. Through sheer will power, he ignored the excruciating pain in his burned hand, and each bottle became a supreme life-or-death challenge as his sweating, aching body kicked its way through the murky air. He would make it—only two to go . . . He felt his hand slipping . . . One bottle away . . . With a final lunge, he grabbed the bottle and swooped onto what had been the vertical surface of a gun mount on the open deck. Yes, heaven!

Then he climbed down into the rising water in so grateful a mood that he hardly realized he was not wearing a life jacket. But he may also have felt a twinge of guilt. His men in the engine room . . . He had not thought the ship would sink and thus could not be blamed for leaving them behind. Still, he had a fighting chance to survive, and they didn't.

Like Dr. Haynes, when he had been "dying" in the wardroom, Lieutenant McKissick heard a voice as he was choking to death in the fumes boiling over the main deck.

"Anybody want to get out?"

"Yes," McKissick cried. "Here!"

He had just staggered out of the stateroom where, with less good fortune than Dr. Haynes, he had found the portholes sealed shut. Through a clearing in the haze, he saw a man standing by the door to the gunpowder storage room.

"Come out this way," the man said.

The lieutenant veered into the room, then crawled through an opening, climbed a ladder to the pointer's booth of Turret 1, and exited onto the open forecastle deck. He fell to his knees, nauseous from the smoke and fumes, and inhaled the fresh air in short, trembling gasps. He was alone; Seaman First Class James Newhall, who worked in the turret, had returned to rescue other men trapped below.

Having been saved himself, McKissick was now determined to join in the effort. He was in the forward section of the ship, and the water was rising swiftly, especially with the bow gone. In the rooms below, fires were raging, and would devour over a hundred men, including all the steward's mates, almost all of the Marines, and most of the naval officers. He had to help save those who might still be alive down there.

Lifting himself up, McKissick, though still dizzy, approached a group of fifteen to twenty men nearby who were milling about uncertain what to do and, seeing no officer around, he took charge.

"Let's get some life jackets," he said. "Then we'll get a hose and try to control the fire below."

McKissick led the men to a gear locker farther aft where life jackets were available, and when all members of the group had their jackets on, they broke out the fire hose and inserted it in a starboard hatch near the captain's main cabin. But not a drop of water dripped out of the nozzle; the fire main had ruptured and there was no pressure.

"Forget the hose!" McKissick shouted. "Let's get those men out of there!"

Several severely burned sailors were helped out of the hatch, but as the ship listed more steeply, the rescue work soon became almost impossible. One man who was unable to walk had to be pulled up by a rope from the starboard side, which already was almost level with the water line, to the raised port side. And once the angle reached about forty-five degrees, even able men could hardly climb the slippery deck to port.

McKissick could hear the crackle of the conflagration below. How many of his buddies were being burned alive down there, or would be drowned? And he was helpless to save them. He struggled to the lifelines high on the port side near Turret 1 and gathered his group around him. Many other sailors nearby were trying to flee aft, since the forward part of the ship, without a bow, was still inching ahead on its one operating engine and would obviously be flooded first. But McKissick didn't see why anyone should linger any longer aboard this dying vessel.

In the flashes of moonlight, the lieutenant glanced around the capsizing ship. His beautiful ship. Slowly, quietly, majestically, it was submitting to the ravages of fire and water and vanishing into legend. As the water began curling around the base of the turret, McKissick decided it was time to let go.

"All right, men," he cried, "over the side!"

And following their Pied Piper, they climbed over the lifelines and calmly walked down the port side into the water.

Though almost maddened with pain himself, Dr. Haynes treated his burned and crippled patients with all the desperate intensity of Moses trying to save his people. He injected morphine, wound bandages, and tied on life jackets as fast as his scorched fingers would allow. But he expected no miracles. This sea wasn't going to part. It was waiting to devour victims, especially the most incapacitated.

Suddenly, the ship keeled, and, as Haynes watched in horror, all of his patients went tumbling down the starboard side into the sea. The doctor himself was thrown to the deck, but managed to crawl to the top of the port side just as the ship rolled to about a ninety-degree angle. He then struggled to the catapult deck, where he tried to cut loose some life rafts lashed to the side of the ship, but the ropes and the toggle pins that held them were just beyond his reach. As elsewhere on the ship, the men in charge of the rafts, waiting for an order to abandon ship before acting, had waited too long. Now, with the vessel virtually on its side, it was almost impossible to release the rafts. Haynes was appalled. The crew would have to face the terrors of the sea with only their life jackets supporting them.

The doctor paused to gather his thoughts and stared into a restless sea that seemed at this moment of catastrophe like a shroud smothering the earth. Had any doctor ever suffered a greater blow? All his patients—in one sudden sweep. He would never see them again, certainly not Marine Private First Class Redd, the man with a cast on his foot who wasn't permitted to debark in Pearl Harbor. The cast would now anchor him forever to the bottom of the ocean.

With many other men, among them Otha Alton Havins, Haynes treaded slowly down the side of the ship and across the red-painted bottom; now it was time to join his patients. Taking a deep breath, he waded into the briny embrace of the sea.

When Ensign Blum regained his footing after falling into a corner with his assistant, he ordered the man, a young Filipino, to get ready to go over the side. The man climbed on top of a gun mount and poised himself to jump.

"Now, Mr. Blum?" he asked, looking down at the ensign.

"Not yet," replied Blum.

Maybe, he felt, he had been a bit hasty. After all, he had never been on a sinking ship before. How could he tell whether it could be saved or not? When the time came for the man to jump, the time would come for Donald Blum, too. And the fellow he had sent down to get a life jacket for him hadn't reported back yet. Anyway, he hadn't heard a single person cry "Abandon ship."

"Now, Mr. Blum?"

"No, wait!"

A miracle could happen—even to an agnostic. But it didn't. When a minute later he put his arm over the side and felt the water, he knew it was time, life jacket or no life jacket.

"Okay, *now*!" he cried.

And the man jumped. Then Blum simply climbed over the lifeline into the sea as if he were stepping into a bathtub. If this was a bad dream, it seemed to him, he had better wake up damn quick!

Ensign Twible, the man Blum had replaced on watch at sky aft, had just left his post to go below when he was shaken by the explosions. His premonition had been correct. The *Indianapolis* was ill-fated. But he himself, he still felt, was not, for God was giving him special protection, and he must now display the power thus bestowed upon him.

As the ship began to list, Twible looked into the sea and "could not believe . . . that we had sunk as low in the water in such a short time. It was almost as if we had the bottom cut out of the ship." He dashed to the main deck, where he found Commander Flynn.

"What should I do?" he asked.

"Go aft," said Flynn, "and make sure the men go to the high side of the ship."

Twible rushed toward the fantail shouting "All hands to the high side!" to frightened throngs of men running in all directions. Suddenly, he realized he had no life jacket. He needed some protection in the sea—why let God do all the work? This concern was short-lived, for there, in front of him, was a familiar figure—one of the men he had prosecuted for going AWOL in San Francisco. Someone, thank heaven, had let him out of the brig, and he was now calmly standing on the deck handing out life jackets. Twible approached him and the two stared briefly at each other. The ensign then walked away with a jacket. God worked in strange ways; the man he had jailed might be responsible for saving his life. If he survived, the ensign vowed, he would recommend the boy for a medal.

Energized by what he saw as the moral resurrection of the young man, Twible continued on aft, slipping and sliding as he struggled ahead, until finally he reached the fantail. There he found about five hundred men, almost half of the crew, hanging on to the lifelines or to each other, two or three tiers deep. When someone lost his grip on a lifeline and started to slip, others would also tumble and then crawl back and grab on again. Some were hysterical, crying, "We're sinking!" "What the hell should we do?" "Where's the captain?"

Twible, always rank-conscious, looked around for a senior officer to give orders but couldn't find one. So it was up to Harlan Twible. He knew the task of saving the lives of almost half the crew was hardly one for a mere ensign, but he was confident; Annapolis had prepared him for this kind of situation. Perhaps that was why God had sent him there.

The men must abandon ship at once, he was convinced, but would they do so without an order from the bridge?—especially since he felt he must violate a cardinal naval rule of survival: When abandoning ship, jump off the high side, where the suction that might pull one down with the vessel would presumably be less. The high side, he judged, was now too high, and the men might fall into the rising screw propellers or on top of each other in the water.

"Men," Twible yelled, "the ship can't be saved. Let's all jump over the starboard side. Then swim away as fast as you can."

The crew ignored him. A rookie ensign they hardly knew ordering them to commit suicide? Some had heard Edward Keyes' cry that they gather on topside, but no word had come from the bridge to abandon ship. Nor had the bugler sounded the order. Why should they listen to someone far less experienced than many of them were? Besides, some did not have life jackets, while a few could not even swim. And hadn't the ship survived the kamikaze attack? The men, in any case, were confused. A little earlier, when some panicked and wanted to go over the side, another officer, crying that the ship would be saved, waved a pistol and threatened to shoot anyone who tried to jump. Now this officer was *ordering* them to jump.

Twible was dismayed. They simply didn't realize that he had received "wonderful training" at Annapolis; that he knew what to do in a crisis. There seemed to be only one way. He would jump over the side himself, and maybe they would follow. Hopefully, they would respect rank in the end "as a straw they could grasp on."

"I'm going over the side, men!" he cried. "And you should all follow me."

With the ship virtually on its side, Twible worked his way down the bulkhead of the aft cook shack and plopped into the water. As he began to swim away, he looked back and saw with satisfaction scores of men leaping in after him. But some of them dropped from the high side and, as he had feared, struck a screw propeller and were either chopped to death or gravely wounded.

Many of the men, Twible knew, would perish. But, as this display of leadership showed, he would save at least some of them, if only they would gather around him and listen to his commands—which, after all, were rooted in heaven and the best textbooks.

·   ·   ·

One of the men who jumped from the fantail was Adolfo Celaya, the Mexican-Spanish youth from Arizona who had joined the Navy to escape the hectic pace of city life. Celaya had been asleep midship on the main deck, expecting to be awakened for the 4 A.M. watch. But as he bounced off the deck during the first explosion, he realized this was no normal wake-up call. What could have happened? Well, at least he had gone to bed fully dressed. Conditioned by his rough early years, he was always prepared for something to go wrong.

And something now had obviously gone wrong. While some of the men near him casually lay down again after the blasts, confident that someone else would repair the damage, Celaya, suspecting disaster, threw a blanket around himself and darted aft toward the fantail, not even stopping when he saw flames blocking his path; he skirted them, burning his legs as he ran.

Celaya was in such a hurry that he didn't give any thought to joining a group of men near the fantail who were desperately trying to toss a twenty-six-foot whaleboat overboard so they wouldn't have to flounder in the water. Fortunately for him. For as the ship suddenly lurched to starboard, the steel cover on the boat slid off and sailed through the air, cutting one man in half. At the same time, the whaleboat itself broke free of the restraining ropes and skidded into a bulkhead, crushing several others to death.

Celaya suddenly realized that his life jacket was in his sleeping compartment below, and was about to weave through the fiery maze to get it when he ran into a comrade, Santos Pena, whom he knew from Tucson.

"Don't go below or you'll never get out," Pena warned. "Stay with me!"

Since he *was* wearing a life jacket, he could hold Celaya up in the water until help came.

The two men ran to the fantail and saw many sailors abandoning ship, following Twible's example. But unlike Twible, the pair decided to jump over the high side, as they had been taught. Celaya glanced into the foamy blackness. A big swimming pool, it seemed.

And in the heat of summer, warm, too—about eighty degrees. Besides, he was a good swimmer, a superior athlete. It wouldn't be so bad. His friend was a reminder of Tucson. All concrete, people everywhere, no space, not even a field where he could run a horse. No wonder he had joined the Navy. But right now, he wished he were back in Tucson.

"Okay, let's go!" Celaya cried.

Pena patted the side of the ship affectionately and, referring to it by its nickname, said, "Good-bye, Indamaru," then jumped the thirty feet into the sea. Celaya immediately followed—and hit something as he landed in the water.

"My God, it must be Pena!" he thought. He called out his friend's name. He shouted it. No answer. He had killed his buddy! All around him, men were screaming, gasping, whimpering, praying, treading, swimming, splashing, but Celaya was now alone—as he had always been.

Also leaping into the sea was Giles McCoy, who had just threaded his way to the forecastle after barely making it out of the brig room below. He grabbed a life jacket from a canvas bag that had been ripped from a bulkhead and, just as he put one arm through it, the ship rolled over. He managed to crawl onto the side of the ship and walk down into the water, still with only one arm in the jacket.

So intent was he on surviving that he hardly heard the cries of men leaping into the void, the crash of objects smashing against bulkheads, the groaning and cracking and whistling of a dying ship. But could he ever banish from his brain the pitiful calls of men who, trapped by fate, would sleep forever in a watertight tomb on the floor of the sea?

Wearing his life preserver, Captain McVay left his emergency cabin and headed for Radio Central below to see if an SOS signal had gotten out. Just then, Captain Crouch, his old friend, walked up to him looking distraught.

"Charlie, have you a spare life preserver?" he stammered.

After the explosions, he had rushed out of the captain's regular cabin, where he was staying, to find out what happened and had left his own behind.

"Yes, I have," McVay replied. "I've got a pneumatic life preserver."

And he stepped back into his stateroom, picked it up, and handed it to a sailor, asking him to blow it up for Crouch. He must take care of his old schoolmate, whom he had persuaded to come on this voyage as a passenger, never imagining that the man would be seriously risking his life. The skipper saw in Crouch a bit of his past —those glorious days at Annapolis when he had dreamt of fulfilling his father's dream that he, too, would become an admiral and perhaps even the commander of a fleet. McVay hastily bade good-bye to his friend and left for Radio Central. The lives of all his men might depend on what he found.

Actually, the captain could have saved himself the trouble, for even his radiomen were not sure whether the SOS had gone out. Commander Janney never reached Radio Central, and the man Lieutenant Orr had originally sent there may not have arrived in time. He rushed in with his message just as the radiomen were rushing out, trying to escape the thickening smoke. They turned around and surged back into the haze to send out the SOS, using a transmitter situated in Radio II nearby. The radio operator, by the dull glow of a flashlight, kept tapping out the message, and the indicators in Radio II all showed that the signal was getting out—with the waning power in the after engine room. Simultaneously, another operator in Radio II itself sent a similar message over a different frequency and the meters also registered.

But had the transmission lines been damaged by the blasts? Had the antennas been knocked down or grounded? And even if the message was getting out, was anybody listening? With the ship going down so swiftly, the message could be repeated only a limited number of times.

Unaware of these efforts to transmit, Captain McVay tried desperately to reach Radio Central. As he put his foot on the first rung of the ladder leading down from the bridge, the ship suddenly jerked to about a twenty-five-degree list, and he was able to get to the signal bridge just below only by hanging on to the railings of the ladder. As the list grew, he crawled to another ladder and continued climbing down, pausing on the communications deck when he saw some sailors about to go over the side without life preservers. It was agonizing enough to have his men abandon ship; he couldn't let them leap to near-certain death. He shouted to the youths: "There's a floater net on the Number 1 Stack—get that! Don't jump over the side unless you have some form of support!" And he added with an optimism he couldn't afford to discard: "The ship should stay in its position for enough time to get that floater net off."

Seconds later, the ship flipped to about ninety degrees.

McVay leaped to the forecastle deck, pulled himself up on the side of the vessel, and started walking aft. He couldn't believe this was happening. In less than fifteen minutes, his ship was floating on its side like a dying whale. But abandon ship? No, he would not. He *could* not. Fantasy engulfed him. Even now he might be able to save the ship, as he had at Okinawa. But he was so tired. Why not just sit down and wait for dawn? Then he could properly survey the situation and decide what to do. He wanted to live, to take Louise in his arms again—but if the vessel sank under him, at least he would be remembered as a captain who went down with his ship, a man worthy of his father's name.

Suddenly, a huge wave, apparently generated by the sinking bow, struck Captain McVay from behind like the arm of God and swept him into the sea.

Captain Hashimoto was perplexed. As his submarine coasted below the surface, too swiftly to permit constant surveillance, all trace of the enemy ship vanished from his periscope. Had he sunk the ship—or had it gotten away? He must have sunk it, for it couldn't have maneuvered out of sight so quickly when he had seen three torpedoes hit it. But he needed proof. He had to find some survivors and interrogate them.

But did he have the time? Other enemy craft might soon respond to an SOS and arrive before his submarine could dive to safety. So, after about thirty minutes under water, *I-58* rose to a level just below the waves, and the commander peered through his periscope again. Still no sign of the ship or of any survivors.

The submarine then nosed all the way up, and Hashimoto and the two Tanakas stood on the bridge, scanning the sea with their binoculars while their boat circled the area. A half-moon still shone down, if through a thin veil of clouds, casting enough light, they hoped, to reveal the faces of the enemy.

As Captain McVay bobbed breathlessly to the surface, he looked up and was seized by terror. The screw propellers, one of them still turning, hovered directly overhead as the stern poked straight up out of the ocean like some prehistoric monster about to dive into the deep. Pathetic clusters of men still clung to the lifelines, and several stood on the blades of the stilled propeller.

As the dying ship held in this position for several dreadful seconds, with the cries of the men still trapped aboard sounding over the crash of plummeting equipment, McVay was convinced that the vessel would fall on him. The beast was about to devour its master. Gaping in awe, he thought to himself, "Well, this is the end of me!" But mixed with his terror was a strange sense of relief, for the decision to live or die, it seemed, had been made for him. Besides, he thought, "it would be much easier if I go down. I won't have to face what I know is coming after this."

McVay's immediate reflex, however, was to survive, and he began swimming away from the ship like an ant scurrying out of the grasp of a spider. Seconds later, he felt the splash of hot oil and water on the back of his neck. He turned around as the monster, gathering speed in a final death plunge, vanished into the black depths with a swish that sent tons of water cascading over the captain and more than eight hundred others who were stranded with him in a boundless sea.

About four hundred people went down with the ship, including

Commander Flynn, Commander Janney, Lieutenant Moore, Lieutenant Orr, and Captain McVay's old Annapolis classmate, Captain Crouch. McVay remained alive. Yet, in a spiritual sense, he, too, had gone down with his ship. The *Indianapolis* had been his responsibility, and now it was lost, with the survivors likely to follow.

Suddenly, some men saw the vague flash of lights on the horizon. A Japanese submarine, they guessed, was coming to finish them off—before they were consumed by the sea.

For Toshio Tanaka, this could be the supreme moment of revenge. If he sighted any survivors, he would advise Commander Hashimoto to machine-gun them all. But he wasn't at all sure that Hashimoto would agree. The commander was older, more conservative, less daring than he; all the man seemed to want were a few witnesses. He would apparently leave the rest for enemy ships to pick up (Hashimoto himself would later claim that this was his intention). But Toshio Tanaka felt that he represented the real spirit of the Japanese cause—even if it was probably a lost one. A samurai would have his vengeance, lost cause or not.

Tanaka meticulously searched wave upon glistening wave for some hint of a human shadow, but, like the others, in vain. Finally, after circling the area once, Navigator Hirokoto Tanaka, knowing that Hashimoto was as fearful as he that the enemy might find them, gave the order for the craft to stop circling and to head northeast—a decision the commander reluctantly approved, though at considerable cost to the morale of some crew members. Not only was Toshio Tanaka disappointed, but the kaitens were bitter—about the whole operation. One confronted Hashimoto with tears in his eyes. How could the commander have deprived him of the chance to blow up a battleship and fulfill his dearest dream? Why had he wasted ordinary torpedoes?

Hashimoto tried to calm the man down. He need not worry. There were other crossroads on the road home and he would have other opportunities. He should be courageous and not be so afraid to live.

The commander himself was battered by conflicting emotions—euphoric that he had at last sunk a great ship for the Emperor, yet haunted by the thought that possibly, just possibly, the ship had gotten away and he had failed again. He tried to banish this thought from his mind. And to confirm to himself that it was indeed a battleship he had sunk, he zealously perused an album of American warships. If he could find just one that resembled his target . . . but none of them seemed to. Well, never mind, both he and Hirokoto thought it was a battleship. And so, when the submarine had submerged again and was about thirty miles from the scene of the attack, he handed his radio operator a coded message to be sent on a standard frequency to naval headquarters in Tokyo: ". . . RELEASED SIX TORPEDOES AND SCORED THREE AT BATTLESHIP OF IDAHO CLASS—DEFINITELY SANK IT."

Then, to celebrate this great coup, Hashimoto, with an enthusiasm dimmed by only the slightest agonizing doubt, ordered that for the crew's next dinner the rather rotten onions be supplemented with canned beans, canned corned beef, and canned eels. The meal was enjoyed by all except the kaitens, who had lost their appetite and were perfectly ready, it seemed, to let the rats eat their share. They pined for the food of heaven, which presumably would be far tastier.

A ship had been sunk? Then where was the SOS?

Captain Layton's men at the CINCPAC combat intelligence office in Guam were baffled. It was early Monday morning, July 30, and they were pondering an intercepted enemy message that had just been decoded. The commander of the Japanese submarine *I-58* boasted that he had sunk a ship. But what type of ship? What was the latitude and longitude where it went down? The Americans had broken the Japanese code, but unfortunately, not the grids reflecting these particular facts.

I-58 didn't seem very important to the Guam experts—even though their files indicated that this submarine was lurking in the general area where the *Indianapolis* was sailing. Since no SOS had been reported, why give special attention to this message when they were so overloaded with enemy reports already?

It had been a busy day; at least five hundred reports had drifted in, and there were only eight people to analyze and evaluate them. They were dizzy from reading about all the glorious activities announced by the submarine commanders, who, as usual, were trying to curry favor with their superiors and mislead their own people by exaggerating and, at times, fabricating their successes. They also wanted, it seemed, to confuse the American forces and learn the location of vessels supposedly sunk by provoking Washington to "prove" that they hadn't been.

One would think that each of these commanders had sunk a battleship—or at least a cruiser. Layton's men didn't believe any of them, and Layton himself was similarly skeptical. The report about *I-58* was too vague to act upon anyway. In due time, of course, it would be routinely relayed to Commodore Carter, Admiral Nimitz' assistant chief of staff for operations in Guam, and Captain Smedberg, Admiral King's assistant chief of naval intelligence in Washington.

The message finally reached Smedberg about ten hours after Layton's men had intercepted it. Actually, Smedberg's office had received the same message from another intercept station and was already translating it. But in Washington, as in Guam, the message was apparently no more impressive in English than it had been in Japanese—even though Smedberg, like Carter, could have looked at his data and virtually pinpointed where the two craft were likely to have been at any given time. No one investigated—or ordered any action.

And so, at least on the first terrible night, Captain McVay and the other survivors would live and die in the shark-infested ocean with no one even aware that they were missing.

VIII

Prelude to Madness

AS SOON AS Giles McCoy hit the water, he found himself trapped in an air bubble caused by the ship's death plunge and was pulled down so deeply into the swirling currents that the pressure, it seemed, would gouge out his eyes and burst his eardrums. He was drowning when, suddenly, he began shooting upward as if fired out of a cannon. He finally surfaced, surrounded by tons of brackish foam from the ship's last gasp.

McCoy vomited a small geyser of oily salt water, then dazedly looked around him; the sea, after devouring the ship, had grown calmer, its appetite satiated for the moment. He felt the awe and wonder that a man might feel upon landing amid the craters and wastelands of Mars. Nothing but long rolling swells as far as the eye could see. A world without people or purpose. Was he the last man alive?

He soon found that he was not. About twenty yards away, McCoy suddenly saw a cluster of about a hundred survivors. He swam over to them, but could hardly distinguish one from another since they all looked like minstrels, their faces covered with fuel oil—as was his own—from an eellike oil slick carried by the waves in the wake of the capsizing ship. But he did recognize Eugene Morgan, a boatswain's mate, who was one of the few sailors he had gotten to know well aboard ship.

While the others were being held up by their life preservers, McCoy still had only one arm inserted through his. Shortly, however, he straddled an ammunition can that drifted by and put his jacket on properly, expecting the can to be his permanent home until help came. But then he spotted a raft with several men in it about fifty yards away. That would be a lot more comfortable.

"I'm going to swim to that raft," he told Morgan.

Morgan tried to dissuade him. "It's too far away," he said. "Stay here. We'll certainly be picked up in the morning."

But McCoy was determined—even though he knew that there were sharks roaming around and that they were drawn to lone victims. He began swimming toward the raft, but the two-inch coating of oil made him feel as if he were plowing through mud, while his life jacket wouldn't permit him to swim under the oil. He thus headed back to Morgan and, removing the preserver, handed it to him.

"Give it to somebody else," he said.

Then he dived under the blanket of oil and once more swam toward the raft. However, each time he popped to the surface for air, the raft seemed to be drifting farther and farther away from him. He was a strong swimmer, but he couldn't swim all night. Maybe Morgan had been right. He thought of his mother; perhaps he shouldn't have so recklessly risked depriving her of a son. Would he ever again hug her, or taste her pumpkin pies? He felt he must live; but gradually his muscles seemed almost to atrophy, while every breath had to be forced out of his aching diaphragm. His eyes, throat, and nostrils, ravaged by the bitter brew of oil and salt water, were afire, and his stomach still convulsed from an enfeebling nausea.

As his body was about to defy his will, McCoy quiveringly reached for a rope dangling from the raft, but he was too weak to hold on. He finally let go and started to drift away when someone grabbed him by the hair and pulled him onto the raft, a foot-wide ring of balsam wood with a latticed wood floor in the center.

Semiconscious as he lay on the slimy rim, he vomited up more scum, then, after some moments, came to his senses and stared into the black faces of about six other men. As a Marine, he had never thought very highly of sailors, but he would be glad to join *these* guys on almost any bloody beach.

Suddenly, one of them cried, "Look, a ship!"

McCoy lifted himself up like an old firehorse at the sound of an alarm, and drew a .45-caliber pistol from the holster still gracing his belt. A shadow was silhouetted against the sky, now briefly moonlit, and seemed to be shaped like a submarine with its conning tower, but he had never seen one that big. It must be a friendly destroyer, he thought. McCoy fired two rounds in the air; the pistol, though dripping wet, worked. Maybe someone would see the flashes. But there was only silence. Finally, the silhouette disappeared into the darkness without flashing a light of its own or sending up a flare. The seventeen men sitting on the raft or hanging on to it with ropes realized in near despair that the sea would remain their bed for the night. A night ringing with the cries of the wounded and, for McCoy, the screams of the doomed in the brig compartment as well.

"Doc! Doc!"

The call echoed over the dancing sea, the cry of a dying world. There were many worlds afloat after the *Indianapolis* went down. Since the ship steamed forward almost until the moment it vanished under the waves, the men who had jumped dotted the ocean over a stretch of several miles. They gathered in many groups, each one isolated from the others and hardly able to see beyond the crest of the nearest wave. None knew that others even existed. Each was a sovereign little empire unto itself with its own rules, its own leaders, its own heroes and renegades.

Dr. Haynes was in the largest group, between three and four hundred men, who struggled to survive without the support of a single raft or floater net. This group soon fragmented into three or four subgroups that coalesced fairly distant from each other. The doctor's world, however, embraced all of these subgroups, for he was needed in each to ease the pain of the wounded and minister to the dead. Fortunately, Haynes had the assistance of Lieutenant Melvin W. Modisher, a fine, compassionate doctor himself, who helped tend the injured and relieve Haynes' awesome burden. Haynes was also grateful that, while everyone was consumed with fear and a sense of doom, the able men were courageous and cooperative. Those with

life preservers held up those without them—until men died, leaving
the preservers behind for the living.

But how long would anyone have the strength or will to help
his comrades if rescue didn't come soon? And the prospects were
not rosy. One radioman in the group shook his head doubtfully
when Haynes asked him about the SOS. The electric power, the
man thought, was off when the distress signal was sent. What would
happen when the life preservers, which now held the men out of the
water a little above the waist, finally gave out? The pneumatic rubber
belt was easily punctured by debris, and lost air quickly anyway.
The kapok life jacket, which fit around the chest, would, according
to experts, remain buoyant for forty-eight hours; after that its fibers
would be too soggy to lend support. The men would thus sink inch
by inch until, finally, their noses would be submerged. Haynes tried
in vain to drive the thought from his mind.

The doctor paddled over to the men who had called him.

"These two guys, can you do anything for them?"

Haynes placed his finger on the pupil of an eye. No reflex. Dead.
The other man, too. Who were they? No one was sure.

"Our personalities [were] gone," Haynes would later write in a
memoir. "We all [looked] the same—grim visages with whites of
eyes and red of mouths surrounded by black oil. But there [was] no
terror in the eyes, no quiver on any lips."

Haynes helped to remove the life jackets of the two men so they
could be worn by others. He wished Father Conway were around
to give final rites. But the father, though about to collapse himself,
was moving from corpse to corpse, uttering one prayer after another.
How could he keep up with all the dead—or with the living, who
needed his words to relieve their pain and anxiety? So Haynes himself
led the group in the Lord's Prayer, while the bodies were let loose
in the sea, to be consumed, in all likelihood, by the sharks circling
around waiting for easy prey.

"Doc, help me! . . . Doc! Doc!"

Other calls. Would they never cease? Haynes could dispatch the
dead to heaven with a prayer, but he often couldn't help the wounded.
There were no medicines, no bandages, no ointments. Yet, he kept

moving among the survivors, from the burned to the crippled to the exhausted to the merely fearful, offering hope, solace, even a little humor. And he warned them relentlessly not to drink the salt water, however great their thirst. They would be plagued with diarrhea, which would further dehydrate them, making them incoherent and delirious; and they would die in agony. There was no fresh water and little food—some potatoes and onions that floated by—but, he assured them, men could live for days without drink or nourishment. Besides, help would be coming shortly. Hold on. Soon they would be with their families.

But many of these men, Haynes knew, would never see their families again. And within twenty-four hours, most of those who had been seriously wounded aboard ship or while jumping off it would die from their injuries or from shock. To stay alive as long as possible, the men would have to stay together, not only to discourage shark attacks, but to keep up morale. Those who were loneliest succumbed the most rapidly to despair and death, and indeed the greatest fear of the survivors was that they would die "as drifters cast from the herd." Thus, the most severely wounded were kept in the center of each group, for they were the ones most likely to drift away, willingly or not.

Haynes was thankful when one of the men found floating by a cork life ring with a long rope attached to it. A seriously injured sailor was placed across it—one less to support—and then more than 150 men took hold of the line. Soon, as if pulled by some superhuman force, the rope coiled itself around the ring, pressing the men together and overcoming their fear that they would involuntarily stray, perhaps while sleeping.

Constantly on watch for strays were such men as Captain Edward L. Parke, commander of the Marine detachment, and Ensign H. C. Moynelo, Jr.; though exhausted, these men ceaselessly rounded up their buddies and brought them back to the "herd," even relinquishing their own life jackets to those who lacked them.

Others used their remaining energy to support the wounded and the jacketless. Lieutenant McKissick was one of these helpers; another was Seaman First Class Garland Lloyd Rich, who, like McKissick, came from a small town in Texas and once played on a football team that the lieutenant coached. Still referring to his old mentor as "Coach," Rich was inspired by McKissick in the water no less than he had been on the field. He drove himself ruthlessly as he swam from one man to another, often together with Haynes, supporting them until they died or someone relieved him.

One man, Aviation Machinist First Class Anthony Francis Maday, held up wounded Commander Lipski for almost twenty-four hours. Dr. Haynes was especially tender with Lipski, who had been so brutally burned that the tendons in his hands were exposed, while his eyes, totally sightless, resembled two fried eggs. He had to be held high so that his raw face and hands would not come in contact with the oil and salt water, which would intensify his pain. Sometimes Haynes held him personally, soothing him with reminiscences of the good times they had shared; the happy moments on liberty when they had sipped whiskey together and talked about their families, their pasts. But the doctor could not suppress morbid thoughts of the immediate future, as everyone sank a little lower, inching every hour toward eternity.

Haynes waited impatiently for daylight. It would be easier to drive such thoughts from his mind when the sun brightened the world and offered renewed hope of rescue. But when morning came, the torment continued, with the demons of night giving way to the demons of light. From about 10 A.M., most of the men suffered from intense photophobia as the glare of the sun reflecting on the oil-covered sea almost blinded them.

"Even when you [closed] your eyes," Haynes would recount, "there [was] no escape, for two hot balls of fire [burned] through your eyelids."

He blessed the men who went around tearing strips of cloth from their comrades' clothing to blindfold them, offering some relief from the sun. And he was also thankful for the oil. Though it made the men sick and helped to blind them, it served as a repellent against the sun, and perhaps the sharks as well.

Day caused suffering, too, because it revealed the ravages of night. Haynes didn't have to count the survivors to know at a glance that in one night dozens of them, perhaps fifty, had vanished. He remembered the soul-searing screams. Had they died of injuries, been pulled down by sharks, succumbed to exhaustion and let themselves drift off to oblivion?

Worst of all, day witnessed the rape of hope. . . .

"A plane!" someone shouted early Monday. "Look! A plane!"

"Where?"

"There—right up there. Honest, I see it. It's there!"

"We all [looked]," Haynes would relate. "There it [was]. We [had] been missed—and we [had] been found."

The men splashed the water with their feet, and one officer spread on the water some green marker dye he discovered in his jacket. That would do it. The plane's crew would see it and radio for help.

"It is a wonderful thought that [ran] through our minds," Haynes would say, "while we [watched] the plane pass over at about 1500 feet."

"He must see us! He must!" a man shouted.

But the plane droned on, becoming smaller and smaller, and finally it was gone, "our hopes with it."

When several other planes later flew over at high altitude, the men remained silent as they stared at the sky, their hopes dashed once more.

"Blind aviators, mates!" a sailor finally cried. "Just a bunch of blind aviators!"

And hopelessness spawned a feeble flurry of humor; those Air Force guys, everybody agreed, could never have survived in the Navy. Laughter. Even as the Navy guys fought to keep their noses above water.

"Doc! Doc!"

How many of these calls could he answer? Haynes asked himself. How many men could he save? Maybe none. But he must try to send a few more to their final peace with some sweet words. He dreaded the new horrors that would blight the day, and then once more the night, when the body, by this time starved, would crave the food necessary to create energy and heat, resulting in terrible chills and, finally, delirium. He wouldn't even try to imagine what might happen if there were still more days and more nights. At what point would the men—would *he*—go mad?

"Doc! Doc! Please!"

Yes, he was coming. Hold on, sailor!

Not every survivor was as altruistic as Dr. Haynes and those who helped him. Adolfo Celaya was one who encountered a less caring group of men. Still recovering from the shock of apparently killing his friend, Santos Pena, when he jumped into the water on top of him, Celaya despondently swam away and grabbed onto a raft that floated by. But though there were only two men on it, they didn't want any company, at least Celaya's.

"Get the hell away!" one of them barked. "Do you wanna turn this thing over?"

Celaya let go, but clung to a rope that hung from the raft. He was crushed. While he could accept death, was he to die humiliated, "cast from the herd"?

Five or six others then swam to the raft and climbed on, too intimidating to be turned back by the original occupants, and more followed. But those already aboard kicked at this new group and men fought each other for every square inch of space on the rim of the raft and in its water-filled interior. When the raft started to overturn, some men leaped off, and the battle began once more. Celaya was not consoled to see that whites could be as ruthless to each other as to a Mexican.

Shortly after dawn, two other rafts and two floater nets supported by corks drifted by. The five conveyances, each overloaded with men crushed under each other in great jumbles of flesh, were lashed together, while scores of swimmers swarmed in to join the group and hold on to ropes suspended from the tiny transports. A new little world of about 150 inhabitants was thus born, a world that still simmered in chaos as men bobbing in the water fought ferociously to join or dislodge others ensconced on minuscule portions of wood or netting.

They fought to escape the horror not only of dangling indefinitely in a deadly void, infinite and bottomless, but of gratifying the rapacious whims of man-eating sharks and other lethal creatures of the deep—barracuda, giant squids, poisonous jellyfish. In fact, it was not long before the saillike fins of the shark circled their world and occasionally made forays into it.

The terrorized men in the water, many of whom could feel the rough texture of sharkskin grazing their feet, were not sure what to do. Some had been told by experts to lie still as if dead, others, to thrash the water as violently as possible—and this seemed to be the most natural reaction. Either way, the sharks hesitated to attack the group, at least during the day. But when a corpse was released to the sea, they were seen pouncing on it and tearing it to pieces as it twisted into its grave—one reason why the men were reluctant to *act* dead. At night, there would be terrible screams in this group, as in others, and a man would unaccountably disappear, while pools of blood would stain the great carpet of oil. If someone strayed very far, the sharks would ultimately get him, dead or alive. The raft, or even the cargo net, thus looked to the swimmers as an oasis might look to a man lost in a burning desert.

In any case, the cries of wounded men in Celaya's group soon mingled with other shouts: "Let the wounded on!" And some of the able survivors on the rafts and nets, impelled by compassion or shame, agreed to cede their precious places to those who suffered most. But with each floating oasis able to hold only fifteen or twenty people, not every injured man was accommodated, and the night still echoed with pathetic calls for help. Some wounded who remained in the water began, in their weakened and unstable condition, to drift away, but the lucky ones were dragged back by Celaya and other heroic men in the group, who reached them before the sharks did.

One of those Celaya tried to save was his crew chief, who had trained him for his fireman's job and was the only other man from their section who survived. The pupil had, in turn, taught his teacher Spanish and developed a close relationship with him. A damn good white! The man had a severely damaged leg and, in his agony, no longer wanted to live.

"Don't worry," said Celaya, "we're going to make it. And then we'll drink a nice cold beer together."

"No," the man insisted. "I can't make it. I have a bad heart."

Celaya tied him to a raft so he couldn't move away again, and in the morning continued to allay his fears with talk of rescue and the bright future that lay ahead.

"No, no," the man responded. "I don't want any punk kid telling me what to do. Damn it, let me go!"

But Celaya refused. He was sure he had already killed one friend. He wouldn't let another go out there into that vast watery graveyard and die, helpless and alone—like a Mexican. He was bitter. Why couldn't his wounded friend find a place on a raft or net? Weren't there any officers around to give orders?

There were. And among them was Lieutenant Redmayne, who was still coasting on a remarkable streak of luck. He had left the aft engine room of the ship about a minute before he would have joined his men in death; he had climbed all the way from the bottom deck to topside while the ship was turning over; and he had managed to escape into the water with a spectacular display of acrobatics.

Then, Redmayne had just gotten into the water when an ammunition can floated by, which he clung to until a life jacket came his way some minutes later. Heading toward him after several more minutes was a raft, apparently the one that Celaya was not permitted to mount; the lieutenant, together with several others, simply climbed aboard, welcome or not.

Redmayne had always cherished authority, but he also cherished the charmed nature of his life. And at this moment of terror, when men were fighting not the enemy but their buddies in a struggle that only the fittest might survive, it would not be prudent to pull rank—or even to mention it. In fact, there was no rank now, for all the men had been reduced to nameless, unidentifiable, black-faced figures in an egalitarian jungle. Anyone who claimed the authority to tell the others how to behave in this anarchistic little world would be distrusted, scoffed at, and possibly dispensed with.

To avoid unnecessary conflict, Redmayne even parted with his most prized possession—his Sunday shoes. He had never enjoyed so perfect a fit, treasuring them almost as much as Cinderella did her glass slippers. And he wanted to keep them even though it was difficult to swim with them on. But when a voice caustically cried out, "Some son of a bitch on this raft is wearing shoes!"—a virtual call to rebellion against the foppish elite—Redmayne knew the clock had struck midnight. He surreptitiously removed them and dropped them into the water. Better his shoes than their owner.

If you couldn't stop a raging fire, Redmayne apparently felt, you waited until the fire died out before starting to rebuild. And he could only rebuild confidence in authority if he waited until the horror had dissipated into a mundane norm of existence. Besides, the men might not understand that he had to stay on the raft because the oil and salt water would add unbearably to the pain he already felt in his burned hand and in his oil-lined stomach—pain somehow exacerbated by the tormenting thought of his men back there in the engine room.

Thus, Redmayne decided that, for a while anyway, he would remain aloof from the panicky struggle on the rafts and conserve his energy. At the propitious moment, he would assert his authority—especially in the rationing of food and water. There were cans of Spam, biscuits, and malt tablets and little wooden barrels of fresh water aboard, and no one must get more than his share.

Actually, Redmayne wasn't sure he would have to take charge; he would not have minded at all if an officer of more senior rank revealed himself. Since no one's face was distinguishable, he might even be sitting next to the captain. He asked the man beside him, "Are you an officer?" No, he wasn't. He asked others around him. Same answer. Finally, after dawn, he found several officers, but all junior to him. One of them was Ensign Twible.

Harlan Twible was Annapolis even as he bobbed in the great swells of the Pacific. He remained fully dressed in khaki uniform, his buttons buttoned, and his socks pulled up; he did knock his shoes off, though—without suffering Redmayne's anguish. However well shoes might fit, he had learned in survival class, they were not to be worn in the ocean. Nor did he ignore many of the other rules. His face was already black with oil, but he smeared additional layers on as protection against the sun, and he forced himself to vomit all the oil and salt water he could instead of waiting for an involuntary reaction, as most of the men did.

Then, as also trained to do, Twible took charge—at least of the men in close proximity to him in the water, where he would remain throughout the ordeal to demonstrate the stoic endurance expected of a Navy man. He had to be cautious, however, for Redmayne was in the group and it wouldn't be proper for him to usurp a senior officer's authority. But at the same time, Redmayne was suffering greatly from his injury and was in no condition to lead these men, many of whom were, in their desperation, getting out of hand and in need of expert guidance.

Twible had personally brought many of the men into the group, gathering them like fallen leaves and persuading them to hold hands to avoid drifting apart. Safety in numbers! he cried—another thing he had learned at the Academy. And, in their confusion, the men obeyed him once more, even though most hadn't the foggiest idea who he was. As he himself would later explain, "I did not know many of the enlisted men due to the fact that I did not have any reason to associate with very many of them." He was, however, "thoroughly indoctrinated" with his "responsibility to the crew," and would try "to keep it from going into a rabble."

Like Redmayne, Twible realized that orders would not necessarily be obeyed. So "when things were starting to get rough," he would "bring them back to sanity" by "leading the people off into prayer." Yes, God was still at work. And with God and Annapolis behind him, he continued to predict that he would survive; in fact, he felt more confident than ever. And who could call him a false prophet? Had he not prophesied, with unfortunate accuracy, that the *Indianapolis* would meet a sad end?

Now if only the men would let him help them survive as well.

. . .

In this same group was Ensign Blum, who, like Redmayne, was not inclined to lose his anonymity, at least not immediately—and for the same reason. Officers were lightning rods for the men when anarchy prevailed, and he wanted to live through this nightmare.

As the *Indianapolis* had gone down, the sandwich Blum had been eating came up, soaked in oil and salt water; still, sick as he was, he swam about two hundred yards in what may have been record time. What, however, should he do now, alone in the middle of the largest ocean on earth with no life preserver and nothing to hang on to? They hadn't prepared him for this at midshipmen's school.

Suddenly, Blum heard voices. Two men were floating nearby, their arms crooked around an inflated rubber life belt. He swam over to them and clamped his own arm around the tube. At last, support. And the men were congenial, too. All assumed that an SOS had gone out and that they would be picked up after daybreak. Blum was apparently the least concerned; the Navy, after all, was an experienced organization that knew what it was doing—except, of course, when it came to granting liberties. So confident of immediate rescue were the three men that they talked not about survival, but about the shore leaves they would get after rescue and the possessions they had lost. Blum had lost three bottles of booze? Poor guy.

In midmorning, the men spotted the tiny armada of rafts and nets and joined the group. Blum, who had by now found a life preserver, tied himself to a raft with the rope hanging from it, and watched as men grappled to climb on. As an officer, should he try to bring order? Who would listen to him? Anyway, he couldn't help them to survive but would be jeopardizing his own survival. No, he would quietly preserve his strength and outlast them all. He felt in tiptop physical shape—even with part of that sandwich still stuck in his queasy stomach.

Nevertheless, he became a bit uneasy when someone paddled up to him and, with a wild look in his eyes, demanded: "Where's my money? I gave it to you for safekeeping."

Who was this man? Blum couldn't tell since the face was black with oil, like his own. The oil, he had been relieved to learn, was the perfect equalizer, the ideal means of achieving anonymity. He didn't even know that among the men around him was his hometown buddy, Ensign Tom Brophy, who was also keeping a low profile. So how could this man now confronting him know who *he* was? Besides, Donald Blum hadn't taken anybody's money.

"I don't have your money," he replied. "Leave me alone."

The man then struck Blum, and the ensign, in dismay, swam to the other side of the raft, followed by his attacker, who tried to hit him again. Though finally losing the man, Blum was no longer so optimistic. This, he thought, was the beginning. The attacker had lost his senses. Unless help came soon—or he woke up—everyone would go mad.

Blum almost felt like joining the men Twible was leading in the Lord's Prayer. But he wasn't sure God existed. All right, no prayer, but simply "heavy wishes." He was upset, though. He believed in people more than in God, but look at some of the people.

"Over here! Over here!"

Where was the voice coming from? Yeoman Havins was exhausted as he thrashed about in the ravenous sea. He wanted to rely on God to save him, but God hadn't saved his older brother, nor had He gotten the surviving brother transferred off the *Indianapolis* in time. But the voice he now heard seemed to be coming from every direction at once, as if from some omnipresent source. Maybe God had remembered him after all.

From the moment Havins had jumped off the ship, crisis followed crisis. As he began swimming away from the plunging vessel, wrapped in a life preserver, a drowning man without support sprang up, choking on oil and salt water, and grasped him around the arms and waist. With Havins unable to extricate his arms, the pair went under three times before the yeoman, with a last burst of strength, finally broke loose. He let his shipmate stay clamped to his waist, hoping to save both of them, but the man couldn't hold on any longer and, as he started going down, grabbed Havins' ankles. Havins desperately flailed the water, and after a few more strokes suddenly felt himself free of his burden. The man had disappeared.

Even swimming alone, Havins could make little headway, since his water-soaked shoes were dragging him down. He tried to untie the soggy laces, but he went under again. Hardly had he surfaced when his rubber life belt went flat, apparently torn by debris. It was time, it seemed, to join his brother. . . . And then the voice.

It continued to call out: "Here! Over here! I have a cargo net!"

Havins cried back: "Whistle so I can find you!" He was finally able to swim to the man, Machinist's Mate First Class John Muldoon, who was hanging on to a rolled-up cargo net. Shortly after he joined Muldoon, two more men, deathly ill from the nauseating ocean brew, were pulled to the net, and then a raft with only one man on it was sighted nearby. The four clinging to the net swam to the raft and climbed aboard. Now there were five against the sea—doubly protected from sharks and other predatory fish by the net, which the men stretched under the lattice-floored raft.

Havins was awed by his good fortune; someone *was* looking after him. His thoughts drifted home. How could his parents have taken the loss of a second son—in a second sinking?

Suddenly, as the raft swung to the crest of a wave, Havins saw another raft with several men on it about a quarter of a mile away. More survivors! He was elated. Please, God, don't stop now! The men in the two rafts paddled furiously toward each other. Who was that calling from the other one? The voice sounded familiar to Havins.

The skipper!

Captain McVay, though until now the proud commander of a cruiser, was satisfied to take charge of a potato crate when one floated by right after the ship's demise. And it didn't take long for him to improve his status. Hardly had he climbed astride the crate when two rafts, one on top of the other, sailed past, having broken loose when the vessel went down.

McVay climbed on the rafts, grateful for his good luck but puzzled that not a paddle or a provision could be found aboard as regulations required. In a way, his good luck added to his anguish. It seemed mockingly obscene—the captain alone with two rafts, while some men out there might not even have life preservers to support them.

How could this have happened? Surely a submarine had torpedoed the ship. But he hadn't been warned that one might be roving in the area. He recalled his talks in Guam with Commodore Carter and the men in the port director's office. They must have had some inkling of the danger—enough to make sure he had an escort at least. Instead, they had lulled him into thinking the risks were minimal. And now, most of his men were probably dead—and *he* was alive. Alive and alone with two rafts!

If he could save just one life now, one life. His men were no longer simply members of his crew, but a part of him. Their agony was his; their death was his, in spirit. He could envision each one he had ever dealt with—what he looked like, what words he had spoken. He had met many of their loved ones when they came to visit the boys at Mare Island. What would he tell these bereaved people now—if he himself survived? . . . Just one life . . .

"Help us! Help us!"

McVay scanned the sea with the one eye he could see through, the other having been temporarily blinded by fuel oil. His prayer had been answered.

"Over here! I have a raft," he called back.

And in a few minutes, three men came swimming up, one of them Quartermaster Third Class Vincent J. Allard, who was helping to prop up two younger comrades. McVay pulled them onto the top raft, then, with Allard's assistance, separated the two rafts and lashed them together, placing the other two men, who could not stop retching and vomiting, in the second one. McVay doubted that the pair would live out the night, and kept watch over them as if they were his own sons. When their condition improved after several hours, he was overjoyed. And he was further cheered to finally discover aboard paddles, food, signaling devices, and other emergency items. Actually not aboard, but attached "underneath" the rafts, which had been floating upside down.

Throughout the night, McVay looked out to sea, searching for more rafts, more men; but the twelve-foot swells made it almost impossible to see anything beyond the next rolling wave, especially with the moon still playing peekaboo behind the clouds. The fuzzy world he gazed at with his one good eye was silent and serene. Yet, only a few hours earlier, he had witnessed the grotesque violence of a huge ship, a floating city, being swallowed whole amid the crash of disintegration and the shrieks of trapped men. Why hadn't those great screw propellers fallen on him, crushed him, ground him up? Then he wouldn't have to face the parents, the wives, the sweethearts, the admirals, or to see the pain in the eyes of his father and wife. . . . Were there no more survivors?

Shortly after dawn, he learned there were—when he sighted Yeoman Havins' group.

Hardly were McVay's two rafts lashed to the third one and the cargo net when the captain bombarded the newcomers with questions. What were their names and ranks? Did anyone need medical attention? Did they see or know of any other groups? Did they know anyone who had died?

Havins and the others were moved by McVay's great concern for them and their comrades. But there was nothing he could do to help. Miraculously, no one aboard was wounded, though some, like the captain himself, were half-blinded from the oil and others could barely see from either eye. The eyes burned whether they stayed open or shut, with the agony subsiding only if they were kept in either state for more than ten minutes at a time. As for other survivors, the men had not seen any. The captain's face dropped. Were nine men, including one officer—himself—the only ones alive?

Though shattered, McVay, to make life seem as normal as possible, tried to sound as if they were simply on maneuvers. He rationed out the little food he had found on the rafts—biscuits, Spam, malted milk tablets—so it could last for ten days. In addition, he had found fishing equipment aboard, and he was a pretty good fisherman. He had found a supply of cigarettes, too, but unfortunately the matches were wet. He had also picked up a drifting water breaker, though with fresh water so scarce, he said, the contents would be given out only when it became "absolutely necessary." He didn't have the heart to tell them that he had tasted the water and found it salty, and thus undrinkable.

McVay then took some paper from someone's wallet and a pencil from another's pocket and began to keep a log, judging the group's position by the sun. He even prepared a two-hour watch list—to maintain naval routine and make sure that someone would be awake if a ship or plane came into view. He might be thrown out of the Navy, but for now he was still the captain and would command a tight raft, or fleet of them.

Suddenly, McVay no longer conveyed the image of a captain, but of the simple fisherman he loved to be, wearing, unstylishly pulled over his ears, a cornucopia-shaped hat fashioned by Allard from a piece of canvas found on one raft. The men all wore such headpieces to protect themselves from the sun. McVay lowered a line into the water and caught one small fish, but immediately recognized it as a poisonous specimen. So he cut it up and used it as bait, then dropped the line again. A big fish came up this time—the biggest he had ever hooked. A shark!

The men looked around and saw about five of the creatures swirling nearby. They were terrified. How could they dangle their legs in the water? What if someone dropped off to sleep and fell in? McVay tried to calm them. And to help give them strength, he led them in prayer, as he would every morning, ad-libbing the words as he went along. He wasn't a religious man, but God certainly came in handy at a time like this.

And so did Otha Havins and another man, Jay Glenn; they helped to raise spirits with melodious renditions of such popular classics as "Oh! Susanna," "Down in the Valley," "I'll Walk Alone," "Rum and Coca-Cola," and "I'll Be with You in Apple Blossom Time." But they were not the Andrews Sisters, and the sharks apparently realized it; they tended to disappear during these frequent concerts —though one of them always stayed for an encore.

He stayed for dinner, too. Every time McVay lowered the line, the shark would be there to pick off the bait or to frighten away other fish. McVay was frustrated. He saw many good-sized schools of fish, especially bonito, or small mackerel, but with the shark haunting the rafts, there was no way he could pull them in. First, fresh water that couldn't be drunk, then cigarettes that couldn't be lit, and now, fish that couldn't be caught. Whatever went awry, though, the captain tried not to show his irritation. These were, after all, minor vexations compared to what other survivors—if there were any—might be enduring.

Besides, McVay wanted to ease, not inflame, anxieties. He was trying to behave properly in these new circumstances; he was living not with fellow officers who had shared similar life-styles, educational backgrounds, and social traditions, but with men of "inferior rank" who were supposed to regard officers with a certain awe. He never would have sipped a dry martini in an officers' club with these men. And though he regarded them almost as his children, especially after the disaster, how well, after all, did he know even his own children?

But now he wanted to know his raftmates, to feel what they were feeling and open his own heart to them, for his bond with them was no longer formalistic, but forged in the fire of catastrophe. And with the arrogance of ambition giving way to the humility of certain ruin, he apparently felt freer now to abandon caste and express emotion. Still, he seemed apprehensive. What did these men, and their comrades who might still be alive, think of him? Did they blame him for the tragedy, lose their respect for him, hate him? After all, he was the captain of the ship, and whatever the causes, he had failed them, leading them into this disaster.

In any case, the living would constantly remind him of the dead, and the dead would never let him forget his sacred duty—to mourn them ceaselessly, and to remember. He would be living with his men, whether in body or in spirit, until his last breath. And so he must know who they were, those who were still alive to tell him.

Sitting on the edge of his raft, McVay asked them about their future plans. Would Havins stay in the Navy?

"I considered such a career," Havins replied, "but I couldn't make my girl, Billie, understand that in peacetime wives go with their husbands and that they're usually together."

Reflecting on his own peacetime experience, McVay chuckled, reluctant to confirm that Billie understood only too well.

He inquired about their families, their girl friends. And they answered freely, but were hesitant to ask him personal questions.

They didn't have to. His own future? Well, he volunteered, he would retire in a few years, hopefully as an admiral; he did not dare say that this seemed very unlikely now. And then he and his wife would really enjoy life together. Louise was quite a woman. Did she love to hunt! They should have seen her during duck season. And fishing? She could catch anything. Wish she were here now. Louise . . . Louise . . . Her name was constantly on his lips.

The men were stunned. Was this their skipper? They knew him as a fair and humane man, a person they respected and could trust, but they never dreamed of exchanging banter about family affairs and personal feelings with him. They were also surprised to find that they could love their skipper not only as a leader but as a buddy. And they were almost as startled to learn that *he* was capable of loving people so ardently—his men, his wife. Who would have imagined?

Conversation was interrupted on one occasion when someone pointed out to sea and cried, "Another raft!"

McVay peered into the distance and saw a raft riding the swells about fifteen hundred yards away. There seemed to be only one person on it, and he was calling for help. Almost simultaneously, he saw another raft bouncing in the waves much farther away with several people aboard. Counting the men in his own little fleet, he judged that perhaps twenty-five or thirty people had survived in all—out of almost *twelve hundred.*

The captain and his men could paddle to the nearest raft in a few hours, but it would take too long to reach the second one; they would surely get blisters on their hands, which would develop into nasty saltwater ulcers, as even the tiniest scratch did. McVay gazed at the men around him and saw that they were all too exhausted to paddle even to the nearest one, too drained from lack of sleep and the uncertainty of rescue.

Uncertainty had led to deep, debilitating pessimism, especially after several planes had flown over that morning and then faded into infinity. The captain and his men had flashed two mirrors, waved two yellow signaling flags, and splashed the water with hands and feet, but to no avail.

Don't worry, McVay had tenderly lied to his men, he personally knew that an SOS message had gotten out. In any case, the ship was due in Leyte the following day, Tuesday; when it failed to show up, a search would immediately be ordered, if one hadn't started already. Meanwhile, they should get some rest before rowing to the nearest raft.

And when the sun broke over the waves on Tuesday, the men, cheered by the thought that help was definitely on the way, set out for the raft, paddling in shifts, and reached it after four and a half grueling hours.

Was he okay? McVay asked the single survivor aboard.

Fine, said the youth, who was amazed to see the captain himself. But after two nights and a day alone in the middle of the ocean, with only sharks and other fish to talk to, he was getting lonely. He hoped the captain didn't mind coming.

McVay smiled as the sailor climbed aboard his raft. He could hardly make out the features on the boy's face, which, like everyone else's, was black from the oil—and he couldn't see very well through his one usable eye, anyway. But it didn't matter. Somehow, this boy was every lost member of his crew, the living and the dead. Every lonely son of his.

No, he didn't mind. And there was plenty to talk about, too— while they waited for a ship to come.

IX

Under No Command

WOULD those damn ships ever stop coming?

Lieutenant Stuart B. Gibson, the port director's operations officer in Tacloban, Leyte Gulf, wondered when he would get some relief. The pressures of his job and the stifling tropical heat were making him testy and uncomfortable. It was Tuesday, July 31—the last day of the month. And what a month it had been. He had had to keep track of about fifteen hundred ships steaming into the harbor; there would be about forty today. Gibson glanced at the daily dispatch from the Harbor Entrance Control Post (HECP) to see which ships had arrived. He had to give berths, fuel, and provisions to each, then report its arrival in coded radio messages to all interested commands and register it on the Ships Present list, which would also be sent to these commands.

One expected ship, Gibson noted, had not arrived—the *Indianapolis*. The day before, Guam had notified his office that this cruiser would pull in at 11 A.M., Tuesday, and he had duly jotted this down in his log. But it was now late afternoon and the *Indianapolis* was missing from the list of arrivals circulated by HECP, which kept several craft at the harbor gateway to observe ship movements.

When the cruiser eventually churned into the Gulf—and Gibson assumed it would—he would routinely add it to the Ships Present list, but he would not report the time it arrived, for port rules stated that "arrival reports shall not be made for combatant ships," only for merchant and naval auxiliary vessels. CINCPAC, as well as the Seventh Fleet, which operated under General Douglas MacArthur in the Southwest Pacific area, laid down these rules in identical letters to all port directors in the Pacific. Why make it easier for a Japanese submarine to learn the movements of a combatant ship? Besides, the radio waves were already overburdened with thousands of reports.

Gibson was not concerned about the *Indianapolis*. Many ships were eight to twelve hours late—and some combatant vessels never arrived. After all, this office dealt mainly with merchant shipping. The port director, in fact, was officially called a senior naval officer of a "merchant ship control staff."

It was the fleet commanders' job to deal with warships, though, of course, the port director was perfectly willing to cooperate—when feasible. Anyway, since the *Indianapolis* was Admiral Spruance's flagship, the admiral might redirect it without notice on some secret mission. In fact, the last Gibson heard, that cruiser was sailing under the direct orders of the President himself. No, the *Indianapolis* was not his responsibility. And since he had been ordered not to announce the arrival of a combatant ship, obviously, it seemed to him, the converse was true: He should not announce its nonarrival either. No port director in the Pacific, he had heard, interpreted the order any other way.

Though Gibson was by no means enamored of the military— and could hardly wait to get back to his wife, infant daughter, and bank manager's job in Richmond, Virginia—he had been working conscientiously in Leyte, where he had been on duty since January. The port director had only recently praised his work and urged him to apply for reassignment to his command. What hypocrisy! This same man had submitted a fitness report on him that directly contradicted what he had told him.

"This officer," the report stated, "performs his duties willingly but is indecisive, frequently becomes bewildered and 'rattle-brained.' He has been a port director watch officer, a duty requiring qualifications which he does not possess to a degree necessary . . . and would do better in a position requiring less originality and responsibility."

The port director, in short, wanted a more experienced Navy man, preferably an Annapolis graduate, for so important a job, and Gibson was a converted bank manager—the kind of instant officer that had to be recruited as the Navy expanded and absorbed its veteran elite.

While Gibson's superior nevertheless recommended him for a promotion, the lieutenant was crushed and "at a loss to explain the basis" of the unfavorable report. Actually, few people who knew Gibson thought of him as a man of daring initiative. If he lacked dynamism, however, he always took pride in doing a competent job and living up to the distinguished name of his family, one of the old aristocratic families of Richmond.

And now there was this "slanderous" fitness report, this "travesty of the truth." Was he to be faulted for obeying every rule explicitly? Did they expect a junior officer to make his own rules? He was glad there was now a new port director, Lieutenant Commander Jules Sancho. Perhaps he would judge him with greater fairness and understanding. Since Sancho was just familiarizing himself with the job, Gibson did not wish to burden him unnecessarily with mundane details—for example, the nonarrival so far of the *Indianapolis*. Nor did he see any need to inform his superiors in the Philippine Sea Frontier (PSF) Command at Toloso, about twenty miles away, which was responsible for protecting Allied shipping not only in Philippine waters but within a vast region that stretched from Indochina to Sarawak—unless, of course, the command asked for information.

This wasn't the port director's headache.

Was it the headache, then, of the Frontier Command leaders? Not according to Captain Alfred M. Granum, operations officer of the command. If or when the *Indianapolis* arrived was not its business. After all, his command, like its subordinate port director's office, dealt mainly with merchant and auxiliary naval ships. Technically, the *Indianapolis* would be under the Frontier's wing as soon as it crossed the "chop" line, an imaginary line dividing the Marianas area of command, with its base at Guam, from the Frontier area of command, with its base at Leyte. Thus, from about midnight, July 29, when the ship was scheduled to cross this line, the Frontier presumably assumed command over it, though, in Granum's view, only on paper. The Frontier's real business was keeping track of 350 to 400 noncombatant ships a day; finding alternate routes for those caught in storms (the principal problem occupying him on this day); and setting up hunter-killer teams to search for Japanese submarines, like the one thought to be lurking in the northern part of the Frontier zone.

Granum wasn't told by his controllers whether the *Indianapolis* had arrived in Leyte Gulf, nor did he ask them. Why should he? Even if he had known the ship was late, he wouldn't have taken special action. There could be any number of reasons for a delay, though one he wouldn't have considered was an attack by an enemy submarine. According to his reports, the main submarine threat did not lie on the route from Guam to Leyte, but on the route from Leyte to Okinawa, where there was heavy shipping for the buildup of an invasion fleet.

Meanwhile, in the chart house, the controllers were plotting the course of every ship in the area, friendly or not, on the operational plotting board, moving the markers every eight hours according to the estimated speed of the ship. Men hustled about shifting the markers, delivering reports, answering telephones. But there was no tension, no sense of urgency. With so many ships to keep track of, they certainly couldn't get excited about the possible nonarrival of any one vessel, especially one over which the command exercised only the vaguest jurisdiction.

Since the *Indianapolis* was due in Leyte Gulf at 11 A.M. that day, the marker for it was moved all the way there—as it was on the plotting boards of the Marianas Command and of CINCPAC itself back in Guam. And since there were no reports to the contrary, the plotters assumed that the ship had arrived on time. Both Guam commands then removed the marker, based on this assumption, though that of the Frontier Command would remain on the board until the vessel appeared on the Ships Present list confirming its arrival—whenever that might be.

If any craft was in danger, Granum felt, surely it would signal an SOS. When would he start investigating a nonarrival? He wasn't sure. After all, the Ships Present list often arrived a day or so late, and sometimes a ship would enter the Gulf without being observed by the Harbor Entrance Controllers.

Nor did Granum want to trouble his superior about the "lateness" of individual combatant ships, any more than Lieutenant Gibson did, particularly since his superior, like Gibson's, was new at the job. Commodore Norman C. Gillette had been Chief of Staff of the Philippine Sea Frontier Command since October 1944, and had temporarily replaced the regular commander, Vice Admiral J. L. Kauffman, only a few days earlier when the admiral went on leave. Gillette himself would later explain his own attitude toward tardy combatant ships: "We did not feel that we were vitally interested or directly responsible or that we should take any unusual action."

This was the fleet commanders' headache.

Rear Admiral L. D. McCormick was a fleet commander, but he already had more than his share of headaches trying to shape up his new command. He had arrived in Leyte Gulf on July 25, about a week earlier, to initiate a training command, Task Group 95.7, which would serve the needs of Task Force 95, operating in the Okinawa area under Vice Admiral Jesse B. Oldendorf. Oldendorf wanted such a command so that he could send his combat-weary crews to Leyte for training and recreation.

Since the *Indianapolis* would soon be joining his task force to prepare for an invasion of Japan, he was not surprised when he received a dispatch from CINCPAC informing him that the crew would report first to Admiral McCormick's group for refresher training. McCormick, however, was puzzled. He knew when the ship was coming, but not why, for he had never seen the first dispatch telling him the reason. And Oldendorf knew why the ship was coming, but not when, for he had never seen the second dispatch from CINCPAC announcing the time of the ship's arrival.

Both admirals were victims of bureaucratic bungling. The communications center at Okinawa, Oldendorf would say later, was "notoriously inefficient in the forwarding of messages," and the center at Leyte was not much better, wrongly addressing the first message to McCormick. Actually, despite the error, McCormick's staff did receive a copy of that message, apparently because the admiral's name was mentioned in the text. But ironically, his aides, thinking that the faulty address indicated the dispatch was intended for someone else, and feeling that it couldn't be very important anyway since it was simply "restricted," not "secret," didn't bother to decode it or even to ask that it be repeated. Without this message, therefore, McCormick could only infer that the *Indianapolis* was coming for training purposes.

But whatever the purpose was, McCormick planned to take some vessels out on training exercises about the time the ill-fated ship was supposed to arrive, and he saw no reason to change the schedule, not even by an hour. Of course, he might wait for it if he had been told exactly why it was coming. But since he was unaware that CINCPAC in fact, had sent this information, he felt the mission could not be very urgent. Apparently, not even urgent enough for him to point out to the subordinate flag officer he left in command that the ship was expected that morning. The officer, he would later argue, had access to all his records and could find this out by himself.

McCormick sailed out of the Gulf with his little fleet about 11 A.M., the exact time the *Indianapolis* was due to enter the Gulf, but no cruiser was in sight. This did not worry the admiral. He did not ask the port director or the Philippine Sea Frontier Command if they knew where the ship was. A waste of time. It would be here—for whatever reason—when he returned. In any case, the *Indianapolis* was not his responsibility. Why should he do the job of the area and Frontier commanders along the route? He would later explain: "They had the means to plot all ships, they had the routing officers . . . and we were not carrying a detailed plot of the *Indianapolis'* trip."

Meanwhile, Admiral Oldendorf, on failing to receive word of the *Indianapolis'* arrival in Leyte, was no more concerned than McCormick, for he had no idea when the ship was due. Often in the past, when it was attached to his division, he "was not informed as to [its] orders." As Admiral Spruance's flagship, it "operated . . .

in a special status, her orders being subject to change without no-
tification."

Thus, Oldendorf would say later, even if he had known the
scheduled time of arrival, he wouldn't have worried about its tar-
diness, for "I would have thought that her orders had been changed
and I had not received the change of orders."

Did Oldendorf feel in any way responsible for checking on the
whereabouts of the *Indianapolis*?

No, why should he? It wasn't his headache.

X

A Way of Life

DOCTOR, if I hold this water in my hands to the sun and evaporate it a bit, will it be safe to drink?"

Dr. Haynes gazed at the crystal clear water the young sailor was cupping in his hands, and he himself had an almost irrepressible urge to feel its coolness as it spilled down his parched throat. It was Tuesday afternoon, about forty hours after the sinking, and under the relentless sun a maddening thirst overwhelmed the survivors. They were immersed in water almost up to their necks, yet they could not drink a drop—or they would go berserk and die. Haynes felt the burning eyes of the men "drill" into him as they waited for his answer.

"No, son," he replied, "that will only make it more salty. You must not drink."

By this time, they would be missed in Leyte. Just a few hours more and they could drink as much as they wished.

But Haynes knew from the crazed look in the eyes of some, especially the younger men with no family responsibilities to steel them, that his words would not be heeded, if they had even been heard. To stop those who began to drink, he struck them, crying; "Don't! Don't! Do you want to die?"

But he finally gave up. What was the use? There were so many of them, and water was everywhere. Man after man took the deadly liquid in his hands and gulped it down, bloating himself with it.

Delirium soon followed. They prattled at first, then thrashed violently with a maniacal energy that the other men, in their exhaustion, could not easily summon. Yet somehow a few did, to save their raving shipmates. Haynes himself helped to buoy up his dear friend, Commander Lipski, one of the last of the severely wounded to remain alive, and listened to his dying words: "I'm going now, Lew. Please tell my wife that I love her and that she should marry again."

Then his head dropped, and Haynes knew he was dead. He hugged the corpse, removed the life jacket, which could serve someone else, and watched the body slide under the waves.

As death claimed ever more men, earthly values yielded to spiritual ones, giving those still alive a certain peace of mind even in the midst of catastrophe. Haynes was thankful that his other friend, Father Conway, was around to help the men embrace God and lead them in prayer. But then, on Tuesday night, the chaplain ceased moving among them. Like many in his flock, he collapsed from exhaustion and became delirious.

Conway was about to float away to his death when he was grabbed by Garland Rich, the young Texan who had played football under Lieutenant McKissick and had, ever since hitting the water, rounded up and supported many of the wounded men. But after holding up the priest for a while and struggling to calm him as he thrashed and babbled gibberish, Rich himself felt ill and too spent to continue his heroic role.

"Doctor!" he called Haynes, who immediately swam over to him. "Doctor, you'll just have to relieve me for a while. I—I can't hold him any longer."

Haynes put his arm through Conway's life jacket to control his wild movements, and embraced his friend, who he knew was dying. The doctor was emotionally drained, especially after watching Lipski sink into the sea. Now another dear friend. How many would die in his arms? There was so much he wanted to tell the chaplain, to thank him for once more—the money that enabled him to go home to see his family, the chance to sing every Sunday the Protestant hymns that had given him strength since childhood, and, most important of all, his efforts to ease the suffering of these people. The father was a man who had served all men; now he was beyond the reach of all men.

And so, it seemed, was Garland Rich, whom Haynes glimpsed some distance away in the moonlight. He had stopped paddling and his head had fallen forward, almost to the surface of the sea. Was Rich dying, too? The doctor agonized. He called for help, but no one heard him, at least no one who was sane enough to respond. What should he do? Which of the two stricken men should he leave to drown?

Meanwhile, Lieutenant McKissick, who, though nearby, had apparently not heard Haynes' call, did hear another faint voice in the night: "Coach, come and help me! Coach, help me!"

Garland Rich! But where was the voice coming from? McKissick desperately scanned the moonlit sea. The men had scattered and no one was in sight. He swam in one direction, then in another, flailing about in near-panic, but his old pupil still eluded him as the voice grew weaker and weaker.

"Garland! Garland! Where are you?" McKissick cried.

He was the boy's coach, wasn't he? He couldn't just let him die.

Neither could Haynes, who was also shouting Rich's name. He knew that mere words could not snatch the youth from the precipice, but there was nothing else he could do. Though Father Conway might himself protest Haynes' decision if he were lucid, the doctor could not steal from his friend even one extra minute of life. And so Haynes helplessly watched while Rich's face dipped into the water and his body drifted away.

"Garland! Garland!" . . . Then only the eternal sound of the waves.

Shortly afterward, Father Conway stopped thrashing and blessed Dr. Haynes in disjointed bursts of rationality. Then he, too, departed—for a land where there would always be enough food to eat and water to drink, and where nobody needed a life jacket or someone to hold his head out of the water.

. . .

That morning there were enough rations even in the land of the living—at least for those in Lieutenant Redmayne's group who reportedly stole some they found on a couple of the rafts and sat stuffing themselves with Spam and malted milk tablets while their intimidated comrades, too listless and feeble to stop them, watched with growling stomachs and gritty throats.

When Ensign Twible heard about this, he was enraged. A shameful injustice! He swam over to Redmayne's raft and told the lieutenant about this breakdown in the modest measure of discipline that, after the initial struggle for places on the rafts, had taken hold of them. The ringleader, he said, headed "a small group that felt they were outside of the Navy and every man was for himself."

Yes, shameful, Redmayne agreed. It was clearly time to unmask himself and take control of the situation. The men in the water were now exhausted and no longer fought each other with their earlier vigor. He thus felt more confident now. Anyway, this might be his last chance to prove to himself, and everybody else, that he was a commander to be reckoned with. He braced himself on the edge of the raft and cried, "I'm Lieutenant Redmayne, the chief engineer, and it turns out that I am the senior officer in the group."

The men listened, but with apathy. Who cared about rank now? In fact, some of the new crew members had never heard of him, while others were resentful. Why hadn't the chief engineer shut off all the engines before the ship went down? They were haunted by the image of that turning propeller grinding up some of their buddies as they jumped overboard. But Redmayne knew he had to assert his authority now or the survivors would never accept it. At the same time, he could not unrealistically raise their hopes of imminent rescue or they might turn against him if he was wrong; he thus described the "worst" scenario.

"By the end of the day," he said, "Leyte will be concerned. My guess is that they will send planes to look for us tomorrow morning. They know our speed and exactly what course to fly. So the planes may sight us before dark tomorrow, and we may see ships by late

Thursday. Before that, the planes will certainly drop us food, equipment, etcetera."

Rescue would most likely come earlier, Redmayne felt, but he couldn't imagine it coming later.

Fortunately, he announced, the men were not without food and water. There were four casks filled with fresh water and some Spam, biscuits, and malted milk tablets aboard the rafts, but no one was permitted to eat or drink until the following day, Wednesday, to make sure the supply would last until rescue came. Redmayne urged the men to bring all food and water to his raft for safekeeping, and was pleased when a few swam over with some of the rations, afraid that the "thieves" might otherwise get their hands on them.

Actually, few really trusted Redmayne either—or for that matter, anyone else. Surely not with commodities that precious. But drained, if not disabled, physically and mentally, the men found it easier now to take orders than to expend their waning energy on protest and resistance. Meanwhile, the "thieves" remained silent as they continued to munch on the forbidden food.

Shortly, Twible swam over to the ringleader's raft to confront him.

"I had no fear of him or the people with him," Twible would say later. "I had been taught how to handle myself. Besides, I knew these people were cowards at heart or they wouldn't be intimidating others. [The ringleader] headed a group that could destroy us all. Panic would have been the end of our chances to survive. If he and his group had been allowed to get away with intimidation, only God knows what would have happened."

Twible pulled near the ringleader's raft. When he saw the food and water that the man was allegedly hoarding, he was in a rage.

"Give it all back!" he yelled.

And he grabbed the rations, then swam to a second raft and seized the food and water the man's cronies were consuming there, returning to the "command" raft with the precious loot in tow.

(The accused "ringleader" denied to the author that he had taken any food or water, arguing that since he was a master-at-arms aboard ship, a policeman who enforced regulations, he had made many enemies, and they were simply seeking vengeance—though Twible, the avowed justice seeker, was not normally a man who scoffed at regulations.)

Whatever the truth, the measure of discipline that extreme exhaustion had brought after the violence was now in danger of crumbling as reality dissolved into illusion. More and more men swallowed salt water, some deliberately, some accidentally—because of the constant splash of the waves against their faces, which were nearing the water level as life belts and jackets gradually lost their buoyancy. Already there were reports of deviant violence: A man on one of the rafts, it was said, had been attacked by crazed shipmates demanding sexual satisfaction.

Twible's answer to such reports of indiscipline was to recite the Lord's Prayer constantly.

"After all," he would say, "I led most of the group into the water and they must have felt I would lead them out." He had to "prevent them from giving up. . . . When all else failed, prayer seemed to bring them back."

Yes, Lieutenant Redmayne was the ranking officer, but his flesh was still afire and his mind still anchored in the engine room with his men. Everyone knew, Twible was sure, that Ensign Twible, with backing from heaven, was the man who would "lead them out."

In the dreadful darkness of Tuesday night, even the most fervent prayer, it seemed, could not have saved the men in Dr. Haynes' fragmented group, which had no rafts, no floater nets, no food, and no fresh water. By now, most of them had lost their minds. Like the sailors in other groups, they had already been suffering from photophobia, nausea, dehydration, neck sores caused by the grating kapok collars, and other ailments. Now, as Haynes had feared, severe chills and high fever—brought on by exhaustion and fluid loss— racked their bodies, accelerating the general dementia. Gradually, the group became "a mass of delirious, screaming men" as they found themselves trapped in a horrifying world of fantasy.

"There's a Jap here!" a man cried. "He's trying to kill me!"

It was a clarion call to madness, sweeping away the last remnants of reason.

"There he goes!" another voice shouted. "Get the Jap! Kill him!"

In Dr. Haynes' words, "The sea [resounded] with yelling, maniacal beings, who, in their mad imaginings, suddenly [turned] against one another. Fights [broke] out, and, in their extreme delirium, men who [had] held each other up now [drew] knives and several [were] brutally stabbed."

The knives flashed in the moonlight as shipmates assaulted each other in an orgy of mayhem and murder; some without knives ripped life jackets off others and held their heads underwater until they drowned. Other men, consumed by fear of comrades they had once trusted, broke away from the group and scattered in all directions. Never had the sharks circling below feasted so well.

"The individual instinct to survive," Haynes would say, "[destroyed] all we [had] done for our common good."

Both Haynes and Marine Captain Parke pleaded with the crazed men to come to their senses and continued to round up those who were swimming off. Finally, Parke collapsed from the effort and, perhaps stabbed or grabbed by a shark, vanished forever.

Meanwhile, two sailors pushed Haynes under the water and held him there, but, miraculously, he managed to scramble to the surface. Now the doctor himself felt the terror, and hallucinations began to ferment in his mind, too. He had to escape his comrades, the same men he loved and felt compelled to save. And as this whole subgroup, so meticulously kept together for two days, disintegrated with the centrifugal force of a bomb blast, Haynes frenziedly swam away toward some unknown shore.

He wanted to move faster, but the waves kept striking him in the face. Who was splashing water on him? Were they joking or were they trying to kill him? He stopped and turned around, his burned hands curled into fists ready to pound his tormentors. But there was no one there. He was alone—alone in the middle of the ocean, with only a bright moon to mitigate the horror of drifting in a dark, unpeopled world to remind him that there would be a dawn.

Suddenly, a voice.

"Who's there?" Haynes called.

He heard a strange jabbering, and then backed away. Was it someone who wanted to kill him?

The hours passed, and he watched the moon edge across the sky to judge the passage of time.

Other voices uttered mad gibberish. Again he swam away. Would daylight ever come? Even the rays of the sun were better than the knives of the night. But how long could he stand the terrible isolation? How long could he fear the men he loved, the men who needed him?

More voices. He must go to them. Let them kill him. There seemed no point, anyway, to life in a world that had lost its soul. But as he tried to swim toward the voices, his strength finally gave out.

"Help me! Help me!" Haynes cried.

He himself had answered this call so often. But madmen, he knew, answered only the call of death.

Giles McCoy was ready to answer the call of death, however reluctantly, but not as a madman. He wanted to join God with a clear mind. And prayer gave him the strength to keep his mind stable, to reject fantasy. It also helped drown out the cries of those he had been forced to leave sealed in their tomb on the ship. The only Catholic in his group, he prayed to himself while fondling a string of beads he found in his pocket.

"What's that?" someone asked him.

"A rosary," said McCoy, who was then urged to pray aloud so the others could repeat the words. And he did—about twenty times a day.

McCoy, who took turns with others sitting on the raft, reflected on his sins, all the "bad words" he had uttered, all the times he had disobeyed his parents. He was cleansing his spirit for the final hour. Unlike Twible, McCoy was doubtful he would survive. Day by day, while the planes flew heedlessly overhead, the men in his group died, succumbing to injuries, the grip of sharks' jaws, suicidal madness, feebleness of mind or body that set them adrift in the smothering night. It now seemed to McCoy that God might be on the verge of calling for him. Determined, however, to be the last to go, he engaged in a kind of macabre game with one of his companions, Seaman First Class Felton J. Outland—who would outlast whom?

"Since I'm a Marine," McCoy boasted, "I'm in better shape than you. But don't worry, I'll take care of you and the others until you die."

"You're not the only tough one in this group," Outland replied. "I'm a pretty tough farmer from North Carolina. I'll outlive you."

But why bet? they agreed. You couldn't collect from a dead man.

Regardless, McCoy, as he promised, did "take care" of his shipmates. He kept them in a group by tying the straps of their life jackets together, held up the injured, let men take turns dozing on his shoulder, and tried, if unsuccessfully, to catch fish with a safety pin and a thread from his shirt, using a malted milk tablet as bait. Most important of all, he brought back the runaways, including one poor hillbilly from Kentucky, Edward Payne, who had drunk salt water and gone raving mad. McCoy slapped him in the face and cried, "Settle down," but the boy simply wept like a child and was set on drowning himself. Finally, some of the others, seeing that McCoy was draining his own strength, urged him to let the youth go.

"Not while I'm alive!" McCoy replied.

Such assurance did not necessarily point to a long life for the demented young man, especially since McCoy, despite his vow to be the last to go, wondered how long he himself could resist the temptation to gulp down sea water. In the first couple of days, hunger had tormented him even though his nausea persisted, and he had yearned for a taste of his mother's pumpkin pie. But all he wanted now was water.

McCoy cupped sea water in his hands and stared at it, as if hypnotized by some huge magic eye. How clear and clean and cool the liquid looked as it glittered in the sunlight like a handful of diamonds. He longed to taste it, to savor it, to fill his being with it. Constantly urinating, he felt that his dehydrated body was drying up; unbearable as his thirst became, though, he couldn't bring himself to drink his urine—as one man was doing. He thought of all the water he had wasted in his life, the water he had recklessly flushed down the toilet. If he ever lived through this, he would drink a gallon a day. Now, perhaps, just a sip. He touched the tiny pond with his tongue. Salty. But could a little salt be that bad? After all, he had a tough constitution. Maybe it wouldn't hurt him.

But then McCoy remembered his mother. Strong, self-educated, wise, a woman who knew how to be happy even though his father, a butter salesman, came home with paltry paychecks. He must discipline himself, she had admonished him. If things went wrong, he must not get upset. And she had said this after having already lost a son. He couldn't die and leave his mother without even one son. McCoy let the water trickle from his hands. Yes, he would live, or at least be the last to die, if die he must. He hoped that God, if He had other ideas, would understand.

"Easy, doctor. Relax, I've got you."

Dr. Haynes stared at the man who had put his arm around his shoulder—and saw a blurred vision of his chief pharmacist's mate, John Schmueck. The man had answered his call for help just as he was about to drift under the surface. Thank God that not everybody had gone mad, that not everybody wanted to kill him. Schmueck towed him over to his subgroup, which was headed by Ensign Moynelo, who, like Parke, Rich, and others, including Pharmacist's Mate Harold Robert Anthony and Yeoman Second Class Victor R. Buckett, risked his life to rescue stragglers.

In this subgroup, fewer men had so far become demented, and those who had, screamed not for blood but for water. Haynes, however, could barely make out a sound now anyway since his mind was filled with the grotesque images of that terrible night. Finally, he slept while Schmueck extended an arm through the back of Haynes' life jacket and hoisted the doctor's body so it could rest on his hip.

Haynes awoke at dawn, Wednesday, and found the sea "mirror calm." Thank heaven, for when he freed himself from Schmueck's grip, he sank to his neck in the water; his life jacket had lost most of its buoyancy, leaving him only about three inches from death. And the closer the lips came to the surface, the stronger the urge was to drink. But Haynes resisted, in part because he felt he would be inviting all the men to commit suicide with him.

Actually, many didn't need an invitation. Someone found an island nearby, a beautiful island with fruit on the trees and clean fresh water in rocky streams. There were even women there, and some looked like Rita Hayworth. With cries of glee, many men began swimming toward the island, among them Ensign Moynelo, who had gone mad while trying to save his men from madness.

Others doubted it was necessary to swim to an island for fresh water. One asked Dr. Haynes, "Doc, if I dive down real deep, will the water be less salty?"

"No! No!" Haynes replied.

Suddenly, someone burst from the sea and shouted: "Doc—I've found her! The ship hasn't really sunk! She's right beneath the surface. I swear she is!"

A number of survivors swarmed around the man as he rambled on: "Do you remember the scuttlebutt in the after living compartment—the one that was always cold, with plenty of good water? I dove down and turned on the scuttlebutt. Honest, I did—and it works. When you drink it, the water is fresh. Fresh water, men! Fresh water!"

His listeners grew hysterical. Fresh water! En masse, they dove toward the "ship," many after ripping off their life jackets. And Haynes wanted to follow. Yes, the ship was there—right under the surface. He could see it with his own eyes! There it was, shimmering as clear as hell. But somehow he restrained himself, taking refuge in his own semirational world.

Most of the men never returned, but some popped up, one crying insanely, "I had a drink from the scuttlebutt! . . . Water, water, all you can drink, right below us!"

Yes, all they could drink! Haynes was lucid enough to know that they had fatally poisoned themselves, and now he could do nothing but wait a few hours to pronounce them dead.

Not everyone drank water—one man filled himself up with tomato juice after swimming to an island where he found barrels of it. Others were finally able to sleep in a bed. When Haynes saw a long, orderly line of men holding on to each other, resembling a bobbing "front of seaweed," he asked one of them, "Why are the men lined up?"

"Shh!" the sailor whispered. "There's a hotel up ahead, doctor, and we're waiting to get in it. But it has only one room—one bed —and we have to wait our turn."

Another man said: "Better get in line, Doc. Each guy gets fifteen minutes in the sack. That's a good deal."

But the only sleep the men would get would be the sleep of death, as, one by one, they suffered screaming fits, then succumbed to the water in the "scuttlebutt." Haynes worked like a robot; he ceaselessly removed life jackets, recited the Lord's Prayer, and released the bodies to the sea, watching as they sank slowly into the depths like diminishing wax figures and finally disappeared. Before, he had worked hard, too, but he was armed with hope. Now the last vestiges of hope had vanished; few men, even the most lucid, thought of rescue anymore. But strangely, without the stress inherent in hope, Haynes found a certain peace in resignation. As he would explain to the author: "You reached the stage where you were not dying anymore, but just going on forever. You adapted yourself to nature. At first, you abhorred your surroundings, then you tolerated them, then you embraced them. Death became a way of life."

"Are you sure of the facts?" Lieutenant McKissick asked the young sailor, a man from his division.

The man had paddled up to him on this scorching Wednesday, telling of a floating dock not far away that serviced seaplanes, and that had barrels of fresh water stacked up on it. But when he had tried to climb onto the dock, a Chinese mess boy had turned him back.

"You are only an enlisted man," the mess boy said, "and so you cannot get up on the dock or have any water."

The man then swam back and excitedly related his story to McKissick.

"Now, because you are an officer," he said, "if you swim with me to this floating dock, we can get some water and find help there."

Since McKissick himself had begun to have fantasies, the story did not seem particularly irrational to him. He did have some qualms, but the young man reassured him.

"Yes, sir, I am positive we can get something to drink there."

Well, in that case . . .

And the two men swam off to find the floating dock, stopping to rest for a while with the group of men Dr. Haynes had joined. When McKissick told Haynes about the floating dock, the doctor was highly skeptical.

"This is not a credible story," he said. "It's simply another hallucination."

"I don't know whether to believe it or not," McKissick replied. "I rather doubt it. But, well, I don't think we have a great deal to lose by trying to find it."

So the lieutenant and his informant continued on their fanciful journey, swimming for what seemed like hours.

"Let's stop and rest," McKissick finally gasped.

He then lost consciousness; when he awoke, he was alone. While he searched for his companion, a man paddled up to him and grabbed his life jacket, trying to tear it off. His own, apparently, had become too waterlogged to use, and he needed another one to keep him alive.

McKissick managed to swim away with his life jacket intact, but he no longer remembered where he was headed. He floated around aimlessly, his mind a haze of incoherent thoughts, his body a mass of enervated flesh.

From the moment the *Indianapolis* was torpedoed, Ensign Blum had never been quite sure if the horror was reality or just a nightmare. By Wednesday, this crisis of perception had grown more acute, and he strove desperately to keep his sanity in the midst of insanity.

When one man, as in Dr. Haynes' group, assured the others that the *Indianapolis* was just below the surface and urged them to dive down to get some fresh water, Blum protested, "No, the ship is not down there."

"You're lying!" someone cried. "I'll show you."

And about half a dozen men removed their life jackets and dove to their death.

Infected by such dementia, Blum himself began to hallucinate. Once, he imagined he was in his family's victory garden picking tomatoes—big, red, juicy tomatoes. How he loved them! But when he bit, there was only his swollen tongue. He began to worry about his mental condition, and about that of his shipmates as well. One man had struck him. The next might stab him. So many had disappeared already. Of the 150 or so men who had first gathered in this group, only about 35 were still here. The rest had simply vanished amid shrieks in the dark. On Tuesday night, the ensign was even able to find space aboard a raft without having to fight for it.

Blum, like McCoy in his group, was determined to be the last survivor. To him, this meant leaving the group while he was still lucid. He found three chief petty officers who were relatively stable, and the four of them devised a plan. They would "borrow" one of the rafts with a portion of the rations and separate from the madmen. After all, if planes were searching for them, there was more chance of the flyers seeing two groups than one (they were unaware that others were afloat elsewhere). If any of the four men showed a serious sign of aberration, they agreed, he would be thrown overboard.

Perhaps they could sell their idea to the other men and Redmayne, the senior officer—for the good of everybody. Their aim, they would say, would be to paddle to Yap, one of the Palau Islands, about five hundred miles away, and seek help there—a feat which Blum, a trained navigator, knew would be virtually impossible.

Blum and his cohorts moved from man to man stressing the merits of such a venture, and then the ensign presented the plan to Redmayne. The lieutenant was wary of it. Was this just a trick to get some of the rations? But his mind was also becoming blurred and he didn't want to reject out of hand any idea, however far-fetched, that could possibly lead to rescue. He would let the group decide.

"Attention, men," he called from his raft. "I've got a proposal here."

And he described it.

"These men," he concluded, "would be taking a raft and about a fourth of our rations with them, so it involves all of us. I'm going to put it to a vote."

Ensign Twible, still in the water, gazed up incredulously at Redmayne. "I was shocked," he would tell the author. "I had never been taught that naval officers took a vote when a decision had to be made."

But he *had* been taught that junior officers never contradicted the orders of senior officers, so he said nothing. Many of the men, it seemed, were as stunned as Twible; nobody in the Navy had ever asked them before to vote on anything. And some of the less sane were puzzled. Why go anywhere when the ship was just below with all the water you could drink? Things weren't really so bad.

Then, as if presiding at a meeting of the Rotary Club, Redmayne said, "All those in favor of letting these guys have the raft and the rations raise your hands."

The majority raised their hands. Blum and his comrades had done a good job of campaigning.

"How many opposed?"

About a half-dozen hands rose, including those of Twible and Redmayne himself.

"The proposal is passed," said Redmayne glumly, lacking only a gavel to make the vote official.

But then the dissenters went to work, barnstorming the community with arguments that the idea was "ridiculous," "stupid," "selfish," an insult to their intelligence. The madmen listened, and Redmayne called for a second ballot. This time most of them voted against the proposal. Blum and his supporters, however, would not accept this reversal. Another quick tour of the precinct and the men were screaming, "Let 'em go! Let 'em go!"

Redmayne could not ignore the new rumblings; he did not want a revolt on his hands.

"It's clear," he said, "that some of you have changed your mind again. We'll have one more vote."

And now the men voted once more to let the Blum party go.

Redmayne reluctantly gave the ensign one-fourth of the food and water, as well as two paddles and two dirty shirts to serve as sails. Blum was delighted as he and his men floated away. No more gibberish or wild cries. The nightmare was getting better.

Redmayne, however, took this as a personal defeat; they had outwitted him. But they would pay a penalty. Though they hadn't disobeyed any orders but had simply profited from his own rules, he would bring them to justice if they—and he—survived. Meanwhile, he must continue to pacify the men. And he did. The big moment had come. As he had promised, he would now distribute the first rations of food and fresh water. He removed a biscuit from a can and tasted it; with a grimace, he threw it down. It was hard and dry and could hardly be swallowed, only adding to his thirst. Meanwhile, the first man to taste the water had to spit it out because it was "dirty and salty." Having to settle for a tiny mouthful of Spam and a malted milk tablet, the men grew more depressed than ever. It had been a terrible day.

But Redmayne did see one tiny nugget of gold amid the stones of failure: the vision of Blum and his friends tasting the biscuits and water!

The vote of unstable men would haunt Lieutenant Redmayne, for some would again change their minds. With one raft less, some swimmers were still unable to find space on the remaining two rafts. And among these men were Adolfo Celaya and his injured friend, whose leg grew more painful by the hour as his wounds festered in the oil and salt water. Celaya was determined to squeeze his buddy onto one of the rafts.

"Lieutenant," he called to Redmayne from the water, "help this man get on a raft. He's badly hurt."

Before Redmayne could answer, Celaya felt someone pushing his head under the surface, where he remained for several moments, almost drowning. Finally, he sprang up, coughing and choking.

"Who did that?" he gasped.

Celaya never did find out. But if he narrowly escaped death himself, it was too late to save his injured friend. He had swum away, and the last Celaya saw of the man, he was atop the crest of a wave about two hundred yards away, waving his arm in apparent farewell. Celaya watched in dazed helplessness, his body too weak to chase him, his mind too scarred for him to cry. First, Santos Pena, and now another dear friend. Gone—and no one else seemed to care. And the man wasn't even a Mexican.

Suddenly, amid the wailing of the waves, Celaya heard two men speaking Spanish, and one of the voices sounded familiar. Santos Pena! He had recently moved to this group from another, though he couldn't be recognized for his oil-blackened face. Celaya was joyous. He hadn't killed his friend from Tucson after all. But the vision of his other buddy waving good-bye would not leave him. Could he have saved the man? Even his joy was tempered by suffering.

On Giles McCoy's raft, the suffering was untempered by any joy. There had been seventeen men in his group and now, on Wednesday night, there were five, and only two were still conscious—McCoy and Felton Outland. The other three, including Edward Payne, the Kentucky hillbilly, lay in comas and would die, it seemed, at any moment.

Even the resilient McCoy wondered whether he could last the night. He and Outland were drained of strength, though both somehow managed to clear their minds whenever fantasy threatened. Each helped the other with his determination to be the last one alive. Who wanted to go out looking like a loser?

"Damn it! We'll see who's going to die first!" McCoy relentlessly challenged his friend.

"Yeah, we'll see!" Outland replied.

But both knew the winner couldn't survive much longer than the loser. And so McCoy continued to prepare himself to die. He had already purged his mind of "evil" thoughts and atoned for all his sins. Now he must cleanse his body. He tore off his T-shirt and jumped into the water, then, with the shirt, tried to scrub the oil from his face and body.

Outland screamed at him: "Get your ass back up here! You'll

wear yourself out—or those goddamn sharks'll get you." He didn't want to win their morbid little game unfairly.

McCoy, however, kept scrubbing. He had to be clean to meet God. And while the dozen or so sharks lurking nearby had frightened him at first, he was used to them by now. Cowardly bastards! They wouldn't dare attack a Marine. But though he expended almost his last reserve of energy, he still could not rid himself of the oil. Finally, he climbed back on the raft, and nearly collapsed.

"You ain't very strong now," said Outland with an air of false triumph. "I'll outlive you sure as hell."

On Thursday morning, Lieutenant Redmayne visited his aunt in England. Suddenly, there was a flood and when he tried to swim to safety, he felt himself drowning. . . .

Redmayne was hallucinating. The spray of water on his face had felt so cool. Should he violate his own rule and taste a few drops? How fresh it was. There couldn't be any harm in trying a little. He scooped up some water and took a sip. And then another. Soon, he began screaming maniacally as the flood waters overwhelmed him. He then calmed down, only to hallucinate again. This time, he had an uncontrollable urge to jump off the raft and dive to the ship. He must get to the engine room! He must save his men!

Ensign Twible, who had taken a Syrette of morphine with him before abandoning ship, grabbed the lieutenant and indelicately jammed the needle into his arm, but to little avail.

"Let me go! Let me go!" Redmayne screamed. "I must get to the engine room!"

If he had been an enlisted man, Redmayne would later say, he would probably have been allowed to dive to his death at this stage, for everyone was so weak, so acclimated to death. But Twible had too great a respect for higher authority to let a superior die, whatever the circumstances. A purely pragmatic matter. After all, the duty of an officer, as he had learned it at Annapolis, was to save the group in critical situations; so by saving an officer, he might ultimately be saving many lives.

But for the time being, Redmayne was in no condition to save anyone, not even himself. As he continued to rave, Twible picked up a biscuit can that floated by and unceremoniously struck him over the head with it. Redmayne fell unconscious, and Twible, though troubled that there would be one less officer, had the chance to lead the struggle to survive.

How many men were left for him to lead? There were dozens floating around his little fleet—but most of them were dead.

In Dr. Haynes' group, the men were scattered over a wide area, also "drifting and dying one by one." Before noon, however, about twenty-five of them gathered and made a daring decision. They would swim to Leyte! Haynes was appalled when he heard of this plan, and swiftly swam over to these men, urging them not to go.

This was sheer suicide! he exclaimed.

No, they could do it, one of the men replied. It would take only a day and a half. And they swam off into infinity.

Meanwhile, Lieutenant McKissick, who was drifting aimlessly nearby, came across another group of men heading toward a new island that had materialized in their fantasy-ridden minds. He joined them in their frenetic search for the illusory promised land, and soon found himself swimming in what seemed to him like shallow water.

"The island!" a man cried triumphantly. "This is the island!"

Where?

"Right under the surface. And look, a hotel! Food, water, everything!"

While some men dived precipitously into the deep, McKissick and other more disciplined survivors floated around insensibly, waiting their turn to go down.

Dr. Haynes was numb as he watched most of the remnants of his once huge group vanish in the waves.

"Those of us who [were] left," he would later recount, "[had] but a little longer to live. Our disintegration [was] almost complete and it [was] difficult to tell whether a man [was] dead or alive."

When he collided with another floating figure, he would know the man was alive only if he opened his eyes. As in Redmayne's group, the dead now outnumbered the living.

"I [knew] we [couldn't] last another night," he would add, "for our noses barely [skimmed] the surface of the water."

On this fourth day in the water, even the men still under Captain McVay's command had almost lost hope of rescue. McVay and his sailors, ensconced on their suite of rafts, were perhaps the most privileged of all the survivors—an accident of fortune that would haunt the captain when he learned of the intense suffering elsewhere. Everyone had more than enough room on his rafts, and sufficient malted milk tablets and Spam to last ten days—stretched to twenty when McVay grew pessimistic about early salvation.

McVay's men were disciplined and relatively stable for another reason as well. The captain was the one officer whom the survivors, with their inbred awe of supreme authority, would not dare defy or attack. True, as hunger and thirst fed their paranoia, some of the men suspected that even he might be holding back some rations for himself. All, however, obeyed his every command, and their respect was strangely reinforced by the new comradely relationship he had developed with them. He had helped them to survive by encouraging conversation that took their minds off their misery. And if the skipper said they would be rescued, they found it hard to believe that so important an authority could be wrong.

But the personal talks and mutual self-revelations ceased as hopelessness set in and minds began to drift; eyesight, if not already impaired, became a blur as the oil matting their hair melted in the sun and dripped down their faces. And the shark that stole all the fish magnified their feeling of futility. Finally, one sailor, using an ineffectual one-inch knife, stabbed the pesky creature between the eyes, provoking it to lash out with its tail and topple the man into the sea, almost upsetting the raft. His comrades managed to pull him to safety virtually out of the jaws of the maddened shark.

Three men in the group were already crying, "We're going to die! We're going to die!" even though McVay assured them: "It's not going to happen! We're going to be saved!"

The captain himself began to have doubts as plane after plane flew over them, blind to their fate. He sought to keep his equilibrium by blocking out thoughts of the future and dwelling on the past.

"I think probably the fact that I enjoyed life," he would later say, "that I thought of many a cocktail hour that you have at home after you have an exhausting day and you come back and take a bath and can relax for a few minutes and get away from the worries of the office. I thought I would certainly like to repeat some of those evenings."

Otha Alton Havins was another survivor in McVay's group who was determined to "stick it out." It was a good thing after all, he realized, that he had not married Billie before casting off from San Francisco; as she had feared, he might have been leaving her a war widow. But it would be unfar of God to take him now. He shouldn't have to die just because some stupid bureaucrat had delayed putting through his transfer orders. Maybe he had angered God when he considered entering the ministry and then decided not to.

Havins was ready to make a deal with God. He gazed into the heavens and announced, "God, if you're punishing me for not going into the ministry, You save these people and I'll go into it."

There was a buzz overhead. Was God answering him already?

XI

Back from the Brink

WHAT Otha Alton Havins heard was not the voice of the Lord, but the Ventura of Lieutenant Wilbur C. Gwinn. Flying a routine patrol mission under Vice Admiral Murray's Marianas Command, Gwinn hardly expected a memorable day. His job was to search for Japanese ships and submarines that were supplying troops isolated on the Palau Islands, but seldom could he find any. The Japanese had few craft of any kind left to send to this backwash area of the war, though occasionally an oil slick betrayed the presence of a submarine—if Gwinn happened to be flying low enough and focused his eyes on the water. Now, as he peered down from three thousand feet, the glassy, undulating surface stretched to the horizon with unblemished uniformity. Nor did his radar home in on any targets.

Gwinn's relaxed manner, humorous eyes, and easy smile hid a deep passion for excitement and challenge. Born on a ranch in Gilroy, California, Gwinn attended the University of California at Los Angeles while working for Douglas Aircraft, where, at the age of nineteen, he supervised sixty-five technicians. On passing the naval aviation examination in 1943, he was commissioned an ensign and served as a test pilot before being sent to the Palau island of Peleliu as a patrol plane commander in squadron VPB-152—the lowest-ranked flyer in the unit.

After flying one thousand hours, Gwinn was wearing a lieutenant's insignia, but sometimes he wished he were back making those dangerous dives as a test pilot. Excitement wasn't just causing death; it was also cheating death. Now he wasn't doing much of either.

At the briefing session that morning, the pilots were told about all the ships at sea in their sector. Just some well-protected American convoys. There was no mention of the *Indianapolis*. The command of the search-and-reconnaissance unit in Peleliu, to which squadron VPB-152 belonged, knew the ship was steaming through but saw no need to inform Gwinn and the other patrol commanders. The pilots had enough to do without being burdened with extraneous detail about big, fast single ships that could take care of themselves. Actually, Gwinn had never heard of any cruiser that was not escorted by destroyers.

Nor did anyone tell Gwinn that an Army Air Force pilot, Captain Richard G. Le Francis, had witnessed a "naval battle" over this area early in the morning of July 31, as he flew his lumbering C-54 from Manila to Guam. A bang-up battle, Le Francis told his superiors when he landed in Guam. Real fireworks. The sky was studded with flashes of light—which he didn't realize were the flares fired by the *Indianapolis* survivors.

Never mind, his superiors replied. That was Navy business. The Army Air Force had its own battles to fight.

At about 8:15 A.M. on Thursday, August 2, Gwinn and his crew climbed into their Ventura for another patrol of the region, but this time with an additional task—they would be testing a new antenna. Almost an unnecessary accessory, it seemed, for there never seemed to be anything important to report.

The antenna became inoperative almost as soon as the plane left the ground, for the weight at its tip had snapped off. Gwinn returned to base, had another weight attached, and zoomed into the sky again, disgruntled that he was now an hour behind schedule.

Gwinn steered the aircraft almost due north and began his search. Plenty of time now to think over coffee about the shortsightedness of the Navy—assigning him to this milk run! But soon, the voice of his radioman, William Hillman, blasted over the intercom, shattering his reverie: The new antenna weight had also fallen off.

That damn antenna! Gwinn rose and, leaving his copilot, Lieutenant Warren Colwell, in control, lurched to the rear of the plane to see what could be done. As he crouched in the tail section, he stared out of the gunner hatch in frustration. The wire, without a controlling weight, was whipping around in the wind. Unless his crew could fix it, he would have to navigate by dead reckoning—a hell of a way to keep to a course.

"Better reel it in," he ordered Machinist Mate Joseph K. Johnson, who was crouching beside him. Maybe a rubber hose fitted around the end would keep it steady.

Suddenly, as Gwinn gazed through the hatch at a slice of sunlit sea, he saw a thin black streak snaking through the waves.

"Joe," he exclaimed, "do you see what I see?"

An oil slick. A Japanese submarine at last!

Gwinn rushed back to the cockpit.

"Have you seen anything below?" he asked Colwell.

"Not a thing."

And the radar hadn't picked up anything either. A submarine must have crash-dived.

"Arm the depth charges!" Gwinn ordered over the intercom. "Open the bomb bay doors!"

He then turned the aircraft toward the oil slick and swooped down to attack.

Yeoman Havins wasn't the only survivor who anxiously gazed into the heavens on hearing a rumble; so did most of the other men strung out along the curling oil slick. But many not already raving mad were simply apathetic or too weak to wave their arms and kick the water as they had before when some dozen other planes had flown over the area.

Indeed, sight of the plane gave rise to new tensions in Donald Blum. What if the pilot saw the survivors and sent for help? Blum's wristwatch—a graduation gift from his mother and father—had dropped into the sea. Would his parents ever forgive him if he returned without it?

Blum was still reeling in confusion from what had turned out to be an abortive sailing adventure to the island of Yap. But he was stable enough now to ask himself why he had ever agreed to a pact with his three raftmates whereby any one of them who showed signs of insanity would be thrown overboard. He had come close to being discarded when he started mumbling to himself, and was saved only when someone bounced a fist off his jaw, bringing him back to his senses. The next time, he could be fodder for the sharks. The wind had also helped Blum cling to reality by prodding the raft back to Lieutenant Redmayne's group after it had moved only a few hundred yards away. Since he felt much safer being an unrecognizable nobody again, part of the group, he was less tense and not as prone to lapses of sanity. But now this plane—how could he go home and face his parents?

Some distance away, Dr. Haynes floated in the water without any such qualms about going home.

"And then we [heard] it," he would recount. "The roar of a plane! Four of us [prayed] that it [was] real and not a last tortuous dream. It [came] near, [passed] over us, and then [grew] smaller in the distance. I [knew] the end [had] sounded. Suddenly, the plane [roared] back. It [was] over my head, skimming the ocean's bosom."

Hundreds of legs, almost paralyzed until this moment, now frantically thrashed the water, and feeble cries wafted over the shiny noon swells: "He sees us!" "We're saved!"

Amid the joyous clamor, few men could discern the dying scream of the man in one group whose leg had almost been sawed off by the razorlike teeth of a shark at the moment of apparent rescue.

From about 150 yards away, some of the survivors could see the open bomb bay doors.

"They're going to drop something!" one man shouted with glee. "Maybe barrels of cold fresh water!"

Lieutenant Gwinn was excited as his Ventura swept down toward the oil slick, his hand gripping the throttle, his lips ready to utter the words "Bombs away!" When the plane had dived to within 150 yards of the northern tip of the slick, he was about to give the order but suddenly noticed tiny black bumps dotting the shiny surface amid an embroidery of froth.

"Secure from bomb run!" Gwinn cried over the intercom, and the plane sped harmlessly by.

What were those bumps? They looked like the knobs on a cucumber. . . . My God . . . people! And now they were waving to him and kicking the water. Were they Americans? If a ship was missing, why hadn't he been told? Or could they be the survivors of a Japanese submarine?

Gwinn steered the plane around for another pass and quickly counted heads—about thirty. And they were in the water without lifeboats. He chilled at the thought that he might have killed dozens of Americans but for a last-second sighting of those black bumps. Whoever they were, he must help them. One more pass, and this time his crew dropped a life raft, kegs of water, life jackets, and a sonobuoy, which allowed them to speak in a one-way conversation with the pilot. He had to find out who they were.

Gwinn saw a wild splashing as men from Dr. Haynes' group scrambled toward the floating items. He could not know that the water cans had ruptured on striking the water, though, when the sonobuoy remained silent, he surmised that the men did not know how to operate it.

Send an urgent message to squadron headquarters, he ordered his radioman. And in a moment, the first dramatic words rode the air waves: "SIGHTED 30 SURVIVORS 011-30 NORTH 133-30 EAST. DROPPED TRANSMITTER AND LIFEBOAT EMERGENCY IFF ON 133-30."

But would the message go through? Gwinn had still not repaired the antenna, and had only been able to get what he hoped was an accurate fix on the location by dead reckoning. How many of the men down there, he wondered, would be alive by the time help arrived?

On the island of Peleliu, a sailor poked his head through the flaps of a tent and said, "There are some flyers down. Better go after them."

Lieutenant Robert Adrian Marks and his crew were about to

answer chow call, but saving survivors, of course, took precedence over sating hunger. Marks was the pilot of a PBY5A Catalina seaplane known as a Dumbo, which belonged to squadron VPB-23. Its main role was to find survivors of ship and air disasters and drop them supplies until rescue craft reached them. But for three days, Marks and his crew had been idly waiting for a mission while flipping the pages of a novel or spinning Glenn Miller records. A nice life, they agreed, but weren't they supposed to be fighting a war?

Anyway, Marks, a tall, slim, mustachioed young lawyer of twenty-eight, wanted to compensate for the "failure" of his last mission on July 30, when he and his men had vainly searched for the survivors of a plane that had been shot down. In this line of work, a man lost a bit of himself if he returned to base empty-handed.

Marks was not accustomed to failure. A native of Ladoga, Indiana, he graduated from Northwestern University Law School when he was only twenty-three, married the daughter of the Chief Justice of Indiana's Supreme Court, and passed the bar by the time the war began. An ensign in the Naval Reserve, he commanded a training ship that attacked the Japanese at Pearl Harbor, and became a Navy flyer in 1942. Thriving on risk—provided it was carefully calculated—he earned a reputation for fearlessness and for demanding that his men be fearless, too. Anyone who lacked courage could end up with permanent latrine duty.

Marks now hurried to command headquarters to find out more about the latest downed "flyers." He learned that Lieutenant Gwinn's superior at VPB-152, Lieutenant Commander George Atteberry, had not relayed to the officer on duty at VPB-23 a copy of Gwinn's radio message, but had instead urged this officer by phone to send a plane on a rescue mission immediately. How many survivors? It wasn't clear from the garbled wording, but there was at least one sighted on a raft.

Nor was it clear to the VPB-23 officer that the mission deserved priority. Already two Dumbos had been dispatched on rescue missions that day, and now Marks' standby plane would have to be used. But what if a really big disaster occurred and there were no planes left to send out? Well, he would take that chance.

Atteberry, neglecting in his rush to answer Gwinn's message, drove over to the PBY unit to personally prod it into action. The crew would have to take off as soon as possible, he told Marks, for Gwinn could circle over the survivors only until 3:30 P.M. or he wouldn't have enough fuel to make it back to base. And the survivors mustn't be led to believe that they were being abandoned.

He would leave as soon as possible, Marks assured Atteberry—but the PBY, he pointed out, was not the fastest plane in the air.

Meanwhile, crew members loaded their Dumbo, code-named *Playmate 2*, with 1,250 gallons of fuel, life rafts, parachute flares, dye markers, and shipwreck kits. It appeared they would be looking for one raft, maybe with only one man to save. But somehow, it seemed, as they rumbled into the sky, they would be saving a little of themselves as well.

Lieutenant Gwinn wasn't sure how many survivors there were to be saved. He decided to follow the oil slick, thinking there might be more than the group of about 30 he had already spotted. As he flew northeast, he saw more black bumps, about 30 more. And when he continued on, the sea was speckled with an additional 70, then with still others scattered in small groups and singles. Over 150 survivors in all! So it couldn't be a Japanese submarine—none carried that many men. Actually, he knew his tally was incomplete, for he could not get an accurate count of all the men piled on top of one another on the rafts.

As Gwinn kept dropping supplies, he was stunned. A major ship must have sunk and apparently no one at the base was even aware of it. Wouldn't an SOS signal have been sent? Wouldn't some command know its ship was missing? Only one thing was clear: Those men floating in the sea wouldn't last much longer. He began to wonder if his message had reached headquarters, realizing that he hadn't yet repaired the antenna.

Gwinn rushed back to the tail section, crawled through it again and, reaching out of the aircraft, grabbed the snapping antenna and pulled it inside. He then tied a rubber hose around the end and, after unreeling it, hurried back to the cockpit and ordered his radioman to transmit a second message: "SEND RESCUE SHIP 11-15N 133-47E 150 SURVIVORS IN LIFEBOAT AND JACKETS. . . ."

Gwinn was worried. What if neither message got through? The survivors might not last the day.

A hundred and fifty survivors! Had to be a ship. But *what* ship?

Captain Granum was perturbed as he read a copy of Lieutenant Gwinn's second message, which he had intercepted. No one had told him that any vessel churning in waters under the Philippine Sea Frontier Command's jurisdiction was overdue. Not that anyone would necessarily tell him, especially if it was a combatant vessel. After all, the arrival or nonarrival of such a craft in the Frontier zone was not really his business. Still, Granum didn't want any disaster reflecting on the command, and neither did his superior, Commodore Gillette.

"Check to see if any ships are overdue," Granum ordered his controllers. And they immediately contacted Lieutenant Gibson at the Leyte port director's office.

Yes, three vessels were overdue, Gibson reported. One of them was the *Indianapolis*, which should have sailed into the port on Tuesday, two days earlier, and joined Vice Admiral McCormick's Task Group 95.7 for training.

The *Indianapolis* hadn't arrived? Granum wasn't worried. It had probably been diverted elsewhere, or joined McCormick's fleet without notifying the port director. The captain cabled McCormick: "HAS THE INDIANAPOLIS REPORTED TO YOU?"

Admiral McCormick had just returned to anchorage from his training tour with several ships. Apparently still unaware that survivors had been found, he was a bit startled when he read Granum's dispatch. The Frontier, after all, should keep track of the vessels passing through its zone of responsibility.

"NEGATIVE," the admiral wired Granum. The *Indianapolis* had not reported to him.

Well, Granum surmised when he read the reply, the *Indianapolis* must have been rerouted, as he had suspected. Nevertheless, a frightening doubt seized him. A hundred and fifty survivors! . . . Then what ship was it?

Whatever its identity, Granum, with Gillette's approval, issued an urgent order to several patrol vessels and planes: Rush to the scene of the disaster to rescue survivors. Let no one charge *his* command with negligence. He coordinated this move with a giant rescue operation already begun by the Peleliu headquarters of Rear Admiral Elliott Buckmaster, Commander of the Western Carolines Sub-Area, who reported to Vice Admiral Murray's Marianas Command.

Alert every damn ship and plane in the region, Buckmaster thundered to his aides, and they scrambled to the communications room to pass the word. Shortly, seven vessels relatively close to the scene were racing to pluck the survivors out of the sea—at all costs.

Yes, at all costs, Admirals King and Nimitz and the other top naval commanders demanded with almost panicky impatience when news of the survivors reached them. What if all those men died? Could there be a worse catastrophe? The atomic bomb would be dropped on Japan in a few days, and the Navy, at the moment of glory, might find itself mired in one of the greatest scandals of the war.

An obvious error, Lieutenant Marks was sure. Probably a mistake in coding.

Marks' PBY was heading toward the drifting survivors when at 2:10 P.M. the pilot intercepted a message from "Gambler Leader"—Lieutenant Commander Atteberry: About 150 survivors were floundering in the sea, Atteberry reported to his headquarters.

On receiving Gwinn's second dispatch, Atteberry had taken off from Peleliu in his speedy Ventura minutes after Marks had departed with orders to relieve Gwinn, who might have to return to base to refuel before Marks' slower plane arrived. Gwinn's first message had concerned Atteberry; the second shocked him, and he decided to fly to the scene personally. He was incredulous until he got there at about 2 P.M. and made a quick count of his own.

Now it was Marks who was incredulous. (He had not seen

Gwinn's second dispatch, which Atteberry was confirming.) Probably another garbled message. But if the report was true, more than a seaplane and one rescue ship would be needed; every vessel in the area should be rushing out there. And when he sighted three ships at about 2:45 P.M., he considered vectoring them to the site of the reported disaster. He decided not to—no one would believe such a nonsensical report.

But then the commander of one of the ships, the destroyer *Cecil J. Doyle*, called him on voice radio—and turned out to be an old friend and colleague, W. Graham Claytor, Jr., a stone-faced man with a will to match. Claytor and Marks knew each other from Indiana, where Claytor was also a lawyer.

Anything up? Claytor asked.

Marks told him of his mission, but with skepticism. After all, wouldn't someone in the Navy know if a vessel carrying at least 150 men had been sunk?

Claytor was puzzled by the report, too. But if it was accurate, the horror those men must be going through! What ship might have gone down? He could not have guessed that it was the *Indianapolis* —commanded by Captain McVay, the husband of his dear cousin Louise.

As Marks' plane roared into the distance, Claytor, though aware that the same submarine that sank the mystery ship might also attack his destroyer, turned the vessel around and, without asking or waiting for orders, sailed swiftly toward the scene—just in case the report turned out to be true.

Homing in on George Atteberry's radio signal, Lieutenant Marks started searching for the "lone raft" he still expected to see. Suddenly, he spotted Atteberry's Ventura circling over the area, and heard his voice booming over the radio: "There are a great many survivors scattered over a large area. So you shouldn't drop any survival equipment until I can show you the entire area, and you can form a judgment of where the equipment can be dropped to best advantage."

Marks was stunned. The report hadn't been garbled after all. And while Gwinn flew back to base with just enough fuel to get there, Marks followed Atteberry and gazed out the window at a whole dying world. Yes, it was true. But now he would have to be ruthlessly practical.

"I felt," he would say, "that the survivors located on rafts or in large groups stood the best chance of survival until help from surface craft arrived, and that the most immediate problem was to get assistance to the singles and to the small groups without rafts."

Marks ordered his crew to drop to these singles and groups three of the four rafts aboard, a shipwreck kit, an emergency ration kit, and some cans of dye marker, which would streak the sea with an identifiable color. As he continued circling, however, he noticed one raft fall open and tear on landing, the emergency ration kit disintegrate in the water, and the shipwreck kit drift unused because the men were apparently too weak to reach it.

Marks' dismay was not abated even when, minutes later, another plane arrived from Peleliu and scattered a load of supplies in the area. A minute fraction of what those men needed.

He would have to send an immediate message, but, since time was so vital, he wouldn't encode it even though the enemy might be listening. At 4:25 P.M., he ordered his radioman, Robert France, to tell headquarters in plain language: "BETWEEN ONE AND TWO HUNDRED SURVIVORS AT POSITION REPORTED. NEED ALL SURVIVAL EQUIPMENT AVAILABLE WHILE DAYLIGHT HOLDS. MANY SURVIVORS WITHOUT RAFTS."

Marks and his crew were transfixed by the scene below, which might have crystallized in a mad painter's mind. They saw men bobbing in the swells like human corks, some with their oil-blackened heads grazing the surface while sharks slithered in their midst, picking them off at random. As radioman France would later write home, "It wasn't the best sight I have ever seen when you stood . . . and watched a great shark swim off with a man."

It was a sight that Marks could bear no longer. He had to go down and save those men. But landing on the twelve-foot swells that were running from the northwest could be like landing on the drifting dunes of a desert, especially with the PBY5A, which, unlike the conventional PBY, had three large retractable wheels that impaired its seaworthiness. He had never tried to land a 5A in open water before, and all attempts made by others in his squadron to do so had been disastrous, triggering an order, in fact, that forbade such landings.

But Marks, knowing that the officer who issued this order could not foresee the present emergency, decided to exercise his own judgment. On all other rescue missions he had simply dropped equipment to survivors and circled until a ship arrived to pick them up. Should he now risk having his plane break up and sink? Was it right to jeopardize the lives of his crew in an attempt to rescue those men down there, who might, after all, be the enemy? Marks felt he would succeed, for he had practiced full stall landings with the PBY extensively. And while this was a PBY5A, he would know how to handle the extra weight in the nose.

Still, Marks was reluctant to make the decision alone. As Lieutenant Redmayne had polled his men in the water when faced with a critical choice, so did Marks. He explained the dangers over the intercom and then asked each crewman whether he favored a landing.

The men were not surprised. They regarded Marks not simply with respect, but almost with awe. As one would say, "He was not the authoritarian that many officers thought they had to be to get the job done, but we knew what he wanted and we were willing to go the extra step to give it to him."

Had he not supported them when the copilot once chastised them for not addressing him as "sir"? Had he not bailed them out when they had gotten into trouble with the shore patrol, though chewing them out afterward? He even gave them cartons of cigarettes and lent them money when they needed it. Now it was time to take that "extra step."

Land, they all agreed.

Marks was moved by this show of confidence, but felt a crushing burden of responsibility. And there was no time to request the authority to land—nor would he take the risk. With ships no doubt steaming toward the area at full speed, his superior might say no. True, he could be court-martialed—if he survived the landing—but there were times when one had to follow the dictates of the soul, whatever the consequences. He informed Atteberry of his intention, then ordered Bob France to send another message to base: "WILL ATTEMPT OPEN SEA LANDING."

The crew members stowed all loose gear, secured electric circuits, and strapped themselves in their ditching stations. Then, before headquarters could reply to his message, Marks, pulling his harness up tight, made a wide turn and put the plane into a power stall. With utter faith in his piloting skill, he headed into the eight-knot north wind toward the heaving blue desert.

"What are those guys doing down there?" Lieutenant McKissick asked himself as he floated around in circles. It was already late afternoon; he had been waiting hours for his turn to dive down to the hotel below the surface so he could drink some fresh water in the rest room. But the men who had already gone down never seemed to come back. Damn unfair! He could pull his officer's rank, of course, but it wouldn't be right. How much water could those men drink, anyway?

Suddenly, McKissick heard a drone overhead and then several great splashes. He looked up and saw a plane dropping things into the water around him.

Why was that plane flying over him? he wondered. He swam over to one of the objects, a deflated life raft that had been folded into a bundle, and the mystery deepened. What was this bundle? Another man swam up and shouted, "Leave it alone! Don't touch it!"

"Why not?" McKissick asked.

"The plane is dropping mail sacks," the man explained. "This is an experimental mail operation and we shouldn't interfere with it."

McKissick examined the life raft but "couldn't figure out how it could have anything to do with the mail." But the man insisted: "Leave it alone! It's mail."

McKissick agreed. He didn't want to go to jail. And as he floated off, he wished that the plane would go away and leave him in peace.

.   .   .

Nearby, Dr. Haynes, like many of the more rational men in the sea, saw the rain of supplies from above as some kind of heavenly miracle. Flawed, to be sure, but a miracle nonetheless. After the first plane, a Ventura, had dropped some objects for survival in the area that morning, Haynes and several comrades, their strength magically renewed, paddled to them—only to find plenty of life jackets, which they didn't need since the dead now provided enough for the living, and cans of water, which they *did* need but couldn't use because they were ruptured.

Their chagrin dissolved, however, when they fully appreciated that they had at last been found. And as they had dared to hope, in the afternoon other planes flew over and more survival supplies plummeted down. One seaplane dropped two life rafts. Rafts! To men who hardly remembered what it was like to feel support under their feet, who had begun to identify themselves as creatures of the sea, rafts symbolized a half-forgotten world where people lived on a firm surface, a world now more illusory than real.

Again rejuvenated, Haynes and several others elatedly swam out to recover them. But how were they to be inflated? No one had the energy to pull the toggle on the air flask.

"Pull! Pull!"

Each man tried, but muscles wouldn't respond. Finally, several pooled their last strength and yanked together; the rafts burst open like giant yellow flowers. But now, how would they climb aboard? Haynes tried to hoist himself onto one, but he might as well have tried to climb Mount Everest. His legs had almost atrophied from extended disuse, and it took several men to lift him high enough so he could fall over the edge. The latticed floor felt alien against his withered flesh after so many weightless days, and within minutes his naked body, completely exposed to the sun for the first time since the sinking, began to wilt.

Somehow Haynes and his helpers managed to drag the sickest and most comatose men to the rafts and dump them aboard.

"Naked, emaciated, they [reminded] me of cadavers in the dissecting room," the doctor would say.

He looked around and found a pint of fresh water. Though he felt like a drug addict anticipating a fix, he would not touch any himself, but poured an ounce at a time into a plastic cup that came with the can and gave it first to those most in need. And while the cup passed through several hands each time, no one cheated—despite a maddening thirst that finally drove even the doctor to contemplate stealing a drop.

Shortly, Haynes and all the others not seriously injured or ill jumped back into the water, like fish squirming off a hook, to shield their bodies from the sun. While they clung to the sides of the rafts, other rescue equipment, including more rafts and even a boat, splashed down, some of it dropped by parachute. But they no longer had the strength to swim to it. Besides, for all their misery, many felt at this moment of salvation strangely relieved by the cool, comforting buoyancy of the habitat they had come to embrace. Was there really any other world?

Of all the times to be without his Bible! Bob France wanted all the spiritual support he could get as he stopped tapping out messages and braced himself against the bulkhead of his radio compartment. As he would later write his family, "In the pocket of my flight jacket I always carry a prayer book and on this hop where I could have used it most I did not have it along."

The Dumbo began to nose gently toward the high rolling swells that reached upward like the knuckles on a forest of fists. Lieutenant Marks, sitting stiffly in the pilot's seat, tried to purge his mind of the images—the ravenous sharks, the floating bodies, the men languidly waving. He tried to forget about the lives that depended on a safe landing.

"We held our breath," France, a native of Baltimore, would write in his letter home, "about the same as you would before going down a roller coaster at Kennywood Park, Mom."

Marks gradually pulled back on the yoke, and as the plane slowed down, he watched the water rushing by just a few feet below. His hands felt the controls grow "mushy," signaling his low airspeed; his eyes calculated the sideways drift; and some portion of his mind coordinated all the "inputs" as he mumbled to himself, "Not yet—not yet—not yet." He had to break the stall at the exact split second necessary to avoid a smash-up.

"Now!" And Marks jerked the yoke back all the way to his chest and crashed into the face of a swell with the plane's nose high so the propellers wouldn't dig into the water. The aircraft rattled and groaned, but it remained intact. And now the roller-coaster ride began. The Dumbo bounced about fifteen feet into the air, then twice more from swell to swell before finally trembling to a halt.

Marks got up and inspected the plane for damage, and soon pencils plugged the holes left by two popping rivets and cotton closed an open seam. The plane, however, seemed otherwise undamaged, as did Marks' reputation for cockpit expertise. But if Marks was an expert pilot, he would now have to be an amateur God.

"When we landed," he would later say, "we realized that we couldn't rescue everyone. We would have to make heartbreaking decisions. We would have to pick and choose among the survivors."

And Marks chose first the single swimmers. He had to save as many of them as possible in the few hours before dusk, since they "were the most likely to succumb to the despair of the night." Yet he had qualms. For he would be able to rescue more men in this limited time if he gathered in the larger groups. But these men, after all, had moral support and encouragement from their companions, and some were on rafts. They could more safely wait for the ships to pick them up. Yes, he would have to be cruel and taxi right past the clusters of men, even if this meant they might wrongly conclude that they were being left to die.

While Marks was a freethinker who believed God was too great to want or to accept worship, he hoped that God would influence the men, if they survived, to forgive him for playing favorites. But would God forgive him for playing God?

"Grab the ring! Grab the ring!"

Lieutenant McKissick looked up and saw a strange sight—a plane was drifting on the water within yards of him. Was this the one that had dropped the mail sacks? He wished it would go away. What did it want of him anyway? Someone, he noticed, was standing in the blister of the plane and shouting.

The ring? What ring? McKissick looked around and saw a life ring attached to a line snaking from the aircraft. Very well, he decided with resignation, let them do what they wanted with him. He clutched the ring, and with a sudden jerk was pulled swiftly through the water. A voice then said, "Welcome aboard!" and he was hoisted up a ladder into the plane.

Where was he? Was this the hotel?

"Here, drink this," a man said, handing him half a cup of water as he languidly lay on the floor of the fuselage.

McKissick gulped down his portion of the sixteen gallons of water aboard the plane, and was then wrapped in a parachute and given some food, though he was too nauseous to keep it down. Gazing around, he perceived the fuzzy images of several other survivors lying near him. He had been one of the first men to be picked up by the plane, which Lieutenant Commander Atteberry, flying overhead as a spotter, had directed to him.

Most of the survivors were, like McKissick, out of their heads, though one, remarkably, welcomed members of the air crew who had sailed out in a rubber raft to reach him with the cheery greeting, "Get me on board that little ol' PBY."

Another man had been unconscious before the plane struck him as it taxied around. Marks had him hauled aboard, thinking he had killed him—though he had actually revived him. The pilot's horror did not diminish as he moved from survivor to skeletal survivor, some of whom were dragged through the water by the life ring for a considerable distance before the plane could come to a halt. (When the motor was cut, much precious time was lost while the aircraft stopped and started again.) Marks was, at the same time, stupefied by what he learned of the tragedy from the first man rescued. He would never forget that man, with the flesh on his arms peeling off like the meat of a boiled chicken as he was pulled aboard.

What ship was he from?

The man was barely able to mumble, "The *Indianapolis*."

With so many survivors floating in the sea, Marks had concluded that the ship that sank must have been fairly large. But a cruiser? Hundreds must have already died.

How many days had the survivor been in the water?

The youth wasn't sure—maybe four or five.

It hardly seemed possible. Marks could not imagine that a man would be able to live that long in the sea, with no food or fresh water, mercilessly exposed to the sun and shark attacks. This was the first word of what had actually happened. He must inform his headquarters immediately—but then he realized that he couldn't. He didn't have a secret code book with him, only a confidential one, and this code could more easily be broken. Could he risk letting the Japanese know what ship they had sunk—if they didn't already know?

At about this time, Commander Hashimoto was bemoaning his luck again. Although he was still trying to convince himself that his submarine had sunk a battleship, he could not be absolutely sure. He desperately wanted another "kill" that would be certain, an insurance hit. He had to *know* that he had fulfilled his obligation to the Emperor and the gods.

On Wednesday, August 1, he had lain in wait for an enemy ship once more—on the Okinawa–Ulithi route, which Navigator Tanaka thought would be bustling with enemy traffic. As the submarine surfaced along the route at about 3 P.M., heading north at 12 knots, Hashimoto sighted a mast on the horizon. He peered through the periscope and saw, about twenty thousand yards away, the hull, bridge, and funnels of an eight-to-ten-thousand-ton westbound ship. An unescorted merchant vessel!

Full speed ahead! Hashimoto ordered with the same guarded optimism he had felt when he sighted the *Indianapolis*.

But the enemy ship was too fast. It faded into the distance, leaving the commander to curse his ill fortune still one more time. The government, trying to cut corners, had fitted out his *I-58* with engines too small to give it the speed he needed to keep up with so fast a ship—if it wasn't heading, like that "battleship," directly toward him. And with the moon "on the wane," he wouldn't be able to attack the merchant vessel at night even if he managed to keep up with it. One more failure. It seemed that he would be returning home again without a single confirmed kill.

Hashimoto was so distraught that he took no notice of a radio report emanating from a Tokyo intelligence unit the following day, August 2: "HEAVY ENEMY . . . TRAFFIC INDICATING LARGE ENEMY WARSHIPS SEARCHING FOR WRECK."

Lieutenant Marks pursued his mission with an almost religious zeal: No others must die. And his crew members found this fervent dedication contagious. Marks' navigator, Ensign Morgan Hensley, a muscular man who had been an amateur wrestler in school, was especially driven. When one survivor missed catching the ring, Hensley, standing in the port blister, reached down and, grabbing the man under the arms, lifted him out of the water and flung him over his head into the plane—a Herculean feat. Aviation Ordnanceman Third Class Earl R. Duxbury also performed heroically, pulling survivor after survivor aboard.

Soon, the hull of the bobbing PBY seemed about to burst, with two men jammed into each bunk and two or three more carpeting every compartment; movement through the plane was almost impossible. More men, nevertheless, were squeezed in, more clumps of human flesh ulcerated with saltwater sores and so soft that bones had torn through the soles of feet that had tried to stand on a firm surface. The stench of urine, excrement, vomit, and oil pervaded the plane, and the moans of misery and madness resonated as if in a mental asylum. Like Lieutenant McKissick, almost all of the men were too unstable to rejoice in their salvation, or even to realize that they had been saved (or, for that matter, lost at sea). Some asked to go to the store for drinks, while others called for their mothers, sweethearts, or wives. Most fell quickly into a stuporous sleep, their first real sleep in days.

Haynes had seen the PBY land some distance from his group and had joyously waited for rescue. He and his companions kept their barely seeing eyes glued to the plane as it drew nearer, stopping to pick up lone survivors here and there. Finally, the Dumbo drifted to within a hundred yards of the group, and the men waved and screamed and cheered, especially when someone leaned out of the plane and waved in recognition. They had been seen! The miracle was actually happening, and rescue was at hand. But then the plane suddenly changed direction. The men were crushed, unable to comprehend this "betrayal." Didn't anybody in the world care about them? They still shouted, but now "shook their fists and wept tears of black despair."

A short time later, however, the PBY pulled up beside the two rafts that Haynes had filled with the worst cases, and these men were lifted precariously onto the wings, where they were secured with pieces of parachute shroud line. Then, an emergency kit containing morphine, first-aid equipment, K rations, and a quart of water was dropped to the other men in Haynes' group, who were now almost all ensconced on rafts and would have to await rescue by a ship.

Haynes was able to ease the suffering of some of these men with the medical supplies, but he could do little for those who, in the last few hours, had lapsed into a critical condition due to the loss of body fluids. There wasn't enough water, he judged, to help them survive for more than a few hours.

Knowing now that rescue was imminent only intensified his torment. After so much suffering, were men to die just hours before they were to be saved? He had to get more water! In a frantic search, he explored every crevice of one raft until he found tucked away a converter that made sea water potable. But how did it work? In the last minutes of daylight, he struggled to read the accompanying instructions.

"Again and again," he would later lament, "I read the instructions . . . , but when I [attempted] to use the equipment my numbed brain [refused] to obey."

Try as he might to desalt the water, it always dripped out of the converter salty. Finally, he gave up and, in a paroxysm of fury and frustration, tossed the converter into the sea. For four ghastly days he had tried to help his dying and demented men, but there was little he could do without medical supplies. Now he had a chance to keep some of them alive until a rescue ship arrived, and he had failed. Suddenly, all the tension bottled up within him burst the emotional dam he had set up to keep himself stable and rational. Dr. Haynes sat down on the edge of the raft, cupped his face in his hands, and bitterly wept.

Night would be a cloak of death for many in Lieutenant Redmayne's group, too. Even Harlan Twible's Annapolis training, it seemed, could not help the men now. The ensign had taken over the reins of leadership a little too late from the disoriented lieutenant, who, late Thursday afternoon, was still unconscious from Twible's blow to the head with a biscuit can earlier in the day. The men were dying so fast that it was difficult to push away their bodies, which littered the water around the rafts. And most of the men still alive were too deranged even to understand Twible's orders.

Yet Twible, still in the water, continued to issue orders. Be patient, men, he rasped. Stay close to the raft and pray to God. He had done all he could—he hadn't closed his eyes for one minute since the sinking. But his thinking, he conceded, had become impaired, and he realized that he wouldn't be able to live much longer. He was, after all, mortal, despite his favored status in the Almighty's book. Yes, after dark, perhaps, only God would be left to help these men.

But God showed Himself even sooner; a lifeboat suddenly parachuted down from one of the planes flying overhead as muted cheers went up from throats almost too parched to utter intelligible sounds. Twible swam to the boat with his last energy, since he knew how to operate the gear in it, and ordered the able men to transfer the injured, including Redmayne. In the craft, he found cans of water and cigarettes, which he passed around amid a silent jubilance dimly reflected in blurred eyes. He also discovered communications equipment, though, to his disappointment, the antenna didn't work.

There was, however, a signal mirror. At Annapolis, Twible had reluctantly learned how to use one, seeing it as a primitive, ineffectual way of signaling, more suitable for boy scouts than for sailors. But now he manipulated this mirror with the dedication of a man holding the last key to survival. He informed the plane that had dropped the lifeboat "as to our condition and why we were in the condition that we were," and indicated what ship the men were from. But a message reflected back only the words: "Slow down!" Apparently, he was not understood.

Before he could try again, he saw that God *had* understood. A couple of hundred yards away, another plane, the PBY that had first dropped supplies, landed and was bobbing toward his group. Suddenly, men who had been almost comatose somehow sprang to life.

"Look, it's coming for us!"

"We're saved!"

Some men, in their joy, started to swim toward the plane.

"Come back! Come back!" Twible cried. "Do you want to die? Wait here! It will pick us up!"

Most of the men, though confused, obeyed. But one "kept raving about something" and then lurched ahead in the direction of the plane—Ensign Tom Brophy. Twible had barely noticed Brophy until now since he was black-faced like everybody else, and had been content to remain incognito during the ordeal; only now, in his apparent madness, it seems, did he finally assert himself, ignoring Twible's pleas.

Ensign Blum would later claim that he never knew his friend was even in the group. In any case, he could not have seen Brophy swim away since, at about the same time, he himself was heading in a different direction. A small inflatable raft had been dropped about a hundred yards away, and when one of the survivors swam over to retrieve it, Blum saw that the man couldn't maneuver it back to the group in the rough water. Should he help him and risk his own life with rescue so near? Some of the men were still floating in the sea, and could certainly use the raft. Besides, he would probably find fresh water and other supplies on board. Oh, what the hell! And he dove into the sea.

After swimming for what seemed like hours, Blum finally joined the man stranded on the raft. With groans and grit, the pair managed to paddle over the great swells and return to the group. Utterly exhausted, Blum opened the six cans of water he found aboard, and he and others indulged in a drinking orgy of a few ounces each. It was better even than the booze that had gone down with the ship. And, it seemed, just as effective. With two or three men sprawled over him on the crowded raft, Blum, his head hanging over one side and his feet over the other, fell into a deep sleep.

So did his comrade, Tom Brophy, a sleep from which he would not wake. He never reached Marks' PBY. Later, Twible would wonder "whether or not Brophy may have thought that the plane had been sent for him. Maybe that was his apparition at that time. He came from a well-placed family."

Ever since late morning, when Captain McVay, Otha Alton Havins, and the others on the skipper's rafts saw Lieutenant Gwinn's Ventura turn around and overfly the area some miles to the south, they all knew that the survivors had been found at last. And Havins knew why, too. God had agreed, it seemed, to strike a deal with him: Havins would enter the ministry after the war and God would save him and his buddies. Little did the others know when McVay led them in the Lord's Prayer at dusk, as he did every evening, that the Lord, at least in Havins' perception, had apparently committed Himself to rescue them.

Still, God was acting in a rather roundabout way. All afternoon long, after the Ventura had appeared, planes were streaking through the sky—but not over the McVay group. McVay was torn emotionally by this strange flying pattern. He felt gratified that more of his men must be alive. But would the rescuers fail to spot *his* little fleet? The search seemed to be moving south while his rafts were drifting north. His men had splashed the water and yelled to the heavens, hoping somehow to attract attention; but no pilot, it appeared, was looking their way.

"A smudge pot!" someone suddenly cried. "Maybe they would see a smudge pot!"

It was still early evening and there was a flicker of hope that the pilots might see it before dark.

How would they make one?

"What about the ammunition can?" McVay said, referring to a large can that the men had retrieved from the sea and hauled aboard one of the rafts a little earlier.

Parts of several life jackets and rubber belts were stuffed into it and a flare was then fired to set the material aflame. Smoke curled slowly into the sky, but in the gray dusk no one, apparently, noticed it, and the chances of anyone doing so lessened by the hour as darkness set in and the rafts and the planes moved in opposite directions.

Meanwhile, Giles McCoy, like Havins, Twible, and many other survivors, was also relying almost entirely on God—if not to save his life, then at least to receive him with open arms. He had purified his mind and cleansed his body to the extent possible. Now, late that afternoon, he lay in his raft and waited for God to do what He felt He must do.

McCoy and his raftmate, Felton Outland, while "competing" with each other to see who could stay alive longer, had lost their once keen sense of awareness. They did not realize yet that planes were circling nearby and that rescue was imminent. But as McCoy stared into the sky, he did see black clouds sail across the gray backdrop of dusk; a few moments later, raindrops began pattering on the sea.

Ever since McCoy resisted drinking the salt water he had cupped in his hands, he had suffered the agony of a narcotics addict trying to kick the habit. Now, at last, fresh water!

"Look, rain!" McCoy yelled to Outland. "We've got to catch some of it!"

McCoy removed his rubber life belt and, with Outland's help, split it open. Perhaps they could trap the drops in this improvised reservoir, enough at least to soothe their arid throats. The sacred tears poured down, and the two men, holding the tube, rejoiced as the drops merged into a steadily rising pool. When the rain abruptly stopped, McCoy lifted the end of the belt to his mouth and let the water trickle down his throat. He gagged. Had he been poisoned? Suddenly, he noticed a powdery preservative coating the inside of the tube; it had fouled the water, rendering it undrinkable.

McCoy despaired; he couldn't understand. Was God perhaps testing his faith before calling for him? He must show that it was unshakable. Yes, he was ready to go if God wanted him, as much as he wished to spare his mother the misery of losing another son. Even so, being a fierce competitor, he still hoped to win the contest with Outland. And it was still likely, he thought, that the three unconscious men in the raft would die before either of them.

McCoy lay down again and awaited the decision. At about 10:40 P.M., as he stared into the distant sky, his gaze fell on an awesome sight. The black clouds that had a little earlier spilled all the wasted water had become a bright pinkish white. Was this some sign from heaven?

"Look at that light!" he shouted to Outland.

His companion looked—and gasped.

"We're not dreaming this, are we?" McCoy asked.

"No, those clouds are lit up."

"A ship must be bouncing a searchlight off them," McCoy exclaimed. "They want us to know they've found us!"

And the two men, he would later say, "cried like babies."

He had passed the test.

If God was rewarding Giles McCoy, He was doing it through Lieutenant Commander Claytor, skipper of the destroyer *Cecil J. Doyle.* For it was Claytor who gave the men a pink cloud as a symbol of hope. Whoever was guiding him, it wasn't his superiors. He was breaking Navy rules repeatedly, but, like Adrian Marks, was ready to risk court-martial if it meant saving even one life.

Claytor had spurned one rule after Marks had told him about his mission, heading for the disaster site before his superiors ordered him to do so. He then falsely reported that he had reversed course at 2:18 P.M., almost an hour and a half after he actually did, to make it appear that he had acted "correctly."

Now Claytor had violated another rule. Though sailing in submarine territory, he had ordered his crewmen to switch on two twenty-four-inch searchlights—one to find the survivors in the water and avoid running them down, and the other, beamed to the heavens, to let them know help was on the way. The danger was that any enemy submarine lurking in the area would find his ship a perfect target. But, given the circumstances, he felt that a calculated risk was warranted. Claytor had been well trained to calculate risks, and to bend rules when conditions so required. A native of Roanoke, Virginia, he had served as president of the *Harvard Law Review* and law clerk to Judge Learned Hand and Supreme Court Justice Louis D. Brandeis.

Claytor realized from the messages Marks and Atteberry routed through him that the initial reports were not garbled, and that so many survivors could only have come from a ship. Further confirming the tragedy were similar intercepted messages from an Army Air Force pilot, Lieutenant Richard C. Alcorn, who landed his PBY in the water a few hours after Marks did.

Alcorn's experience especially worried Claytor. Because the pilot had come down just after dark, he could find only one survivor. He switched on his lights, but had to turn them off quickly when other rescue planes, thinking the survivors were signaling their location, started dropping heavy supplies that nearly smashed into his PBY. As Alcorn dared not taxi around without lights for fear of running into somebody, his rescue effort soon ended, and he stormed off for home in frustration.

Even though his own searchlight was illuminating the *Doyle*'s path, Claytor feared, as Alcorn had, that he might hit survivors. Thus, as he drew closer to the disaster area, he vectored in on the signals coming from Marks' Dumbo, since he knew it had picked up many men whom he could take aboard right away without having to move around.

With the help of a parachute flare dropped by a circling plane, the *Doyle*, at about fifteen minutes after midnight, edged its way toward the PBY. Meanwhile, in the race against death, six other vessels were plowing through the waters from various points and would arrive throughout the night: the destroyers *Madison* and *Ralph*

Talbot, the destroyer transports *Bassett, Ringness,* and *Register,* and the destroyer escort *Dufilho*. But the first to reach the scene was the *Doyle*. And as soon as it slowed to a halt near Marks' Dumbo, Claytor ordered several men to lower a whaleboat and head for the plane to bring back the rescued men. The ship then began to drift slightly in the rolling swells, its lights beaming. . . .

Dr. Haynes stared incredulously at the blinding apparition. Was this the flash of death or the glow of deliverance? In a moment, he knew, when he found himself dwarfed by the shadowy outline of a ship that suddenly knifed through the gleaming haze. The ship's searchlight played across the little raft.

"But even [then]," Haynes would later report, "we [did] not feel elated. There [were] no cheers, for the ship [was] just another episode in a situation that [was] going to go on and on forever."

One naked sailor on his raft didn't even want to board the vessel unless he was "guaranteed" a drink of water.

"Son," a voice from the ship's bridge called out, "we have all the water you can drink."

But the sailor remained skeptical.

"If you ain't got no drinkin' water," he cried, "just shove off and leave us alone."

Haynes and his men were helped up a ladder by the ship's crew and lifted onto the deck, but their legs buckled under the weight of their emaciated bodies as they tried to walk on the unfamiliar solid surface. After five days in the water, they felt more like aquatic animals than human beings. Most had to be dragged or carried through a passageway to compartments that had been prepared for them. As Haynes entered a compartment, he was handed a glass of water, which he gulped down in one ecstatic swallow. Lieutenant Commander Claytor then entered and asked him: "What ship are you off?"

Haynes gazed at Claytor with astonishment. The man didn't know?

"You're looking," he murmured, "at what's left of the *Indianapolis*."

The doctor, who had resisted blacking out for four horrendous days, now fainted—and Claytor, in his shock, almost did, too. The *Indianapolis*—Charlie McVay's ship! What had happened to his cousin's husband? Claytor knew how devoted Louise was to McVay and dreaded the thought of giving her the news—if the captain hadn't survived.

Claytor now continued to act independently. Commodore Gillette, Commander of the Philippine Sea Frontier, had ordered the first vessel on the scene to advise him urgently of the "identity of ship survivors" and the "cause of sinking." Gillette and his operations officer, Captain Granum, who had discovered only a few hours earlier that the *Indianapolis* had never arrived in Leyte, were now nervously waiting to learn if this was the ship that had been sunk; their careers could hinge on the answer.

Claytor, apparently unaware of their intense personal stake in the matter, sent a message instead through normal channels, addressed to the Commander of the Western Carolines, who, he figured, would inform them in any case: "HAVE ARRIVED AREA. AM PICKING UP SUR-VIVORS FROM USS INDIANAPOLIS. . . . TORPEDOED AND SUNK LAST SUN-DAY NIGHT."

Claytor realized that this historic message would rock the Navy to its foundations. But if the tragedy was too momentous to be fully comprehended this soon, he understood it vividly in personal terms. He knew Louise. If Charlie was dead, life would be all but over for her as well.

Life was almost over for the men crowded on Donald Blum's raft, when suddenly, at about 1:30 A.M. Friday, they were caught in the glare of a powerful light. An amplified voice then rumbled in the night: "Who are you?"

Blum, who had been asleep, awoke with a start and, as he pushed aside the men sprawled over him, found himself nearly blinded by the beam, though he could make out the barrel of a machine gun aimed at his raft. Was this a dream within a dream?

"Who are you?" the voice repeated.

"We're from the *Indianapolis*," someone on the raft cried.

The cruiser USS *Indianapolis*

U.S. NAVY

Charles B. McVay III with wife Kinau and son Charles IV

Captain Charles B. McVay III (left rear), Seaman Charles B. McVay IV (right rear), and Admiral Charles B. McVay II

KINAU McVAY WILDER

U.S. NAVY

The submarine *I-58*

Commander Mochitsura Hashimoto

Lieutenant Hirokoto Tanaka

Captain Toshio Tanaka

Ensign Harlan
M. Twible

Lieutenant
Charles B.
McKissick

Lieutenant
Richard B.
Redmayne

Dr. Lewis
L. Haynes

Ensign Donald
J. Blum

Yeoman Otha A. Havins

Fireman Adolfo V. Celaya,
during recovery period

Marine PFC Giles G. McCoy (right) recovering after rescue with Seaman Glen L.
Milbrodt (left) and Seaman Louis P. Bitonti

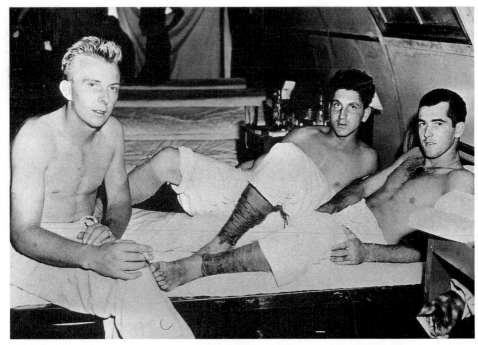

GILES G. MCCOY

GILES G. MCCOY

U.S. NAVY

Commander W. Graham Claytor, Jr.,
skipper of the destroyer *Cecil J. Doyle*,
who helped to rescue survivors

Secretary of the Navy James Forrestal

Fleet Admiral Ernest J. King

Fleet Admiral Chester W. Nimitz

U.S. NAVY

U.S. NAVY

Lieutenant Wilbur C. Gwinn (left front) and his crew: Lieutenant Warren Colwell (right front), AOM2T Harold Hickman (left rear), Chief Radioman William Hartman (center rear), and AMM1c(T) Joseph Johnson

Lieutenant R. Adrian Marks (extreme right rear) and his crew. Front row: Aviation Radioman Roland A. Shepard, AMM3c Richard W. Bayer, Seaman Warren A. Kirchhoff, Aviation Radioman Robert G. France, AOM Earl Duxbury; back row: AMM2c Donald M. Hall, Ensign Morgan F. Hensley, Ensign Irving D. Lefkowitz

GILES G. MCCOY

U.S. NAVY

Lieutenant Marks destroys his
battered PBY seaplane

Hashimoto testifying at the McVay trial

Indianapolis survivors aboard USS *Ringness* after rescue

GILES G. MCCOY

Charles McVay III and
his wife Louise at
1960 reunion of
USS *Indianapolis* survivors

GILES G. MCCOY

Mochitsura Hashimoto
and his wife Nobuko at
their shrine in Kyoto

DAN KURZMAN

There was a shocked pause. Ensign Jack Broser, commanding a whaleboat from the *Bassett*, the second ship to reach the disaster site, was skeptical. The *Indianapolis*? If a cruiser had gone down, his skipper would have known about it and told him. Perhaps they were Japs posing as Americans. He stared at the faces—black! Was this a disguise? Did they have a bomb ready to blow up his men? A resident of New York, he asked, "Where do the Dodgers play?"

"In Brooklyn," a voice warbled.

Another pause, and Blum riveted his eyes on the man behind the machine gun, realizing that his group might be taken for the enemy. Was he to be killed by his own Navy? He furtively slid into the water, expecting to hear a deadly rattle.

But instead, Blum found himself being fished out of the water by the strangers and dragged into their boat, where he rejoined his raftmates. He thanked God, or whoever was running the universe, that none of them had, in their madness, answered "Chicago" or "Philadelphia."

The boat then chugged around as the crew searched for other men, and shortly returned to the *Bassett* with a full load. Blum was the first to set foot on the deck, since he was the only one strong enough to climb the cargo net unassisted. Crewmen ushered him to the bridge, where he found Lieutenant Commander Harold J. Theriault, the ship's captain. Again the question that reflected one of the greatest blunders in American naval history: "What ship are you from?"

And again the incredulity when the reply was given.

"How many of you are in the water?" Theriault asked.

Blum hesitated. Yes, how many? Were the survivors in his group the only ones? "I don't know," he said.

Did he want anything to eat or drink?

"Yes," Blum replied, "a big glass of tomato juice."

Meanwhile, he was taken to a water fountain and could not stop drinking. But there was still room for the juice. A man then approached him carrying a large bowl.

"What's that?" Blum asked.

"Hot tomato soup."

Hot soup? How often out there in the water had he dreamed of feeling a cold glass of juice trickle down his leather-dry throat. Would a fish drink hot soup? He took the bowl and threw it overboard.

"Cold tomato juice, please," he said.

He would see to it that this nightmare ended on the proper note.

Meanwhile, the *Bassett*'s whaleboat was running a kind of shuttle service, as it picked up swimmers and men from Marks' PBY and from rafts, delivered them to the ship, and then went out searching for more. Among those rescued were Adolfo Celaya, Richard Redmayne, and Harlan Twible.

Celaya, who had hurt his back when he jumped from the *Indianapolis*, was helped aboard the *Bassett* and onto a bunk, where he lay in a rosy half-world. His thirst was for the new, exciting life that awaited him. The experience in the water had demonstrated, if in grotesque relief, that the quality of a man was not determined by rank, class, wealth, or color, but by the nature of his soul.

Still . . . what would the sailors who were coming to take him to the shower say when they found that, scrape as they might, the oil-blackened skin would never become white?

Lieutenant Redmayne was still unconscious when he was lifted from his raft to the whaleboat, finally awakening when the craft pulled up to the *Bassett*.

"Where are we?" he mumbled, thinking he was still aboard the *Indianapolis*. "Are we entering the harbor at Guam?"

"Yes, sir," someone humored him.

But when he had been placed on a stretcher, lifted to the deck, and carried to a compartment with immaculately white bulkheads that shone under bright lights, he started to have doubts. The *Indianapolis* was clean, but never like this. Looking down from his second-tier bunk, he saw a Marine sergeant he recognized.

"Sergeant," he said, "are we in heaven?"

The sergeant smiled. "No, sir, Mr. Redmayne. We've been rescued."

The lieutenant was relieved. He had begun to worry. His oil-stained body was soiling the crisp white sheets and it just wouldn't have been right to mess up heaven.

Harlan Twible knew he was still on earth because he had not shut his eyes since the night before the sinking. Besides, God, he felt, favored him and would not pluck him away prematurely. Otherwise, would he have survived in his condition? He had lost forty pounds, and when sailors had carried him aboard the ship and cut him out of his waterlogged life jacket, he found that he was paralyzed from the waist down, at least temporarily, and had shrapnel lodged in his side from the explosions.

If he had been aware of his paralysis before, he might have lifted himself aboard a raft with the other wounded and lost the invincible aura of the Annapolis officer that had inspired men to survive. He had worked for four days to save what he could of his little world. Now, on the fifth day, he would rest.

At about 2 A.M., a jangling telephone awakened Captain Granum from a restless sleep. Someone from his office was on the line. A message had come in from the *Bassett*'s skipper, Lieutenant Commander Theriault, whom the Philippine Sea Frontier Command had sent on the rescue mission with orders to report the identity of the ill-fated vessel directly to the PSFC. Granum and his superior, Commodore Gillette, did not want the message to go through a maze of channels before reaching them, and with good reason, considering that Claytor's earlier dispatch identifying the *Indianapolis* had still not arrived.

Yes, what was the message? Granum asked impatiently.

"Survivors are from USS *Indianapolis* . . . which was torpedoed twenty-ninth July [sic]. Continuing to pick up survivors. Many badly injured."

Just as he and the commodore had suspected. A terrible tragedy.

. . .

Captain McVay, who had dropped off to sleep during a night of bitter frustration, awoke after daylight Friday and anxiously scanned the horizon. The flealike planes were still circling over the water, but they seemed to be flying ever more south while his rafts drifted ever more north. After so many grueling hours in the air, the pilots would no doubt feel that every man still alive had been found, and would be returning to base soon. He and his raftmates, it seemed, were doomed.

With all hope abandoned, McVay decided that since there was no longer anyone to signal, he would use his last flare to light the single dry cigarette in the carton that had been retrieved earlier from the sea. Let the boys enjoy a last puff before they died. Someone fired the flare into the cloth material in the ammunition can, which had stopped burning during the night, and a new smoldering blaze lit the cigarette. As the men passed it around, they did not have to be told why McVay had used the last flare for this rather frivolous purpose.

Still, Otha Alton Havins did not give up on God. A deal, after all, was a deal. Suddenly, there was a new drone overhead. The men saw a plane flitting nearby in what seemed like a search pattern, and began waving and yelling, but there was no sign of recognition. No flyover, no waggling wings. They had to signal the plane quickly —but how could they? The new smudge pot had already gone out, and there were no more flares. That last puff on the cigarette, it appeared, had been fatal. And when the plane flew off, death seemed inescapable. Even Havins was ready to concede that there might have been a misunderstanding between him and God.

Then, at about 10:30 A.M., Havins noticed a blur on the horizon. What was it?

"Look, over there!" he cried, pointing toward the blur. "Am I hallucinating, or is that a ship?"

"If you're hallucinating," someone replied, "then I am, too. That's a goddamn ship, and it's coming right at us!"

Everyone turned to Captain McVay, and his smile seemed to confirm that it was; he hadn't looked this happy since the sinking.

"I told you we'd be saved," he said.

Havins was ecstatic. God had answered his prayers. Now he would honor his part of the bargain and enter the ministry when he got home.

"Thank you, Lord," Havins intoned, lifting his eyes to heaven.

And shortly, the ten men in the group were being pulled or carried aboard the *Ringness*, which had reached the disaster area that morning. It was Lieutenant Marks' squadron leader, Lieutenant Commander M. V. Ricketts, who had spotted the group as he flew overhead a little earlier. And the ship had headed directly for it, guided by radar that pinpointed the location of an ammunition can filled with the half-burned remains of life preservers that had been used to light a cigarette.

Saved! But Captain McVay, strangely, was no longer smiling. Yes, he was happy for his boys. And much of his life, his life with Louise, lay ahead. But would even Louise's love and devotion compensate for the terrible anguish he feared he might now bring to his family and himself?

With anxiety dampening his joy, McVay stumbled to the bridge and stammered out his story to Lieutenant Commander William C. Meyer, skipper of the *Ringness*, as if trying to purge his soul of guilt. Meyer then drafted a report to Guam, but McVay added two words: "not zigzagging." Meyer objected. Why mention this in the initial message? Without an explanation, headquarters might draw the wrong conclusions. But McVay insisted that those words be used.

Thus, the message sent to CINCPAC read: "HAVE 37 SURVIVORS ABOARD INCLUDING CAPTAIN CHARLES MCVAY III. STATES BELIEVES SHIP HIT 0015, SANK 0030 . . . 30 JULY. POSITION ON TRACK EXACTLY AS ROUTED PD [PORT DIRECTOR] GUAM. SPEED 17, NOT ZIGZAGGING. HIT FORWARD BY WHAT IS BELIEVED TO BE TWO TORPEDOES OR MINE FOLLOWED BY MAGAZINE EXPLOSION."

Reliving the tragedy added to McVay's pain. All those people dead—and he was the captain. But were the perils of the sea to be the worst he would face?

·　　·　　·

Captain McVay and his men were not the only survivors who had felt abandoned. Giles McCoy and Felton Outland thought they would be left behind, too. The pink cloud that had so exhilarated them the previous night had long since dissolved into a mist of renewed hopelessness. If the planes had found survivors, *they* were not among them. Since dawn, the two men could see the aircraft circling in the distance and could even detect faraway ships—none of them steaming in their direction.

Hours passed, and the pair grew even weaker. No water, no food. How could they survive another night? Suddenly, late in the afternoon, as their eyes swept the sea and the sky, there was nothing—nothing but a world shaded in blue, murmuring with the rhythm of eternity. The planes and the ships were gone!

"The bastards missed us," McCoy groaned. "We're finished."

About 4 P.M., the two men, as they lay in the raft waiting to leave the world, suddenly heard a familiar sound—the whir of a motor. It grew louder and louder. They gazed up and there, sailing over them, was a PBY.

"Those guys in the blister are waving at us!" McCoy cried.

He must have passed another test.

Shortly, a vessel crawled out of the horizon. When it had come within fifty feet of the raft, a crewman threw ropes to the occupants, while another swam over to pull the raft toward the ship. The three unconscious men on the raft were lifted aboard, but McCoy and Outland tried to climb up the hanging ladder without assistance, only to fall back onto the raft. Helped up now, McCoy, his pride wounded, pushed the man away.

"I can walk by myself," he announced.

He had never felt so weak, but that made the challenge all the more enticing. He was a Marine, after all. He would show these sailors. Hardly had he taken a step, however, when he fell flat on his face. Again humiliated, he tried to rise, but his flaccid leg muscles did not react. With tears in his eyes, he lay on his stomach, panting in frustration. Well, with a little limbering up, he'd outrun the whole crew. And he kissed the deck before being carried on a stretcher to a compartment, where he was placed in a bunk and, to his further shame, spoon-fed water by some mother-hen sailor.

Meanwhile, the rescuing vessel—the *Ringness*—headed for Peleliu. It would arrive a bit late, since it had been delayed when it picked up McCoy and his raftmates—the last men from the *Indianapolis* to be found alive. They had been discovered just after the *Ringness* was ordered to leave for Peleliu to deliver Captain McVay and the other survivors it had picked up. With dusk near, the ships remaining in the area would make an envelope sweep after dark, but the night would be black, overcast, and frequently squally, and finding a lone raft would be almost impossible.

God, it seemed, had pulled McCoy back from the very brink.

Early that morning, Lieutenant Marks had climbed to the bridge of the *Doyle*, briskly saluted Lieutenant Commander Claytor, and said, "Sir, I request that you destroy my airplane by gunfire."

Marks felt he had no choice. During the night, fifty-six survivors had been moved from the PBY to the whaleboat to the *Doyle*. And each time the boat rode the swells and crashed against the plane, deep scars and slits would deface the aircraft and wing struts. Also, oil was leaking out from rents in the bottom of the plane that were caused by the landing, while the fabric in the wings had torn under the strain of men walking on them with their pitiful burdens. Thus, when the last survivors had debarked, Marks conferred with his crew and got a consensus: With all its breaks, breaches, and bruises, the plane could not take off. The men salvaged whatever gear they could and called for the whaleboat to come for them. Then, on boarding the *Doyle*, Marks made his put-the-plane-to-rest request to Claytor, who would later that day leave for Peleliu with ninety-three survivors.

The pilot painfully watched from the deck as the ship's guns fired at his dear Dumbo. Had it not obeyed his every command, saving countless lives in its distinguished career? When the aircraft at first refused to sink, it was almost like witnessing the execution of a loved one who wouldn't die. Finally, the plane vanished in a whirlpool of bubbles.

Marks went down to the wardroom, and was not cheered by an encounter there with Dr. Haynes, who had been sleeping on a couch.

In a sudden release of emotion and nervous tension, the doctor burst into tears and, between sobs, compulsively spoke of his ordeal.

Marks, who had been sitting at a table writing an official report of his activities, listened for a few minutes and then interrupted: "Doctor, why don't you rest? Your voice is almost gone. You can tell about it tomorrow."

No, he had to talk now, however exhausted, dehydrated, and feverish he might be. For before Haynes "[could] find rest," Marks would later recall, "his story [had to] be told in all its tragic detail."

But if Haynes sought comfort in telling his story, Marks sought comfort in winning Haynes' approval of his own role in the story. He remembered the doctor and his men waving frantically, splashing with their feet, crying out to him, "Please save us!"—and his decision to deliberately pass them by to rescue lone swimmers, though he would later pick up the worst cases in the group. Now, with this decision weighing heavily on him, he asked Haynes: "[Did I make] a horrible error? Should I have taken your men aboard?"

"Lieutenant," Haynes replied in a raspy voice that was hardly more than a whisper, "you were right! You did right to pass us by!"

These words had a magic effect on Marks, but as he turned back to his report, he still wondered how best to explain his actions.

"Doctor," he said hesitantly, "I couldn't get my plane off this morning. She was too badly damaged to fly, so we had to sink her by gunfire. Now I've got to explain why I landed."

Marks paused, searching Haynes' countenance. "Doc, can I quote you as saying my open-sea landing was necessary to save you fellows?"

XII

The Price of Salvation

DONALD BLUM awoke late Friday morning to the squeaks and groans of a ship plowing through rough water. The *Bassett*, brimming with 151 survivors, had at 6 A.M. started steaming toward the Philippine island of Samar, where the men would be treated at a new military hospital before sailing home.

Blum squeezed the mattress he had slept on in the officers' quarters. It was springy and dry. Where was the water-filled raft? Had he simply imagined the shipwreck and the sharks, the mirages and the madness, the hunger and the heat? But then he smelled the oil that oozed from every pore in his body, and he knew that it had all happened. No dream could smell that bad.

During the night, the other survivors on the ship had been carried to canvas cots lining the deck, but Blum had visions of a more luxurious cruise. Since he was ambulatory and the madmen were now under control, he decided it was finally time to pull rank. So he stumbled down to the officers' quarters, found a vacant compartment, and flopped onto the mattressed bunk. Here he would not be treated like an Arabian prince with the crew catering to his every wish and whim, as he would be on deck. And he might not be served his favorite foods and have his body scrubbed clean—he would have to do it himself. But oh, the cool, gentle feel of the mattress against his sore-ridden flesh.

Blum awakened after several hours' sleep and went to the shower, using kerosene to help him scrape off the clinging oil. Then, clad only in a clean pair of shorts someone had given him, he staggered to the wardroom for breakfast, the first food other than malt pills and Spam that he would consume since the half-eaten sandwich he had regurgitated during the sinking.

But when he got to the wardroom, he found, to his despair, that breakfast was no longer being served. Did the Navy think he had gotten out of the habit of eating? A chief called him over to his table.

"How about a cup of coffee, sir?"

Blum sat down and nearly choked with the first sip.

"What's in this coffee?" he gasped.

"Torpedo alcohol—two hundred proof. We use it for propelling torpedoes."

Just what Blum needed. Not as good as the whiskey that he had lost when the *Indianapolis* went down, but not bad. Who wanted Wheaties for breakfast, anyway? He swiftly drained the cup, and in a few moments was almost as comatose as he had been at times in the water. Blum got up and reeled back to his bunk. He would sleep soundly, secure in the knowledge that no enemy submarine could escape torpedoes that used so powerful a propellant.

At dawn the next day, Blum was still groggy when the *Bassett* pulled into Guiuan Harbor at the island of Samar. Barges carried the men, most of them on stretchers, to shore, from where they were driven to a hospital in the hills. As soon as they arrived, doctors and nurses furiously tried to heal wounds to body and mind—though they were too late to save two of the most gravely injured men.

One of the survivors who needed a great deal of healing was Lieutenant Redmayne. Still somewhat unstable, he suffered from severe claustrophobia and nightmares that caused him to flail the air violently with fists intended for some unseen foe. His burned hand actually pained him more now that he was out of the water, and so did the bump on his head from Ensign Twible's biscuit-can blow. When Twible had almost recovered from his paralysis—and from

the effects of a half glass of beer he had wrung out of his doctor—
he limped over to see Redmayne. The lieutenant, sitting up in bed,
growled as he felt the large protrusion on his head: "Some son of a
bitch was out to get me. Look at this bump."

Twible smiled. "I did it," he confessed. "You went nuts and
wanted to dive to the engine room. I had to stop you."

Redmayne was stunned. Twible had saved his life!

"I hope I keep this bump all my life," he said. "I never want to
forget how lucky I was."

After they had rested sufficiently, Redmayne, Twible, Blum, and
two other officers were gently led, one after the other, into a room
and subjected to the Navy's first official interrogation about the
tragedy. How did it happen? Why did it happen? Each of the men
recalled what he could, rambling, stumbling over words in an emotional outpouring of the horrors trapped in his mind.

The interrogators listened in shocked silence. Then they warned:
All this information must remain secret until a full inquiry was held
and the Navy decided that the time was ripe for disclosure. The
security of the United States was at stake.

The American public, after all, might criticize the Navy and
demand punitive measures—perhaps even a housecleaning at the top.
And just when the war's end seemed within reach, thanks in large
measure to the Navy's triumphs.

While naval officers on the island of Samar were trying to forestall
public criticism of the Navy, a naval officer on the island of Peleliu
was inviting such criticism. Captain McVay held a press conference
in Peleliu on Sunday, August 5, the day after the *Ringness* arrived
there with a load of survivors.

The newsmen had just been flown in to see him, though their
stories could not be filed until the Navy gave the okay. They gathered
in Base Hospital No. 20, the medical way station for men picked up
by the *Ringness*, the *Doyle*, and the *Register*. McVay, who had never
been known to publicly criticize the Navy before, now vented feelings that had been smoldering in him for days.

"We were due at our anchorage [in Leyte] at 1100 hours," he said. "I should think by noon or 1300 they would have started to worry. A ship that size practically runs on train schedule. I should think by noon they would have started to call by radio to find out where we were, or if something was wrong. So far as I know, nothing was started until Thursday."

McVay paused, and all the physical and mental suffering he and his men had undergone seemed caught in eyes wailing with anguish, seething with anger.

"This is something I want to ask somebody myself," he went on. "Why didn't this get out sooner?"

Throughout his voyage on the *Ringness*, and now in Peleliu, McVay painfully pondered this question, mulling it over with fellow officers, including Captain Meyer aboard the ship and Captain Eugene Oates, an old friend he met in Peleliu. As he sat on the porch of Oates' Quonset hut amid whispering palms and stared hypnotically at the sea, he could still see the faces of his boys etched with foam on every breaking wave. He had always loved the sea, but now it was simply a vast hungry graveyard. And the bright sunshine that had always brought the world to life, giving it warmth, color, and beauty, was merely the mocking smile of death. Nor was the once comforting quilt of night less deceptive, with the moon and stars still gaily poking through what was now a dark shroud.

Why hadn't anyone warned him of the danger? Why hadn't someone known that the ship had gone down? Who was at fault? They would certainly blame him, even though he was guiltless. They would hang him in the sunshine so that others might hide in the shade. But he would fight them relentlessly—within the bounds of protocol and tradition, of course; he was, after all, still a Navy man. But McVay realized that whatever happened, he would not find peace. If he lost the fight, his career and reputation would lie in ruins, and he would bring shame to Louise, his father, his sons. And if he won, it would be a hollow victory. So many of his crew, his boys, were dead. And he had been their skipper.

· · ·

When Navy Secretary James Forrestal learned of the *Indianapolis* tragedy, he could only agonize over the ironies intrinsic to war. On August 6, the day after McVay's press conference, he sat at his desk in the Pentagon facing piles of reports that cast the Navy in two contrasting lights. One from Navy Captain Parsons aboard the *Enola Gay* reflected Navy pride in the success of the atomic bomb attack on Hiroshima that day, possibly the final blow in a war that had seen the most momentous victories in naval history. But another report badly tarnished this pride, telling of the *Indianapolis* tragedy, apparently the greatest disaster in that history.

Actually, Forrestal was more worried about a possible World War III than about naval pride. In his eyes, war with the Soviet Union was nearly inevitable after the defeat of Japan, and he feared that the Truman administration would approve a plan to unite the three armed services—a plan that he was convinced would weaken America's ability to fight such a war. General George C. Marshall, the Army Chief of Staff, who he felt was blind to the potential Russian menace, favored a united force, failing to understand the need for an independent Navy. And now Marshall might use he *Indianapolis* episode as proof that the Navy needed to be reined in.

Of course, Forrestal did have Fleet Admiral King, the Navy Chief of Operations, on his side—even if the Secretary did resent strong men in positions of power. He found them to be stubborn and sneering, and did not wish to be dependent on their strength. At the same time, he seemed intimidated, almost obsequious, in their presence, and often resorted to a "labored camaraderie," as one observer put it. He called the admirals by their nicknames and, corrupting his own Princetonian eloquence, emulated their rather tough, inelegant manner of speech even as he yielded to their views—in particular those of King.

Forrestal had been trying to appear tough since childhood. In his teens, he even donned boxing gloves and entered the amateur ring to assert his manhood, and when he once suffered a broken nose, he preferred to retain the pugilistic image it gave him rather than have it surgically corrected.

Forrestal now thumbed through the latest reports on the *India-*

napolis disaster. It would be kept a secret for another week or so. By then, he apparently felt, the war would be over, since the atomic dust would have settled and clearly signaled the Japanese that further resistance would be futile. (He had nevertheless wanted the bomb to be dropped on a forest outside Tokyo to demonstrate its power before it was used to destroy a city. After all, the United States would need Japan as an ally in the coming war with Russia, and the Japanese might not cooperate if their cities were atomized.)

Now the *Indianapolis* tragedy could bring a new threat to the nation's security, at least indirectly. When the public learned of it, he apparently feared, there would be screams for blood, perhaps even his own; and he was needed to help mobilize the nation for the new conflict. Moreover, the disaster appeared to play right into the hands of those pressing for military union. Seldom, it seems, had Forrestal felt as powerless and dependent on others for rescue. He would have to ask Admiral King to help him find a way to clear the Navy's name.

Admiral King was as pleased to give help as Secretary Forrestal was reluctant to ask for it. The admiral, with other members of the Joint Chiefs of Staff, had largely run the war, exercising their greatest influence after Harry Truman became President. King, whose vanity was reflected in his ruggedly handsome face, felt it was only natural that Forrestal should listen to an admiral, especially in wartime. Besides, after having reached his lifelong goal—command of the most powerful Navy in history—he clearly didn't want posterity to rank him under any naval civilian.

Thus, as reports of the *Indianapolis* tragedy trickled into his Pentagon office, he grew alarmed. The timing couldn't have been worse. With the war about to end, his main job was to make sure that the Navy he led got the elephant's share of the credit for victory. And now this catastrophe.

King's devotion to his Navy was total. Like Forrestal, he hadn't favored dropping the atomic bomb on a Japanese city, though not because he was reluctant to antagonize Japan too deeply. The bomb, he simply felt, didn't have to be used to force Japan to surrender. His fleet had already blown the Japanese Navy out of the water, and all it had to do now was blockade and starve the country into submission. But the bomb had been dropped, and now history might not appreciate the full importance of the Navy's role in the war—and, he apparently feared, might even remember him mainly for what could be the greatest American naval sea disaster ever.

Until now, King's record had been stained only once, when he had been a junior officer; he was reprimanded by a man he could never forget—Admiral Charles B. McVay II. King would, of course, overcome this setback, but now again he was being haunted by a McVay—the admiral's son! By losing his ship and triggering an unprecedented disaster, Captain McVay had jeopardized the good name of the Navy, King's Navy. Something had to be done, King decided. Admiral Nimitz himself might have to take the heat if necessary. As King would write Forrestal on September 25, the "responsibility" for the ambiguous order on reporting ship arrivals "lies with the Commander in Chief, U.S. Pacific Fleet." King also sent a thinly veiled reprimand to Nimitz himself: "ASSUME THAT UNESCORTED SHIPS OR CONVOYS ARE NOT BEING ROUTED OVER KNOWN POSITIONS OF ENEMY SUBS WITH ASSIGNED OFFENSIVE MISSIONS BUT RECENT LOSS OF *INDIANAPOLIS* APPEARS TO BE A CASE IN POINT."

Admiral Nimitz did not have to read King's message to feel the rising heat. Nearly nine hundred men under his command had met the most grisly fate—one that might be ascribed more to the negligence of his officers than to the fortunes of war. He apparently feared that the public could turn up the thermostat even more, and King's message seemed to hint that he could be left to sizzle.

A placid man with a rosy complexion and whitish blond hair, Nimitz, though a tough sailor, had a gentle sense of humor and a fervent love of flowers, which he zealously planted himself in his garden at home and outside his headquarters in Pearl Harbor. But if the symbols of peace helped him to deal with the horrors of war, nothing could temper the horror of the reports he had received on the *Indianapolis* dead. After the survivors had been rescued, ships and planes swept the disaster zone in a massive search for bodies. But most were so decomposed and shark-bitten that after the first few were brought aboard, the rest were examined on the pickup boats, identified (when possible), then immediately sunk with weights. Now Nimitz chillingly read the results of this body-seeking expedition. A report from one ship, the USS *French*, described some of the corpses found that day:

"Medium size, medium build, appears to be rather young. Very advanced stage of decomposition and appeared to have been partially eaten by sharks."

"Body unclothed except for a pair of socks unstenciled. . . . Very badly mutilated by sharks."

"Body clad in dungaree trousers only. Badly mangled by sharks."

"Fully clothed with dungaree shirt and trousers, skivvy drawers, shoe and sock on left foot (right foot missing)."

As Nimitz read the reports, he suffered what he would describe as the worst trauma in his military career, a career that had peaked in this war with the command of the largest armada of ships, planes, and men ever assembled. It was painful indeed to read these ghastly details, page after page, describing his dead sailors, boys who might have been saved and gone back to their wives, sweethearts, parents, most of whom would never even have the consolation of knowing that the remains of their loved one had been positively identified (it had been impossible to take fingerprints since the skin had peeled off the hands, if the sharks had not removed them). And to die during what might be the last week of the war!

There were perplexing questions that had to be answered:

Why did the *Indianapolis* go down, and how was it possible for its men to be in the water for almost five days without anybody knowing about it?

Aside from the responsibility of Captain McVay for losing his ship, had there been bureaucratic bungling, overconfidence, or carelessness on the eve of victory?

Had some of his men misconstrued his rules, or had his rules been deficient?

Nimitz was a compassionate man. Only with reluctance had he supported use of the atomic bomb, feeling, as a classical old warrior, that it was not a legitimate weapon of war. Killing a hundred thousand civilians in the blink of an eye was not the way he wanted to fight. Military "logic," however, had finally triumphed over compassion, and now the war was ending. But he could not celebrate. Hundreds had died in the *Indianapolis* tragedy—statistically, of course, a mere fraction of the tens of thousands who had fallen in this war, and a trifling number compared to the whole city of people that had suddenly vanished in the bomb blast over Hiroshima. Yet he could never forget the sailor with the unstenciled socks or the "rather young" man who had been eaten by sharks—who needn't have died.

Still, no matter how egregious the errors committed by some of his officers, he felt that any man could have made them. As a young officer, Nimitz was himself court-martialed and reprimanded for running a ship aground, though with iron dedication he had managed, like King, to overcome this handicap and rise to a top command. The memory of this mishap gave him a sense of caution that would not permit him to reach decisions until he exhaustively discussed them with his staff and commanders.

Recognizing his fallibility, Nimitz never boasted or claimed a victory he had not won. Where would he be without men like Admirals Spruance, William F. Halsey, Richmond Kelly Turner, and John McCain, without the many officers of lesser rank who had helped carry the United States to the brink of victory—among them Captain McVay?

The admiral felt that he must be fair with those responsible for this tragedy, as the Navy had been with him in the past—as he hoped it would be in the future. After all, he could still be chosen to succeed Admiral King as Chief of Naval Operations if the inquiry he would order didn't reflect too gravely on his commanders—or himself.

Admiral Nimitz wanted the inquiry to be held without delay so that the Navy could reveal the details of the disaster to the public as soon as the war ended and military censorship was lifted. Thus, hardly had Hiroshima crumbled when the survivors in Peleliu were hoisted or carried aboard the hospital ship *Tranquility* bound for Guam. There many of them would be questioned before continuing the voyage home. Two men were not taken aboard; they had died in Peleliu.

When the nurses on the ship had tucked their patients into crisply sheeted beds, Lieutenant Commander Atteberry entered the ward, accompanied by a shy, smiling young aviator.

"Men," he said, "how'd you like to meet the guy who found you?"

The survivors shouted and cheered and Lieutenant Gwinn grinned. They limped over to him, grasped his hand, and tearfully embraced him. Seldom had perfect strangers so loved each other at first sight. Surely Gwinn was the instrument of God. None could doubt that if he had not seen them when he did, they all would now be shark-mutilated skeletons.

Happy as he was for his men, Captain McVay wondered if Gwinn had really done *him* a favor. With the ship due to land in Guam the next day, it was hard to believe that barely more than a week had passed since the *Indianapolis* had cast off from there with assurances that it would be facing no serious danger. He now stood by the railing and peered into the hazy, blue distance as if into a lost age that had existed in another lifetime, an age full of joy and hope in which he had found Louise and would soon become an admiral as his father so fervently wished. What an ideal life had lain ahead . . . only a few days earlier.

On Tuesday, August 7, the survivors debarked in Guam and were driven to Base Hospital No. 18, where Admiral Spruance moved from bed to bed, pinning the Purple Heart on their pajamas. Shortly, they were reunited with those who had been taken to Samar and then flown here to join in the investigation. There were embraces, jokes, talk about home, and also silence, the silence of men who wanted to forget.

Captain McVay was one of these men. He wanted to forget for a few days, at least until the inquiry started and he would be forced to relive the entire ordeal. He approached Giles McCoy in the hospital one day and said, "You look pretty strong. Do you feel well enough to do something?"

McCoy was still recovering from severe sunburn, dehydration, a back injury, and saltwater ulcers on his limbs, and his legs were bandaged since much of the skin had peeled off. But yes, he was ready to "do something."

"Well, how about being my driver?"

And soon McCoy was driving the captain around the island, sometimes for meetings with naval officials, but often on tours into the hills. McVay would ask McCoy to stop occasionally, then would get out to survey the harbor and villages below and gaze dreamily into some hidden heaven.

"Beautiful sight, isn't it?" he once mused.

But McVay could never escape relity for long. Once, he emerged from a meeting, climbed into his jeep, and angrily rasped, half to himself, half to McCoy, "Those bastards are really trying to get me."

McCoy drove him back to the hospital. The landscapes that had so enthralled the captain now only reminded him of a peace and tranquility that he could never again fully enjoy. He wished the court of inquiry would finally meet and finish up with him.

Captain McVay's agitation grew with every passing day as delay followed delay. The court was originally to meet on August 9, but on that Wednesday an American plane dropped an atomic bomb on Nagasaki and the Russians invaded Manchuria. And it wasn't easy for some members of the court to abandon their posts while the last shots were being fired, especially a combat officer like Vice Admiral Charles A. Lockwood, Jr., who commanded the Pacific submarine fleet and would head the court. McVay himself was caught up in the excitement, but his inability to take part in the unfolding drama only added to his depression. After serving his country so devotedly throughout the war, he was, at the moment of victory, a captain without a ship, who, he felt, was about to be discredited, destroyed.

And his anxiety was not eased by his own sense of guilt, however innocent he knew himself to be.

Some of McVay's men found that their easygoing, even-tempered skipper was now quick to anger. He had come out of the disaster loving his men more but tolerating their mistakes less. And Donald Blum was especially aware of this tendency. He spent his first days in Guam resting, writing letters, making out forms. One form dealt with claims for personal property that had been lost n the disaster. As he and two of the officers who had roomed with him aboard the *Indianapolis* filled out this form, Blum asked his companions half-seriously, "Do you think I should put in for my whiskey?"

"You smuggled whiskey aboard?" a shipmate responded.

"Yeah, three bottles. I hid them in that space between the two corner desks under some suitcases."

"That's where I put mine!" the man exclaimed. "I lost six bottles."

"I hid mine there, too," the second shipmate groaned. "A whole case!"

Blum was shocked. What an incredible waste! There had been enough liquor in that compartment to open a nightclub! All of it gone, and the Navy, he was sure, wouldn't pay them a dime. Still, he might sound out the captain, who, after all, loved his liquor, too. But he decided it would be futile, especially after he shot to the top of the skipper's "shit list."

Blum had been assigned to mail duty, a job that required him to drive a jeep to the post office, return mail addressed to the deceased, and bring back the rest for distribution in the hospital. He reveled in this job because he had the jeep to himself when he finished his work, and there were a lot of pretty girls in Guam. Weak as he was, he was determined to make up for the ban on shore leaves aboard the *Indianapolis* and for all the time he had lost floating around in the sea. Fate, however, continued to plague him.

On one occasion, Blum aroused the ire of Admiral Nimitz himself when he sped past the admiral's car in his jeep.

Nimitz ordered an aide to find out who the "reckless driver" was, and the next day, McVay summoned Blum.

"What's all this about?" the captain demanded after informing him of the admiral's displeasure.

Blum departed minus his job and his jeep, and was restricted to the hospital area. Grounded! Once again, no girls, no fun. But soon his griping turned to gratitude. He and the other able men were moved to a rest camp, where they could do some skeet shooting, play tennis, guzzle at the bar, eat choice food, and picnic on a beautiful beach strewn with sympathetic nurses. More like a country club— and Jews weren't excluded from this one. Okay, this made up for the lost booze. All the admirals in the Navy couldn't drag him away from here, Blum vowed. But some did; he was called to testify at the inquiry.

Shrouded in secrecy, the inquiry finally opened on August 13 in an atmosphere tense with anger, impatience, and frustration. So rushed and unready was the court that the judge advocate, or prosecutor, Captain William Hilbert, admitted that it was "starting the proceedings without having available all the necessary data." Nor, it seems, the necessary dedication at this heroic moment in history to a task related to unprecedented naval bungling.

Besides Captain McVay and Ensign Blum, forty-one witnesses from scattered Pacific bases sat in the corridor of CINCPAC headquarters waiting to testify, one by one, in the large "courtroom" office. They included Lieutenant Redmayne, Ensign Twible, Admiral McCormick, Lieutenant Gibson, Commander Sancho, Captain Granum, Commodore Gillette, Commodore Carter, Lieutenant Waldron, and Captain Naquin.

Perhaps the most notable missing witness was Admiral Murray, commander of the Marianas, who was Naquin's superior and the man in command of the area where the *Indianapolis* had sunk. He was one of the three judges! Murray would help decide whether he and *his* men had been negligent in the briefing of McVay—a prospect that did little to raise McVay's spirits. As an "interested party," or potential defendant, the captain would be able to listen to all the evidence. He would thus find himself immersed in tragedy at the very moment the rest of the Free World was exploding in joy.

At 7 P.M., August 15, in the White House, President Truman, with his wife and his Cabinet glowing by his side, announced the momentous news: Japan had surrendered! The nation went wild. People danced in the streets, auto horns blared, confetti flew.

One hour later, who could hear, who wanted to hear, the radio announcer as he hoarsely interrupted the greatest holiday of the age with a news report that some ship had been sunk. All that was over. The boys were coming home! Thus, drowned out in the tumult, as the Navy perhaps calculated, was the concise, emotionless Navy Department communiqué: "The U.S.S. *Indianapolis* has been lost in the Philippine Sea as the result of enemy action. The next of kin have been notified."

A little earlier, Thomas D'Arcy Brophy, Sr., and his wife were driving near Montreal, where Brophy had visited a branch office of his advertising agency. When they turned on the radio and learned that the war was over, they could barely contain their joy. Tom Jr. was coming home! To his father, young Tom was a reflection of himself, and all his hopes were wrapped up in the boy. He was destined to emulate his father.

The elder Brophy was a success indeed. He was chairman of Kenyon and Eckhardt, a large New York advertising agency, and was an organizer of the American Heritage Foundation, a trustee of leading hospitals, a director of medical societies, and a member of some influential government councils and committees. His son, he felt, would wield the same power, and he would start on the road up as soon as he returned. Yes, Tom was coming home. What a homecoming he would get!

In the midst of the radio-borne frenzy, Brophy drew up to the curb to telephone his Montreal office. He entered a public phone booth and dialed the number.

Any messages?

There was one. . . .

A minute later, Brophy walked out of the phone booth and, ashen-faced, plodded hesitantly back to the car. How would he tell his wife, he wondered, as the sounds of celebration still emanating from the radio mingled with the words that mercilessly rang in his ears—"We regret to inform you . . ."

At about the same time, east of Okinawa, Commander Hashimoto stood on the bridge of the submarine *I-58* and, symbolically, it seemed, scanned the horizon to the setting sun. Yet, oddly, he was almost as elated as the Americans dancing in the streets. For in the last few days, he had finally become "certain" that he had sunk at least one ship for the Emperor.

On August 10, he had sighted a convoy escorted by two destroyers. It was time, Hashimoto reluctantly decided, to keep his promise to the surviving kaitens and send them to a glorious death. This might be their last chance, for he knew that the war was drawing to an end, though he tried to suppress the thought. Three days earlier, his English-speaking diving officer, who had heard the American news on the radio, reported to him that a special type of bomb had been dropped on Hiroshima and that the city had been utterly destroyed. But Hashimoto refused to listen, since such news could only lower his morale and that of his men. Only Toshio Tanaka listened, and the report made him regret even more that he hadn't found the survivors of the sunken "battleship" so that he could personally have machine-gunned them in the water. He pined for another opportunity.

Now, it seemed, he might have it. With the joy of vengeance in his heart, Tanaka, on Hashimoto's orders, sent two kaitens skimming toward immortality. Hashimoto then peered through his periscope and saw only an infinite sea unmarked by any ship. He didn't actually see the two destroyers dive into the depths and, again to Toshio Tanaka's disappointment, he decided not to lose time searching for survivors, but to flee immediately from the other ships in the convoy. Still, at least one of the vessels must have sunk, Hashimoto figured. And Toshio Tanaka agreed, if only to justify the dark gratification he felt. Hashimoto prayed for the souls of the departed warriors, and headed toward home.

Two days later, on August 12, the commander spotted an enemy merchant ship escorted by a destroyer. There were two kaitens left. He picked one, who, blessing his luck, was soon sailing toward the merchantman. But the destroyer apparently saw the kaiten's periscope and made a depth-charge attack. Hashimoto's hands grew "clammy with sweat" as he watched and prayed. An explosion! But who had hit whom? When the water had subsided and the smoke cleared, the merchant vessel was gone. Exultation and relief. Again, no one saw the ship plunge; but surely one of those brave kaitens struck home. The morale of the crew soared, and Hashimoto felt confident once more that he had repaid *chu* to His Imperial Majesty. But his joy was short-lived.

On August 15, the commander was called to the hatch by his communications officer and thought he "had never seen a man so sad."

"Please come down a minute," the officer said.

Hashimoto followed him to the wardroom, where the man drew him into a corner and, handing him a news report, groaned, "Look what's come."

The commander read the report in silence and froze. Japan had surrendered? It couldn't be true, he assured himself, though he had long known this moment was inevitable. It was some newspaper stunt. After all, he'd received nothing official. Trying his best to appear calm, he said: "This may be a broadcast to confuse us. Destroy it! Bring all future dispatches directly to me and don't tell anyone!"

He must not shock the crew, which was in a delirious mood after the last presumed hit. The news of surrender was so disconcerting that it might cause crew members to make a fatal error, menacing them all. Hashimoto returned to the bridge and stared again at the setting sun, churning with mixed feelings—relief, sadness, desperation. Of course that report was true. What should he do now? Return to Japan—and surrender to the enemy? Where else was there to go?

It was futile to flee, he decided; he would continue on to Japan and give up. But he would keep the terrible news secret until the submarine reached home waters and would no longer need to submerge. There was still one kaiten left. Let him scream. Now there was no need for him to die.

Shortly, the communications officer came up with a radio message from general headquarters in Tokyo, and Hashimoto read what he had already surmised. Japan had accepted the Potsdam Declaration demanding surrender.

"DO NOT ATTACK ENEMY EXCEPT IN SELF-DEFENSE," the dispatch ordered.

Hashimoto put down the message and felt he must at least tell his officers. He called them to the bridge and gave them the news, ordering them not to inform the crew. The officers wanted to cry, but no one dared to. Hashimoto now worried about the fate of the Emperor. Would the Americans destroy the soul of Japan? Toshio Tanaka worried about the physical survival of Japan. Would the "barbarians" sack the nation? But Navigator Hirokoto Tanaka had no feeling at all. He didn't worry about things he couldn't control. He had survived, hadn't he? Just as he knew he would. And he would survive under the Americans as well. He was too clever for them.

For Captain McVay, though, the war was not over. He knew a bitter struggle lay ahead, not to save his career—that was certainly over—but to avoid a disgrace that he did not deserve. Almost masochistically, he accepted moral responsibility for the tragedy that he knew would haunt him for the rest of his life; but why should he be a scapegoat for others? From his talks with naval officials in the past few days, he suspected that the Navy he loved was, in fact, about to "betray" him, to use him to cover up negligence in high places. He had to clear his name, not simply for himself, but for his father and Louise. Yet in the end, he found that he could not really fight, for he had been trained since his Annapolis days to accept the Navy's decisions, right or wrong. Otherwise, he would not be worthy of the honor of serving as a naval officer.

As the first witness before the court of inquiry, McVay was asked the obvious questions.

Had the *Indianapolis* zigzagged the night of the disaster?

No, it had not. But the bad weather didn't require it to do so, and no one had warned him about any submarine menace.

Had he given the order to abandon ship?

Yes, but he wasn't sure the order had reached many men, since all communications had broken down.

After McVay described how he had dealt with the crisis, no one, to his relief, offered any hint that he might have acted improperly.

Some of McVay's officers were called and they all supported the captain's testimony, to the extent they knew the facts. When a question was asked about the "ringleader" in their group who stole rations on the rafts, Redmayne and Twible, sticklers for discipline, identified the man and said they wanted him punished. But Blum replied that he knew nothing about it. And eventually, when several witnesses disputed the accusations, the case against the "ringleader" was dropped. Who could tell who might have been hallucinating at the time?

Could Blum confirm a report that someone made sexual advances to men aboard the rafts?

Oh, no, he replied, he didn't know anybody who would do something like that.

Blum had decided that he would volunteer as little information as possible. He suspected that they were looking for a scapegoat, and for all he knew, they were setting him up to be one. Jews, after all, he had been told, weren't too popular in the Navy.

The focus of so many questions on events that took place after the sinking nourished McVay's feeling that the court was perhaps not trying to hang him after all, but would punish the real blunderers. In fact, as he listened to the testimony of others, he noted that there seemed to be relatively little interest in what happened aboard ship. But he was apparently worried about Admiral Murray. Why wasn't he answering questions instead of asking them?

The military witnesses were called to testify one by one, and the sphere of responsibility was tossed from one officer to the next as if it were a football loaded with dynamite.

Officers of the Philippine Sea Frontier Command took the stand:

Commodore Gillette, Captain Granum, Lieutenant Commander Sancho, and Lieutenant Gibson. CINCPAC was at fault, they charged, for although it issued an order *not* to report arrivals of combatant ships, it never mentioned what to do about nonarrivals —so it was "naturally" assumed that they shouldn't be reported either. Sancho, at the same time, pointed out that Gibson, his subordinate, had never told him that the *Indianapolis* was overdue.

Commodore Carter of CINCPAC answered the PSF witnesses: True, an order about nonarrivals had not been issued, but as a matter of common sense they should have been reported by Gibson's office as well as by Admiral McCormick's command.

Admiral McCormick of Task Group 95.7 also lobbed the ball back to the PSF officers: Why didn't *they* keep track of the ship? He himself would have done so, but the cable informing him that the *Indianapolis* was to train under his command was incorrectly decoded by members of his staff and was never delivered to him. Not his fault, of course.

Officers of the Marianas Command, Captain Naquin and Lieutenant Waldron, claimed innocence, too, and were not pressed. Their commander, Admiral Murray, was, of course, one of the judges. Yes, Naquin agreed, he did have information about the four submarines on an offensive mission and the sinking of the *Underhill*, but he still thought that the threat was "negligible." Waldron also thought the threat was negligible—for Naquin never told him about those submarines or the sinking.

No one ashore, it seemed, shared any responsibility for the tragedy.

On August 17, while Captain McVay waited anxiously to learn his fate, Commander Hashimoto waited just as anxiously to learn his. He was distraught as his submarine floated into the special kaiten base on an island off Kure. At last it was time to face the truth.

"Clear lower deck—everybody aft!" he called over the intercom.

When the crew had assembled aft on the upper deck, Hashimoto pulled a sheet of paper from his jacket pocket and, with trembling voice and tears in his eyes, read aloud the Imperial dispatch announcing the end of the war.

Some of the men broke down and wept; some remained inscrutable, trying to hide their feelings; and some seemed relieved that the inevitable had finally happened and they could now go home. When Hashimoto finished reading, only a few muffled sobs broke the silence. Without another word, he boarded a motorboat that took him ashore to report to a senior officer on the valiant deeds of his kaitens, who, except for the one survivor, had been fortunate enough to escape the indignity of defeat.

Hashimoto then sailed on to Kure, where he was met by a group of submarine officers who, despite the Imperial order, were determined to continue the fight. The commander refused to join them. Oppose the Emperor's wishes? Unthinkable!

"We have no more fuel for our submarines," he argued. "So how can we continue? No, His Imperial Majesty has spoken. We have no choice. We must surrender."

The officers were silent, their faces gray with agony. Yes, they finally agreed, there was no choice.

And after reporting to his commanding officer, Hashimoto stepped into a jeep and was driven to his half-destroyed house. He would bring his wife and children out of hiding and try to provide for them as best he could—until the moment of disgrace when *they* would come for him, perhaps to shoot him as a war criminal.

A few days later, on August 20, as the inquiry in Guam drew to an end, Captain McVay declined to make a closing argument. Since he was not accused of anything, there was nothing to deny. The hearing had gone better than he had expected. No charges. No hostile questions. Until this moment, he had been extremely pessimistic, but now he felt that the judges might place the blame where it belonged—on those who had failed to check on the whereabouts of the *Indianapolis*. A court-martial seemed out of the question. America had lost over seven hundred ships in the war, and not one of their skippers had been court-martialed. The judges, no doubt, realized that if they were to single him out, it would be obvious that the Navy was looking for a scapegoat.

McVay thus dared to hope that the velvet-gloved treatment he had so far received at this hearing was a presage of lenience for him, and he was unshaken even when the judge advocate stated unequivocally: "Any officer found negligent should be punished!"

But then, as he sat in the hearing room for the last time, he was shocked to learn that the velvet gloves had an abrasive lining. The judge advocate was piling "fact" upon "fact," building up to a set of "false" conclusions:

- Lieutenant Waldron had warned him of the submarine menace, and yet the captain did not zigzag on the fatal night.
- Visibility was good on that night, making it even more essential for him to zigzag.
- He delayed sending out an SOS message.

McVay sat quietly, listening in disbelief. "The judge advocate was wrong on all three counts!" he cried to himself in bitter rage.

Despite his fury and dismay, McVay clung to a straw of optimism as the court began apportioning the blame. It recommended:

That Lieutenant Gibson be sent a Letter of Admonition, a lesser censure than a reprimand, for failing to report the nonarrival of the *Indianapolis* in Leyte;

That Admiral McCormick be ordered to discipline his staff for not decoding the cable that explained why the *Indianapolis* would be reporting to him.

Although McVay felt that Gibson and McCormick's men, whatever their own responsibility, were being made scapegoats for their gold-braided superiors, the judges, by recognizing that people ashore had made blunders, might conclude that the skipper wasn't responsible for the disaster. Still, this could be wishful thinking, he realized, and the court might well recommend that he, too, be given a letter of censure, demolishing his career, as he had long anticipated.

McVay's surge of optimism *was* wishful. The captain listened in shock as a judge rasped out the court's recommendation in his case: Not only should he receive a Letter of Reprimand, but he should be brought to trial by general court-martial for performing his duties inefficiently and endangering lives through his negligence.

The captain's only thought was, why had he survived the ordeal?—an oft-asked question that now became a masochistic tool of torture. It seemed unimaginable. He would go down in history as the only American skipper ever to be court-martialed for losing his ship in battle—and he was the son of one of the country's greatest admirals. How could he leave for home and face his father? How could he drag him and Louise through the hell of a court-martial trial?

McVay decided to fly to Hawaii and see Admiral Nimitz. Maybe the admiral would understand. He had to understand. But the captain knew how the Navy operated. The senior commanders had to protect their reputations at all costs; the Navy wouldn't allow its top brass to be tarnished. So, for the good of the Navy (and thus the country), he might have to be sacrificed. And perhaps there was justice within this injustice. For was he not, after all, the skipper of hundreds of men now rotting in the sea, half-eaten by sharks?

In early September, all the remaining survivors packed their newly issued gear and got set to leave on the last lap to paradise—home. Most had physically recovered from their terrible ordeal, but many, though no longer hallucinating, were still plagued with recurring nightmares, sometimes waking with sweaty brows and trembling hands. Some even had an urge to violence.

Lieutenant Redmayne, who had thought he entered heaven when he was rescued, now often experienced such moments of hell, intensified by the claustrophobic condition that had dogged him even before the sinking. Yet, as the senior surviving officer still in Guam, he was resolved to return to the United States at the head of the crew. He was still only a lieutenant, but he hadn't forgotten that the Navy owed him a promotion to lieutenant commander, even if he no longer had a ship to power.

When the time came to leave, Redmayne called five ensigns together and issued them orders. Each would be in charge of a busload of about sixty men.

"The buses will take us to the pier," he said. "Make sure everyone is present. They're waiting for us in San Diego and no one must be left behind."

"Yes, sir!"

The buses arrived at the pier and the men soon filed aboard the aircraft carrier *Hollandia*. The public address system then called for muster, and each of the ensigns gathered his men and reported to Redmayne.

Donald Blum, one of them, cried out, "All accounted for, sir."

Redmayne was irritated. This was just like Blum! The lieutenant still thought he might have him court-martialed for "borrowing" one of the rafts during the disaster, even though he himself had approved the move, if reluctantly. Redmayne didn't want anyone accounted for; he wanted to know that everyone was *present*.

"Yes, sir."

Once the *Hollandia* was underway, the ship's doctor informed him that one man in Blum's group hadn't reported to him for a checkup.

Redmayne summoned Blum. Where the hell was that man?

"I'll take care of it, sir."

But the doctor soon complained again, and Redmayne now sent an officer to investigate. Shortly, he gave Redmayne the report: The missing man was still in Guam! Blum had neglected to take muster on his bus.

Enraged, Redmayne gave the news to the ship's captain, who roared, "I'll have Blum court-martialed!"

The captain would have to stand in line, Redmayne thought. But would it be wise to return home as conquering heroes—with one of the few surviving officers in the brig?

Hmm . . . Very well, said the captain when he understood Redmayne's dilemma. Confine him to quarters for ten days.

Yes, a good idea. It was pretty severe punishment, after all.

Well, Redmayne informed Blum with barely suppressed glee, he was finally getting what he deserved. He couldn't move out of his room for ten days.

Blum grinned. Honest? No work? No duties? What a good Navy! A great opportunity to make up for lost sleep. Room service, too.

As he lazily stretched out on his bunk, he wondered what time they would bring him dinner.

Actually, most of the men aboard felt as if they were on a holiday cruise, with only light duties and plenty of time between tasty meals to loll in the sun with beer in hand and home in mind. But there would be no holiday for Adolfo Celaya. His superior kept assigning him to jobs lifting heavy crates, and Celaya was resentful. He suspected that his Mexican heritage singled him out for these arduous assignments, since few whites were given such tasks. Anyway, the heavy work sharpened the pain in his back, which he had injured when jumping from the ship.

Finally, on being assigned to a third hard work detail, he rebelled.

"I can't do any more work," he told his superior. "My back hurts and it's getting worse."

The man sent him under guard to the ship's doctor, who examined him and, ignoring the patient's complaints, concluded there was "nothing wrong" with him.

When Celaya still refused to work, he was given seven days in the brig on a bread-and-water diet.

But they were only two days away from San Diego, Celaya pointed out.

Then he'd finish his term ashore.

Celaya was despondent, and, as he sat in his cell brooding, he relived the five days he had spent in the water with the dead, the wounded, the insane. He could still see his friend bouncing in the swells, waving to him before he sank into the depths. Why hadn't he joined the man? Somehow the vastness of the ocean, the eternal peace it implied, seemed preferable to these ghastly walls that were relentlessly closing in on him, suffocating him, crushing his spirit.

Finally, from the porthole, Celaya could hear music in the distance. San Diego! Home, at last, just as he had imagined while floating half-dead in the water. Actually, not quite as he had imagined. While the others would be greeted by a brass band, he expected to be greeted by machine guns.

.   .   .

"California, here we come . . ." The brass band on the San Diego dock beat out the strains of this nostalgic song as the survivors moved down the gangplank on the sunny afternoon of September 26. They were embraced by WAVES, accosted by reporters, surrounded by military and city officials, then lifted into jeeps for a parade that crawled down Broadway.

The crowds were disappointing, for San Diegans had been given little notice of the homecoming. But no matter. To Redmayne, who sat in the lead vehicle waving his cap to the people, even a *little* adulation seemed like an impossible dream come true. Only a few weeks earlier, he had been in a virtual coma in the middle of the ocean, hours away from death, and now he was being welcomed home like a conquering admiral. Maybe this was heaven after all.

The procession drove on to Camp Elliot, and, after a few days of processing there, Redmayne and most of the others were free to go home on a month's leave.

Giles McCoy had an especially happy homecoming. When his train pulled into the St. Louis station, he saw his parents searching for him amid the teeming crowds on the platform. His mother stared at him as he approached. Was that her son? She hardly recognized him. Thirty pounds underweight, with his recently oil-coated head shaven, he just didn't look like Giles. But then they fell into each other's arms, while his father "felt him all over" to see if he was "in one piece." An official telegram had informed the parents that their son had suffered only from "submersion," and Giles himself had assured them on the phone that he was "fine"—but why not make sure?

"Son, you're skinny," his mother sobbed, "but don't worry, I'll fatten you up."

And then home, where McCoy gorged himself on pumpkin pie. It tasted even better than the imaginary kind that had helped to keep him alive in the water.

But there would be no pie for Adolfo Celaya—only bread and water. He had been escorted off the ship as a prisoner under guard, and placed in a barracks in the camp. In the morning, however, he ate breakfast in the mess hall with the other survivors and was overjoyed. Apparently, he was being set free; they must have finally realized that they had made a mistake. But then an officer approached him.

"Celaya, come with me," he ordered. "I'm taking you to the brig."

Celaya was horrified. Five more days in the brig?

"No, seven more. The two on the ship didn't count. You're starting all over."

Celaya was thrust into an eight-foot-square cage made of chicken wire, and again put on the skimpy prison diet. Gradually, his starved body, already enfeebled by the ordeal at sea, grew weaker. In the water, he had managed to remain sane even among the insane, but by the sixth day in the cage he began to slip. He felt humiliated, abandoned. They hadn't even the decency to put him in a real cell intended for human beings. Instead, they had thrown him into a "chicken coop"—as if he were a creature without mind or feelings, raised for slaughter. He would prove that he had feelings.

Ripping some wires from the cage, he twisted them into a noose, but when he tried to hang himself, he found that the wire ceiling was too low. The final humiliation—they wouldn't even let him die with dignity.

The next day, in desperation, Celaya called for a chaplain.

"Help me, Father!" he pleaded. And he told him his story.

"You only have a day to go," the priest said sympathetically. "You must hold on."

He then slipped Celaya some cookies, adding, "Keep your mind occupied. Think of someone you love."

And that night, Celaya thought of his horse, his boyhood companion. He even talked to the animal.

"Where are you now?" he asked.

"Don't worry about me, I'm all right," the horse replied. "They haven't taken me to the glue factory yet."

And then Celaya spoke to one of his cows.

"Now don't move . . . and give me lots of cream, please."

How good the milk tasted.

. . .

At home in Washington, D.C., Captain McVay, languishing in a limbo of uncertainty, was almost as depressed as Adolfo Celaya. His wife Louise had greeted him with love and compassion, and his father had, too, in his own way. The son felt greatly relieved when this rigid-minded admiral, who had coldly presided over the ruination of many a Navy man for committing even minor offenses, assured him of his solid support. Yet the captain was apparently chagrined by the unfamiliar look of sadness, even grief, in his father's eyes, eyes that had seldom reflected emotion before.

The captain had seen Admiral Nimitz in Pearl Harbor and explained his innocent role in the disaster, and Nimitz had seemed sympathetic. But McVay remembered times when he himself had been sympathetic to men accused of some offense, even as he ordered their punishment. He grew fatalistic. As he would tell *The New York Times*: "I was in command of the ship and I am responsible for its fate. I hope they make their decision soon and do what they want to with me."

While McVay could sometimes avoid his father's gaze, he couldn't avoid the gaze of those who had lost loved ones in the tragedy, and he envisioned them staring at him, many not simply with sadness, but with terrible hatred. He dreaded to read the letters from parents, wives, sweethearts that were stacked high on his desk, and he shook every time the telephone rang, especially on holidays. Like the howls of wounded wolves, the voices echoed incessantly in his psyche:

"Merry Christmas. Ours won't be merry because you killed our son."

"Why did you survive while my husband didn't?"

"God will punish you for this crime."

Shattered by such recriminations, his soul churning with qualms of guilt though his mind pleaded innocent, McVay would cry, "Oh, goddamnit! Why are they doing this to me?"

Louise tried to comfort him. It was natural, she assured him. They were half-mad with grief, and had to vent it somewhere. She helped him to cope with these attacks, and to ease his own suffering.

The captain would sit down and answer every loved one, even the angriest and the most desperate. To the widow of Casey Moore, the damage control officer he had sent below to help put out the fires, he wrote:

"Your mourning is for your husband . . . I mourn for all the men. During our leave . . . I grew to know wives and children, and I grieve for them. All those days [in the water] I called the roll in my mind and I could see every single man. So shall I see them every day of my life, and I am sure my punishment will be that I will live a long, long time."

But there was little he could say to the bereaved that would ease their misery and rage. He could not answer the most agonizing question of all: Why did this have to happen? Perhaps it would take his court-martial to give them peace, and help him to find peace, too.

No parent was wounded more deeply than Thomas D'Arcy Brophy, the father of Tom Jr., who had vanished in the ocean as he tried in his madness to swim to Lieutenant Marks' seaplane. Brophy could not accept his beloved son's death. Engraved in his mind was that moment he called his office and learned the tragic news, then staggered out of the roadside phone booth feeling that he himself had died. A boy so brilliant, so handsome, so popular. And now he was gone.

How had Tom died? To find out, Brophy sought out as many survivors as he could. One man, feeling sympathy for the father, spoke admiringly of the son. Tom had died a hero, trying to help others. The father felt a touch of relief. Yes, that was Tom. But he had to learn more about how he died—and why.

Rushing to Washington from his home in New York, he burst into McVay's temporary office at the Navy Department and demanded to speak with the captain. But McVay, already reeling from the brutal letters and phone calls plaguing him day and night, apparently felt he could not face another bereaved accuser that day. Besides, in his moody moments, he could be aloof, even snobbish.

He had an important engagement, McVay told Brophy, and couldn't see him at that time. Brophy trailed him in his car, and was enraged to find that the "important engagement" was a cocktail party. He had wanted to discuss the death of his boy with "the man who killed him," and the man had brushed him aside so he wouldn't be late to a party!

He would destroy McVay, Brophy vowed. And he set out to do so, using his ample political clout. He released his fury on Navy Secretary Forrestal and other authorities, and even on President Truman. McVay would later tell Harlan Twible that Brophy, according to his sources, had "used all his leverage" to get Truman to make sure that he was court-martialed.

Whatever Truman's reaction, there were receptive ears in the capital, and McVay began to suspect this when Twible this time furnished *him* with information. After recovering at home from his injuries, Twible had been assigned to the naval gun factory in Washington, where he met an old acquaintance—Admiral King's son, Ernest Jr., or Joe. And Twible repeated Joe's words to the captain —words that Joe King today denies he uttered:

"My dad's going to get McVay."

Admiral Nimitz had a different view, which crystallized about the time Captain McVay arrived in Washington in early September: McVay was a good officer and did not deserve to have his career destroyed. He may have made mistakes—but who didn't? After all, Admiral King had indicated that he was unhappy with Nimitz's own role in the *Indianapolis* tragedy. And Nimitz apparently realized that he should have ordered his staff to clarify the rules for reporting nonarrivals, an order he belatedly issued now. But if he rejected the recommendations of the inquiry panel, he seemed to fear, he might be accused of trying to weasel out of his own share of the blame.

Still, Nimitz felt that he could not in fairness order the court-martial of McVay. He had not court-martialed any of the hundreds of other commanders who had lost ships during the war, some under questionable circumstances. The only charge that could reasonably be made against McVay was negligence due to his failure to have his ship zigzag. And even this charge would be dubious, for the routing orders given him in Guam left the matter of zigzagging to his discretion, and such orders took precedence over the Navy's standing rule, which made zigzagging mandatory. Thus, he would be guilty only of bad judgment, if he was guilty at all. And bad judgment was not normally an offense that called for a court-martial.

No, he wouldn't make an exception now. And so, on September 6, Nimitz wrote a letter to the Judge Advocate General of the Navy:

> The Commander in Chief, U.S. Pacific Fleet, does not agree with the court in its recommendation that Captain Charles B. McVay III, U.S. Navy, be brought to trial by general court-martial. . . . His failure to order a zigzag course was an error in judgment, but not of such nature as to constitute gross negligence. Therefore, a Letter of Reprimand will be addressed to Captain McVay in lieu of a general court-martial.

At the same time, Nimitz ordered that a Letter of Reprimand also be issued to Lieutenant Gibson for the "careless and inefficient manner in which [he] performed [his] duties," and that a less severe Letter of Admonition be sent to Gibson's boss, Lieutenant Commander Sancho. Nimitz was softer on Admiral McCormick, who would, in fact, shortly be promoted from rear admiral to vice admiral. He was simply required, as the court of inquiry had recommended, to discipline his staff for not decoding the cable that informed McCormick why the *Indianapolis* would be reporting to him.

When Admiral King read the letter regarding McVay, he was perturbed. Nimitz, he apparently felt, did not realize that the good name of the Navy was at stake, that perhaps the biggest scandal in its history could leave an indelible smudge on its impeccable image. Something had to be done to resolve the crisis. The bereaved relatives, especially Brophy, were knocking on all the doors in Washington, demanding punishment for those responsible. And at the head of their list was the most visible culprit, the captain of the ship, who had dared to survive. But if McVay was a cause of the crisis, perhaps he could be a solution as well.

McVay, King seems to have thought, would understand the ne-
cessity of sacrifice. He had, after all, admitted that his ship was not
zigzagging when it was hit. Nor could King ignore the implications
of McVay's remark after his rescue that somebody in the Navy had
fouled up by not ordering a search for survivors. Such a charge clearly
could lead to trouble.

In any case, King decided on a move that, if successful, could
demolish Captain McVay. And he began the demolition process on
September 25, when he wrote Secretary Forrestal:

> I cannot agree with the opinion of Commander-in-Chief, U.S. Pa-
> cific Fleet, that the failure of Captain McVay to order a zigzag course
> was an error in judgment. . . . I recommend that the Secretary of the
> Navy direct the following action: Captain Charles B. McVay be brought
> to trial by general court-martial in accordance with recommendation
> 1.A of Court of Inquiry in this case.

And since the facts emerging at the Guam hearings were skeletal,
King urged that a full-scale investigation of the disaster be held to
add some flesh to the bones.

It would be very embarrassing if Captain McVay was exonerated
simply because the evidence did not carry enough weight.

Secretary Forrestal pondered his dilemma with the same cautious
wiliness he had once displayed as a boxer. He had to avoid a scandal
that might threaten his chances of keeping the Navy independent.
But would the court-martial of Captain McVay, which Admiral King
recommended, help the cause, or hurt it? The press would highlight
it for weeks, relentlessly drilling the Navy's greatest blunder into
the public's mind—and into the President's as well.

On the other hand, if there was no court-martial, people might
focus their anger on the admirals—and himself. Tom Brophy had
certainly made it clear: The bereaved families would not rest until
the "guilty" were punished.

Nor did Forrestal seem confident that the "thorough investigation" King also recommended would serve his purpose. What if he
authorized the court-martial of McVay and the facts unearthed ab-

solved him of serious negligence? After all, Admiral Nimitz didn't believe the man's offenses called for a court-martial. The Navy would be accused of trying to make McVay a scapegoat, possibly further jeopardizing its future.

Complicating Forrestal's dilemma was his reluctance to defy Admiral King and his other top military advisers. Finally, Vice Admiral Louis Denfield, Chief of Naval Personnel, suggested to the Secretary a way to avoid embarrassment if any new facts unearthed exonerated McVay: Hold off on his trial until the investigation was completed.

When King approved this idea on November 10, Forrestal concurred. It did seem the fairest—and safest—thing to do. He called his special assistant, Edward Hidalgo, into his office and, characteristically pointing a finger at him, said: "Eddie, I've been reading about the McVay case in the papers. We don't need that kind of publicity. Do whatever you can to put an end to it. Find out the truth. Work with Forrest to get rid of this sensationalism."

He would do his best, Hidalgo replied.

And shortly, he met with Vice Admiral Forrest Sherman, Chief of Naval Operations for Air, and Admiral C. P. Snyder, the Navy Inspector General, to plan a new full-scale inquiry.

But that same day, King had second thoughts, perhaps feeling that if the investigation should exonerate McVay, the troublemakers might demand that someone else be punished. In any case, only hours after he had advised Forrestal to delay McVay's trial until the inquiry had ended, he penciled a memo to Snyder: "Comment on the feasibility of bringing C. O. *Indianapolis* to trial *now.*"

Snyder replied: "Captain McVay feels that due to the exhaustive manner in which this office is conducting its investigation, additional facts favorable to his case may be developed. Should you desire to bring Captain McVay to trial before my investigation is completed, it is, in my opinion, entirely feasible to do so."

Two days later, on November 12, King got in touch with Forrestal, and the Secretary reluctantly agreed that, given the extraordinary circumstances, the court-martial of Captain McVay should proceed without delay.

XIII

For the Good of the Navy

I'M CAPTAIN RYAN, and you are going to testify against Captain McVay!"

Captain Thomas J. Ryan, Jr., the short, cocky, forty-four-year-old judge advocate who would prosecute Captain McVay and conduct the trial, addressed Giles McCoy, one of the men sent to Washington after his leave was over to testify at the court-martial. Ryan, a lawyer who headed the Department of Ordnance and Gunnery at Annapolis, was known as an easygoing, fun-loving Irishman who loved liquor as well as law, but he took this job seriously. For beneath the carefree veneer, according to some associates, was a simmering ambition.

Yes, he was a friend and former classmate of McVay's, and he hated to ruin the man's career. But he had his own to consider. He had already won two Navy Crosses as a destroyer squadron commander in the New Georgia and Russell Island campaigns, and he would shortly take command of the cruiser USS *Providence*. Now, a victory in a case so crucial to his superiors could open the road to the top. If McCoy was smart, he would play the Navy game, too. But McCoy was too honest to be smart.

"No, you're wrong," he replied. "I think a lot of Captain McVay. He is my skipper and I'm not going to testify against him."

Ryan's pink face turned red. McVay was being charged on two

217

counts: failing to zigzag during good weather, and waiting too long to order the crew to abandon ship. And all Ryan wanted McCoy to say was that there had been no call to abandon ship.

Did McCoy hear the call? he asked.

McCoy was cautious. "There was so much noise," he responded, "that I couldn't have heard a bugle if someone had blown it in my ear."

The red tint grew deeper. "You're still in the service, McCoy," Ryan snapped, "and I am a Navy captain."

But McCoy wouldn't be intimidated. Only hours before, he had been in a barroom brawl with some sailors who had made disparaging remarks about the Marines, and he had had to have a cut over his eye stitched. Anyway, after surviving five days of horror in the waters of the Pacific, he felt he could survive anything.

"I've been through a lot," he said. "So do what you want with me."

Ryan softened his tone and shoved a sheet of paper across his desk. It stated that there had been no call to abandon ship. "This is what I want you to say," he ordered.

But McCoy would not budge.

"Then get out," Ryan barked. "I'll see you later when you take the oath."

On departing, McCoy, his face morose, asked a Marine officer who had accompanied him: "I think the captain is going to cause me trouble if I don't read his testimony. Could he court-martial me?"

"We won't let that happen," said the officer.

Nevertheless, McCoy felt betrayed. He had been proud to fight for his country, and now some of the top military officers wanted to make his skipper a scapegoat to cover up their own blunders. This wasn't the kind of justice for which so many of his buddies had died.

Captain Ryan was agitated, too. A Marine Pfc had refused to buckle under to him, to a man who held not only two Navy Crosses but the Congressional Medal of Honor and the Legion of Merit. The Medal of Honor was awarded to him for his courageous role in saving people during the 1923 earthquake that destroyed Tokyo, where the Navy had sent him to learn Japanese. He had carried many victims to safety, including one young woman he snatched from a bath in a burning hotel.

The Navy leaders, some people thought, had chosen Ryan to prosecute this case because of his many medals, which would presumably give the prosecution the greatest possible credibility. And Ryan was grateful for their faith in him. But it was clear that he couldn't depend on McVay's crewmen to testify as he wished. Whom could he depend on? Perhaps the man who sank the ship. McVay had admitted that his vessel had not been zigzagging; the Japanese commander could confirm that this "blunder" had made the *Indianapolis* an easy target. His dramatic presence might be the key to McVay's conviction. A Japanese officer would have no reason to protect an American commander, and would probably be afraid to displease the prosecuting authorities anyway.

Ryan's superiors agreed that the man could be a valuable witness. Although McVay, his lawyers, and the press might object to having a Japanese officer take the stand at the court-martial of an American officer, Ryan could explain that the man would not testify *against* the captain, but would simply verify some important facts. With the stakes so high, almost any gamble, it seemed, was worth taking.

An urgent message thus went out from Admiral King's office to U.S. naval headquarters in Tokyo: Find the commander of the submarine that sank the *Indianapolis* and bring him to Washington immediately!

Though the war had been over for three months, Commander Hashimoto was still in charge of the submarine *I-58*. Now, finally, he had taken the craft from Kure, where it had been docked, to Sasebo for transfer to the Americans. Since his partially ruined house in Kure was still habitable, he had until now slept and eaten at home while spending the day aboard the submarine, which he used as an office.

Many of Hashimoto's men, including Toshio Tanaka and Hirokoto Tanaka, had been living on the craft, either because their homes had been destroyed or because they were needed to help the commander make out numerous reports for American naval inspectors, who wanted to know every detail about the makeup and missions of the Japanese submarine fleet. Finally, the reports were completed, and it was time to take leave of the boat that symbolized to them the last remnant of a lost glory.

Hashimoto had written honest accounts, even though many of his friends feared that if he revealed which submarine had attacked which target, as he was instructed to do, he and perhaps others would be charged with war crimes.

Nonsense! Hashimoto replied, though privately wondering whether they could be right. Sinking an enemy ship was a normal action of war. The Americans he had met were reasonable men, and they would not consider this a war crime. He had even told them how he had sunk a battleship of the *Idaho* class. Why should he hide this? He was proud of this achievement—though deep in his mind doubt still lingered. Could the "battleship" have escaped?

The Americans now realized that he had, in fact, sunk a ship, but that the "battleship" had really been a cruiser—the *Indianapolis*. So when Captain Henri Smith-Hutton, an intelligence officer in Tokyo, was ordered to find the commander of the mystery submarine, he called in Rear Admiral Nakamura, the Japanese in charge of naval demilitarization, and relayed the order: Find Hashimoto.

Nakamura was alarmed. Was Hashimoto to be charged with war crimes?

No, Smith-Hutton replied, he was simply to be a witness at the court-martial of an American naval officer.

Nakamura, though incredulous that a Japanese would be called to testify at the trial of an enemy officer, soon located Hashimoto in Sasebo, where he was arranging to transfer his submarine to the Americans. And later that day, November 27, the *I-58* commander was reading the admiral's telegram: "PREPARE FOR A TRIP TO WASHINGTON TO APPEAR AT MILITARY TRIAL AS WITNESS. LEAVE FOR TOKYO URGENTLY WITH ALL BATTLE REPORTS."

Hashimoto was perplexed. Was this a trick? Was he really to be a witness—or a defendant? He placed his trust in the gods. Leaving

Toshio Tanaka in charge of the submarine, he returned to his home in Kure; his wife, wondering whether she would ever see him again, silently packed the few white shirts he had. Then he was off to Kyoto to see his parents, before continuing on to Tokyo.

By the time Hashimoto arrived three days later, Nakamura and other Japanese naval officials in the capital were frantic.

"We thought you had run away," Nakamura said. "Do you want to get us all into trouble?"

Hashimoto apologized. Why, he asked, was he being sent to the United States as a witness?

Because, he was told, he had sunk a cruiser—the *Indianapolis*—and the captain of the ship was being court-martialed. The *Indianapolis*? Hashimoto had never heard of it. So it wasn't a battleship after all. Well, at least he now knew for sure that he hadn't gone through the war without sinking a single ship. And a cruiser, after all, wasn't bad.

For all his rush, Hashimoto spent three more days in Tokyo while the Americans arranged for a flight; finally, escorted by an American officer, he stepped aboard a C-54. It was just after midnight—December 7. Exactly four years earlier, he had set out on another voyage to America—as a proud "conqueror"; now he was making the same trip as a humiliated "prisoner." He wished he could understand the logic of the gods.

A few days earlier, on December 3, Captain McVay awakened in his apartment on a cold, cloudy morning and must have wondered about the logic of *his* God. The day that he had once hoped to avoid through a swift, heroic death had finally come. Today his court-martial would begin, and death would come slowly.

But McVay worried more about Louise, for he knew that she agonized as deeply as he did over the tragic events that had poisoned their lives. When he had left San Francisco on the fateful voyage, he imagined returning to share with her an admiral's future, filled with joy and promise. But now, even if he was exonerated, nothing would be the same. The harsh reality was that most of his men had died on a ship he commanded; even if the desperate letters stopped coming and the hysterical phone calls ceased, their faces would flash though his mind forever as a reminder that he must never again know peace.

Adding to his misery was the sight of his battle-hardened father weeping; the admiral could not even bear to come to court. And the old man's agony was all the greater since the trial would take place in the Washington Navy Yard that had once been under his command. Nor would the captain's two sons be there to help comfort their father. Charles IV was studying at Stanford (after making up for his poor high school record), and Kimo was still in the Army, based in Hawaii.

Louise made sure that her husband's Navy blues were impeccably pressed, his shoes immaculately shined. He must show the world that he was a proud perfectionist, a man incapable of the kind of negligence he was being charged with. Pale but composed, McVay left the apartment with Louise at about 9:30 A.M., and they were soon speeding across the city in a taxi, which dropped them in the Washington Navy Yard in front of Building 57, the site of the trial.

Normally, courts-martial were held in secret, but not this one. The public must know that the culprit responsible for the *Indianapolis* tragedy would be punished if found guilty. About a fourth of the spectators' seats in the makeshift courtroom were filled with curious people who would have the rare opportunity to see a military officer humiliated. Louise seated herself toward the front, and McVay strode to the defense table, where he sat tensely twisting his class ring while conferring with his chief counsel, Captain John P. Cady, a tall, congenial man with quizzical eyes and a pleasant smile.

Actually, Cady's smile was rather forced now, for he found little joy in this assignment. He was not asked whether he wanted this case; he was ordered to take it simply because he happened to be available. An Annapolis graduate, he had received a law degree from George Washington University in 1932 but had failed the bar examination, having been too busy on sea assignment to study seriously for it. Now a staff officer working in Washington, he found that he didn't really want to be a lawyer, certainly not in this case, which would place him and his modest legal qualifications in the public spotlight.

Still, the Navy apparently felt that if a brilliant, ambitious lawyer like Captain Ryan was needed to prosecute McVay, a reluctant law graduate like Captain Cady, with just enough legal training to pass as a lawyer, was an acceptable choice to defend McVay. The defendant himself didn't object to Cady. Almost any lawyer, he thought, could present the facts of the case, for they were obvious enough. Anyway, the Navy would act not on the facts, but in its perceived best interests. McVay had to agree, as a Navy traditionalist, that these interests were far more important than the interests of any individual.

As soon as the court had filed in, Cady, a chain-smoker, snuffed out his cigarette, stood up, and, with a calculated sense of indignation, objected to the trial. The accusation that McVay hadn't given the order to zigzag, he fiercely argued, stated only a conclusion, not an offense.

"Overruled!" responded the court. The charges were "in due form."

Cady then asked for more time "to properly prepare the case for the defense," and the court adjourned until the next day. McVay was relieved. One more day to recover from the shock of final realization that everything he held dear in life was in the balance; one more day to ready himself for a punishment that he knew would be unjust, yet somehow deserved.

The following day, McVay was in court again, less pale now and perhaps slightly more confident, for the first day's exposure to the trial had strangely proved less terrifying than the anticipation of it. The men who were accusing him, it seemed, were almost as frightened and vulnerable as he. And if they lost, they could not even console themselves with the thought that defeat might actually help to purge their souls.

McVay faced the seven judges and pleaded not guilty to all charges. Then the first witness for the prosecution was called— Lieutenant Waldron, who had given Captain McVay his routing instructions in Guam and had just flown in from there.

RYAN: Was the question of zigzagging discussed with McVay?

WALDRON: [It was] discussed with the navigator [Commander Janney], and indication was made that the ship should zigzag at the commanding officer's discretion.

The cross-examination began.

CADY: What was your reply to Captain McVay's request for an escort from Captain Naquin's office?

WALDRON: The reply was, "Escort not needed by the *Indianapolis*."

CADY: Were the enemy contacts shown in the intelligence brief as given . . . greater in number or about as usual?

WALDRON: They were about normal; on the average of three or four a week.

CADY: Did they indicate to you any excessive enemy submarine activity?

WALDRON: No, sir; they didn't.

CADY: I take it that, in your opinion, at the time of your discussion with Captain McVay, the passage from Guam to be routed according to your instructions was a perfectly normal and routine situation.

WALDRON: At the time, it was routine.

McVay was pleased. The first prosecution witness confirmed his claim: He had been led to believe that the fatal voyage would be perfectly routine and that the dangers would not be great, justifying to a large degree his decision not to zigzag.

Shortly, Lieutenant McKissick was taking the oath. He had flown home in the same plane that had let McVay off in Hawaii, and had since recovered from his madness.

RYAN: As officer of the deck on the night of the sinking, did you receive any orders while you were on watch?

McKISSICK: Yes, sir. I received orders from the captain the latter part of my watch that at the end of evening twilight we would cease zigzagging and resume base course.

Now Cady interrogated the witness.

CADY: Did you question the orders . . . to stop zigzagging at the time they were given to you?

McKissick: No, sir. I did not question the orders . . . I didn't feel like it was anything unusual. . . . At the time I came off watch, there was no moon. The visibility was very poor. It was a very dark night. . . . At times . . . it was impossible to recognize men that were standing five to ten feet of you, [but] at other times the visibility seemed to be better.

Cady: Was it customary on the ship to cease zigzagging after evening twilight?

McKissick: Well, yes, sir, it was customary, if the visibility was poor . . . ; we did it all during the war.

Cady: Can you testify whether or not the standing orders contained any instructions to the officer of the deck to notify the captain in case of any change in weather conditions, visibility, or so on?

McKissick: I can testify definitely that those instructions were in the standing night orders. . . . I had no hesitation . . . in notifying the captain of such events. . . . It was my practice.

However, on that night McKissick saw nothing significant to report to the captain. He noted no meteorological change or any danger in the sighting of an enemy submarine about two hundred miles away, as reported in the dispatch he had seen while on duty.

McKissick (continuing): We received dispatches all through the war much to the same effect. When any of [the submarines] were that far away, we didn't feel unduly alarmed at such a report.

Cady: Did you hear an order to abandon ship?

McKissick: No, I didn't.

Cady: Did this mean that such an order could not have been given?

McKissick: No, sir. That order could very definitely have been given and I would not hear it. . . . [In any event, the men] had ample time to get topside and prepare to abandon the ship.

McVay's face brightened. Another good witness.

As Lieutenant Redmayne was called to testify, his eyes still reflected signs of the terror that so often gripped him in his sleep.

Ryan: What was the weather on the night of July 29?

Redmayne: It was intermittent moonlight, with the visibility good when the clouds weren't in front of the moon, and the visibility poor when the clouds were in front of the moon.

Cady moved in for the cross-examination.

> CADY: Did it appear to you that you should have been zigzagging?
> REDMAYNE: No, sir.
> CADY: Were you concerned when Commander Janney reported to you and other officers that a hunter-killer team was searching for an enemy submarine ahead?
> REDMAYNE: No, I wasn't particularly worried about it.

The lieutenant seemed agitated by the intensity of the grilling. Now he was being asked about the engine room. Why did he leave it? Ryan wanted to know, apparently trying to show that McVay had not made a vigorous enough effort to communicate with him —and possibly seeking to discredit his own witness for giving answers less than helpful to his cause.

> REDMAYNE: I left the engine room because we had no communications with the bridge, and I did not know what the captain wanted done with the engines.

The judge advocate relentlessly pursued his quarry.

> RYAN: Were the conditions in that engine room at the time you left sufficiently desperate for you, on your own initiative, to tell your men to abandon the only remaining safe source of power on that ship?
> REDMAYNE: I didn't consider the conditions bad enough for the engine room to be abandoned.

The nightmare continued even in the day.
Dr. Haynes was a more relaxed witness.

> RYAN: Did you hear or receive any orders concerning "abandon ship" which would normally have emanated from the captain or the officer of the deck?
> HAYNES: No, I did not.

The cross-examination:

> CADY: Could the word have been passed to prepare to abandon ship without you having heard it?
> HAYNES: Yes, it could have.

The doctor recalled how Commander Janney had "jokingly" remarked at the dinner table "that we were going to pass by a submarine during the night. . . . It was the usual jovial conversation you have around a wardroom table."

> CADY: What were the conditions of visibility?
> HAYNES: I didn't notice; I believe it was very dark . . . I would like to say that under Captain McVay's command, the *Indianapolis* was a very efficient, trim fighting ship, and I would be honored and pleased to serve under him again.

Perhaps the most succinct witness was Ensign Blum, who was still determined to say as little as possible for fear of somehow making a scapegoat out of himself.

The prosecution began gently:

> RYAN: Did anything unusual occur during the night of 29–30 July, 1945? If so, what was it?
> BLUM: The ship sank.
> RYAN: Did you at any time receive any word or orders to abandon ship?
> BLUM: No.

Cady, curiously, did not ask him if the order might have been given without his hearing it—and Blum wasn't volunteering anything. Nor did Cady succeed in eliciting even the most general information.

> CADY: Did you see any moon from your station?
> BLUM: I don't remember.
> CADY: Did you see any moonlight?
> BLUM: I don't remember that.
> CADY: Was it cloudy?
> BLUM: I don't remember that.

The court reporter would report:
"The judge advocate did not desire to reexamine this witness."
"The court did not desire to examine this witness."
"The witness said that he had nothing further to state."
"The witness was duly warned and withdrew."

And the courtroom resounded silently, it seemed, with a collective sigh. How did a man so devoid of memory ever become a naval officer? Blum might have answered: By knowing what to forget and when to shut up.

Giles McCoy had a better memory, though he wished he hadn't. He would tell the truth, while portraying the skipper in the best possible light. As he expected, the prosecution was icy.

> RYAN: Did you ever have, during this period from the explosions and when you were going over the side, any occasion to notice the weather or visibility conditions?
>
> McCoy: Yes, sir. When I was going over the side . . . I guess the clouds just cleared the moon, and it was bright.

The implication was that visibility wasn't good before he went over the side.

Apparently with their pretrial encounter in mind, Ryan avoided asking McCoy whether he had heard an order to abandon ship, or whether such an order might have been issued without McCoy hearing it.

Cady, however, did refer to the issue.

> CADY: Did you hear any word passed through the brig compartment, "All hands, topside," or words to that effect?
>
> McCoy: No, sir.

But he wasn't given the chance to add what he had said at his meeting with Ryan—that in all the chaos he couldn't have heard "a bugle if it were blown in my ear."

It was now that memory became especially painful.

> CADY: Were any other people in the [brig] compartment with you?
>
> McCoy: Well, yes, sir, there was people sleeping down there.
>
> CADY: Did you notice whether they were still there when you left?
>
> McCoy: Yes, sir, they were starting up the ladder, sir.

McCoy did not add that some were too badly injured to be carried up before the hatch was closed.

Ensign Twible, when questioned, had no doubts about the weather.

TWIBLE: When I had gone on watch, it was quite light, but later on in the evening it got so dark that I had to request that the gun captain inform me if there was a man on the shield looking out over the sea, and . . . when it came time for me to be relieved and my relief didn't get up there, I looked down towards the quarterdeck and noticed . . . shapes down there, but I couldn't tell whether it was one man or two.

CADY: Did you see any moon that night on watch?

TWIBLE: I can't recall that I did. . . . There were breaks in the clouds, because I can definitely remember seeing the moon after I got into the water, but I could say that the sky was heavily overcast.

CADY: Were you able to see the horizon?

TWIBLE: No, sir, I wasn't.

Nor did Twible hear any word to abandon ship—except his own. He had passed the word on his "own initiative."

But if many didn't hear McVay give the order, one person who did was Coxswain Edward Keyes, who had been sent below to call all the men to topside.

CADY: Keyes, did you observe the captain give the order to abandon ship?

KEYES: Yes. . . .

After he had returned to the bridge from below, Keyes said, the captain "hollered down . . . for the men to abandon ship."

When Captain Naquin took the oath, the defense attorney took aim.

CADY: Why did the *Indianapolis* sail from Guam without escort?

Naquin never got to answer, for Ryan objected to "this line of questioning on the ground that such testimony was incompetent, irrelevant, immaterial, and not germane to the issues in this case." In other words, it seemed the finger might point not at McVay, but at less dispensable commanders.

Objection sustained! the court ruled.

The defense was thus forced to take a different tack.

CADY: What was your estimate of the risk of enemy submarine activity along the Peddie route?

NAQUIN: I would say that it was a very low order. . . . The risk was very slight. . . . There were literally dozens of [reports], but the actual submarine activity against us was at a very low ebb.

CADY: Was there at any time any question in your mind of diverting the *Indianapolis* after she sailed?

NAQUIN: There was not.

Later, Ryan asked Captain Granum about the submarine danger.

GRANUM: There was no more than a normal hazard that could be expected in wartime.

The defense attorney trod carefully in his cross-examination.

CADY: Was there ever any actual confirmation of the presence of an enemy submarine in the Philippine Sea Frontier at about this time along the Peddie route?

GRANUM: In this area, no.

The question arose whether zigzagging was really necessary to avoid enemy torpedoes. Cady called to the stand Captain Glynn Robert Donaho, a veteran submarine commander whose boat had sunk or damaged twenty-eight enemy vessels during the war.

CADY: Based on your experience, what is your opinion of the value of zigzagging of a target as affecting the accuracy of torpedo fire?

DONAHO: With our modern submarines, fire-control equipment, high-speed torpedoes, a well-trained control party, and with torpedo spreads, I didn't find that zigzagging affected the results.

Ryan was dismayed by this reply. In his cross-examination he moved relentlessly from one question to the next.

RYAN: Now, assuming that [a] target was making seventeen knots [and changing course by 45 degrees] and that you felt that you could not come to the surface and chase, when do you think you would have had another chance to fire at this target?

DONAHO: It takes five seconds to make an observation, and about five seconds for the integration to take effect, and I could have fired within 10 seconds.

RYAN: Now . . . we have assumed that this target makes a change of course of 45 degrees. Assuming that that had been away from you, would your spread have been as likely to hit as if it had not turned?

DONAHO: Yes, sir.

Captain Ryan was clearly frustrated. He would make a final attempt to shake his witness's testimony.

RYAN: Is it a reasonable inference from what you have just said that zigzagging as an antisubmarine measure is of no value to surface ships?

DONAHO: On the contrary, you always expect a target to zig, and you anticipate what is going to happen on the next leg. I have personally found that a target not zigzagging would have confused me.

Ryan sat down, apparently wondering why he had asked that last question. But to his obvious relief, he received help from Cady. Just as it appeared that the defense had been given an enormous boost, Cady inexplicably asked a question he, too, no doubt wished later he had not posed.

CADY: Is it disconcerting to you as a submarine commander to have a ship, a target, zigzag?

DONAHO: Yes, because just before firing, a zigzag throws your calculations off, and you have to get a new setup.

But, though Donaho appeared to contradict himself on this point, he made it clear that zigzagging would not have prevented a hit.

While still somewhat dubious that anyone's testimony would decisively influence the court officers, Captain McVay exuded renewed confidence when he was called upon to testify.

CADY: Did you give any instructions regarding zigzagging to the officer of the deck before turning in?

McVAY: I did not. The conditions were such that I did not believe that zigzagging was necessary. Visibility was poor. There was no moon. . . . I had in my standing orders the conditions under which the ship should zigzag, though I did not specifically have in there to start zigzagging when . . . the visibility was good. [In any case], I got no impression [in Guam] of any unusual conditions in the area. . . . I considered the supervisor and officer of the deck . . . that night competent officers, and I believe that if conditions had been such as to require them to zigzag, they would have done so and informed me.

CADY: Then your doctrine as laid out in your standing night orders had been demonstrated effective; is that correct?

McVAY: That is correct.

CADY: Were you able to see any damage from the bridge?

McVAY: I could not see any damage at all. It was too dark. . . . I didn't know what the damage was until I was told by the executive officer.

CADY: Did you see any moonlight after the explosion?

McVAY: No, sir, I did not. In fact, it was so dark on the bridge I couldn't recognize anybody.

CADY: When did you see the moon?

McVAY: Sometime later on that morning, after I had been in the water an hour or so. The moon apparently came out [from] behind the clouds.

Now the focus shifted to the second charge against the captain. The prosecution began the questioning:

RYAN: Did you personally order the word passed, "All hands, abandon ship"?

McVAY: I told the officer of the deck to pass the word, "All hands, abandon ship." I personally told him that.

RYAN: Do you know what means he utilized to carry out your orders?

McVAY: He had no means other than word of mouth to get that word about the ship. . . . Since the public address system was out and all forms of communications were out, it would've been, in my opinion, impossible to get word to every part of the ship . . . in the short time available.

The *Indianapolis* had simply sunk too quickly.

"Where is Indianapolis?"
The star witness of the trial, Mochitsura Hashimoto, arriving at

Oakland Airport en route to Washington, asked his guard to point to the city on a wall map of the United States. He was still basking in the knowledge that he had *definitely* sunk a cruiser by that name.

The guard placed a finger on the map and replied: "This is Indianapolis. Isn't that the name of the ship you sank? How many hits did you make?"

"Three," Hashimoto boasted.

But now he wondered if that glorious attack might not lead to his own inglorious demise. True, the enemy had treated him humanely so far, in fact, almost like a comrade. During the trip, his Japanese-speaking American escort, a naval lieutenant, had proudly displayed his ability to write his name in Japanese; crew members had invited him into the cockpit and shown him how to operate the aircraft; a WAVE had just driven him and his escort on a tour of San Francisco; and the U.S. Navy had even given him a hundred dollars to buy gifts for his family. Incredible! Almost as incredible as the scheme to bring him to Washington to testify for the prosecution at the trial of the American commander whose ship he had sunk. He still wondered if this might be some kind of trick.

The American commander was just as incredulous when he learned that Hashimoto was being brought from Japan. An enemy responsible for killing so many of his men would testify "against" him? The prosecution was humiliating not only him personally, McVay felt, but the U.S. Navy and the nation as a whole. And when the news was made public on December 8, just before Hashimoto's plane touched down in Oakland, many newspaper editorialists and members of Congress agreed. Day after day, headlines were revealing Japanese atrocities committed during the war, and side by side with these stories was another: A "Jap officer" was being given an opportunity to "slander" an American officer.

By the time Hashimoto arrived in Washington, public fever was running so high that there was genuine fear that his life could be in danger. Amid a glitter of camera flashes, he and his guards burrowed their way through a crowd of reporters, who were bombarding him with questions. Why did Japanese soldiers prefer suicide to capture? Did the Japanese worship the Emperor as Americans worship God?

Hashimoto was bewildered, since he had never given much thought to such matters. Practically carried from this bedlam into a waiting car, he was rushed to a well-guarded hotel.

The next day, Hashimoto was bundled off to the Washington Navy Yard, where he found himself sealed off on the third floor of the single officers' dormitory. He was regarded as neither a war criminal nor a prisoner of war, an officer assured him, but he was being protected for his own good, since many bereaved families "did not have a kind feeling" toward him. Hashimoto understood, and was even appreciative. Besides, it was midwinter, and he savored the steam heat in his room, a luxury he did not enjoy at home.

"You will be treated as a lieutenant," the officer said. "Have you any requests to make?"

"Well," Hashimoto replied, "I didn't have much time to pack my things for this trip. So I would like to get some clothes."

Within hours, his room resembled a haberdashery, with hats, shoes, shirts, and other attire strewn across the bed. Hashimoto could hardly believe it. And they didn't even present him with a bill! Maybe he would live to see his wife and children again after all.

That afternoon, fantasy dissolved into reality when he was escorted to the courtroom for preliminary questioning to determine his credibility and competence. Captain Ryan and other prosecution lawyers queried him about his background, the visibility on the night of the sinking, the kind of torpedoes he used, and other technical questions. Then a question of more gravity: Did the *Indianapolis* zigzag as it approached him?

"I didn't see any radical zigzag movement," Hashimoto said through an American interpreter, "but there apparently was some small movement. Since it was night, it was difficult to make an accurate judgment."

Ryan seemed to be disappointed. Why couldn't the man just say the ship wasn't zigzagging? He might testify now that it wouldn't have made any difference.

Hashimoto met the next day with Captain Cady and his assistants, and was drilled with similar questions. To clarify his statement about the weather, he even drew a picture showing the moon and the clouds. The visibility, he said, as he had at his meeting with Ryan, was "relatively good" for about ten thousand meters in the direction of the moon. But in other directions it wasn't very good, and he could "hardly discern the horizon."

This answer appears to have disturbed Ryan, for if the visibility "wasn't very good" except in one direction, the judges might feel that McVay was justified in ceasing to zigzag. But the same answer may have troubled Cady as well, precisely because the visibility was "relatively good" in one direction, the direction where the *Indianapolis* happened to be.

> CADY: Was the target zigzagging?

The reply, strangely, was more ambiguous than before.

> HASHIMOTO: I am not clear about that.
> CADY: Would it have made any difference to you whether the ship was zigzagging or not?
> HASHIMOTO: It would not have made any difference.

Cady could only wonder why he had opposed the man's appearance at the trial.

Thus, while Ryan was debating whether he should ask Hashimoto to testify after all, Cady, it seemed, was now perfectly willing to have him called—though it would be tactically wise to feign repulsion at the appearance of an enemy alien as a witness "against" an American officer. Ryan finally decided to take the risk; with all the publicity about Hashimoto, the prosecution might be more damaged if he didn't appear than if he did, even if he gave unhelpful testimony. For his failure to appear could be seen as an admission that the man backed McVay's contentions.

Hashimoto was thus brought once more before Ryan, who now wanted to finish with the man's testimony as quickly as possible. The prosecutor didn't want him taking time at the witness table shuffling through documents.

"Try to the extent possible not to look at your documents as you talk," he advised Hashimoto. "Memorize the important items."

Hashimoto went back to his room and memorized these items,

feeling this was the least he could do for those who had furnished
him with a free wardrobe.

On the morning of December 13, Hashimoto was taken to the
courtroom again, this time as the star of the real show. He entered
an adjoining room and found himself seated next to a number of
sailors, who greeted him with curious stares, some of them reflecting
shock and even hatred.

"Who are these men?" Hashimoto asked his escort, a towering
Marine captain who made him look dwarfish.

"They're survivors of the *Indianapolis*," the escort replied. They
were also waiting to testify.

Hashimoto had an "uncomfortable feeling." They probably
wanted to kill him—just as he had wanted to kill them when he fired
his torpedoes. He stole glances at these young men and pondered
the irony of fate. After he had sunk their ship, he searched for survivors to interrogate but could not find any. Now here they were,
waiting to be interrogated—by the Americans.

Inside the courtroom, which bulged with more than 150 people
who had come to see this unique confrontation between the two commanders, Ryan stood up and stated that the next witness for the prosecution would be Mochitsura Hashimoto, "Japanese enemy alien."
Cady immediately objected.

"If the court please," he said, "I wish to make formal objection
to the idea of calling one of the officers of the defeated enemy who,
as a nation, have been proven guilty of every despicable treachery,
of the most infamous cruelties, and of the most barbarous practices
in violation of all the laws of civilized warfare, to testify against one
of our own commanding officers on a matter affecting his professional ability and judgment.

"I am sure I express the feeling of every American citizen, especially those who so recently fought against the Japanese, in protesting at this spectacle. This objection is not, and cannot, be based
on any legalistic grounds, since our lawmakers have never imagined
through the centuries of Anglo-Saxon law any such grotesque proceedings."

As Cady sat down, there was a rustle of emotion in the jam-packed room. Though the defense attorney couldn't be unhappy about what he expected Hashimoto to say, he would make the most of the prosecution's "blunder" in bringing him from Japan. For his part, Ryan, hoping to dampen the effect of Cady's words, rose quickly to reply: "If the court please, the judge advocate regrets exceedingly that emotional aspects to the introduction of this witness are being stressed in this court. It is not the intention of the judge advocate . . . to ask this witness to give any opinions as to the honor or the actions of the accused in this case.

"The witness is being called to testify as to the facts within his knowledge, which, I believe, are necessary to a decision in these proceedings. I have no intention to ask the witness other than, in effect, where and when he was at or about the time of this incident, what he saw, what he did, and how he did it."

Ryan paused and listened to the silence, which gave him hope— they were paying attention, weighing his words. He continued: "In order to guarantee accurate answers to such questions as may be asked him, we intend to request the court to swear him with the oath according to our law, and the oath which will bind him in his own country, which will make him subject to prosecution if . . . he does not give true evidence before this court.

"It is also a matter of record . . . that there are many cases of members of our armed forces having been tried by courts-martial and in the proceedings of those courts-martial enemy aliens testified before the court."

Ryan then cited a previous court-martial to show that it was the testimony that mattered, regardless of who the witness was. He quoted from the transcript of the trial:

"The judge advocate did not introduce two important witnesses [for they] were notorious prostitutes and . . . their testimony would be valueless. . . . The judge advocate erred in not calling these witnesses, [for] even though they were notorious prostitutes . . . this would not necessarily render their testimony valueless. The credence to be given the testimony . . . of all witnesses is for the court and not the judge advocate to decide."

Cady interrupted: "If Hashimoto is going to be called, I will also

make legal objection on the grounds of competency, since his nation
is not of Christian belief, thus affecting [his] ability to take the oath
as a witness to tell the truth. I submit to the court how, under the
circumstances, can there be any pains or penalties of perjury upon
such a witness, an enemy alien of a defeated nation, who has no
standing in this country at all? There are numerous questions asto
the veracity of the Japanese as a race, and it is a question for the
court to determine how he may be placed upon oath or affirmation
to tell the truth."

Ryan responded: "If the court please, if there is any question
about how the witness Hashimoto could be held to the pains and
penalties of perjury, if there is any evidence indicating that he has
perjured himself, I have no doubt that the naval authorities will turn
this witness over to the proper civilian authorities, and he can then
suffer such pains as the court would adjudge in this country, and
then he could get it again in his own."

Cady, who had obviously realized from the first that he could
not prevent Hashimoto from testifying even if he wished to, now
said: "It appears that the proper procedure would be to bring in the
proposed witness and to examine him as to his understanding of the
truth and falsehood, the meaning of perjury, and his belief in punishment following upon falsehood."

The judge agreed, then announced that since Hashimoto believed
in gods unknown to them, it was proper to give him the American
Navy oath without the phrase "so help me God," and to require
him only to "affirm" rather than to "swear" to tell the whole truth.
It was also proper, the court ruled, to give him the Japanese Navy
oath as well.

"The Jap Navy was destroyed or something," Cady grunted, to
the laughter of the spectators. Why take a Japanese Navy oath when
there was no Japanese Navy?

Hashimoto now shambled into the courtroom and became the
object of intense scrutiny. Was this the ferocious Japanese warrior
of the headlines—this meek-looking, disheveled little man with a
rather frightened look in his eyes? After bowing deeply to the two
interpreters and to the president of the court, Hashimoto took a seat
at the prosecution table. He looked around at the spectators with

discomfort. They were staring at him, it seemed, as if they were in a zoo peering at some kind of rare oriental bird.

As he glanced at McVay, Hashimoto still couldn't believe that it was the American commander who was on trial and that he, the defeated enemy, had been bundled all the way from Japan to give testimony that might incriminate the man. If Japan had won the war, it was unimaginable that a Japanese court would call an American commander to testify in the trial of a Japanese officer. In fact, he could not recall any Japanese commander who had ever been court-martialed for losing a ship. Odd, the Americans.

Hashimoto may also have felt a certain vengeful satisfaction; he sank the ship that had made possible the killing of over a hundred thousand people in Hiroshima. What poetic justice! But he nevertheless felt a strange sympathy for McVay, a feeling that stemmed not only from a sense of professional respect, but from a touch of gratitude. For the captain had, after all, given him the opportunity to sink his first—and perhaps only—enemy ship for the Emperor.

Hashimoto's presence in the courtroom was as incredulous to McVay as it was to Hashimoto, though the captain had known that the man would be a witness. He saw in Hashimoto's presence more than personal mortification, which, however painful, was a kind of masochistic therapy for his apparent guilt feeling. The sight of his enemy renewed memories of those who died at the hands of this man. McVay felt no personal animosity toward him; Hashimoto had only been performing his duty, and he had fired his torpedoes with skill. But Hashimoto was the source of the horror and humiliation, and now he would testify against him.

As Cady questioned the witness, the interpreter translated:

CADY: Hashimoto, what is your religious belief?
INTERPRETER: He is a Shintoist.
CADY: What do you know of the meaning of truth and falsehood?
INTERPRETER: He says he is fully aware of the difference between truth and falsehood.
CADY: What happens to you in your religion if you tell a falsehood?
INTERPRETER: Should he happen to utter any falsehood, he will have to pay for it; that is to say, he will be punished for it.
CADY: Does your religion include a belief in the life hereafter?

    INTERPRETER: He believes that the soul exists after the death.
    CADY: And that this punishment for falsehood will be in the here-
after?

Hashimoto was startled by this theological question, which, he
felt, the ordinary believer should not be asked to answer. But he
replied nevertheless.

    INTERPRETER: He believes that . . . he will be punished during his
    life for any falsehood or wrongdoing that he may utter, or wrongdoing
    that he may do, but that upon his death there will be forgiveness.
    CADY: Do you have any knowledge of Christianity?
    INTERPRETER: Yes, he has some slight knowledge of Christianity.
    CADY: Do you know what perjury means?
    INTERPRETER: He has full knowledge of it.
    CADY: Is there punishment in Japanese law for perjury?
    INTERPRETER: He says he doesn't know all the details, but he knows
    that he is of the opinion that they are punished.

    With the preliminary questioning over, the court ruled that Ha-
shimoto understood the taking of the oath and that he was competent
to testify. The president of the court then administered the American
pains-and-penalties oath to him, and the oath binding upon a Japanese
in his own courts. When the witness had signed the first in English
and the second in Japanese, he sat down with a feeling of relief. But
new tension soon gripped him. Now he must help determine the
fate of the man whose ship he had sunk—the handsomely uniformed
man at the defense table whom he eyed as he absorbed the improb-
ability of the scene. Did anyone ever hear of a victor who had to
pray for a good word from the vanquished?

    But if Hashimoto empathized with McVay, he did not regret his
attack on the man's ship. In fact, he had a "pleasant feeling" when
he saw a model of the *Indianapolis* perched on the table in front of
him. Yes, that was the ship he had sunk for the Emperor.

    As Captain Ryan began to question Hashimoto, an electric hush
settled over the courtroom amid expectations of dramatic revelation.
But not a spark flashed in the silence. Ryan merely probed into the
witness's background and the technical aspects of his attack, asking

him to get up and, with navigation instruments, plot on a large chart the routes of the two vessels and the spot where the violent encounter occurred. And with the judges gathering around him, he complied. In view of Hashimoto's answers at the pretrial examination, it was not surprising that Ryan asked no questions about the weather or the zigzag movements of the *Indianapolis*, though these were the ones most closely related to the charges.

Captain Cady, in his cross-examination, posed equally marginal questions at first, but then dealt with the central charge.

> CADY: Was the target zigzagging at the time you sighted it?
>
> INTERPRETER: At the time of the sighting of the target, there was an indistinct blur and he . . . was unable to determine whether or not it was zigzagging.
>
> CADY: Was it zigzagging later?
>
> INTERPRETER: There is no question of the fact that it made no radical change in course. It is faintly possible that there was a minor change in course between the time of sighting and the time of attack.

Hashimoto, who could understand some English, felt his statement had not been interpreted accurately and, sympathizing with McVay, wanted to be fair to him. He turned to the interpreter and complained about the interpreted statement. He didn't say, he claimed, that "it is faintly possible that there was a minor change in course" before the attack. He had said what he had told Ryan and Cady in the preliminary interviews: There were small zigzag movements. How else would he have seen only one mast at first, and then two?

The interpreter, according to Hashimoto, shrugged and replied: "I was giving a brief, simple answer. It's enough."

Hashimoto still insisted on an accurate translation, and even tried to protest to the judges; but, unable to express himself well enough in English, he realized that his plea was fruitless and waited for the next question. It was the key one.

> CADY: Would it have made any difference to you if the target had been zigzagging on this attack?
>
> INTERPRETER: It would have involved no change in the method of firing the torpedoes, but some changes in the maneuvering.

Cady was apparently taken aback. In the preliminary interview, Hashimoto had stated flatly: "It would not have made any difference." Had the interpreter again translated Hashimoto's words inaccurately? Had the witness simply neglected to clarify his statement? Whatever the answer, Cady, inexplicably, did not press him for clarification.

Understandably, neither did Ryan when he resumed his questioning. And he still didn't ask Hashimoto about the weather—though the witness, in reply to a question about his use of radar, volunteered the information that "prior to surfacing, the visibility was good."

Once more, Cady failed to elicit from the witness what he had stated in the preliminary interview—that visibility was actually poor *except* in the direction of the moon. The court record thus states, "The accused did not desire to recross-examine this witness."

Both lawyers seemed relieved when Hashimoto stood up, bowed to the court, and, with his escort at his side, quickly left.

Finally, on December 19, after fifty-seven witnesses had testified, many of them in the choppy, traumatic monotone peculiar to the miracle survivor, it was time for closing arguments. Captain Ryan showed signs of strain. Had his decision to call an enemy alien to testify boomeranged? Had Captain Donaho's expert testimony strongly influenced the judges? They were, he knew, all true Navy men, who respected the letter of every rule more than they did simple logic, which sometimes clashed with the rule. And so Ryan would cite specific points of damaging testimony to show how Captain McVay deviated from Navy rules.

Yes, Ryan said, McVay may have given the order to abandon ship, but not in a timely or efficient manner. He had brushed aside Commander Casey Moore's report that "the compartments up forward were flooding fast." As a result, many men, if they heard the order at all, jumped into the water without having the time to find life preservers and drowned; a messenger who was supposed to have been sent to the engine room with the order to "kill headway" never arrived; and nobody closed any watertight doors. The commanding officer was ultimately responsible for all of these failures, Ryan averred, and he rattled off the page and question numbers of the testimony to "prove" each point. He was so zealous in this attempt that the statement cited sometimes had little or no relation to the charge being made.

And why hadn't McVay ordered his officers to zigzag when "there was intermittent moonlight?" Why did he rely "on ship doctrine [which permitted subordinates to make their own decisions as circumstances dictated] to compensate for his failure to issue specific orders to commence zigzagging . . . if . . . visibility improved?"

When Ryan had completed his argument, Captain Cady crushed the inevitable cigarette in an ashtray, stood up, and proceeded to answer the damaging points, while focusing on the "reasonableness" of McVay's actions. But he, too, was uncomfortable. McVay, he silently conceded, may have technically violated the rule that ships must, in relatively clear weather, zigzag at all times in a combat area, even in less dangerous waters—though the question of the weather that night was controversial. And Cady, like Ryan, knew how important rules were to a true Navy man, especially if a violation should lead to disaster. He didn't seem to realize, as Admiral Nimitz apparently did, that the rule on zigzagging would not apply in this case since McVay's routing orders gave him discretion on the matter and took precedence over others. In any case, he never made this vital point in court but merely appealed to "common sense."

What was negligence? It was, Cady declared, "the failure to exercise the care which an ordinarily prudent man would use under the circumstances in the discharge of [his] duty." And the evidence, he said, "shows that [McVay] had capable and experienced officers on watch, that his standing and night orders provided for the contingencies involved . . . and that he himself was on the bridge before and after the critical time of moonrise. . . . [This] is not disputed. It is not apparent what more any ordinarily prudent commanding officer could do than this."

Why didn't McVay act on Casey Moore's report? "Firstly, because the list at that time was slight; second, because he knew . . .

Moore had had time to make only a most hurried inspection; thirdly, because of his natural and commendable desire to save the ship if possible."

Besides, "testimony is abundant that the actual orders to abandon ship reached practically every part of the ship. . . . Compartments below had been cleared. All hands able to be moved were topside. Orders had been issued to get down life jackets, rafts, and floater nets. . . . There was ample time for everyone who was alive to get topside."

Cady paused, then asserted forcefully: "When a ship is hit and sinks within fifteen minutes, timeliness ceases to have much meaning. Only a well-trained, alert, and level-headed crew could have done so much in so short a time."

And daringly pointing an invisible finger at the "brass," who did not even know the ship was missing, he noted that most lives, after all, were not lost "upon the sinking of the *Indianapolis*, but in the water."

The trial finally drew to a close and the members of the court filed out to deliberate. McVay was heartened; his lawyer, though having committed some mistakes, had done a credible job, and he could see from the hopeful expression of his wife and friends that they were encouraged, too. Was it possible that he might soon be living a normal life with Louise? The thought was at first exhilarating, but it soon dissipated. Even if he avoided personal disgrace, in the context of the horrors that had devoured so many of his men, this wouldn't really matter very much. Whatever the decision, McVay knew, he would be haunted by the ghosts that had seized his soul.

As the minutes passed, McVay sat with his wife in an adjoining room awaiting the decision. Louise, pressing his hand, tried to comfort him. It would turn out all right, she assured him. Everybody, even the newsmen, she had heard, felt that he would be exonerated.

McVay, with his intimate understanding of naval logic, still did not think he would be exonerated, but he did believe that the prosecution had failed to prove its case. On the other hand, the defense had shown that no enemy vessel was sighted even though lookouts were competently doing their job; that all necessary safety precautions were taken aboard the ship; that radio distress messages were transmitted on at least one frequency, even though they may not have gotten out; and that lifesaving and other emergency equipment had been correctly maintained, though the Navy had provided him with poorly equipped life rafts, leakable wooden water breakers, badly packaged medical supplies, and food unsuited to emergency conditions.

Most important of all, many of his men had testified that they had received orders to abandon ship in time to get safely over the side, or that such orders could have been given without their hearing it; and a highly decorated submarine commander, as well as Hashimoto himself, had at least intimated that zigzagging wouldn't have saved the ship.

But the captain remained silent, gazing into space, like a man seeking peace in some distant world. He dearly loved his wife, but he wondered if it was right for her to share his misery. Every time they kissed, embraced, made love, he would curse himself for enjoying the pleasures that so many of his men would never again know on earth.

Finally, the call came. The court convened and McVay took his seat at the defense table.

Would the accused please stand.

McVay rose and stood stiffly with his chest thrust out, the ribbons on his blue uniform gleaming, his stern, handsome face as expressionless as it had been when a Silver Star was pinned on him. Only the once sparkling eyes seemed different; they stared straight ahead at the seven unsmiling men sitting before him—yet, it seemed, without really seeing them. The men he saw were smiling, joking, full of dreams. . . .

In the tense silence, a judge's voice sounded with the monotony of a train click-clacking along a shiny track:

"The specifications of the second charge not proved. And that the accused, Charles B. McVay, 3rd, Captain, U.S. Navy, is of the second charge not guilty; and the court does therefore acquit the said Charles B. McVay, 3rd, Captain, U.S. Navy, of the second charge."

Most of the spectators were jubilant, but Captain McVay's face remained immobile. He realized what most of the spectators did not—that he had, in fact, been found guilty and unfit to command in the Navy. Although the court had proclaimed him innocent of the second charge—failure to order his men to abandon ship in a timely manner—it did not clear him of the first charge—"hazarding" the ship through failure to order it to zigzag. And since the Navy, he knew, never announced that a defendant was guilty until his case had been fully reviewed, the court's silence on the first charge was tantamount to a verdict of guilty. McVay sat down almost unaware, it seemed, that Captain Ryan was offering into evidence the defendant's fitness record.

This record, Ryan said, apparently not wishing to humiliate McVay any more than was necessary, "contains only one unfavorable entry, a Letter of Reprimand concerning the loss of the U.S.S. *Indianapolis*, but otherwise this record of the accused deserves the rating of outstanding during his entire commissioned service."

If McVay did hear these words, there was no hint of it on his pale, frozen countenance. He had been proud indeed of his "outstanding" record, but now it was all over—his career, his life. Yet he wasn't surprised, or even sorry for himself. But his father, his wife—they were now among the casualties of the *Indianapolis*.

Once the court had been cleared, McVay stood up, and with Louise at his side, as silent and morose as her husband, he started for the door. Suddenly, Ryan rushed up to him.

"Charlie," he said, "I want you to know there was nothing personal in this and I wish it had come out the other way."

McVay stared at Ryan, as if in startled recognition. His old classmate at Annapolis, Tom Ryan. What great days they had spent together. What dreams they had dreamed. How proud "Rabbit" McVay had been to be a naval officer.

"Whatever the verdict," McVay replied in the cool, controlled tone of a man who might have just been assigned an attack mission, "it is for the good of the service."

Ryan had known of the court's decision before McVay did, for during the recess he had been summoned to the deliberating room and asked to record not only McVay's acquittal on the second charge, but to note, "The specification of the first charge proved. And that the accused, Charles B. McVay, 3rd, Captain, U.S. Navy, is of the first charge guilty."

Now, when McVay had left the courtroom, Ryan was recalled by the court.

"Please record the sentence of the court," he was ordered.

And Ryan recorded: "The court . . . sentences . . . Charles B. McVay, 3rd, Captain, U.S. Navy, to lose one hundred (100) numbers in his temporary grade of captain and to lose one hundred (100) numbers in his permanent grade of commander."

Ryan now knew what his victory meant. McVay could never advance in the Navy.

But he must have felt relief from his own heavy burden when the judges asked him to record a recommendation to the appeals court: "In consideration of the outstanding record of the accused and our belief that no other commanding officer who lost his ship as a result of enemy action has been subjected to a court-martial, we strongly recommend Charles B. McVay, 3rd, Captain, U.S. Navy, to the clemency of the reviewing authority."

Each of the judges then somberly signed the record—one paragraph to please the top command, it seemed, the other to appease their conscience.

The next day, commentaries and editorials abounded.

• The *New York Herald Tribune*: "Some reporters were so sure that the court would dismiss both charges against Captain McVay that they had stories announcing his acquittal prepared before the court convened for announcement of the verdict."

• The North American Newspaper Alliance: "Is the Navy trying to hide something? Is it trying to make a scapegoat of Captain McVay?"

• The *Army and Navy Bulletin*: "Responsibility for the debacle . . . must be fixed several echelons higher than a lone commanding officer. For if 800 to 900 men escaped from the sinking ship . . . then the Jap submarine accounted for less American lives than did the negligence of the high command."

At the Secretary of the Navy's office, one of the letters piled up on Forrestal's desk read typically: "I urge clemency for Captain McVay. If he was guilty, most of your war-time commanders were guilty, I among them. Even the typed instructions left . . . some latitude for judgment as to when ships should zigzag"—F. G. Murrell."

Meanwhile, the families of some of the dead were not appeased by the conviction. They wanted more heads in addition to McVay's.

And then there was Congress.

"It seems to me," cried Representative Henry D. Larcade, Jr., of Louisiana on the floor of the House, "that instead of Captain McVay being brought to trial, that those responsible for . . . not sending rescue craft until five days after the disaster should have been the ones to summon for court-martial."

Representative Edith Rogers of Massachusetts was appalled that the prosecution had called Hashimoto to testify. No other country would do such a deplorable thing, she said. And she introduced a resolution to expunge the witness's testimony from the record, though this resolution would die in committee since most members of Congress had no stomach to fight the U.S. Navy.

But dead or alive, the resolution deeply disturbed Forrestal and his Navy chiefs, for it seemed to question their motives. The Secretary apparently began to wonder about the wisdom of having held a trial before the Inspector General's investigation was complete. If McVay was shown to be innocent, Forrestal would have to overturn the conviction, and people might start asking why he had not postponed the trial.

On December 23, four days after the court-martial ended, Forrestal anxiously sent a memorandum to Admiral C. P. Snyder, the Inspector General: When would his report be ready?

Several days later, Forrestal got the reply: The investigation, involving interviews with fifty witnesses and 616 pages of testimony, was now complete. The following week, when the bulky report arrived, Edward Hidalgo read it carefully and then whipped off a memorandum to Forrestal with some conclusions.

On the basis of the report, Hidalgo asked rhetorically, should the Secretary reverse McVay's conviction?

> This alternative is not expedient, . . . although you have it in your power to reverse the conviction without advancing any particular reasons. Therefore, I consider this to be strictly a legal problem in which the Secretary of the Navy acts in a capacity comparable with that of an appellate court. Measured by this test there seems to have been sufficient evidence to support the court's finding:
>
> 1. That McVay was responsible for the safety of his ship;
> 2. That the ship was not zigzagging;
> 3. That in accordance with the U.S. Fleet Orders it should have been zigzagging.
>
> *It is true that the causal nexus between the failure to zigzag and the loss of the ship appears not to have a solid foundation.* In fact, a good percentage of the testimony on this issue was given by a witness for the defense (Captain Donaho) who, in effect, stated that zigzagging merely increased the difficulty of an attack. The fact remains, however, that the technical charge on which McVay was convicted was that of "hazarding" his ship—not of causing its loss or sinking.

He had spoken with another legal expert, Hidalgo continued, who favored

> additional language [in the response to McVay's appeal] to the effect that McVay was convicted of a super-technical charge, etc. It is felt, however, that such language would tend to lead into implications of apology for ever having tried McVay.

In other words, though the charge against Captain McVay might be "super-technical," the Navy couldn't admit it without arousing suspicion that the trial was a travesty of justice. Nor did the memorandum note the fact that McVay's routing orders took precedence over the standing zigzag rule, and that the captain, therefore, may not have committed even a "super-technical" violation of the rule.

Forrestal, heeding Hidalgo's advice, clung to the thread of rationale for the conviction. After all, both Admiral Denfield and Admiral King backed the verdict. But because of McVay's excellent past record, and apparently their own troubled consciences, they recommended that his sentence be remitted. Now, at least, this smudge would not bar him from getting more Navy stripes. Yes, a logical compromise. McVay's conviction would stand—but he wouldn't be penalized.

The problem was, such action would satisfy neither those who wanted McVay exonerated nor those who wanted him punished. Naval leaders still feared that both groups would demand the prosecution of other Navy brass who might be implicated, too. After giving this matter considerable thought, Hidalgo wrote in a memorandum to the Secretary on February 16:

> We must squarely face a seemingly inevitable question as to whether the Navy is to conduct additional investigations, and, if not, what disciplinary action has been taken in addition to the McVay trial. My present understanding is that our investigations are at an end. If true, we should say so frankly.

Forrestal apparently concurred. But he had to be careful in choosing the men who would be disciplined. There would be no more trials, with possibly embarrassing revelations. Letters of Reprimand or Admonition would suffice. He already had a recommended list from Admiral Nimitz: Letters of Reprimand to Commodore Gillette and Captain Granum, and a Letter of Admonition to Captain Naquin. Admiral King made sure that Lieutenant Gibson and Lieutenant Commander Sancho were added to the ignominious list of names.

The Navy Secretary and his men wanted to see the aftermath of the *Indianapolis* vanish as quickly as the ship had. So Admiral Sherman wrote a report entitled, "Narrative of the Circumstances of the Loss of the U.S.S. *Indianapolis*," which described the causes of the tragedy. In a few days, a press conference would be held and the document would give reporters all the answers they needed.

Unfortunately, however, the Secretary and his men weren't sure what all the answers were. Forrestal and Hidalgo grappled with their doubts. Could Naquin be disciplined without their admitting that his superiors should be, too? Should the report mention that McVay was not told of the four Japanese submarines or the sinking of the *Underhill* in the area?

They weighed every word, every paragraph. Two of the most explosive paragraphs read:

> There were indications that at least four Japanese submarines were reported operating at sea on offensive missions [in June and July 1945]. This specific information, however, although known to Captain Naquin, . . . did not reach the operations officer or the routing officer at . . . Guam. For this failure, Captain Naquin has been held responsible.
>
> On 27 July . . . McVay . . . visited the Advance Headquarters of [CINCPAC] and . . . was . . . given no information regarding enemy activity to the westward of Guam. . . . At the port director's office . . . he discussed with [a routing] officer details of his routing and of limited enemy activity in the area. . . . *He was not informed of the presence of the four Japanese submarines to the westward.*

These statements amounted to an admission by the Navy that Captain McVay had left Guam without having the vital information he needed to protect his ship from a submarine attack—the heart of McVay's defense. They were deleted from the Narrative, and a new paragraph was inserted:

> On July 27, . . . McVay . . . visited the office of the port director, Guam, in connection with his routing to Leyte. Later that day the navigator of the *Indianapolis* also visited the port director's office. . . . Information of possible enemy submarines along the route was contained in the routing instructions and was discussed with the navigator.

What did the revised Narrative thus mention? The useless, outdated intelligence brief "contained in the routing instructions" that told of merchant ships observing possibly phantom submarines and fleeting periscopes.

What did it leave out? The urgent information that Naquin withheld from McVay about four Japanese submarines on offensive missions and the sinking of the *Underhill*.

Now Forrestal and Hidalgo wrestled with the next question: Should Gibson and Sancho be mentioned in the Narrative?

Gibson had already received a Letter of Reprimand, and Sancho a Letter of Admonition, as a result of the Guam inquiry. But Gibson protested that he was completely blameless, since he had received no orders to report the nonarrival of combatant ships in Leyte.

Admiral McMorris, Nimitz's chief of staff, however, was unimpressed by Gibson's argument. A good naval officer, he felt, should always have his antennae working to pick up distress signals. The reprimand, he said, should "be not withdrawn." And Admiral King concurred.

But Edward Hidalgo did not want a public argument that could get embarrassingly out of hand. Why not just mention the titles of the offices held by Gibson and Sancho? He would write the Secretary:

> There is a strong feeling among men who commanded our ships in the South Pacific area that the failure to report the arrival of a ship not only was the accepted and common practice, but was a procedure entirely consistent with CINCPAC instructions. [Also,] fairness would seem to require the naming of *all* or *none*. Other parties are involved in errors of judgment, etc., at Guam and elsewhere who appear to deserve no special claim to anonymity.

This appraisal apparently upset Forrestal. True, others were no doubt "involved in errors of judgment," and the list was long—long enough to seriously damage the Navy's image:

- Commodore Carter failed to warn McVay of the submarine danger and issued the faulty order regarding the arrival of combatant ships.
- Captain Layton, the combat intelligence officer in Guam, and his counterpart in Washington, Captain Smedberg, neglected to investigate the intercepted report from the submarine *I-58* that it had sunk an enemy warship.
- Admiral McCormick, like the Philippine Sea Frontier Command officers, did not try to find out why the *Indianapolis* was overdue in Leyte.
- Admiral Oldendorf, who knew the ship was coming but not when, made no inquiries after a reasonable time had passed.
- Admiral Murray did not keep tabs on his subordinate, Naquin, to insure that the man informed him of any submarine menace—especially one that, according to the Inspector General's report, "would

have appeared to have been sufficient reason [for Murray's command]
to have diverted the *Indianapolis* from her routing."
• And finally, Admirals King and Nimitz and their Chiefs of Staff had
approved the ambiguous ship arrival order and had not required that
combatant ships be escorted.

Forrestal was firm. For the good of the Navy, he seems to have
felt, no admiral or subordinate whose testimony might reflect on an
admiral could be censured.

On the other hand, didn't some lower-grade officers have to be
named in order to *protect* the admirals—not to mention the Secretary,
who was ultimately responsible for the failures of the Navy? This
apparently seemed a reasonable solution to Forrestal even though the
Inspector General had written to King: "It cannot be accepted that
the primary failure was due to a garbled message heading or the
stupid interpretation of an order by an Acting Port Director. It was,
rather, a failure of coordination and integration of intelligence by
several senior commands."

In any case, Forrestal was, as usual, reluctant to lock horns with
King, and King wanted scapegoats. But it seemed only fair to the
Secretary that he at least listen to Stuart Gibson after the man's intense
campaign to clear himself.

One February afternoon, a few days before the press conference,
Gibson, now a civilian, was relaxing at home in Richmond, Virginia.
He was about to start on a new job in a bank and was enjoying the
few free days still left after his discharge from the Navy.

Gibson had virtually given up hope that he would ever get the
Navy to delete from his file the reprimand he had received after the
Guam hearings. He had written and phoned naval authorities, plead-
ing that they reconsider his case, but the answer was always vague
—"We'll see," or "Call us again." Well, what the hell, he was no
longer in the Navy, and who would see the reprimand, anyway?
His ego and his sense of justice had been bruised, but it simply wasn't
worth worrying about.

Yet the "injustice" continued to rankle. It was all Admiral King's fault, he felt. And King was part of a rotten system that had to depend on scapegoats to protect arrogant admirals like himself.

"The Navy," Gibson said bitterly to his wife, "is acting as both judge and jury."

Nevertheless, he tried to forget the whole sordid affair and make up for all the time he had lost being away from his wife and three children. Also, he had a new job to think about, and he would do well at it, he was sure. He was a dedicated worker—whatever the Navy said about him.

The telephone rang and Gibson answered it. Silence. Then: "You want me in Washington—tomorrow?" When he hung up, he told his wife, "It was the Navy. They want to speak with me."

"About what?"

Gibson didn't know, but he assumed it was about his attempt to clear his name. He could hardly believe it: They were sending a special plane to take him to Washington in the morning!

The next morning, after the short plane trip, Gibson was startled to find himself being ushered into the office of Secretary Forrestal himself. When he had seated himself amid numerous admirals, Forrestal thumbed through a file and asked him several questions. He just wanted to clarify some of the points Gibson had made in his letters, he said with no hint of hostility.

He wasn't unique, Gibson pointed out. As far as he knew, there wasn't one port director who reported the nonarrival of combatant ships. Why should he be singled out? He hoped he would be exonerated.

Forrestal seemed sympathetic, though the admirals remained expressionless.

Why had he been brought to Washington?

Well, there was to be a press conference, and it was desirable to get as much information as possible.

A press conference? It would probably concern the McVay court-martial, Gibson surmised.

When the meeting ended, Gibson was optimistic that perhaps the reprimand he had received in Guam would be remitted after all. And then he could finally put all his anguish behind him.

·   ·   ·

On February 23, 1946, Fleet Admiral Nimitz, who had replaced King as Chief of Naval Operations after a long-planned resignation several days earlier, stood before a large gathering of reporters in the Pentagon. He looked rather uncomfortable, as if he wished he were back home planting flowers; he apparently knew that he wasn't revealing the entire truth. The important thing was to keep the public from thinking ill of its Navy. After distributing copies of the Narrative Nimitz said: "There is no thought of exonerating anyone in the Navy who should be punished for his performance of duty in connection with the sinking of the *Indianapolis* and the attending loss of life."

As for himself, the admiral stated, "to the extent that a Commander in Chief should be held responsible for failures or errors of judgment on the part of subordinates, I must bear my share of responsibility."

A letter he had received from E. Connelly, the father of one of the dead, had elicited this "confession." He read from the letter:

> "We have searched the press and other publications diligently for acknowledgment by you for your part in the mistake and inefficiency connected with the sinking of the U.S.S. Indianapolis. To date we have seen nothing. On behalf of the . . . bereaved families you owe it to us, and yourself, to make a public statement."

Nimitz, who had approved the order regarding arrivals of combatant ships that had misled officers of the Philippine Sea Frontier Command, was now making a public statement—but his name would, of course, be absent from the list of people to be disciplined. Indeed, he had been promoted to the top post in the U.S. Navy.

Now one reporter dared to ask: "I was wondering why Captain McVay was court-martialed, and the officers responsible either directly or indirectly for the unusual length of time in which a search was not instituted were let off, so to speak, with a reprimand, rather than a finding of 'guilty' in a court-martial."

Admiral Sherman, one of those conducting the press conference, only replied: "Well, I can't say as to the reasons which led to that decision."

But the Narrative did seem to say "as to the reasons":

The *Indianapolis* was scheduled to have arrived at Leyte at 11 A.M., July 31. It is probable that under normal conditions, no concern as to her nonarrival would have been felt until she was eight or nine hours overdue. Several additional hours would have elapsed . . . to check her movements so that, in all probability, *search for her would normally not have commenced until she would have been approximately 24 hours overdue.* That would have been some time in the forenoon of August 1. The survivors were actually sighted at about 10:25 A.M. . . . on August 2, by a plane on routine patrol.

Thus, even without negligence, it was pointed out, hundreds would have been dead by the time help arrived under the flawed system then in effect. And since negligence would account for only one day's death toll, it was not logical to judge too harshly those responsible for the delay, the Narrative seemed to say, ignoring the fact that only by chance were the survivors spotted at all. Furthermore, according to the Narrative, "failure to evaluate accurately a report made by a Japanese submarine did not necessarily have a bearing on the prosecution of the war as a whole and was actually of only local significance." Negligence, after all, contributed to the death of only 880 men.

Who, then, would be disciplined? The Narrative listed the culprits and explained why each one was on the list.

Commodore Gillette and Captain Granum, who were told of their coming notoriety only hours before the press conference, received Letters of Reprimand for not giving "closer personal attention to the work of [their] inexperienced juniors (Sancho and Gibson)," and permitting "a loose state of organization within" their command.

Yet Gillette's superior, Vice Admiral Kauffman, had commended the commodore for his "initiative, tireless effort, and administrative ability," while Granum, only two months earlier, in October, had been awarded the Legion of Merit with a citation that read: "For exceptionally meritorious conduct in performance of outstanding service . . . for protection of all shipping."

Lieutenant Commander Sancho, who was not told in advance that he would be publicly named, had received a Letter of Admonition because he was unaware that the *Indianapolis* had never arrived in Leyte though it "was his duty . . . to keep himself informed of such matters."

And Lieutenant Gibson had received a Letter of Reprimand for failing to investigate the nonarrival of the ship and to make an "immediate report of the fact to his superiors." Nonarrivals, the Narrative said, "were expected to be reported"—even though, it admitted, "no such order was issued, permitting the inference [to be] drawn . . . that since arrival reports were not to be made for combatant ships, by the same token neither were reports of nonarrivals to be made."

The Narrative then revealed that "this matter has since been clarified in terms which cannot be misinterpreted." This statement was, in essence, an admission that Admiral Nimitz and other high officers had been negligent in failing to make the original order clear. But whether it was clear did not, in their opinion, exempt the subordinate officers who misinterpreted the order from being punished for this negligence.

Gibson, who was relaxing at home on this Sunday reading the newspaper with the radio on, suddenly thought he was hearing things—his name. He turned the radio louder and heard a newscaster quoting the Narrative. His negligence, the man said, had contributed to the death of 880 people! Nothing was said about the faulty order he was obeying.

"My God!" Gibson cried.

He couldn't believe it. Only a few days earlier, he had been sitting in Secretary Forrestal's office and no one had told him that his reprimand would stand, and even be made public. Someone could at least have warned him so that he would have had a chance to prepare an answer. He came from one of the oldest families in Richmond, and now it was disgraced. How could his wife face her friends? How would his children be accepted in school? What would happen to his career? He was especially vulnerable because he was about to start on a new job. The newspapers would be calling him any moment now, and he didn't know what to tell them.

With these thoughts cascading through his mind, Gibson rushed to the telephone in panic and called his brother, George, who was a lawyer.

He needed help, he cried. Should he sue the Navy for slander? Ask for a congressional investigation?

He didn't have the connections in Washington, George said. But he could recommend an attorney who did have them. Gibson immediately called the man and explained his situation.

"I'll take the case," said the attorney, "but it will cost you every cent you have. It'll be long and you probably won't win. And if you do, nobody will remember that you were exonerated. With all the running publicity, you'll be remembered as the man who sank the *Indianapolis*. Drop it."

Gibson slowly put down the phone, dazed, devastated.

What should he do? he asked his wife, who he knew was a fighter.

If they had the money, she would want to fight, she said. They owed it to the children. But with their modest savings, would the battle be worth it?

No, the lawyer was right. Stuart Gibson knew he was innocent. His wife knew it. And his children would believe it. Nothing else really mattered. He would drop it. When the news media began calling, however, he paused, still asking himself whether he should spill out his fury. Instead, in a broken voice, he simply answered, "No comment."

In any case, Captain McVay led every story. The Narrative stated succinctly that the Secretary had approved the recommendations of the court, but that Admiral King had remitted McVay's sentence and restored him to duty.

Would the captain then be able to advance in the Navy? a reporter asked Admiral Denfield at the press conference.

Denfield chose his words carefully: "Well, of course, anybody that has a court-martial and has lost his ship—there is always a question whether we will give him another one or not."

Admiral Nimitz, who had opposed the court-martial in the first place, then clarified the answer with the discomfort of a man who had swallowed nails: "The conviction was not remitted; the *sentence* was remitted."

Apparently in appreciation for McVay's stoic "acceptance" of this permanent stigma, the Navy two months later awarded the captain the Bronze Star for the courage he had displayed at Okinawa. The announcement, however, was made not through its national public relations channels, but, quietly, through the Potomac River Naval Command, which released items of local interest.

XIV

Toy of Treachery

THE STORY of the *Indianapolis* did not end with the remittance of Captain McVay's sentence and the censure of four other officers. While Lieutenant Gibson and Lieutenant Commander Sancho, both now civilians, decided not to fight the "injustice" done them, Captain Granum and Commodore Gillette, as career officers in the Navy, bitterly fought back.

Like Gibson earlier, Granum and Gillette wrote letters to the Navy Inspector General with pens that oozed with anger and dismay. No, their organization was not "loose." They supervised their men rigidly, but it wasn't the duty of these officers to check on the whereabouts of a combatant ship. As Gillette put it, "For an organization to take upon itself responsibilities not assigned to it . . . would create confusion and court disaster."

Blame the commander of the Eastern Carolines Sub-Area for sending out search planes that flew so high that survivors couldn't be sighted, Gillette suggested. Blame the CINCPAC combat intelligence officer for incorrectly evaluating Hashimoto's intercepted cable that revealed he had sunk an American ship. But don't blame the Philippine Sea Frontier Command, which was only acting according to orders.

"It was the unbelievable coincidence of many circumstances that combined in an unbelievable manner to produce delay in the rescue,"

Gillette wrote. And now the media was calling him "criminally responsible" for the loss of all those lives. Was it fair?

The Inspector General, however, was adamant. The Philippine Sea Frontier officers, he said, were guilty of negligence, "whereas . . . other failures . . . were due to faulty judgment."

This distinction fit in well with Washington's desire to remove from the top naval echelons any significant taint of guilt for the disaster. Better the officers of the "backwash" Philippine Sea Frontier Command than the sacrosanct brass of CINCPAC and the Pentagon.

Gillette would still not give up. To hell with the Inspector General. In July 1946, he wrote directly to Secretary Forrestal, whom he had earlier met to protest his punishment. Forrestal had then conceded that it was unjust to deny him an opportunity to defend himself. Wouldn't the Secretary agree that "the Philippine Sea Frontier was not charged with the security of combatant ships?"

Four months later, in December 1946, Forrestal replied—in letters to all four censured members of the Philippine Sea Frontier. He was now convinced, the Secretary wrote, "that the disciplinary action heretofore taken in your case was more severe than the circumstances warranted." Consequently, the letter of censure "is hereby withdrawn."

The vindicated men felt a tremendous sense of relief—but only temporarily. For there was no press conference, no public announcements. This was, after all, private Navy business. And if the public would always regard the men with disdain for "killing all those boys," they would simply have to be strong enough to endure the pain.

Forrestal himself apparently had a lower endurance level. Since his conscience, it seems, had been bothering him, he may have felt a sense of relief, too—but it was also temporary. For setback followed setback. He lost his job as Navy Secretary after the war; he lost his struggle to prevent union of the three armed services; and he lost the argument to prepare for a new war that would keep the Communists from taking over the earth. Overwhelmed by the growing pressures, Forrestal gradually went mad and committed suicide in 1949.

· · ·

Members of the *Indianapolis* crew, however, would vigorously fight the vestiges of their madness. One who would suffer worse than most was Adolfo Celaya, even after he was released from the "chicken coop" in which he had languished after the ship docked in San Diego.

When Celaya finally arrived on leave at his modest home in Florence, Arizona, he could barely face his father. With returning servicemen being welcomed like conquering heroes in neighboring homes, how could he explain that the agony in the water had been followed by the agony ashore, that he had been treated like a criminal?

Night after night, Celaya dreamed that he was still in the water, choking, drowning as someone pressed his head under, or trapped in a cage that grew smaller, ever smaller, until he could no longer move. He would awaken in a sweat, gasping for breath, and then restlessly turn in his bed, unable to go back to sleep as fuzzy dream turned into vivid memory.

In his misery, Celaya began to frequent bars, though he had seldom drunk before. At last he could sleep, but the nightmares only grew more grotesque, driving him to guzzle still more alcohol. After his leave, Celaya desperately sought an immediate discharge from the Navy, which, he felt, had almost destroyed him. He even feigned madness (he was, in fact, half-mad) and was hauled off to the hospital in a straightjacket. Given his discharge, he returned to Florence, where he once more haunted the bars—until one night he drank himself into unconsciousness and had to be carried home.

When Celaya awoke, the horror and humiliation of his degradation finally gave him the strength to break out of the cage he had never really left. Vowing not to touch alcohol again, he no longer viewed himself as a hopeless misfit in a wretched world. He was suddenly eighteen, and as nightmares about the past gradually dissolved into dreams about the future, he returned to his old high school to complete his education. With the aid and encouragement of the school basketball coach, he once more became a star on the court, even making the all-state team. The coach then helped him to enroll in San Jose State College, where he played basketball and studied physical education, as he had planned. Perhaps he would become a coach.

But after graduating, Celaya gave up this dream, feeling a Mexican would face too many obstacles in the coaching field. He remained in the San Jose area, where he married, worked at several jobs, and saved up enough money to open a heating and air-conditioning shop. Today, he and his son are prosperous business partners. Occasionally, Adolfo still has bad dreams, but now when he awakens, he realizes his horse was right. Ride with the vicissitudes of life—until they send you to the glue factory. And he gets out of bed and gulps down not a can of cold beer, but a glass of creamy milk.

Richard Redmayne would also have recurring nightmares; sometimes he would dive down to join his men in the engine room of the *Indianapolis*, at other times, flee from attacking dogs. He would awaken screaming, and on occasion find that he had battered his wife in bed. He has become so claustrophobic that he will seldom even travel in a plane; the least dip might cause him to cry out, "My God, we're dead!"

Still, Redmayne did not lose his love for authority, and applied for a commission in the regular Navy after the war. The long-awaited promotion to lieutenant commander came through at last, and Redmayne spent twenty-six years in the service, retiring as a captain in 1967. He opened an antiques shop in Kittery Point, Maine, then went into the real-estate business. He now lives in Maine and Naples, Florida, together with his wife, Trude, and the ghosts of the men in the engine room.

After the *Indianapolis* tragedy, Dr. Haynes felt the Navy was so much a part of him that leaving it seemed almost tantamount to jumping ship. So after recovering from his exhaustion, he left for Bremerhaven, West Germany, to watch over the U.S. naval forces based there. Before long, his burned fingers grew sufficiently nimble to permit him to wield a scalpel as a surgeon, the job he coveted. He eventually served as chief surgeon and director in several naval and civilian hospitals, and won the American Medical Association's Hoekken Award for developing a process for preserving blood by freezing it.

In 1978, Haynes retired, and has since divided his time between his home in the Boston area and one in Naples, Florida—next door to Redmayne. He lives with his second wife—his first died in 1969—and is sporadically visited by five children, fourteen grandchildren, and four great grandchildren.

Nevertheless, Haynes still finds himself longing for the company of his drinking partner, Stanley Lipski, and his spiritual partner, Father Conway. They are still dying in his arms, but he cannot save them, nor any of the others who are calling him—"Doc! Doc! Over here! Don't let me die!"

Giles McCoy had a tempting offer to stay in the Marines, since his heroic role in the tragedy had shown the corps that he had the makings of a brilliant commander. How would he like to go to officers' training school and, once he had his bars, be shipped off to China? McCoy was almost lured by the exotic appeal of the Far East. But he woke up one morning and decided that he had had enough of the military.

After his miraculous survival, he didn't want to burden God with the task of protecting him in new wars. Besides, he was disillusioned with the service after what he considered the "railroading" of Captain McVay. What was more important to the top brass, he asked himself—honor or self-interest? He was repulsed by the answer. Finally, his back still pained him, and he might not make a very good Marine any more.

In fact, because of this problem, McCoy could no longer play baseball. He had been the star of his high school team and had hoped to play for a major-league team, but now all he could do was watch others hit the ball and wonder if he couldn't have hit it a little farther.

Then, another miracle! He went to a chiropractor, and, after several weeks' treatment, his condition improved dramatically. He began to play with an unaffiliated minor-league team, and then for farm clubs of the St. Louis Browns during two summers, though he never quite made the parent team.

So impressed was McCoy with this new manifestation of God's power that he decided to enroll in a chiropractic college and become a chiropractor himself. This was an opportunity to help others who suffered as he had. And he went on to have a highly successful practice in Boonville, Missouri, until he retired with his wife, Betty, to dabble in real estate and play golf at his summer home in Palm Coast, Florida.

But there was one thing neither he nor God could cure—his maddening thirst. Deprived of fresh water for so many days at sea, he has since craved it almost as intensely as he had when he was afloat, and his thirst is virtually insatiable. Whenever he goes hunting, for example, he is forced to stop along the way at houses and ask for water. He doesn't waste a drop, and still regrets the need to flush water down the toilet.

But McCoy has wanted to save more than water. He has wanted to save memories of one of history's greatest tests of human endurance and will. In the late 1950s, he and his old raftmate Felton Outland set up a committee to arrange for reunions of the *Indianapolis* survivors. To find the addresses of the men, they sent letters to dozens of automobile license bureaus around the country and placed advertisements in leading military magazines. Finally, in 1960, the first reunion took place, appropriately at a hotel in Indianapolis, and more than half the survivors showed up, embracing, slapping backs, exchanging memories. They ignored the horror, for how could they speak of that?

That was precisely what they must do, McCoy insisted. How many of them, for all their courage and heroism, had been suffering all these years, silently hiding in their hearts terrible stories of selfishness, greed, and moral weakness. Now was the time to tell all to each other, to cleanse the heart and the mind of the last vestiges of madness. He had spoken with two psychiatrists and they had advised him that this was the best therapy. So McCoy gathered the men in a room, and each told his story, some weeping, some fighting emotion, spilling out facts like computers, all of them reliving dreadful moments, and then draining their souls of them.

One survivor especially moved McCoy—Edward Payne, whom he had saved several times when Payne had tried to swim away from their raft. The man had come to the reunion from the hills of Kentucky, selling a cord of wood and two goats to pay for transportation; McCoy contributed an additional sum, with the hotel picking up the room and dinner bill. Almost unrecognizable with his hair snipped around the bowl his wife had placed on his head, Payne wept on McCoy's shoulder as he begged forgiveness for his mad behavior. And McCoy embraced him almost as firmly as he had when he dragged him back to the raft.

Since 1960, McCoy has supervised a reunion in Indianapolis every five years, and the emotion has never seemed to dwindle. (Glenn G. Morgan of Houston, Texas, McCoy's successor as head of the association, will arrange future reunions.) But though the memories have been no less vivid at successive meetings, the survivors are better able to handle them now. Still, only to a degree. Giles McCoy himself was barely able to keep his eyes from tearing as he described in a stream of consciousness the terrors he and his comrades endured. At times, when he broke off, he seemed to be listening even during moments of silence. Was he listening to the cries of the men hopelessly trapped by circumstance in the brig compartment of the *Indianapolis*?

Harlan Twible, the quintessential Navy man, remained in the service through the Korean War, but then, because of health problems stemming from the disaster, decided to hang up his uniform and enter civilian life. In 1958, Twible became vice president of the Hayes Corporation, an electrical control manufacturer in Michigan City, Indiana; after twenty-two years, when he was only fifty-four, he retired to Florida with his wife. He has suffered three coronaries since World War II because of his depleted physical reserves. But always the optimist, he feels that the tragedy had a positive side.

"The lifetime of experience that I acquired in four days," he would say, "the decisions that I made as a young naval officer, made other decision-making in later life simple and rather insignificant. It undoubtedly made my twenty-two years as a corporate executive easier."

Twible, unlike many of the other survivors, has never expressed wonder at his salvation. Lieutenant Gwinn happened to sight the survivors by sheer accident? It was no accident.

"I never once doubted but that I would live through this ordeal in the water," he says. "I believe that it was the fact that I knew I would live through it that allowed me to work as well as I did."

It was just a matter of applying the rules he had learned at the Naval Academy—and if they didn't work, those he had learned at Sunday school.

Otha Alton Havins, on returning to his home in California after the war, was determined to keep the vow he had made to God—to enter the ministry if he and the others in Captain McVay's group were saved. But first he had some unfinished business. Billie, his girl friend, who had turned down his multiple proposals of marriage while he was in the service, now welcomed him back with a resounding yes. They married in 1946, and found themselves facing a grave financial problem. Havins thus worked as a barber during the day and as a clerk at night, earning enough to enroll in the Fort Wayne Bible College in 1951. Four years later he was ordained a minister and spread the word of his own incredible salvation for the Missionary Church Association until 1965, when he retired because of a heart ailment (apparently a result of the sea ordeal) and engaged in real estate from his home in Salinas, California.

Through God, Havins has remained close to his brother, who went down with the *Arizona*, and to his buddies who went down with the *Indianapolis*. God has also helped him to overcome the resentment he felt toward the Navy bureaucrats who had not transferred him elsewhere as they had promised before the cruiser sank. He should have known, he feels, that God was aware of the injustice and would not let him go down with a ship he wasn't supposed to be on.

Charles McKissick, once out of the Navy, hung up an optometrist's shingle in McKinney, Texas, where he practiced until his recent retirement. To McKissick, the *Indianapolis* never really died. It is still alive in his consciousness. He remembers each room and compartment, the rhythm of its motors, the beauty of its clipper bow. He remembers the pride he felt to be a member of the crew, the moment of agonizing disbelief when it lurched to a vertical position, as if to sail into the sky, and sliced into its ocean grave.

Sometimes the vision seems to be a mere fantasy—until he hears the faint echo of a voice: "Coach, coach, help me!"

On arriving home in Scarsdale, New York, Donald Blum lived his own fantasy. He stuffed himself with tomatoes he picked in his parents' victory garden, then stumbled into his mother's kitchen and filled the still empty crannies of his stomach with her rich cooking. He slept late, after long nights in the local bars. Girls, girls, girls. And then there was one—Sandra. He married her in 1951.

When he could find time, Blum worked for his father's engineering firm, and eventually he took it over. His "learning difficulty" did not keep him from becoming a top-rate engineer, and on "retirement," a consulting engineer in great demand.

Blum still loves the water and often goes boating, making repairs himself without fear of being deafened by a loudspeaker ordering him to drop his hammer and act like an officer and a gentleman. He prides himself on his survival, for he has learned that it isn't normal for a person to thrash around in the ocean for five days and remain alive.

Though Chuck Gwinn is not one of the survivors, he would surely win a popularity contest among them. And when he turns up at an *Indianapolis* reunion, his back is usually sore from numerous affectionate slaps. For all of them know that if he had not spotted them when he did, no one would be alive to hold a reunion.

Gwinn, after the war, worked as a hydraulic, electrical, and construction engineer for San Jose's East Side Union High School District, retiring in 1985. He is content in the knowledge that few other people have ever been given the chance to save so many lives.

Adrian Marks, like Gwinn, regards his role in the rescue of the *Indianapolis* survivors as the highlight of his life. And before retiring as a lawyer in Frankfort, Indiana, in 1988, he fought vigorously to obtain benefits and recognition that have been denied them. In one 1980 affidavit addressed to "Some Bumbling Bureaucrat in the Veterans Administration and to Anyone Else Who Gives a Damn," he demanded medical treatment for a particular survivor—and got it.

Although Marks shrugs off thoughts of the risks he took to save the men, the thrill of the rescue possesses him.

"I met you forty years ago," Marks would tell the survivors in an emotional speech at the 1975 reunion. "I met you on a sparkling sun-swept afternoon of horror. I have known you through a balmy tropic night of fear. I will never forget you. . . . I suppose that through the years . . . at least ten thousand times my memory has recalled some portion of the day when our fates were crossed. . . . I am humbled by the thought that I have seen true greatness in our time."

This statement mirrors the sentiment of members of Adrian Marks' own crew when they talk about their commander and the time he defied the odds to land in the sea so that all of them might live in peace with themselves for the rest of their lives.

In Japan, Hirokoto Tanaka was soon at peace with himself, despite his country's defeat. He had, after all, won a personal victory; the Americans had failed to kill him. He had had the will and the skill to survive, just as Japan would—even though, to his dismay, the Emperor had announced that he was not divine after all.

Hirokoto has often thought of the glorious moment when he sighted that "battleship." Yes, he had been a good sailor—he knew how to make sure a ship didn't get away. But his "samurai" days were over. He had to be practical now, especially after he married in 1947. So he took a job with a haberdashery firm selling clothes and, being as stable on land as he was at sea, stayed there until he retired in 1978. Hirokoto Tanaka was a good salesman. He knew how to make sure a customer didn't get away.

Peace did not come as easily to Toshio Tanaka. When he learned that the *Indianapolis* had carried parts of the atomic bomb to the Far East, he was rabid.

"If I had known," he would say, "my hatred of those American sailors would have multiplied." Yes, he would have killed them. "This is how war is. War drives people mad."

But Toshio Tanaka's madness gradually receded before reality and he learned to accept American occupation. The Emperor, after all, still sat on the throne. It wasn't important that he had renounced his divinity; Tanaka never thought of him as a god anyway, but simply as a symbol of Japanese nationalism. And with the symbol surviving, Japan would be powerful again.

To help nourish the seed of revival, he became an officer in Japan's paramilitary Maritime Self-Defense Force in 1953. Now retired, he hopes Japan will one day field another great Navy—with American help!

Commander Hashimoto was amazed by the Americans. While penned up in his dormitory during Captain McVay's court-martial trial, he was treated more like an honored guest than an enemy officer who had caused the death of so many American boys.

Hashimoto was pressured only once—on Christmas. One of his guards, a bit drunk, demanded that he help him finish off a bottle of whiskey, though the commander seldom imbibed anything but sake. The guard's superior, however, was so mortified that to make up for this indignity he invited the commander out for a night on the town.

Finally, after twenty days in the United States, Hashimoto was flown back to Japan, laden with gifts that his guards and escort officers had given him for his family. His wife could hardly believe it: Gifts? She had wondered if he would return alive.

After a brief rest at home, Hashimoto was at sea again—the skipper of a ship carrying Japanese soldiers to Japan from outlying areas. And in the early 1950s, he was back in the submarine business, supervising construction for the Maritime Self-Defense Force. He marveled at all the modern equipment the Americans had made available. If only his *I-58* had been so amply equipped, he would surely have sunk more American ships. The thought called to mind that exhilarating moment when he saw flames shooting from the *Indianapolis*.

In 1974, at the age of sixty-four, Hashimoto was a sailor once more—a captain of a Japanese merchant ship—when he suddenly found himself the victim of an ironic twist of fate. While heading for the United States one foggy day (this time carrying not torpedoes but automobiles), his ship collided in Japan's Inland Sea with a Liberian freighter, sinking it and killing all but two of twenty-six Korean seamen aboard.

This sinking Hashimoto did not celebrate. He was brought to trial, charged with negligence—as Captain McVay had been exactly twenty-nine years earlier—and forced to resign from his job. He slouched back to his home in Kure to ponder his disgrace and seek the forgiveness of the gods for the deaths the accident had caused— although he blamed his radar man for this tragedy.

In fact, Hashimoto would soon be cohabiting with the gods. A brother who had inherited the Shinto priesthood from their deceased father had died, and Hashimoto stepped into the saintly sandals. He would finally fulfill his father's wish, giving up the sea for hallowed land, even though he still somewhat dreaded the thought of leaving the temporal world. Anyway, who would give him another ship now?

Thus, in 1976, Hashimoto and his family left for Kyoto where, at his shrine, he would pray every day for the health and well-being of visitors and beautify his gardens to make sure the gods would find the place hospitable.

Like Hashimoto, Charles McVay found that there was no ship at sea waiting for him after *his* disgrace, but there was a new job in New Orleans. Rear Admiral A. S. Merrill, Commandant of the Eighth Naval District, asked him to be his chief of staff. Merrill remembered McVay well, for McVay had been his student at Annapolis and had earned the Silver Star while serving with his task force.

McVay was fascinated with the special flavor of New Orleans and its surroundings. Besides his home in the city, he bought a rustic house in the magnificent wilderness of the bayou, where he went fishing or duck hunting with Louise whenever he could escape from the office. Louise still lived to please him. As a visitor would relate: "She had servants but she would go down to the basement and hand-scrub his collars and cuffs. Meals were served beautifully. Even a bowl of soup was served with elegance. . . . [Smokers] dreaded dirtying her silver ashtrays. . . . She was a perfectionist where Charlie was concerned."

But even an adoring wife couldn't stop the slow destruction of this once vibrant, fun-loving man. He seldom whistled any more, and often when Louise or someone else was speaking, he would suddenly drift off into oblivion, and return after several moments to the real world, smiling his empty smile to conceal his brief flight into some terrifying solitude. What right did he have to enjoy life when 880 of his men were lying in their watery graves? Yes, he deserved to be court-martialed, however unjust the charges. As he would tell the wife of one of his drowned officers over lunch: "That I have been punished makes me feel that I have paid a small installment for my men and my ship."

But Louise would urge him: "Charlie, Charlie, let's forget the past. Live in the present. Think of the future."

And McVay would try again to adjust to a world he no longer

understood, a world that no longer understood him. Had the *Indianapolis* been God's punishment for all his sins of the past? One of his biggest sins, he felt, was his neglect of his children; he had never been much of a father. McVay was thus glad to be able to help his younger son Kimo, just out of the Army, to resume his education.

He shouldn't worry, even if he didn't have the necessary credits for college, McVay advised his son. He happened to be a friend of the director of admissions at Tulane University. And in 1947, Kimo moved in with his father and stepmother while attending classes at Tulane. His stay, he soon found, would be no vacation.

"Kimo," they ordered, "make your bed." "Kimo, wash your dishes." "Kimo, pick up your things."

Just like in the Army—or the Navy. They ran a tight ship. Kimo could understand why they had an ideal marriage. His father had brought the Navy home, and Louise happily catered to it.

Knowing that the road to promotion was forever blocked, McVay left the Navy in 1949 at the age of fifty. Ironically, he at last became Rear Admiral McVay, technically fulfilling his father's dream—though this "graveyard promotion" only served to remind him, and his father, of the "disgrace" he had suffered while on active duty.

McVay got a job representing an insurance firm, then an employee-benefit consulting company, and enjoyed being largely his own boss. Yet he remained at heart a sailor, wearing fatigues at home, barking orders to his son, living a disciplined life. And though the Navy had made him a scapegoat and ruined his future, he missed its "integrity," which contrasted with the "degrees of honesty" he found in the business world.

But McVay wouldn't be in touch with the Navy again until 1960, when Giles McCoy sent him an invitation to speak in Indianapolis at the first reunion of the survivors. He "dreaded this thing," McVay would say later. Hate mail was still coming in from bereaved loved ones blaming him for the death of a husband or son. How could he now face those who still lived? They would accuse him, taunt him, humiliate him.

Don't be silly, Louise admonished him. He was their captain. They still loved him just as he loved them. He *must* go.

And so he did. But he trembled as his plane landed in Indianapolis. Would he be greeted by shouts of "Murderer!"? By placards telling him to go home? As he stepped out of the plane with Louise at his side, he saw about a hundred people clustered at the door of the airport terminal. But in a moment, the pounding of his heart gave way to the shouting of his shipmates—welcoming him like a conquering hero. McVay broke down and wept.

The next day, he was wearing a badge identifying him as a "captain," for he had argued that he "was an honest-to-goodness captain and never was really a rear admiral." McVay, still handsome but balding and more lined now, described at one meeting of the survivors his role in the tragedy—and was thunderously applauded. The "captain" beamed. He had been forgiven by the living, if not by the relatives of the dead. Perhaps now he could lead a more normal life.

Kimo had graduated from college and gone back to Honolulu, but returned to New Orleans for a visit a few years later, in 1956— this time with a wife and a five-year-old son, Mark. As soon as they arrived, McVay and Louise virtually adopted Mark. As Kimo's wife, Betsy, would say: "I got to know two people who were adoringly devoted to each other. Each was the other's whole life. Little Mark was the only one who could intrude. They adored him. Weekends, they went to their country place on the bayou. We went with them and Dad took little Mark fishing. I think he dreamed of giving Mark all that he hadn't given to his own sons."

The years passed, and in 1961, Louise, usually so energetic, began taking naps and grew progressively more lethargic. McVay took her to the doctor, and tests were taken. The results came through— incurable cancer. Overcome with grief, McVay wrote to Kimo and Betsy, telling them the news. Would they please bring Mark to see Louise before she died.

When the couple arrived at the hospital, Betsy would recall, she "was horrified to see this once so strong woman reduced to nothingness. She did recognize Mark and actually smiled. It was really the only thing Dad could do to bring her any joy. Dad told me very matter-of-factly that he had told the doctors to keep her heavily medicated but to do nothing to save her. He just didn't want her to be in pain or to be aware of what was happening to her. I sensed that Dad was in shock."

Weeks later, the call from the hospital came. Louise was gone.

"Dad came in to tell me," Betsy would recount, "then disappeared into his room and came back with two bracelets given to his mother by the Empress of China."

McVay gave the bracelets to Betsy and, still Navy to the core, asked her to sign for them.

At Louise's funeral, McVay himself resembled death. His once splendid face was gaunt and gray, and his eyes, focusing inward, it seemed, reflected a soul seared to the roots. Most of his crew had died. His father had passed away in 1959, a tragic, brokenhearted figure. And now his dear Louise. Like some irresistible human magnet, little Mark became the recipient of all the love McVay had lavished on his wife, all that he wished he had lavished on his sons. But Mark would soon be leaving with his parents. And then he would be alone again, as he had been when a great wave had thrust him into an infinite sea.

As McVay contemplated the arid future, Betsy one day brought him a stack of letters that had accumulated. He thumbed through them, glancing at the name of the sender, then returned one to her. The letter, written in a childish scrawl, had been sent by someone whose name he did not recognize.

"Why don't you open it?" Betsy asked.

"No, I don't want to."

Betsy sensed why. He couldn't take another of those letters from a bereaved family, reminding him how he had "killed" their boy.

"You must open it," Betsy insisted. He had to conquer his fear.

"No! No! Leave me alone."

"Then, can *I* open it?" she asked.

McVay hesitated for a moment, then nodded his agreement.

Tension gripped him as Betsy tore open the envelope and silently read the letter. Finally, Betsy looked up, smiling. It was from a little neighborhood child saying she was sorry about Louise.

"The relief in Dad's eyes was overwhelming," Betsy would say.

Fearful of leaving McVay alone, Betsy persuaded him to go to New York to visit friends and relatives there. In New York, he went to see a cousin, who mentioned to him that a mutual female friend was also in mourning.

Who was this friend? he asked.

Vivian Smith.

Vivian? McVay's eyes brightened. A vivacious beauty, she had lived a few doors away from him in Washington when his father had been based there. They had grown up together and had dated in the 1930s after McVay divorced Kinau. But Vivian had married another naval officer, then divorced him and went to New York, where she became a famous Powers model. In 1947, she married Winthrop Smith, board chairman of the Merrill Lynch brokerage firm. And now Smith had died, about the same time as Louise.

Why not go to Litchfield, Connecticut, and see Vivian? McVay's cousin suggested. Perhaps they could console each other.

McVay was soon reunited with Vivian after almost thirty years. With a certain shock, he did not find the poised, carefree beauty he had once known, but a rather frumpish woman of fifty-eight, with a smile more forced than carefree. Vivian had always been independent; when she was a high-fashion model, she supported her sister and her three children, as well as her own son until he graduated from college. With her marriage to the wealthy Smith, and her entrée into a life of superluxury, self-indulgence, and social arrogance, her free spirit was unleashed in bursts of fiery temper at anyone who would dare challenge her demands or her preeminent status in Litchfield society.

But McVay saw only the Vivian of his youth. Yes, she had lost her beauty, but he, after all, was not the dashing young officer he had once been. He recalled the hours she had spent at his home after his divorce playing with the children, the evenings at the officers' club. He had thought he loved her.

Perhaps he did. And here she was now, single again—at the very moment he needed someone to talk to, someone he knew and could entrust with the secrets in his tormented soul, who would understand his agony and help him conquer it. They dated once more—just like old times. Vivian found McVay a distinguished escort who was popular with her friends, even though he had little money. And McVay found Vivian at least a partial antidote to his loneliness and grief, and she even made him laugh once in a while. Louise had only recently died, but would she not wish him to find some relief from his misery?

Shortly, McVay and his old sweetheart were married and he moved into her magnificent colonial-style mansion in affluent Litchfield. But both of them, it seemed, soon realized they had married a memory, and regretted their decision. McVay had hoped to find a suitable job in the area, but was unable to, and spent much of his time serving as Vivian's escort to parties and teas that utterly bored him. The social whirl reminded him of his life with Kinau—except that she was born into the Hawaiian aristocracy and did not need to impress herself or anyone else, but, as a naturally happy person, sought fun for fun's sake. Vivian, it seemed, was unhappy and sought the rather empty satisfaction of topping the social register.

Furthermore, Kinau had never tried to dominate or belittle her husband, and loved him as a human being if not as a model husband. Vivian, on the other hand, soon made it clear that he was, after all, only a sailor (however highly ranked), and must learn to adjust to her elite life-style. She also discouraged him, it appears, from inviting his two sons and their families to "her" home. She may have played with them as children, but they were not socially acceptable now. And in his growing depression, McVay did not put up a struggle, even though he longed to see them—especially his grandchild Mark.

On one occasion, Vivian did accompany him to Washington, where they met for an hour or two with Charles IV and his wife. The son sensed his father's unhappiness, and was shocked by her manner toward him. "Come here!" she would call. "What do you think you're doing?" she would demand.

McVay, however, was not without affection in Litchfield. He made friends at the exclusive Sanctum men's club, where he played bridge every Wednesday afternoon. And he did find several people at home who cared about him. Vivian's teen-age son, Winthrop Smith, Jr., had deeply resented him when he first moved in, wondering how his mother could marry another man, especially so soon after his father's death. But he gradually grew to like, and even love, McVay, who, in his loneliness, reached out to him. McVay dug a pond for Winthrop, and taught him how to fish, and even created a marsh so they could shoot ducks together—though once a year he would visit the bayou alone and nostalgically engage in these sports with the ghost of Louise at his side. At the same time, he developed a close relationship with Vivian's son by her first marriage, Gordon Linke.

McVay also found another friend at home—the maid, Florence Regosia, a gentle woman with red hair and blue eyes. Sometimes he spent more time talking with her while mixing drinks in the butler's pantry than he did with his wife in the drawing room. During these talks, he would often lose himself in the past.

His mother had cooked the most delicious dishes, he told her. His father had been very strict, but a great man. His elder son, he always regretted, had been unable to stay in the Navy because of his poor sight. As for Louise, she could do everything—fish, hunt, cook. He could still taste her shrimp creole. She had "stuck by" him all during the trial—every moment.

While McVay, in his own way, loved Vivian's sons and Florence, he still felt a special love for Mark, and was hoping to visit him and his family—when the news came one day in 1965: Mark had died of a brain tumor.

Mark?! Only nine years old—dead? McVay couldn't believe it. Had God saved him so that he might die many deaths? Would there never be an end to his dying?

McVay would answer this question on the snowy day of November 6, 1968. It was Wednesday, his day to play bridge at the club. Florence knocked on his door.

"Lunch is ready, Admiral McVay," she called.

"I'll be right down," he replied.

Florence was concerned about him. Though he usually tried to appear cheerful, he couldn't hide his depression the last several days. She could see it in the pensive, almost mournful expression on his face. What was troubling him—his lost men, Louise, Mark, the marriage that was barren of warmth and understanding? Florence was glad he was going to see friends after lunch, and perhaps forget his problems for a few hours. She went downstairs, set the dining-room table, and brought a bowl of vegetable soup and a turkey sandwich from the kitchen. Vivian was upstairs and her husband would be eating alone today since he was pressed for time.

McVay shortly entered the room, but strangely stood by the door with his hands behind his back.

"You are going to play bridge this afternoon, aren't you?" Florence asked.

"Yes."

"Well, don't you want some lunch first?"

"Yes, I'll have it."

Florence then went to the kitchen, and soon returned to find the soup and sandwich still there, but McVay gone.

Was he feeling all right? Florence ran upstairs and knocked on his door. No answer. She opened the door and walked in. On the night table, she saw the holster for his service revolver, which he had kept. The gun was missing.

"Oh my God!" Florence cried.

She dashed downstairs and looked through a window toward the garage. McVay's car was still there; he hadn't gone to the club. She heard shots—but it was the hunting season, of course. At that moment, there was a pounding on the back door. Perhaps it was he. Florence rushed to open it and her face dropped when she saw the caretaker, Al Dudley.

"I don't know what's happened to Admiral McVay," she said.

Dudley was pale, his eyes glassy with tears.

"It's terrible," he exclaimed. "He's lying out front. He shot himself in the head. Don't go out there! Don't look at him!"

Aghast, Florence dashed to the dining-room window, which faced the front garden, and there she saw him sprawled on the grass, blood from his head seeping into the crystal white snow. At his fingertips was a little toy sailor that he had carried around for good luck.

Rear Admiral Charles B. McVay III died a few hours later in the hospital. Ironically, unlike his Japanese counterpart, Hashimoto, he had chosen the traditional Japanese way of solving insoluble problems. He had a simple private funeral. His two sons and their wives were there, but were virtually ignored by Vivian, who would apparently never forgive her husband for killing himself on her front lawn, humiliating her before the world—at least her world. She claimed that her husband had died in a "hunting accident," but few would believe that he had gone hunting on the front lawn—with a service pistol. Within a few weeks, Vivian changed her name back to Smith.

The name McVay, however, would live on—not only in the hearts of the seamen who loved their skipper, but in the consciences of the cynics who used him to protect themselves. The ashes of Charles McVay, like those of Louise, were scattered over the Gulf of Mexico as he had requested, and he is back in the soothing embrace of his beloved. But will even an eternity of love be enough to ease the pain of the terrible wound inflicted on him by the Navy he had so cherished?

EPILOGUE

T HE COURT-MARTIAL conviction of Charles McVay was an unfortunate episode in the illustrious history of the U.S. Navy, and today still casts a shadow over its image. Even more than forty years later, naval officials are not eager to reveal all the facts. While I was able to obtain many of the documents dealing with the case, some are still unavailable to researchers, even if requested under the Freedom of Information Act. When I asked naval officials for the transcript of the Guam court of inquiry hearings on the *Indianapolis* disaster, an important source of information, they simply replied that it was not in naval files and did not explain where it might be or why it was missing. To learn the contents, I had to rely mainly on interviews.

It is perhaps not surprising, therefore, that efforts by McVay's family and survivors of the *Indianapolis* tragedy to overturn the skipper's conviction, or at least to obtain a Presidential Unit Citation to honor his name, have met with total resistance from naval authorities. When Giles McCoy, as chairman of the Indianapolis Survivors Association, urged President Ford in 1975 to award a citation to the survivors, Rear Admiral James W. Nance, the assistant vice chief of naval operations, wrote back:

> The history of the U.S.S. *Indianapolis* and her accomplishments are
> indeed impressive. However, when considering these accomplishments

with those of other equally fine ships, they are not considered to be of a degree to warrant award of the Presidential Unit Citation.

In fury, McCoy replied:

> We receive your answer and comparison as being most disrespectful. You made no attempt at giving a fair review. You did not look into the history before and after the death of the great ship USS *Indianapolis*. There is no conceivable way to classify our events as similar to any other equally fine ships. . . . Due to the negligence of the Naval Operations Department, we spent a total of five days in . . . life jackets and during the last three days lost at least 75 percent of our crew. There would have been 100 percent lost had we not been accidentally found by pilot Lieutenant Charles Gwinn on the fourth day.
>
> Not until now did we intend to downgrade the Navy Department, but your letter, sir, was most dishonoring to our memories of the great naval force serving our country then and now.
>
> We realize that you have all the power against us in fighting this 30-year-old thorn in your side. You will not bury us with the *Indianapolis* nor with our deceased Captain Charles B. McVay III. We the remaining survivors and the souls of our shipmates [who were] lost . . . will be back to haunt you. . . .

And McCoy, as good as his word, has continued to haunt the Navy. In 1980, he renewed his request for a Presidential Unit Citation to President Reagan's new Secretary of the Navy—Edward Hidalgo. He was the man who had advised Secretary Forrestal thirty-five years earlier not to overturn Captain McVay's conviction or to make it seem that the Navy was apologizing for it even though the evidence against the captain might be "super-technical."

Hidalgo responded:

> Your desire to receive a Presidential Unit Citation is fully understood. However, . . . the Chief of Naval Operations determined that although the USS *Indianapolis* had a fine record prior to her sinking, she did not meet the criteria for [such an award].

McVay's son, Kimo, meanwhile, has investigated all possibilities for public vindication of his father. His hopes soared when Louise McVay's cousin, Graham Claytor, who helped to save many survivors, became Secretary of the Navy under President Jimmy Carter, but he proved powerless to rectify the injustice. Nor did a plea to President Ronald Reagan in 1983 bear fruit. A White House assistant replied:

> I have been advised that all avenues of appellate review have long since been exhausted. No authority exists for the Secretary of the Navy or the Judge Advocate General to change the findings of the court-martial in your father's case. The Pardon Attorney's Office, Department of Justice, has also advised that Presidential pardons are not awarded posthumously.

One route he could take, Kimo was told by Senator Daniel Inouye of Hawaii, would be to petition the Board for the Correction of Naval Records to expunge all mention of his father's court-martial from his military record. This action would produce a "legal fiction" that would permit one to be "technically correct in saying that (the skipper's) record is clean."

Another possibility, the senator said, lay in a joint congressional resolution expressing the sense of the Congress that an injustice had been done; it would be signed by the President and become public law. But this solution, Kimo was warned, is "exceedingly rare and would have difficulties in committee and on the floor of both Houses of Congress." And in any case, it wouldn't nullify the conviction.

McVay's sons and the survivors still demand full, and not simply "fictional," vindication of the skipper—in addition to presidential recognition of the ship's fine record as a special tribute to the man and his crew. It is perhaps because such actions would amount to an apology and admission of error that naval leaders are loath to take them.

But McVay's supporters are asking if the American democratic system is so inflexible that an injustice cannot be rectified; if the U.S. Navy, which so gloriously helped to conquer the enemy, is incapable of conquering itself. These supporters feel that unless the President and Congress can find a way to exonerate McVay and compensate his crew, the living and the dead, a black mark could stain the honor of the Navy long after the skipper's name is engraved in naval lore as a victim not only of the Navy's worst sea disaster, but possibly its worst moral disaster as well.

APPENDIX

Crew of
the USS *Indianapolis*

(asterisks denote survivors)

Abbott, George Stanley, S1
Acosta, Charles Mack, MM3
*Adams, Leo Harry, S2
Adams, Pat L., S2
Adorante, Dante W., S2
*Akines, William Roy, S2
Albright, Charles Erskine, Jr., Cox
*Allard, Vincent J., QM3
Allen, Paul Franklin, S1
Allmaras, Harold Dean, F2
*Altschuler, Allan Harvey, S2
Alvey, Edward Suites, Jr., AerM2
Amick, Homer Irwin, S2
*Anderson, Erick T., S2
Anderson, Lawrence Joseph, SK2
Anderson, Leonard Ole, MM3
Anderson, Richard Lew, F2
Anderson, Sam General, S2
Anderson, Vincent Udell, BM1
*Andrews, William Robert, S2
Annis, James Bernard, Jr., CEMA
Anthony, Harold Robert, PhM3
Antonie, Charles Jacob, F2
*Anunti, John Melvin, M2
Armenta, Lorenzo, S2
*Armistead, John H., S2
Arnold, Carl Lloyd, S1

Ashford, Chester Windell, WT2
*Ashford, John T., Jr., RT3
Atkinson, J. P., Cox
Aull, Joseph Harry, S2
*Ault, William Frazier, S2
Ayotte, Lester James, S2

Backus, Thomas Hawkins, Lt. (jg)
Baker, Daniel Albert, S2
Baker, Frederick Harold, S2
Baker, William Marvin, Jr., EM1
*Baldridge, Clovis Roger, EM1
Ball, Emmet Edwin, S2
Ballard, Courtney Jackson, SSMB3
Barenthin, Leonard William, S1
Barker, Robert Craig, Jr., RT1
Barksdale, Thomas Leon, FCO3
Barnes, Paul Clayton, F2
Barnes, Willard Merlin, MM1
Barra, Raymond James, CGM2
Barrett, James B., S2
Barry, Charles, Lt. (jg)
*Barto, Lloyd Peter, S1
Barton, George Stewart, Y3
*Bateman, Bernard Byron, F2
Batenhorst, Wilfred John, MM3
Batson, Eugene Clifford, S2

Batten, Robert Edmon, S1
Batts, Edward Daniel, StM1
*Beane, James Albert, F2
*Beaty, Donald Lee, S1
Becker, Myron Melvin, WT2
Beddington, Charles Earnest, S1
Bedsted, Leo A. K., F1
Beister, Richard James, WT3
*Belcher, James R., S1
*Bell, Maurice Glenn, S1
Bennett, Dean Randall, HA1
Bennett, Ernest Franklin, B3
Bennett, Toney Wade, St3
Benning, Harry, S1
*Benton, Clarence Upton, CFCP
*Bernacil, Concepcion Peralta, FC3
Berry, Joseph, Jr., StM1
Berry, William Henry, St3
Beukema, Kenneth Jay, S2
Beuschlein, Joseph Carl, S2
Biddison, Charles Lawrence, S1
Billings, Robert Burton, Ens.
Billingsley, Robert Frederick, GM3
Bilz, Robert Eugene, S2
Bishop, Arthur, Jr., S2
*Bitonti, Louis Peter, S1
Blackwell, Fermon Malichi, SSML3
*Blanthorn, Bryan, S1
*Blum, Donald Joseph, Ens.
Boege, Raynard Richard, S2
Bogan, Jack Roberts, RM1
Bollinger, Richard Howard, S1
*Booth, Sherman Chester, S1
Borton, Herbert Elton, SCB2
Boss, Herbert George, S2
Bott, Wilbur Melvin, S2
Bowles, Eldridge Wayne, S1
Bowman, Charles Edward, TC1
Boyd, Troy Howard, GM3
Bradley, William Hearn, S2
Brake, John, Jr., S2
*Brandt, Russell Lee, F2
Braun, Neal Frederick, S2
*Bray, Harold John, Jr., S2
Brice, "R" "V", S2
Bridge, Wayne Aron, S2

Bright, Chester Lee, S2
Briley, Harold Vinton, MaM3
Brinker, David A., Pfc (*Marine*)
Brooks, Ulysess Ray, CWTA
Brophy, Thomas D'Arcy, Jr., Ens.
Brown, Edward Augustus, WT3
*Brown, Edward Joseph, S1
Brown, Orlo N., Pfc (*Marine*)
Bruce, Russell William, S2
Brule, Maurice Joseph, S2
*Brundidge, Robert Henry, S1
Bruneau, Charles Albino, GM3
*Buckett, Victor Robert, Y2
Budish, David, S2
*Bullard, John Kenneth, S1
*Bunai, Robert Peter, SM1
Bunn, Horace G., S2
*Burdorf, Wilbert John, Cox
Burkhartsmeier, Anton Tony, S1
Burkholtz, Frank, Jr., EM3
Burleson Martin LaFayette, S1
Burrs, John William, S1
Burt, William George Allan, QM3
*Burton, Curtis Henry, S1
Bush, John Richard, Pvt. (*Marine*)
Bushong, John Richard, GM3

Cadwallader, John Julian, RT3
Cain, Alfred Brown, RT3
Cairo, William George, BUG1
Call, James Edward, RM3
Cameron, John Watson, GM2
Camp, Garrison, StM2
Campana, Paul, RdM3
*Campbell, Hamer Edward, Jr., GM3
*Campbell, Louis Dean, AOM3
Campbell, Wayland Dee, SF3
Candalino, Paul Louis, Lt. (jg)
Cantrell, Billy George, F2
Carnell, Lois Wayne, S2
Carpenter, Willard Adolphus, SM3
Carr, Harry Leroy, S2
Carroll, Gregory Krichbaum, S1
Carroll, Rachel Walker, Cox
Carson, Clifford, F1

Carstemsen, Richard, S2
*Carter, Grover Clifford, S2
*Carter, Lindsey Linvill, S2
*Carter, Lloyd George, Cox
*Carver, Grover Cleveland, S1
*Cassidy, John Curron, S1
Castaldo, Patrick Peter, GM2
Castiaux, Ray Vernon, S2
Casto, William Harrison, S1
Cavil, Robert Ralph, MM2
Cavitt, Clinton Columbus, WT3
*Celaya, Adolfo Valdo, F2
*Centazzo, Frank Joseph, SM3
*Chamness, John Desel, S2
Chandler, Lloyd Nyle, S2
Chart, Joseph, EM3
Christian, Lewis Enock, Jr., WO
Clark, Eugene, CK3
*Clark, Orsen, S2
Clements, Harold Preston, S2
*Clinton, George William, S1
Clinton, Leland Jack, Lt. (jg)
Cobb, William Lester, MoMM3
Cole, Walter Henry, CRMA
Coleman, Cedric Foster, Lt.
   Comdr.
*Coleman, Robert Edward, F2
*Collier, Charles Rives, RM2
Collins, James, StML
Colvin, Frankie Lee, SSMT2
Condon, Berna Theodore, RdM1
Connelly, David Fallon, Ens.
Conrad, James Patrick, EM3
Conser, Donald Lynn, SC2
Consiglio, Joseph William, FC2
Conway, Thomas Michael, Lt.
   (chaplain)
Cook, Floyd Edward, SF3
Cooper, Dale, Jr., F2
Copeland, Willard James, S2
*Costner, Homer Jackson, Cox
Countryman, Robert Earl, S2
*Cowen, Donald Rodney, FC3
Cox, Alford Edward, GM3
*Cox, Loel Dene, S2
Crabb, Donald Calvin, RM2

*Crane, Granville Shaw, Jr., MM2
Crews, Hugh Coachman, Lt. (jg)
Crites, Oval D., WT1
Cromling, Charles J., Jr., Sgt.
   (Marine)
Crouch, Edwin Mason, Capt.
   (Passenger)
Crum, Charles Junior, S2
Cruz, Jose Santos, CCKA
Curtis, Edwin Eugene, CTCP

Dagenhart, Charles Romeo, Jr.,
   PhM2
Dale, Elwood Richard, F1
*Daniel, Harold William, CBMA
Daniello, Anthony Gene, S1
Davis, James Clark, RM3
Davis, Kenneth Graham, F1
Davis, Stanley Gilbert, Lt. (jg)
Davis, Thomas Edward, SM2
Davis, William H., Pfc (Marine)
Day, Richard Raymond, Jr., S2
Dean, John Thomas, Jr., S2
*DeBernardi, Louie, BM1
DeFoor, Walton, RdM3
DeMars, Edgar Joseph, CBMA
DeMent, Dayle Pershing, S1
Denney, Lloyd, Jr., S2
*Dewing, Ralph Otto, S1 FC3
*Dezelske, William Bruce, MM2
Dimond, John Nelson, S2
Dollins, Paul, RM2
Donald, Lyle Herbert, EM1
Doney, William Junior, F2
*Donner, Clarence W., RT3
Dorman, William Burns, S1
Dornetto, Frank Paul, WT1
Doss, James Monroe, S2
Doucette, Roland Ordean, S2
*Douglas, Gene Dale, F2
Dove, Bassil Raymond, SKD2
Dowdy, Lowell Steven, CWO
Drane, James Anthony, GM3
*Drayton, William Harry, EM2
Driscoll, David Lowell, Lt. (jg)
*Dronet, Joseph E. J., S2

Drummond, James Joseph, F2
Drury, Richard Eugene, S2
*Dryden, William Howard, MM1
Dufraine, Delbert Elmer, S1
Dunbar, Jess Lee, F2
Dupeck, Albert, Jr., Pfc (*Marine*)
Durand, Ralph Joseph, Jr., S2
Dycus, Donald, S2

Eakins, Morris Bradford, F2
Eames, Paul Herford, Jr., Ens.
Eastman, Chester Steve, S2
*Eck, Harold Adam, S2
Eddinger, John William, S1
Eddy, Richard LeRoy, RM3
Edwards, Alwyn Curtis, F2
Edwards, Roland James, BM1
E'Golf, Harold Wesley, S2
Elliott, Harry William, S2
Elliott, Kenneth Albert, S1
Emery, William Friend, S1
Emsley, William Joseph, S1
Engelsman, Ralph, S2
Epperson, Ewell, S1
Epperson, George Lensey, S1
*Erickson, Theodore Mentzer, S2
Ernst, Robert Carl, F2
*Erwin, Louis Harold, Cox
*Ethier, Eugene Edwin, EM3
Eubanks, James Harold, S1
Evans, Arthur Jerome, PhM2
*Evans, Claudus, GM3
Everett, Charles Norman EM2
Evers, Lawrence Lee, CMMA
Eyet, Donald Archie, S1

Fantasia, Frank Alfred, F2
Farber, Sheldon Lee, S2
Farley, James William, S1
*Farmer, Archie Calvin, Cox
*Farris, Eugene Francis, S1
Fasthorse, Vincent, S2
*Feakes, Fred Atkinson, AOM1
*Fedorski, Nicholas Walter, S1
Feeney, Paul Ross, S2
*Felts, Donald "J," BM1

*Ferguson, Albert Edward, CMMA
Ferguson, Russel Myers, RT3
Figgins, Harley Dean, WT2
Firestone, Kenneth Francis, FC2
Firmin, John Alden Homer, S2
*Fitting, Johnny Wayne, GM1
*Flaten, Harold James, WT2
Fleischauer, Donald William, S1
Fleshman, Vernon Leslie, S2
Flynn, James Madison, Jr., S1
Flynn, Joseph Ambrose, Comdr.
Foell, Cecil Duane, Ens.
*Fortin, Verlin Leverre, WT3
*Foster, Verne Elmer, F2
*Fox, William Henry, Jr., F2
*François, Norbert Edward, F1
Frank, Rudolph Anthony, S2
Franklin, Jack Ray, RdM3
Freeze, Howard Bruce, Lt. (jg)
French, Douglas Orrin, FC3
French, Jimmy Junior, QM3
Fritz, Leonard Albert, MM3
Frontino, Vincent Fred, MoMM3
Frorath, Donald Henry, S2
Fuchs, Herman Ferdinand, CWO
Fuller, Arnold Ambrose, F2
Fulton, William Clarence, CRMA
*Funkhouser, Robert Morris, ART2

*Gabrillo, Juan, S2
Gaither, Forest Maylon, FC2
*Galante, Angelo, S2
*Galbraith, Norman Scott, MM2
*Gardner, Roscoe Wallace, F2
Gardner, Russel Thomas, F2
Garner, Glenn Richard, MM2
*Gause, Robert Pritchard, QM1
Gause, Rubin Conley, Jr., Ens.
*Gemza, Rudolph Arnold, FCO3
*George, Gabriel Vincent, MM3
Gerncross, Frederick Joseph, Jr.,
   Ens.
*Gettleman, Robert Alfred, S2
*Gibson, Buck Warren, S1
Gibson, Curtis Woodrow, S2
Gibson, Ganola Francis, LM3

Gilbert, Warner, Jr., S1
*Gilcrease, James, S2
Gill, Paul Edward, WT2
Gilmore, Wilbur Albert, S2
Gismondi, Michael Vincent, S1
*Gladd, Millard, Jr., MM2
Glaub, Francis Anthony, GM2
*Glenn, Jay Rollin, AMM3
Glovka, Erwin Samuel, S2
Godfrey, Marlo Roy, RM3
Goeckel, Ernest Stanley, Lt. (jg)
*Goff, Thomas Guy, SF3
Golden, Curry, StM1
Golden, James LaVonne, S1
Gonzales, Ray Adam, S2
*Gooch, William Leroy, F2
Good, Robert Kenneth, MM3
Goodwin, Oliver Albert, CRTA
Gore, Leonard Franklin, S2
Gorecki, Joseph Walter, SK3
Gottman, Paul James, S2
Gove, Carroll Lansing, S2
*Gray, Willis Leroy, S1
Greathouse, Bud R., S1
Green, Robert Urban, S2
*Green, Tolbert, Jr., S1
Greene, Samuel Gile, S1
*Greenlee, Charles Ians, S2
*Greenwald, Jacob, 1st Sgt. (Marine)
Greer, Bob Eugene, S2
Gregory, Garland Glen, F1
Greif, Matthias Daniel, WT3
Gries, Richard Charles, F2
Griest, Frank David, GM3
Griffin, Jackie Dale, S1
*Griffith, Robert Lee, S2
Griffiths, Leonard Sylvester, S2
Griggs, Donald Ray, F1
Grimes, David Elimer, S2
Grimes, James Francis, S2
Grimm, Loren E., Pfc (Marine)
Groce, Floyd Vernon, RdM2
Groch, John Thomas, MM3
Guenther, Morgan Edward, EM3
Guerrero, John Gomez, S1
Guillot, Murphy Umbroise, F1

Guye, Ralph Lee, Jr., QM3
Guyon, Harold Lewis, F1

Haberman, Bernard, S2
Haduch, John Martin, S1
Hale, Robert Baldwin, Lt.
Hale, William Franklin, S2
Hall, Pressie, F1
Halloran, Edward George, MM3
Ham, Saul Anthony, S1
Hambo, William Perrin, PhM3
Hammen, Robert, PhoM3
Hamrick, James Junior, S2
Hancock, Thomas A., Pfc (Marine)
Hancock, William Allen, GM3
Hankinson, Clarence Winfield, F2
Hansen, Henry, S2
*Hanson, Harley Clarence, WO
Harland, George Alfred, S2
Harp, Charlie Hardin, S1
Harper, Vasco, StM1
*Harrell, Edgar A., Corp. (Marine)
Harris, James Davis, F2
Harris, Willard Eugene, F2
*Harrison, Cecil Manly, CWO
Harrison, Frederick Elliott, S2
Harrison, James McLaurin, S1
*Hart, Fred Junior, RT2
Hartrick, Willie Boomer, MM1
*Hatfield, Willie, S2
Haubrich, Cloud David, S2
Hauser, Jack Isaac, Sk2
*Havener, Harlan Carl, F2
*Havins, Otha Alton, Y3
Hayes, Charles David, Lt. Comdr.
Hayles, Felix, Ck3
*Haynes, Lewis Leavitt, Lt. Comdr.
Haynes, Robert Albert, Lt.
Haynes, William Alexander, S1
Heerdt, Raymond Edward, F2
Heggie, William Arnold, RdM3
Heinz, Richard Anthony, HA1
*Heller, John, S2
Heller, Robert Jacob, Jr., S2
Helscher, Ralph John, S1
Helt, Jack Edward, F2

Henderson, Ralph Lewis, S1
Hendron, James Raymond, Jr., F2
Henry, Earl O'Dell, Lt. Comdr.
*Hensch, Erwin Frederick, Lt.
Hensley, Clifford, SSMB2
Herbert, Jack Erwin, BM1
Herndon, Duane, S2
*Hershberger, Clarence Lamar, S1
Herstine, James Franklin, Ens.
Hickey, Harry Todd, RM3
Hicks, Clarence, S1
Hiebert, Lloyd Henry, GM1
Hill, Clarence Max, CWTP
Hill, Joe Walker, StM1
Hill, Nelson Page, Jr., Lt.
Hill, Richard Norman, Ens.
*Hind, Lyle Lewis, S2
Hines, Lionel Gordon, WT1
*Hinken, John Richard, Jr., F2
Hobbs, Melvin Dow, S1
*Hodge, Howard Henry, RM2
Hodgins, Lester Byron, S2
Hodshire, John William, S2
Hoerres, George Joseph, S2
Holden, Punciano Aledia, St1
Holland, John F., Jr., Pfc (Marine)
Hollingsworth, Jimmie Lee, StM2
Holloway, Andrew Jackson, S2
Holloway, Ralph Harris, Cox
Hoogerwerf, John, Jr., F1
*Hoopes, Gordon Herbert, S2
Hooper, Prentice William, S1
Hopper, Roy Lee, AM1
*Horner, Durward Richard, WO
Horr, Wesley Alan, F2
Horrigan, John Gerard, F1
*Horvath, George John, F1
*Hoskins, William Orson, Y3
*Houck, Richard Eugene, EM3
Houston, Robert Garvis, F1
Houston, William Howard, PhM2
Hov, Donald Anthony, S1
*Howison, John Donald, Ens.
Hubbard, Gordon R., Pfc (Marine)
Hubbard, Leland R., Pfc (Marine)
*Hubeli, Joseph Francis, S2

Huebner, Harry Helmut, S1
Hughes, Lawrence Edwin, F2
*Hughes, Max M., Pfc (Marine)
Hughes, Robert Alexander, FC3
Hughes, William Edward, SSML2
Humphrey, Maynard Lee, S2
Hunter, Arthur Riles, Jr., QM1
Huntley, Virgil Clair, CWO
*Hupka, Clarence Elmer, Bkr1
*Hurley, Woodrow, GM2
Hurst, Robert Huntley, Lt.
Hurt, James Edward, S2
Hutchison, Merle Byron, S2

Igou, Floyd, Jr., RM2
Izor, Walter Eugene, FL

Jackson, Henry, StML
*Jacob, Melvin C., Pfc (Marine)
*Jacquemot, Joseph Alexander, S2
Jadloski, George Kenneth, S2
Jakubisin, Joseph Sylvester, S2
*James, Woodie Eugene, Cox
Janney, Johns Hopkins, Comdr.
*Jarvis, James Kenneth, AM3
Jeffers, Wallace Mansfield, Cox
Jenney, Charles Irvin, Lt.
Jensen, Chris Alstrum, S2
*Jensen, Eugene Wenzel, S2
Jewell, Floyd Raymond, SKV1
Johnson, Bernard John, S2
Johnson, Earl Rankin, BM2
Johnson, Elwood Wilbur S2
Johnson, George Glen, S2
Johnson, Harold Bernard, S1
Johnson, Lewis Eugene, S1
Johnson, Ray Francis, MM1
Johnson, Scott Albert, F2
Johnson, Sidney Bryant, S1
Johnson, Walter Marion, Jr., S1
*Johnson, William Albert, S1
*Jones, Clinton Leroy, Cox
Jones, George Edward, S2
Jones, Jim, S2
Jones, Kenneth Malcolm, F1
*Jones, Sidney, S1

Jones, Stanley Fairwick, S2
Jordan, Henry, StM2
Jordan, Thomas Hardin, S2
Josey, Clifford Odell, S2
Jump, David Allen, Ens.
Jurgensmeyer, Alfred Joseph, S2
*Jurkiewicz, Raymond Stanley, S2
*Justice, Robert Eugene, S2

Karpel, Daniel Larence, BM1
Karter, Leo Clement, Jr., S2
Kasten, Stanley Otto, HA1
*Katsikas, Gust Constantine, S1
Kawa, Raymond Philip, SK3
*Kazmierski, Walter, S1
Keeney, Robert Allan, Ens.
*Kees, Shelous Eugene, EM2
Keith, Everett Edward, S1
Kelly, Albert Raymond, S2
*Kemp, David Poole, Jr., SC3
*Kenly, Oliver Wesley, RdM3
Kennedy, Andrew Jackson, Jr., S2
Kennedy, Robert Arthur, S1
Kenny, Francis Joseph Patrick, S2
Kenworthy, Glenn W., Corp.
  (*Marine*)
Kephart, Paul, S1
*Kerby, Deo Earl, S1
Kern, Harry Gilbert, S1
Key, S. T., EM2
*Keyes, Edward Hiram, Cox
Kight, Audy Carl, S1
Kilgore, Archie Clinton, F2
Killman, Robert Eugene, GM3
Kinard, Nolan Dave, S1
Kincaid, Joseph Ercel, FC2
*King, A. C., S1
King, Clarence, Jr., StM2
King, James Thomas, S1
King, Richard Eugene, S2
King, Robert Harold, S2
Kinnaman, Robert Harold, S2
*Kinzle, Raymond Arthur, Bkr2
Kirby, Harry, S1
Kirchner, John H., Pvt. (*Marine*)
Kirk, James Roy, SC3

*Kirkland, Marvin Foulk, S1
Kirkman, Walter William, SF1
*Kiselica, Joseph Frederick, AMM2
*Kittoe, James William, F2
*Klappa, Ralph Donald, S2
*Klaus, Joseph Frank, S1
Klein, Raymond James, S1
Klein, Thiel Joseph, SK3
Knernschield, Andrew Nick, S1
Knoll, Paul Edward, Cox
Knott, Elburn Louis, S1CQ (FC)
Knudtson, Raymond Arthur, S1
Knupke, Richard Roland, MM3
*Koch, Edward Chris, EM3
Koegler, Albert, S1
Koegler, William, SC3
Kolakowski, Ceslaus, SM3
Kollinger, Robert Eugene, S1
Konesny, John Matthew, S1
Koopman, Walter Frederick, F2
Koppang, Raymond Irwin, Lt. (jg)
Kouski, Fred, GM3
Kovalick, George Richard, S2
*Koziara, George, S2
Kozik, Raymond, S1
Krawitz, Harry Joseph, MM3
*Kreis, Clifford Eddie, S1
*Kreuger, Dale Frank, F2
*Kreuger, Norman Frederick, S2
Kron, Herman Edward, Jr., GM3
Kronenberger, William Maurice,
  GM3
Kruse, Darwin Glen, S2
Krzyzewski, John Michael, S2
Kuhn, Clair Joseph, S1
Kulovitz, Raymond Joseph, S2
*Kurlick, George Robert, FC3
*Kuryla, Michael Nicholas, Jr., Cox
Kusiak, Alfred Meciuston, S2
Kwiatkowski, Marion Joseph, S2

Labuda, Arthur Al, QM3
La Fontaine, Paul Sylvester, S1
Lakatos, Emil Joseph, MM3
Lake, Murl Christy, S1
Lamb, Robert Clyde, EM3

Lambert, Leonard Francis, S1
Landon, William Wallace, Jr., FCO2
*Lane, Ralph, CMMA
*Lanter, Kenley MacKenzie, S1
*La Paglia, Carlos, GM2
La Parl, Lawrence Edward, Jr., S2
Lapczynski, Edward William, S1
Larsen, Harlan D., Pfc (Marine)
Larsen, Melvin Robert, S2
Latigue, Jackson, StM1
Latimer, Billy Franklin, S1
Latzer, Solomon, S2
Laughlin, Fain Heskett, SK3
*Laws, George Edward, S1
Leathers, William Ben, MM3
LeBaron, Robert Walter, S2
*Lebow, Cleatus Archie, FCO3
*Leemerman, Arthur Louis, RdM3
Lees, Henry W., Pfc (Marine)
Leluika, Paul Peter, S2
Lestina, Francis Joseph, S1
Letizia, Vincencio, S2
Letz, Wilbert Joseph, SK1
Levalley, William Delbert, EM2
Leventon, Mervin Charles, MM2
Le Vieux, John Joseph, F2
Lewellen, Thomas Edgar, S2
Lewis, James Robert, F2
Lewis, John Robert, GM3
Linden, Charles Gerald, WT2
Lindsay, Norman Lee, SF3
Link, George Charles, S1
Linn, Roy, S1
Linville, Cecil Harrison, SF2
Linville, Harry Junior, S1
Lippert, Robert George, S1
Lipski, Stanley Walter, Comdr.
Little, Frank Edward, MM2
Livermore, Raymond Irving, S2
Lloyd, John Francis, WT2
Loch, Edwin Peter, S2
*Lockwood, Thomas Homer, S2
Loeffler, Paul Eugene, Jr., S2
*Loftis, James Bryant, Jr., S1
Loftus, Ralph Dennis, F2

Lohr, Leo William, S1
Lombardi, Ralph, S1
Long, Joseph William, S1
Longwell, Donald Jack, S1
*Lopetz, Sam, S1
*Lopez, Daniel Balterzar, F2
Lorenc, Edward Richard, S2
*Lucas, Robert Andrew, S2
*Lucca, Frank John, F2
Luhman, Emerson David, MM3
Lundgren, Albert Davis, S1
Luttrull, Claud Ancil, Cox
Lutz, Charles Herbert, S1

*Maas, Melvin Adolph, S1
Mabee, Kenneth Charles, S1
*Mace, Harold A., S2
MacFarland, Keith Irving, Lt. (jg)
Machado, Clarence James, WT2
*Mack, Donald Flemming, Bug1
*Maday, Anthony Francis, AMM1
Madigan, Harry Francis, BM2
Magdics, Steve, Jr., F2
Magray, Dwain Frederick, S2
*Makaroff, Chester John, GM3
Makowski, Robert Thomas, CWTA
*Maldonado, Salvador, Bkr1
*Malena, Joseph John, Jr., GM2
Malone, Cecil Edward, S2
Malone, Elvin, C., S1
Malone, Michael Leo, Jr., Lt. (jg)
*Malski, Joseph John, S1
Maness, Charles Franklin, F2
Mankin, Howard James, GM3
Mann, Clifford Eugene, S1
Mansker, LaVoice, S2
Mantz, Keith Hubert, S1
Marciulaitis, Charles, S1
Marple, Paul Thomas, Ens.
Markmann, Frederick Henry, WT1
Marshall, John Lucas, WT2
Marshall, Robert Wallace, S2
Martin, Albert, S2
Martin, Everett Gilliland, S1
Marttila, Howard W., Pvt. (Marine)

Massier, George Arcade, S1
Mastrecola, Michael Martin, S2
Matheson, Richard Robert, PhM3
*Matrulla, John, S1
Mauntel, Paul John, S2
*Maxwell, Farrell Jacob, S1
McBride, Ronald Gene, S1
McBryde, Frank Eugene, S2
*McCall, Donald Clifton, S2
*McClain, Raymond Bryant, BM2
McClary, Lester Earl, S2
McClure, David Leroy, EM2
McComb, Everett Albert, F1
McCord, Edward Franklin, EM3
McCorkle, Ray Ralph, S1
McCormick, Earl William,
  MoMM2
*McCoy, Giles G., Pfc (Marine)
McCoy, John Seybold, Jr., M2
*McCrory, Millard Virgil, Jr., WT2
McCroskey, Paul Franklin, S1
McDaniel, Johnny Alfred, S1
McDonald, Franklin Gilreath, Jr.,
  F2
McDonner, David Pious, Jr., F1
McDowell, Robert Earl, S1
*McElroy, Clarence Ernest, Jr., S1
*McFall, Walter Eugene, S2
McFee, Carl Synder, SC1
*McGinnis, Paul Wendle, SM3
McGinty, John Matthew, S1
*McGuiggan, Robert Melvin, S1
McGuire, Denis, S2
McGuirk, Philip Arthur, Lt. (jg)
*McHenry, Loren Charles, Jr., S1
McHone, Ollie, F1
McKee, George Edward, Jr., S1
McKenna, Michael Joseph, S1
*McKenzie, Ernest Eugene, S1
McKinnon, Francis Moore, Y3
*McKissick, Charles Brite, Lt. (jg)
*McKlin, Henry Theodore, S1
*McLain, Patrick Joseph, S2
McLean, Douglas Bruce, EM3
McNabb, Thomas, Jr., F2
McNickle, Arthur Samuel, F1

McQuitty, Roy Edward, Cox
*McVay, Charles Butler, III, Capt.
*McVay, Richard Calvin, Y3
Meade, Sidney Howard, S1
Mehlbaum, Raymond Aloysius, S1
Meier, Harold Edward, S2
Melichar, Charles Harry, EM3
Melvin, Carl Lavern, F1
Mencheff, Manual Angel, S2
*Meredith, Charles Everett, S1
Mergler, Charles Marlen, RdM2
Messenger, Leonard J., Pfc (Marine)
*Mestas, Nestor A., WT2
Metcalf, David William, GM3
*Meyer, Charles Thomas, S2
Michael, Bertrand Franklin, Bkr2
Michael, Elmer Orion, S1
Michno, Arthur Richard, S2
Mikeska, Willie Wodrew, S2
*Mikolayek, Joseph, Cox
*Milbrodt, Glen LaVerne, S2
Miles, Theodore Kerr, Lt.
Miller, Artie Ronald, GM2
Miller, George Edwin, F1
Miller, Glenn Evert, S2
Miller, Samuel George, Jr., FC3
Miller, Walter Raymond, S2
Miller, Walter William, B1
Miller, Wilbur Harold, CMMP
Mills, William Harry, EM3
*Miner, Herbert Jay, RT2
Minor, Richard Leon, S1
Minor, Robert Warren, S2
Mirich, Wally Mayo, S1
Mires, Carl Emerson, S2
Miskowiec, Theodore Francis, S1
*Mitchell, James Edward, S2
Mitchell, James Hamilton, Jr., Sk1
*Mitchell, Kenneth Earl, S1
*Mitchell, Norval Jerry, Jr., S1
Mitchell, Paul Boone, FC3
Mitchell, Winston Cooper, S1
Mittler, Peter John, Jr., GM3
Mixon, Malcom Lois, GM2
*Mlady, Clarence Charles, S1
*Modesitt, Carl Elsworth, S2

*Modisher, Melvin Wayne, Lt. (jg)
Moncrief, Mack Daniel, S2
Monks, Robert Bruce, GM3
Montoya, Frank Edward, S1
Moore, Donald George, S2
Moore, Elbert, S2
Moore, Harley Edward, S1
Moore, Kyle Campbell, Lt. Comdr.
Moore, Wyatt Patton, Bkr1
*Moran, Joseph John, RM1
*Morgan, Eugene Stanley, BM2
*Morgan, Glenn Grover, Bgm3
Morgan, Lewis E., S2
Morgan, Telford Frank, Ens.
*Morris, Albert Oliver, S1
Morse, Kendall Harold, Lt. (jg)
Morton, Charles Wesley, S2
Morton, Marion Ellis, S2
*Moseley, Morgan Millard, SC1
Moulton, Charles Calvin, S2
*Mowrey, Ted Eugene, SK3
Moynelo, Harold Clifton, Jr., Ens.
Mroszak, Francis Alfred, S2
*Muldoon, John James, MM1
*Mulvey, William Robert, BM1
Munson, Bryan C., Pfc (Marine)
Murillo, Sammy, S2
Murphy, Allen, S2
Murphy, Charles T., Pfc (Marine)
*Murphy, Paul James, FC3
Musarra, Joe, S1
Myers, Charles Lee, Jr., S2
Myers, Glen Alan, MM2
*Myers, H. B., F2

Nabers, Neal Adrian, S2
*Naspini, Joseph Anthony, F2
Neal, Charles Keith, S2
Neal, George M., S2
Neal, William F., Pfc (Marine)
Neale, Harlan Benjamin, S2
*Nelsen, Edward John, GM1
*Nelson, Frank Howard, S2
Neu, Hugh Herbert, S2
Neubauer, Richard, S2

Neuman, Jerome Clifford, F1
Neville, Bobby Gene, S2
Newcomer, Lewis Willard, MM3
Newell, James Thomas, EM1
*Newhall, James Franklin, S1
*Nichols, James Clarence, S2
Nichols, Joseph Lawrence, BM2
Nichols, Paul Virgil, MM3
Nielsen, Carl Aage Chor, Jr., F1
Nieto, Baltazar Portales, GM3
*Nightingale, William Oliver, MM1
Niskanen, John Hubert, F2
*Nixon, Daniel Merrill, S2
*Norberg, James Arthur, CBMP
Norman, Theodore Raymond, GM2
Nowak, George Joseph, F2
Nugent, William Gerald, S2
Nunley, James Preston, F1
*Nunley, Troy Audie, S2
Nutt, Raymond Albert, S2
*Nuttall, Alexander Carlyle, S1

*Obledo, Mike Guerra, S1
O'Brien, Arthur Joseph, S2
O'Callaghan, Del Roger, WT2
Ochoa, Ernest, FC3
*O'Donnell, James Edward, WT3
Olderon, Bernhard Gunnar, S1
*Olijar, John, S1
O'Neil, Eugene Elbert, S1
Orr, Homer Lee, HA1
Orr, John Irwin, Jr., Lt.
*Orsburn, Frank Harold, SSML2
Ortiz, Orlando Robert, Y3
Osburn, Charles William, S2
Ott, Theodore Gene, Y1
*Outland, Felton James, S1
*Overman, Thurman David, S2
*Owen, Keith Nichols, SC3
Owens, Robert Seldon, Jr., QM3
Owensby, Clifford Cecil, F2

*Pace, Curtis, S2
*Pacheco, Jose Cruz, S2
Pagitt, Eldon Ernest, F2

Pait, Robert Edward, BM2
*Palmiter, Adelore Aurthor, S2
Pane, Francis William, S2
Parham, Fred, St2
Park, David Ernest, Ens.
Parke, Edward L., Capt. (*Marine*)
*Paroubek, Richard Anthony, Y1
*Pasket, Lyle Matthew, S2
Patterson, Alfred T., S2
Patterson, Kenneth George, S1
Patzer, Herman Lantz, EM1
*Paulk, Luther Doyle, S2
*Payne, Edward Glenjoy, S2
Payne, George David, S2
*Pena, Santos Alday, S1
Pender, Welburn Morton, F2
*Perez, Basilio, S2
*Perkins, Edward Carlos, F2
Perry, Robert J., S2
Pessolano, Michael Richard, Lt.
Peters, Earl Jack, S2
*Peterson, Avery Clarence, S2
Peterson, Darrel Erskine, S1
Peterson, Frederick Alexander,
 MM3
Peterson, Glenn Harley, S1
Peterson, Ralph R., S2
Petrincic, John Nicholas, Jr., FC3
Peyton, Robert Carter, StM1
Phillips, Aulton Newell, Sr., F2
*Phillips, Huie Harold, S2
Pierce, Clyde Alton, CWTA
Pierce, Robert William, S2
Piperata, Alfred Joseph, MM1
Pitman, Robert Fred, S2
Pittman, Almire, Jr., St3
Pleiss, Roger David, F2
*Podish, Paul, S2
*Podschun, Clifford Albert, S2
*Pogue, Herman Crawford, S2
Pohl, Theodore, F2
Pokryfka, Donald Martin, S2
*Poor, Gerald Melbour, S2
Poore, Albert Franklin, S2
Potrykus, Frank Paul, F2
*Potts, Dale Floyd, S2

Powell, Howard Wayne, S2
Powers, R. C. Ottis, S2
Poynter, Raymond Lee, S2
Praay, William Theo, S2
Prather, Clarence Jefferson,
 CMMA
Pratt, George Roy, F1
*Price, James Denny, S1
Priestle, Ralph Arthur, S2
Prior, Walter Matthew, S2
Puckett, William Charles, S2
Pupuis, John Andrew, S1
Purcel, Franklin Walter, S2
Pursel, Forest Virgil, WT2
Pyron, Freddie Harold, S1

*Quealy, William Charles, Jr., Pr2

Rabb, John Robert, S1
Ragsdale, Jean Obert, S1
Rahn, Alvin Wilder, SK3
Raines, Clifford Junior, S2
Rains, Rufus Brady, S1
*Ramirez, Ricardo, S1
Ramseyer, Raymond Clifford, RT3
Randolph, Cleo, StM1
*Rathbone, Wilson, S2
Rathman, Frank Junior, S1
*Rawdon, John Herbert, EM3
Realing, Lyle Olan, FC2
Redd, Robert F., Pvt. (*Marine*)
*Redmayne, Richard Banks, Lt.
Reed, Thomas William, EM3
Reemts, Alvin Thomas, S1
Reese, Jesse Edmund, S2
*Reeves, Chester O. B., S1
Reeves, Robert Arnold, F2
Regalado, Robert Henry, S1
*Rehner, Herbert Adrian, S1
*Reid, Curtis Franklin, S2
*Reid, James Edgar, BM2
*Reid, John, Lt. Comdr.
*Reid, Tommy Lee, RdM3
Reilly, James Francis, Y1
Reinert, Leroy, F1
Reinold, George H., Pfc (*Marine*)

Remondet, Edward Joseph, Jr., S2
*Reynolds, Alford, GM2
Reynolds, Andrew Eli, S1
Reynolds, Carleton Clarke, F1
Rhea, Clifford, F2
Rhodes, Vernon Lee, F1
Rhoten, Roy Edward, F2
Rice, Albert, StM1
Rich, Garland Lloyd, S1
*Rich, Raymond A., Pfc (Marine)
Richardson, John Richard, S2
Richardson, Joseph Gustave, S2
Rider, Francis Allan, RdM3
*Riggins, Earl, Pvt. (Marine)
Riley, Junior Thomas, BM2
*Rineay, Francis Henry, Jr., S2
Roberts, Benjamin Ellsworth, WT1
Roberts, Charles, S1
*Roberts, Norman Harold, MM1
Robison, Gerald Edward, RT3
*Robison, John Davis, Cox
Robison, Marzie Joe, S2
Roche, Joseph Martin, Lt.
Rockenbach, Earl Arthur, S2
Roesberry, Jack Roger, S1
Rogell, Henry Tony, F1
*Rogers, Ralph Guy, RdM3
*Rogers, Ross, Jr., Ens.
Roland, Jack Anderson, PhM1
Rollins, Willard Eugene, RM3
Romani, F. J., HA1
Roof, Charles Walter, S2
Rose, Berson Horace, GM2
Rose, Francis Edmund, Pfc
   (Marine)
Ross, Glen Eugene, F2
Rothman, Aaron, RdM3
Rowden, Joseph Geren, F1
Rozzano, John, Jr., S2
Rudomanski, Eugene William, RT2
Rue, William Goff, MM1
Russell, Robert Avery, S2
*Russell, Virgil Miller, Cox
Rust, Edwin Leroy, S1
Rutherford, Robert Arnold, RM2
Rydzeski, Frank Walter, F1

*Saathoff, Don William, S2
Saenz, Jose Antonio, SC3
Sain, Albert Franklin, S1
Salinas, Alfredo Antonio, S1
Samano, Muraldo, S2
Sampson, Joseph Raymond, S2
Sams, Robert Carrol, StM2
Sanchez, Alejandro Vallez, S2
*Sanchez, Fernando Sanchec, SC3
Sand, Cyrus Harvey, BM1
Sanders, Everett Raymond,
   MoMM1
Sassman, Gordon Wallace, Cox
*Scanlan, Osceola Carlisle, S2
Scarbrough, Fred Richard, Cox
Schaap, Marion John, QM1
Schaefer, Harry Winfield, S2
Schaffer, Edward James, S1
Scharton, Elmer Daniel, S1
*Schechterle, Harold Joseph, RdM3
Scheib, Albert Eddie, F2
Schewe, Alfred Paul, S1
Schlatter, Robert Leroy, AOM3
Schlotter, James Robert, RdM3
*Schmueck, John Alton, CPhMP
Schnappauf, Harold John, SK3
Schooley, Dillard Alfred, Cox
Schumacher, Arthur Joseph, Jr.,
   CEMA
Scoggins, Millard, SM2
Scott, Burl Down, StM2
Scott, Curtis Marvin, S1
Scott, Hilliard, StM1
*Seabert, Clarke Wilson, S2
Sebastian, Clifford Harry, RM2
Sedivi, Alfred Joseph, PhoN2
Selbach, Walter Herman, WT2
Sell, Ernest Frederick, EM2
Sellers, Leonard Edson, SF3
Selman, Amos, S2
*Setchfield, Arthur Lawrence, Cox
Sewell, Loris Eldon, S2
*Shaffer, Robert Patrick, GM3
Shand, Kenneth Wallace, WT2
*Sharp, William Hafford, S2
Shaw, Calvin Patrick, GM2

*Shearer, Harold James, S2
Shelton, William Enloe, Jr., SM2
Shields, Cecil Norris, SM2
Shipman, Robert Lee, GM3
*Shown, Donald Herbert, CFC
*Shows, Audie Boyd, Cox
Sikes, Theodore Allan, Ens.
Silcox, Burnice Rufus, S1
Silva, Phillip Gomes, S1
Simcox, Gordon William, EM3
Simcox, John Allen, F1
*Simpson, William Edward, BM2
Sims, Clarence, Ck2
*Sinclair, James Ray, S2
Singerman, David, SM2
Sipes, John Leland, S1
*Sitek, Henry Joseph, S2
Sitzlar, William Clifton, F1
*Sladek, Wayne Lyn, BM1
*Slankard, Jack Crocker, S2
Smalley, Howard Earl, S1
*Smeltzer, Charles H., S2
Smeraglia, Michael, RM3
Smith, Carl Murphy, SM2
Smith, Charles Andy, S1
*Smith, Cozell Lee, Jr., Cox
Smith, Edwin Lee, S2
Smith, Eugene Gordon, BM2
*Smith, Frederick Calvin, F2
Smith, George Robert, S1
Smith, Guy Nephi, FCO2
Smith, Henry August, F1
Smith, Homer Leroy, F2
*Smith, James Wesley, S2
Smith, Kenneth Dean, S2
Smith, Olen Ellis, CM3
Snyder, John Nicholes, SF2
Snyder, Richard Redhaffer, S1
Solomon, William, Jr., S2
Sordia, Ralph, S2
*Sospizio, Andre, EM3
Sparks, Charles Byrd, Cox
Speer, Lowell Elvis, RT3
*Spencer, Daniel Frederick, S1
Spencer, James Douglas, Lt.
*Spencer, Roger, S1

Spencer, Sidney Ancil, W0
Spindle, Orval Audry, S1
*Spinelli, John Anthony, SC2
Spino, Frank J., Pfc (Marine)
Spomer, Elmer John, SF2
*Spooner, Miles Lewis, Pvt. (Marine)
Stadler, Robert Herman, WT3
*Stamm, Florian Marian, S2
Stanforth, David Earl, F2
Stankowski, Archie Joseph, S2
Stanturf, Frederick Robert, MM2
Stauffer, Edward H., 1st Lt.
   (Marine)
Steigerwald, Fred, GM2
*Stephens, Richard Park, S2
*Stevens, George Golden, WT2
Stevens, Wayne Allen, MM2
*Stewart, Glenn Willard, CFCP
Stewart, Thomas Andrew, S2
Stickley, Charles Benjamin, GM3
Stier, William George, S1
Stimson, David, Ens.
Stone, Dale Eugene, S2
Stone, Homer Benton, Y1
Stout, Kenneth Irwin, Lt. Comdr.
St. Pierre, Leslie Robert, MM2
Strain, Joseph Mason, S2
Straughn, Howard V. Jr., Corp.
   (Marine)
Streich, Allen Charles, RM2
Strickland, George Thomas, S2
Strieter, Robert Carl, S2
Stripe, William Stanley, S2
Strom, Donald Arthur, S2
Stromko, Joseph Anthony, F2
Stryffeler, Virgil Lee, F2
Stueckle, Robert Louis, S2
*Sturtevant, Elwyn Lee, RM2
Sudano, Angelo Anthony, SSML3
Suhr, Jerome Richard, S2
Sullivan, James Patrick, S2
Sullivan, William Daniel, Ptr2
*Suter, Frank Edward, S1
Swanson, Robert Herman, MM2
Swart, Robert Leslie, Lt. (jg)
Swindell, Jerome Henderson, F2

Taggart, Thomas Harris, S1
Talley, Dewell Emanuel, RM2
*Tawater, Charles Hoyt, F1
Teerlink, David Sanders, CW0
Telford, Arno John, RT3
Terry, Robert Wayne, S1
*Thelen, Richard Peter, S2
Thielscher, Robert T., CRTP
*Thomas, Ivan Mervin, S1
*Thompson, David Alvin, EM3
Thomsen, Arthur A., Pfc (*Marine*)
Thorpe, Everett Nathan, WT3
*Thurkettle, William C., S2
Tidwell, James Freddie, S2
Tisthammer, Bernard Edward,
    CGMA
Toce, Nicolo, S2
Todd, Harold Orton, CM3
*Torretta, John Mario, F2
Tosh, Bill Hugh, RdM3
Tracy, Richard I., Jr., Sgt. (*Marine*)
Triemer, Ernst August, Ens.
Trotter, Arthur Cecil, RM2
Trudeau, Edmond Arthur, Lt.
True, Roger Glenn, S2
Truitt, Robert Edward, RM2
Tryon, Frederick Braum, Bug2
Tull, James Albert, S1
*Turner, Charles Morris, S2
Turner, William Clifford, MM2
Turner, William Henry, Jr.,
    ACMMA
*Twible, Harlan Malcolm, Ens.

*Uffelman, Paul, R., Pfc (*Marine*)
Ulibarri, Antonio De Jesus, S2
Ullmann, Paul Elliott, Lt. (jg)
*Umenhoffer, Lyle Edgar, S1
Underwood, Carey Lee, S1
*Underwood, Ralph Ellis, S1

*Van Meter, Joseph William, WT3

Wakefield, James Newell, S1
Walker, A. W., StM1
Walker, Jack Edwin, RM2
*Walker, V. B., F2
Wallace, Earl John, RdM3
Wallace, John, RdM3
Walters, Donald Henry, F1
Warren, William Robertson, RT3
Waters, Jack Lee, CYA
Watson, Winston Harl, F2
*Wells, Charles Orville, S1
Wells, Gerald Lloyd, EM3
Wennerholm, Wayne Leslie, Cox
Wenzel, Ray Gunther, RT3
Whalen, Stuart Denton, GM3
Whallon, Louis Fletcher, Jr., Lt. (jg)
White, Earl Clarence, TC1
White, Howard McKean, CWTP
*Whiting, George Albert, F2
Whitman, Robert Taft, Lt.
*Wilcox, Lindsey Zeb, WT2
Wileman, Roy Weldon, PhM3
Willard, Merriman Daniel, PhM2
Williams, Billie Joe, MM2
Williams, Magellan, StM1
Williams, Robert Louis, WO
Wilson, Frank, F2
Wilson, Thomas Beverly, S1
*Wisniewski, Stanley, F2
Wittmer, Milton Robert, EM2
*Witzig, Robert Marian, FC3
Wojciechowski, Maryian Joseph,
    GM2
Wolfe, Floyd Ralph, GM3
Woods, Leonard Thomas, CWO
*Woolston, John, Ens.
Wych, Robert A., Pfc (*Marine*)

Yeaple, Jack Thomas, Y3

*Zink, Charles William, EM2
Zobal, Francis John, S2

NOTES

Full data on printed material can be found in the Bibliography. Interviewees (Ints.) are identified in the Acknowledgments.

CHAPTER I

1–2 Courtroom confrontation: Ints. John P. Cady, Mochitsura Hashimoto
2–7 McVay's background to World War II: Kinau Wilder, *The Wilders of Waikiki*; ints. Charles B. McVay IV, Kimo McVay, Kinau Wilder
7–8 McVay and Louise Claytor: Ints. W. Graham Claytor, Betsy McVay, McVay IV, K. McVay

CHAPTER II

9–10 Haynes' background: Int. Lewis L. Haynes
11–12 Redmayne's background: Int. Richard Redmayne
12 McVay's orders: Dan Kurzman, *Day of the Bomb*; Charles B. McVay III, speech to *Indianapolis* survivors reunion, July 30, 1960; int. Gordon Linke
13 Parsons and the bomb: Kurzman
14 McVay and his men (quotes): McVay's testimony, Naval Inspector General's investigation
14–15 McVay and his father: Int. McVay IV
15 History of the *Indianapolis*: Navy Department, *Dictionary of American Naval Fighting Ships*, vol. III; *U.S.S. Indianapolis CA35 Survivors Memorial Reunion* (pamphlet), 1985
16–17 Donald J. Blum: Int. Donald J. Blum
17–18 Havins' vow: Int. Otha Alton Havins
19 Celaya's dream: Int. Adolfo Celaya
19–20 The secret cargo: Kurzman; ints. Grover Carver, Celaya, Robert R. Furman, Giles McCoy
21 Message from King: Int. Haynes

CHAPTER III

24–26 Debt to the Emperor: Int. Hashimoto
26–28 Hashimoto's naval career: Mochitsura Hashimoto, *Sunk*; int. Hashimoto
28–30 Birth of the kaiten: Edwin P. Hoyt, *The Kamikazes*; Rikihei Inoguchi and
Tadashi Nakajima, *The Divine Wind*; ints. Hashimoto, Hirokoto Tanaka, Toshio Tanaka
30–32 Toshio Tanaka and the "barbarians": Int. Toshio Tanaka

CHAPTER IV

33–34 Sitting on the bomb: Int. McCoy
34 The kamikaze strike: Int. McCoy and other crew members
34–35 The "artillery" officers: Ints. Blum, Furman, and others from crew of *Indianapolis*
35 Did McVay know about the bomb?: McVay speech, July 30, 1960; ints. Furman,
G. Linke
35 McVay and Haynes: McVay's testimony, Naval Inspector General's investigation
36–37 Judging against the usual: Int. Blum
37 Havins' new disappointment: Int. Havins
37 Redmayne's good luck: Int. Redmayne
37–38 McVay's reverie: Ints. members of crew
38–39 The betrayal of Blum: Int. Blum
39 McVay favors training course in Guam: McVay's testimony, Naval Inspector
General's investigation

CHAPTER V

41 Hashimoto and the Taimon Group: Hashimoto; int. Hashimoto
41–43 The confident Hirokoto Tanaka: Int. Hirokoto Tanaka
43–45 McVay meets Carter: Testimony, McVay and James B. Carter, Naval Inspector General's investigation
44–45 Carter knew of submarine danger: Testimony, Carter and William R. Smedberg III, Naval Inspector General's investigation
44 McMorris' view of submarine danger: Charles H. McMorris' testimony, Naval Inspector General's investigation
45 Why Carter didn't inform McVay: Carter's testimony, Naval Inspector General's investigation
45 McVay and Spruance: McVay's testimony, Naval Inspector General's investigation
45 Anderson's message: Samuel Clay Anderson's testimony, Naval Inspector General's investigation
46 Naquin's secrets: Oliver F. Naquin's testimony, Naval Inspector General's investigation; int. Naquin
46–48 McVay and the routing officer: Testimony, McVay and Joseph Waldron,
Naval Inspector General's investigation

CHAPTER VI

49–51 Did kaitens hit target?: Hashimoto; ints. Hashimoto, H. Tanaka, T. Tanaka
51 Wrecking Blum's morale: Int. Blum

51 Wait until the next island: Int. Havins

52 The intelligence brief: McVay's testimony, Naval Inspector General's investigation

52–53 The submarine joke: Haynes' testimony, Naval Inspector General's investigation; ints. Haynes, Redmayne

53–54 McKissick and the warning message: Charles B. McKissick's testimony, Naval Inspector General's investigation

54–55 McKissick's love for his ship: McKissick tape

55–56 McVay's order on zigzagging: Testimony, McVay and McKissick, Naval Inspector General's investigation; McKissick tape

56–57 McVay on the bridge: McVay's testimony, Naval Inspector General's investigation (including quotes)

57 McVay disbelieves dinner conversation: Ibid.

57–58 Hashimoto searches for a ship: Hashimoto; int. Hashimoto

58–59 Redmayne on watch: Int. Redmayne

59–61 Twible, God, and Annapolis: Harlan M. Twible, Résumé of the Life of Harlan M. Twible (including quote: "He was not too conversant . . ."); int. Harlan M. Twible (including quote: "You're Naval Academy . . .")

61–63 Hashimoto sights ship: Hashimoto; ints. Hashimoto, H. Tanaka, T. Tanaka

64 Nothing to report: Int. Blum

64–65 Waste of a good Marine: Int. McCoy

65–66 A hit at last: Hashimoto; ints. Hashimoto, H. Tanaka, T. Tanaka

CHAPTER VII

67–69 McVay rushes to bridge: McVay's testimony, Naval Inspector General's investigation (including quotes); McVay Narrative, Sinking of USS *Indianapolis*

69–71 Redmayne dashes to engine room: Redmayne's testimony, Naval Inspector General's investigation; int. Redmayne

71–72 McCoy in the brig room: McCoy's testimony, Naval Inspector General's investigation; int. McCoy

72–73 Haynes seeks to escape fire: Haynes' testimony, Naval Inspector General's investigation; int. Haynes

73–74 McKissick seeks to escape fire: McKissick's testimony, Naval Inspector General's investigation; McKissick tape

74–75 Havins helps victims: Int. Havins

75–77 Haynes tries to save victims: Haynes' testimony, Naval Inspector General's investigation; int. Haynes

77–78 Blum's nightmare: Int. Blum

78 McCoy escapes from brig area: McCoy's testimony, Naval Inspector General's investigation; int. McCoy

78–80 McVay decides to abandon ship: Testimony, McVay (including quotes) and Edward Keyes, Naval Inspector General's investigation; McVay Narrative

80–81 Hashimoto euphoric but anxious: Hashimoto; ints. Hashimoto, T. Tanaka

81–82 Redmayne escapes from engine room: Redmayne's testimony, Naval Inspector General's investigation; int. Redmayne

82–84 McKissick leads men over side: McKissick's testimony, Naval Inspector General's investigation; McKissick tape

84–85 Haynes loses his patients: Haynes' testimony, Naval Inspector General's investigation; int. Haynes

85 Blum abandons ship: Blum's testimony, Naval Inspector General's investigation; int. Blum

85–87 Twible takes control: Twible's testimony, Naval Inspector General's investigation; résumé, Twible's life; int. Twible

88–89 Celaya abandons ship: Int. Celaya

89 McCoy abandons ship: Int. McCoy

89–91 McVay swept into sea: McVay's testimony, Naval Inspector General's investigation; McVay Narrative

91–92 Hashimoto searches for survivors: Int. Hashimoto

92–93 McVay watches ship go down: McVay's testimony, Naval Inspector General's investigation; McVay Narrative

93–94 Failure to find survivors: Hashimoto; ints. Hashimoto, T. Tanaka, H. Tanaka

94–95 The intercepted message: Naval Inspector General, memorandum re intercepted message, February 27, 1946; T. E. Van Metre, memorandum, re intercepted message, November 2, 1945; testimony, E. T. Layton and W. R. Smedberg III, Naval Inspector General's investigation

CHAPTER VIII

97–99 McCoy swims to raft: Int. McCoy

99–104 Haynes tries to comfort men: Haynes, "We Prayed While 883 Died," *Saturday Evening Post*, August 6, 1955; Haynes' account of survivors following sinking, to Naval Inspector General, November 26, 1945; int. Haynes

104–106 Celaya in the water: Int. Celaya

106–107 Redmayne at midnight: Int. Redmayne

107–108 Twible waits to take charge: Résumé, Twible's life; int. Twible

109–110 Blum fights to survive: Int. Blum

110–111 Five against the sea: Int. Havins

111–117 McVay's new command: McVay's testimony, Naval Inspector General's investigation; McVay Narrative; int. Havins

CHAPTER IX

119–121 Gibson and the *Indianapolis*: Forrest Tucker, Fitness report on Gibson, February 22, 1945; Gibson, letter to Tucker's superior officer protesting adverse fitness report, May 23, 1945; Gibson, letter to Chief of Naval Personnel in reply to letter of reprimand, September 24, 1945; ints. Betty Gray Gibson, Richard F. Newcomb, John P. Williams

121–123 Under the Frontier's wing?: Alfred M. Granum, letter to CINCPAC, September 1, 1945; Naval Inspector General, letter to Chief of Naval Operations concerning reprimand to Granum, April 22, 1946; Naval Inspector General, letter to Chief of Naval Operations concerning reprimand to Commodore N. C. Gillette, April 10, 1946; testimony, Granum and Gillette, Naval Inspector General's investigation.

123–125 The undelivered message: L. D. McCormick, letter to CINCPAC, September 22, 1945; testimony, McCormick and J. B. Oldendorf, Naval Inspector General's investigation

CHAPTER X

127–129 The death of three: Haynes, *Saturday Evening Post*, August 6, 1955; Haynes' account of survivors to Naval Inspector General, November 26, 1945; McKissick tape; int. Haynes

130–132 A lack of trust: Int. Redmayne, Twible, source requesting anonymity

132–134 Dementia and death: Haynes, *Saturday Evening Post*, August 6, 1955; Haynes' account of survivors to Naval Inspector General, November 26, 1945; int. Haynes

134–136 McCoy and the magic eye: Int. McCoy

136–138 An island full of women: Haynes, *Saturday Evening Post*, August 6, 1955; Haynes' account of survivors to Naval Inspector General, November 26, 1945; int. Victor R. Buckett, Haynes

138–139 The floating dock: McKissick tape; int. Haynes

139–142 Blum leaves the group: Résumé, Twible's life; ints. Blum, Redmayne, Twible

142–143 Celaya and his friends: Int. Celaya

143–144 McCoy prepares to meet God: Int. McCoy

144–145 Redmayne hallucinates: Ints. Redmayne, Twible

145–146 Swimming to Leyte: Haynes, *Saturday Evening Post*, August 6, 1955; McKissick tape; int. Haynes

146–147 McVay and his raftmates: McVay's testimony, Naval Inspector General's investigation; McVay Narrative; int. Havins

CHAPTER XI

149–151 Gwinn sights "submarine slick": Wilbur C. Gwinn, report to Commander, Fleet Air Wing 18, August 3, 1945; int. Gwinn

151–152 Blum "fears" rescue: Int. Blum

152 Haynes group sights plane: Haynes, *Saturday Evening Post*, August 6, 1955; Haynes' account of survivors to Naval Inspector General, November 26, 1945; int. Haynes

152–153 Gwinn calls for help: Gwinn's report to Commander, Fleet Air Wing 18, August 3, 1945; int. Gwinn

153–155 Marks sent on rescue mission: Adrian R. Marks, statement regarding rescue of survivors, to CINCPAC; Marks, address before USS *Indianapolis* survivors' reunion, August 2, 1975; Marks, letters to author, November 3, December 23, 1988; Earl P. Duxbury, notes on Marks and rescue of survivors; int. Duxbury, Robert France, Marks

155–156 Gwinn drops supplies to survivors: Gwinn's report to Commander, Fleet Air Wing 18, August 3, 1945; int. Gwinn

156–157 Frontier joins in rescue operation: McCormick, letter to CINCPAC, September 22, 1945; testimony, Granum, Gillette, McCormick, Naval Inspector General's investigation

157–158 Marks talks with Claytor: Marks, statement to CINCPAC; Marks, address before survivors' reunion, August 2, 1975; int. Claytor

158–161 Marks attempts sea landing: Ibid; Marks, letters to author, November 3, December 23, 1988; Duxbury, notes on Marks and rescue of survivors; France, letter to his family, September 20, 1945; int. Duxbury, France

161 McKissick and the "mail sack": McKissick tape

162–163 Haynes group recovers rescue equipment: Haynes, *Saturday Evening Post*, August 6, 1955; int. Haynes

163–164 Marks lands plane in sea: Marks, statement to CINCPAC; Marks, address before survivors' reunion, August 2, 1975; Marks, letters to author, November 3, December 23, 1988; Duxbury, notes on Marks and rescue of survivors; France, letter to his family, September 20, 1945; ints. Duxbury, France

164–166 Marks rescues McKissick and others: Ibid; McKissick tape

166–167 Hashimoto fails to sink merchant vessel: Hashimoto; int. Hashimoto

167–169 Marks and Haynes' group: Haynes, *Saturday Evening Post*, August 6, 1955; Haynes, letter to author, December 30, 1988; Marks, statement to CINCPAC, August 5, 1945; Marks, address before survivors' reunion, August 2, 1975; Marks, letters to author, November 3, December 23, 1988; Duxbury, notes on Marks and rescue of survivors; France, letter to his family, September 20, 1945; ints. Duxbury, France, Haynes

169–171 The swims of Twible, Blum, and Brophy: Résumé, Twible's life; ints. Blum, Twible

171–172 McVay, Havins, and the smudge pot: McVay's testimony, Naval Inspector General's investigation; McVay Narrative; int. Havins

172–173 Foul water and pink clouds: McCoy, letter to author, January 17, 1989; int. McCoy

173–176 Claytor rescues Haynes: Richard C. Alcorn, report to Sub-Area Operations, Rescue Operations, August 2–5, 1945; Claytor, report on rescue of survivors of USS *Indianapolis*, August 2–4, 1945; Haynes, letter to author, May 15, 1989; Haynes, *Saturday Evening Post*, August 6, 1955; William H. Jones, "No-Nonsense Lawyer Claytor Knows When to Bend the Rules," *Washington Post*, January 21, 1977; ints. Claytor, Haynes

176–178 Blum's rescue: Int. Blum

178 Celaya's rescue: Int. Celaya

178–179 Redmayne's rescue: Int. Redmayne

179 Twible's rescue: Int. Twible

179 Granum learns the truth: Harold J. Theriault, cable to Granum, August 3, 1945; Granum's testimony, Naval Inspector General's investigation

180–181 Rescue of McVay's group: McVay's testimony, Naval Inspector General's investigation; McVay Narrative; Jim Anderson, "Tragic Indianapolis Story Told"; *NCVA Cryptolog* (Eugene, Ore.); int. Havins

182–183 McCoy's rescue: Int. McCoy

183–184 Haynes eases Marks' conscience: Haynes, *Saturday Evening Post*, August 6, 1955; Haynes, letter to author, May 15, 1989; Marks, letters to author, November 3, December 23, 1988; int. Haynes

CHAPTER XII

185–186 Blum's potent breakfast: Int. Blum

186–187 Rescued officers interrogated: Ints. Redmayne, Twible

187–188 McVay meets the press: Richard F. Newcomb, *Abandon Ship!*; press conference transcript, August 5, 1945; int. G. Linke

189–190 Forrestal agonizes over sinking: Kurzman; Arnold A. Rogow, *James Forrestal*; int. anonymous source

190–191 King ponders whom to blame: Thomas B. Buell, *Master of Sea Power: A Biography of Fleet Admiral Ernest J. King*; Kurzman; Fleet Admiral Ernest J. King, memorandum to the Secretary of the Navy Concerning the Court of Inquiry's Inquiry into All the Circumstances Connected with the Sinking of the USS *Indianapolis* and with the Delay in Reporting the Loss of That Ship, September 25, 1945; King, order to Naval Inspector General to investigate the sinking and the delay in reporting it, October 18, 1945; ints. McVay IV (re his grandfather's reprimand of King), source requesting anonymity

191–193 Nimitz suffers worst trauma: E. B. Potter, *Nimitz*; Potter and Chester W. Nimitz, *The Great Sea War*; Nate White, "This Man—Nimitz," *Christian Science Monitor*, October 20, 1945; King, memorandum to Navy Secretary, September 25, 1945; Nimitz, remarks on recommendations of the court of inquiry, September 6, 1945; Report, Bodies

Found by USS *French*, August 6–7, 1945; Nimitz press conference, transcript, February 23, 1946

193–195 McVay anxious about future: Newcomb; ints. Gwinn, McCoy

195–197 McVay vents anger on Blum: Int. Blum

197–198 The inquiry opens: Newcomb; Record of Proceedings of a Court of Inquiry Convened at Headquarters, Commander Marianas, Guam, August 13, 1945; ints. Blum, Naquin, Redmayne, Twible

198–199 Message for Brophy: Navy Department press release, loss of USS *Indianapolis*, August 14, 1945; "Ensign Lost in Sinking of *Indianapolis*, July 30," *New York Times*, August 21, 1945; "Thomas Brophy, Ad Executive, Dies Trying to Save 2 Children," *New York Times*, July 30, 1966; ints. Blum, Twible

199–201 Hashimoto learns of Japanese surrender: Hashimoto; ints. Hashimoto, H. Tanaka, T. Tanaka

201–203 The inquiry proceeds: Raymond B. Lech, *All the Drowned Sailors*; Newcomb; Record of Proceedings of a Court of Inquiry; int. Blum, Naquin, Redmayne, Twible

203–204 Hashimoto goes home: Hashimoto; ints. Hashimoto, H. Tanaka, T. Tanaka

204–206 The court's recommendations: Lech; Newcomb; Record of Proceedings of a Court of Inquiry; ints. Naquin, Twible, G. Linke (to whom McVay confided his attitudes)

206–208 The last lap to paradise: Ints. Blum, Redmayne

208 Celaya in the brig: Int. Celaya

209 The homecoming: Ints. McCoy, Redmayne

209–210 Celaya's torment: Int. Celaya

211–213 McVay's torment: Katherine D. Moore, letter to Senator Spark M. Matsunaga (McVay quote), September 28, 1984; ints. Blum, Ernest King, Jr., G. Linke, McVay IV, K. McVay, Twible

213–214 Nimitz opposes McVay court-martial: Nimitz, memorandum to Judge Advocate General re court of inquiry, September 6, 1945

214–215 King recommends McVay court-martial: King, memorandum to Navy Secretary, September 25, 1945; int. McVay IV

215–216 The hesitant decision to court-martial McVay: King, directive to Naval Inspector General to investigate *Indianapolis* sinking and aftermath, December 6, 1945; King, memorandum to Navy Secretary approving delay of court-martial, November 10, 1945; King, memorandum to C. P. Snyder, Naval Inspector General, re feasibility of immediate court-martial, November 10, 1945; Snyder, report to King, November 10, 1945; T. E. Van Metre, memorandum to Naval Inspector General concerning investigation of the *Indianapolis* case, November 10, 1945; int. Edward Hidalgo

CHAPTER XIII

217–219 Ryan confronts McCoy: Congressional Medal of Honor citation, Thomas J. Ryan, Jr.; ints. John P. Cady, McCoy, source requesting anonymity

219–221 Hashimoto called to Washington: Ints. Hashimoto, H. Tanaka, T. Tanaka

221–223 Court-martial—the first day: Record of Proceedings of a General Court-martial Convened at the Navy Yard, Washington, D.C., by Order of the Secretary of the Navy, December 3, 1945 (pp. 1–2); ints. Cady, G. Linke, McVay IV

223–224 Waldron testifies: Record of Proceedings, McVay court-martial

224–225 McKissick testifies: Ibid. (pp. 30–44)

225–226 Redmayne testifies: Ibid. (pp. 45–62)

226–227 Haynes testifies: Ibid. (pp. 64–74)

227–228 Blum testifies: Ibid. (pp. 162–65)

228 McCoy testifies: Ibid. (pp. 172–81)

228–229 Twible testifies: Ibid. (pp. 324–25)

229–230 Keyes, Naquin, and Granum testify: Ibid. (pp. 106–12, 329–31, 332–33)

230–231 Donaho testifies: Ibid. (pp. 334–43)

231–232 McVay testifies: Ibid. (pp. 349–63)

231–234 Hashimoto arrives in Washington: Lech; Newcomb; ints. Cady, Hashimoto

234–240 Hashimoto's competence: Record of Proceedings, McVay court-martial (pp. 256–65); ints. Cady, Hashimoto

240–242 Star of the show: Ibid. (Record, pp. 266–76)

242–244 Closing arguments: Ibid. (Record, pp. 373–81); int. Cady

244–247 The judgment: Ibid. (Record, pp. 382–85); "McVay: The Court Decides," *Newsweek*, December 31, 1945; " 'The Good of the Service,' " *Time*, December 31, 1945; int. Cady

247–250 Reaction and remittance: Forrestal, memorandum to Snyder, December 23, 1945; Snyder, memorandum to Forrestal, January 2, 1946; T. G. Murrell, letter to Forrestal, January 11, 1946; Forrestal, letter to Murrell, January 22, 1946; Edward Hidalgo, memorandum to Forrestal, February 13, 1946; int. Hidalgo

250–253 The Navy seeks cover: "Narrative of the Circumstances of the Loss of the USS *Indianapolis*"; Snyder, memorandum to King, November 30, 1945; Snyder, memorandum to King, Discussion of Facts in the Further Investigation of the Sinking of the USS *Indianapolis* and the Delay in Reporting the Loss of this Ship; Vice Admiral Forrest Sherman, memorandum to Admiral Ramsey, Rough Draft of Narrative of the Circumstances of the Loss of the USS *Indianapolis*, February 20, 1946; Hidalgo, memorandum to Forrestal, February 2, 1946; Hidalgo, memorandum to Forrestal, February 16, 1946; Nimitz, memorandum to King recommending reprimands, n.d.; int. Hidalgo

253–254 Preparing the sacrifice: Narrative; ints. B. Gibson, Williams

255–258 Nimitz meets the press: Narrative; J. L. Kauffman, letter to Chief of Navy Personnel re Gibson, October 26, 1945; transcript, news conference, February 23, 1946

CHAPTER XIV

261–262 Forrestal's compromise: Rogow; Gillette, letter to Naval Inspector General re his reprimand, March 16, 1946; Granum, letter to Naval Inspector General re his reprimand, April 3, 1946; C. A. Lockwood, Jr. (Naval Inspector General), memorandum to Chief of Naval Operations re reprimand of Gillette, April 10, 1946; Lockwood, memorandum to Chief of Naval Operations re reprimand of Granum, April 22, 1946; int. Hidalgo

263–264 Celaya—beer and milk: Int. Celaya

264 Redmayne—ghosts and glory: Int. Redmayne

264–265 Haynes—loyalty and loneliness: Int. Haynes

265–267 McCoy—thirst and therapy: Int. McCoy

267–268 Twible—frailty and faith: Int. Twible

268–269 Havins—marriage and mission: Int. Havins

269 McKissick—fantasy and reality: McKissick tape

269 Blum—God and greed: Int. Blum

269–270 Gwinn—love and luck: Int. Gwinn

270 Marks—justice and greatness: Marks, address before survivors' reunion, August 2, 1975; Marks, letters to author, November 3, December 23, 1988

270–271 H. Tanaka—sailor and salesman: Int. H. Tanaka

271 T. Tanaka—bitterness and acceptance: Int. T. Tanaka

271–273 Hashimoto—friendship and disgrace: Lyle Nelson, "Sea Story Sequel 29 Years Later," *Honolulu Star-Bulletin*, August 13, 1974; int. Hashimoto

273–275 McVay pays installment: Jack Averitt, "U.S.S. Indianapolis Captain 'Dreaded' Survivor Reunion," *Indianapolis News*, July 30, 1960; Gerry La Follette, "Tragedy Still Hurts—After 15 Years," *Indianapolis Times*, July 30, 1960; Betsy McVay, letter to author, September 28, 1988; Katherine D. Moore, letter to Senator Spark M. Matsunaga (quoting Captain McVay in luncheon conversation), September 28, 1984; ints. McCoy, K. McVay

275–277 The death of Louise: B. McVay, letter to author, September 28, 1988; int. K. McVay

277–279 Marriage on the rebound: Ibid; ints. G. Linke, Jocelyn Linke, McVay IV, Florence Regosia, Winthrop Smith, Jr., E. Seward Stevens

279–281 McVay's final death: Ints. G. Linke, Regosia, Smith, Jr., Stevens

281 A soul without peace: Ints. McVay IV, K. McVay

EPILOGUE

283–285 Seeking justice: James W. Nance, letter to McCoy, July 24, 1975; McCoy, letter to Nance, August 6, 1975; Hidalgo, letter to McCoy, April 15, 1980; Anne Higgins, Special Assistant to President Reagan, letter to K. McVay, September 12, 1983; Senator Daniel K. Inouye, letter to K. McVay, September 23, 1983; ints. Claytor, McCoy, McVay IV, K. McVay

BIBLIOGRAPHY

This book is based largely on information obtained from interviews with over one hundred people in the United States and Japan (many are listed in the Acknowledgments), scores of letters, diaries, and memoirs, and hundreds of official documents, many under the Freedom of Information Act. For background, I also perused over fifty books and hundreds of newspaper and magazine articles. A select bibliography follows.

BOOKS

Amrine, Michael. *The Great Decision*. New York: Putnam, 1959.

Bailey, Charles W., and Knebel, Fletcher. *No High Ground*. New York: Harper, 1960.

Benedict, Ruth. *The Chrysanthemum and the Sword*. Boston: Houghton Mifflin, 1946.

Bernstein, Barton J., ed. *The Atomic Bomb*. Boston: Little, Brown, 1976.

Blow, Michael. *The History of the Atomic Bomb*. New York: American Heritage, 1968.

Brown, Anthony Cave, and MacDonald, Charles B., eds. *The History of the Atomic Bomb*. New York: Dial, 1977.

Buell, Thomas B. *The Quiet Warrior: A Biography of Admiral Raymond A. Spruance*. Boston: Little, Brown, 1974.

———. *Master of Sea Power: A Biography of Fleet Admiral Ernest J. King*. Boston: Little, Brown, 1979.

Clark, Ronald W. *The Birth of the Bomb*. New York: Horizon, 1960.

Colegrove, Kenneth W. *Militarism in Japan*. Boston: World Peace Foundation, 1936.

Costello, John. *The Pacific War*. New York: Rawson, Wade, 1981.

Couhat, Jean Lebayle, ed. *Combat Fleets of the World 1976–77*. Annapolis, Md.: Naval Institute Press, 1976.

Craig, William. *The Fall of Japan*. New York: Dial, 1967.

Feis, Herbert. *Japan Subdued: The Atom Bomb and the End of the War in the Pacific*. Princeton, N.J.: Princeton University Press, 1961.

Fetridge, William Harrison, ed. *The Navy Reader*. New York: Bobbs-Merrill, 1943.

Forrestel, E. P. *Admiral Raymond A. Spruance, USN*. Washington, D.C.: U.S. Government Printing Office, 1946.

Gibney, Frank. *Five Gentlemen of Japan*. New York: Farrar, Straus & Young, 1953.

Hashimoto, Mochitsura. *Sunk: The Story of the Japanese Submarine Fleet, 1941 –1945*. New York: Henry Holt, 1954.

Helm, Thomas. *Ordeal by Sea*. New York: Dodd, Mead, 1963.

Hoyt, Edwin P. *How They Won the War in the Pacific*. New York: Weybright & Talley, 1970.

———. *The Kamikazes*. New York: Arbor House, 1983.

Ingram, Luther Gates, Jr. *The Deficiencies of the United States Submarine Torpedo in the Pacific Theater: World War II*. Unpublished thesis, San Diego State University, 1978.

Inoguchi, Rikihei, and Nakajima, Tadashi. *The Divine Wind*. Annapolis, Md.: U.S. Naval Institute, 1958.

Ito, Masanori. *The End of the Imperial Japanese Navy*. New York: Norton, 1956.

Karig, Walter; Harris, Russel L.; and Manson, Frank A., eds. *Battle Report: Victory in the Pacific*. Vol. 5. New York: Rinehart, 1949.

Kurzman, Dan. *Kishi and Japan*. New York: Obolensky, 1960.

———. *Day of the Bomb*. New York: McGraw-Hill, 1985.

Lech, Raymond B. *All the Drowned Sailors*. New York: Stein & Day, 1983.

Millot, Bernard. *Divine Thunder*. New York: McCall, 1971.

Morison, Samuel Eliot. *Victory in the Pacific 1945*. Boston: Little, Brown, 1968.

Navy Department. *Dictionary of American Naval Fighting Ships*. Vol. III. Washington, D.C.: U.S. Government Printing Office, 1968.

———. *Almanac of Naval Facts*. Annapolis, Md.: U.S. Naval Institute, 1969.

Newcomb, Richard F. *Abandon Ship!* New York: Henry Holt, 1958.

Potter, E. B. *Nimitz*. Annapolis, Md.: Naval Institute Press, 1976.

———, ed. *Sea Power: A Naval History*. Annapolis, Md.: Naval Institute Press, 1981.

———, and Nimitz, Chester W. *The Great Sea War*. Engelwood Cliffs, N.J.: Prentice-Hall, 1960.

Reischauer, Edwin O. *Japan, Past and Present*. New York: Knopf, 1964.

Rogow, Arnold A. *James Forrestal*. New York: Macmillan, 1963.

Silverstone, Paul H. *U.S. Warships of World War II*. Garden City, N.Y.: Doubleday, 1966.

Thomas, Gordon, and Morgan-Witts, Max. *Enola Gay*. New York: Stein & Day, 1977.

Yokota, Yutaka, and Harrington, Joseph D. *Suicide Submarine*. New York: Ballantine, 1962.

PERIODICALS

American History, August 1975. "Texas to Tokyo Bay: C. W. Nimitz in the Pacific." P. S. Weddie.
———, June 1985. "Lost at Sea." Michael Mueller.
EB Topics (General Dynamics), January 10, 1980. "Navy Commissions U.S.S. *Indianapolis*."
Life, June 14, 1943. "Pearl Harbor Salvage."
Nature, September 14, 1966. "Torpedoes: Their Use and Development During the War."
NCVA Cryptolog (Eugene, Ore.), Spring 1984. "Tragic *Indianapolis* Story Told." Jim Anderson.
Newsweek, August 27, 1945. "Nobody Looked."
———, December 10, 1945. "The Indianapolis: Why?"
———, December 24, 1945. "A Jap Bears Witness."
———, December 31, 1945. "McVay: The Court Decides."
———, March 4, 1946. "The Navy Relents."
Popular Science, September 1943. "Why DE [Destroyer Escort] Boats are Death to Subs."
Reader's Digest, April 1957. "There Was a Man." William L. Worden.
Saturday Evening Post, August 6, 1955. "We Prayed While 883 Died." L. L. Haynes with G. W. Campbell.
Time, August 27, 1945. "Men Against the Sea."
———, December 10, 1945. "The Captain Stands Accused."
———, December 24, 1945. " 'Such Grotesque Proceedings.' "
———, December 31, 1945. " 'The Good of the Service.' "
———, March 4, 1946. "End of the Indianapolis Case."
U.S. Naval Institute Proceedings, January 1962. "Kaiten—Japan's Human Torpedoes." Yutaka Yokota and Joseph D. Harrington.
Warship International, vol. 13, no. 1. "Attacking the Indianapolis—A Re-Examination." Carl Boyd.

NEWSPAPERS

Chicago Tribune, August 3, 1976. "Shark Terror Relived After Ship Sank." John Gorman.
Christian Science Monitor, October 20, 1945. "This Man—Nimitz." Nate White.
Focus on Education (San Jose, Calif.), June 1985. "World War II Hero Retiring."
Honolulu Advertiser, December 10, 1974. "The 'Hanging' of Captain McVay." Cobey Black.
———. July 29, 1983. "Did Skipper of 'Indy' Get a Bum Rap?" Jim Borg.
Honolulu Star-Bulletin, August 13, 1974. "Sea Story Sequel 29 Years Later." Lyle Nelson.

Houston Post, July 29, 1978. "What Ever Happened to Survivors of '45 Sinking?"

Indianapolis News, July 30, 1960. "U.S.S. Indianapolis Captain 'Dreaded' Survivor Reunion." Jack Averitt.

Indianapolis Star, April 11, 1960. "5 Days Spent in Sea Lived Again by Cruiser Survivor." John H. Lyst.

———, July 24, 1960. "In Memory of Those Who Served." Michael J. Quinn.

———, July 31, 1960. "150 Survivors Here in Reunion Mark U.S.S. Indianapolis Sinking."

Indianapolis Times, July 30, 1960. "Tragedy Still Hurts—After 15 Years." Gerry La Follette.

———, July 31, 1960. "U.S.S. Indianapolis Crew Relives War Tragedy." Gerry La Follette.

———, August 4, 1960. "McVay Learned Integrity in Navy." Gerry La Follette.

Navy Times, September 24, 1975. "Sharks: What We Don't Yet Know Definitely Can Hurt Us." Gregory Simpkins.

The New York Times, August 21, 1945. "Ensign [Brophy] Lost in Sinking of Indianapolis July 30."

———, July 30, 1966. "Thomas Brophy, Ad Executive, Dies Trying to Save 2 Children."

———, November 8, 1968. "C. B. M'Vay 3d, 70, Retired Admiral."

———. Other articles: August 15, 18, 1945; November 28, 1945; December 4–7, 9–12, 14–16, 19–20, 22, 1945; January 5, 1946; February 24, 1946; April 9, 27, 1946; November 8, 1968.

St. Louis Post-Dispatch, July 27, 1945. "Navy's Greatest Disaster." Gary Ronberg.

———, July 27, 28, 1975. "Thirst, Sun, Sharks and Despair." Gary Ronberg.

San Jose Mercury, July 30, 1975. "The Day Young S.J. Pilot Made History." Michael Cronk.

The Washington Post, November 14, 1968. "Adm. Charles McVay Dies at 70."

———, January 21, 1977. "No-Nonsense Lawyer Claytor Knows When to Bend the Rules." William H. Jones.

———, August 5, 1975. "Remembering the Hunger and Thirst, the Sharks and the Screams. . . ." Steven Norwitz.

World War II Times, June–July 1986. " 'I Have Seen Greatness!' " R. Adrian Marks.

DOCUMENTS

Alcorn, Richard C., Commanding Officer, 4th Emergency Rescue Squadron, Flight D Detachment. Report to Sub-Area Operations. Rescue Operations 2–5 August 1945. August 6, 8, 1945.

Anderson, M. A., Commander, Western Carolines Sub-Area. Report to Commander in Chief, U.S. Fleet. Rescue and Search for Survivors of USS *Indianapolis* (CA 35) and Recovery, Identification, and Burial of Bodies; Bodies Found by USS *French*, August 6–7, 1945.

———. Report to Island Commander, Peleliu. Identification and Disposal of Bodies and Personal Effects Found on Bodies by U.S. Naval Vessels Engaging in Search for Survivors from USS *Indianapolis*. August 11, 1945.

———. Report to Commander in Chief, U.S. Pacific Fleet and Pacific Ocean Areas, Advance Headquarters. Rescue and Search for Survivors of USS *Indianapolis* and Recovery, Identification, and Burial of Bodies. August 15, 1945.

Atteberry, G. C., Commanding Officer, Patrol Bombing Squadron 152. Report to Commander, Western Carolines Sub-Area. Sighting and Air-Sea Rescue of *Indianapolis* Survivors. August 9, 1945.

Atteberry, G. C.; Gwinn, W. G.; and Marks, R. A. Transcript of press conference. August 6, 1945.

Blackman, J. L., Memorandum for Operations Officer, Western Carolines Sub-Area. Extracts from VPB-23 Duty Officer's Log. August 2–6, 1945.

———. Memorandum for Air Operations Officer, Sub-Area. Operations of VPB-23 to Date on *Indianapolis* Rescue. August 4, 1945.

———. Memorandum for Air Operations Officer, Comwescar Sub-Area. VPB-23 Search Operations. August 7–8, 1945.

Blum, Donald J., to Chief of Naval Personnel. Casualty Report, U.S. Fleet Hospital #3149. August 5, 1945.

Brief in the General Court-Martial Case of Captain Charles B. McVay, 3rd, U.S. Navy, Tried on 3 December 1945.

Brown, W. S., Commanding Officer, USS *Ralph Talbot*. Report to Commander, Western Carolines Sub-Area. Search and Recovery of Survivors, August 6, 1945.

Carver, Grover. Letter to author. March 24, 1988.

CINCPAC. Wartime Pacific Routing Instructions. 1945.

———. (Advance Headquarters) Messages from Commander Forward Area, Central Pacific, concerning escort of vessels. February 9, March 14, April 21, May 11, December 13, 1945.

———. Navy Department messages on shipping rules. March 14; April 8, 22; May 1, 12, 15, 21; June 11, 17; August 3, 1945.

———. Order to *Indianapolis* to report to Port Director, Guam, for onward routing to Leyte. July 26, 1945.

———. Extracts from War Diary, Enemy Submarines. July 28, 1945.

———. Reply to C. P. Snyder concerning List of Ships That Left Guam for Leyte 26, 27, 28 July 1945. November 5, 1945.

Claytor, Graham, Commanding Officer, USS *Cecil J. Doyle*. Memorandum Report on Rescue of Survivors of USS *Indianapolis*. August 2–4, 1945.

———. Report to Commander Western Carolines Sub-Area on Search Conducted August 5–9, 1945.

Colclough, O. S., Judge Advocate General of the Navy. Memorandum for the Secretary of the Navy. Report on General Court-Martial in the Case of Captain C. B. McVay, III. November 29, 1945.

Cushman, Charles A., Assistant Judge Advocate General, Letter to Mrs. Alexander T. Moore. November 9, 1984.

———. Letter to Senator Jim Sasser. November 9, 1984.

Doran, Walter F., Military Aide to the Vice President. Letter to Kimo McVay. September 19, 1983.

Duxbury, Earl P. Notes on Lieutenant Marks and rescue of *Indianapolis* survivors.

Edwards, R. S., Vice Chief of Naval Operations. Memorandum for the Secretary of the Navy concerning the return to Japan of witness Mochitsura Hashimoto. January 3, 1946.

"Father of the Dead." Letter to Secretary of the Navy James Forrestal. March 30, 1945.

Forrestal, James, Secretary of the Navy. Memorandum to C. P. Snyder, Naval Inspector General, asking status of *Indianapolis* investigation. December 23, 1945.

———. Memorandum to Judge Advocate. General Court-Martial. Charges and Specifications in Case of Captain Charles B. McVay, III, U.S. Navy. November 29, 1945.

———. Letter to T. G. Murrell in reply to letter pleading for clemency for Captain McVay. January 22, 1946.

France, Robert. Letter to his family. September 20, 1945.

Furman, J. R., Commanding Officer, USS *Register*. Report to Commander, Western Carolines Sub-Area. Search Operations of U.S.S. *Register* for Survivors of USS *Indianapolis*. August 8, 1945.

Gibson, Stuart B. Letter to Forrest Tucker's superior officer protesting adverse fitness report. May 23, 1945.

———. Letter to Chief of Naval Personnel concerning reprimand in case of USS *Indianapolis*. September 24, 1945.

Graham, W. M. Radio Transmissions, to Commander Marianas. July 28, 29, 1945 concerning enemy submarines. November 28, 1945.

Granum, Alfred M. Letter to CINCPAC concerning loss of USS *Indianapolis*. September 1, 1945.

Gwinn, Wilbur C., Patrol Bombing Squadron 152. Report to Commander, Fleet Air Wing 18, concerning sighting of survivors of USS *Indianapolis*. August 3, 1945.

Haynes, Lewis L., Memorandum to Naval Inspector General. An Account of Survivors Following the Sinking of the USS *Indianapolis* with Recommended Changes in Life Saving Equipment. November 26, 1945.

———. Letter to author. December 30, 1988.

———. Letter to author. May 15, 1989.

Hidalgo, Edward. Memorandum to the Secretary of the Navy making recommendations on press statement regarding the sinking of the USS *Indianapolis*. February 2, 16, 21, 1946.

———. Memorandum to the Secretary of the Navy discussing charges against Captain McVay. February 13, 1946.

———, Secretary of the Navy. Letter to Giles McCoy. April 15, 1980.

Higgins, Anne, Special Assistant to President Ronald Reagan. Letter to Kimo McVay. September 12, 1983.

Hollingsworth, A. F., Commanding Officer, USS *Helm*. Report to Commander Western Carolines Sub-Area. Search for Survivors, 4–5 August 1945.

Hoover, Vice Admiral J. H., Commander Marianas. Operation plan. July 23, 1945.

USS *Indianapolis* (CA-35). The Final Sailing List. July 1945.

———. Survivors List. July 30, 1945, to July 30, 1985.

———. *Survivors Memorial Reunion* (pamphlet). August 2–4, 1985.

Inouye, Senator Daniel K. Letter to Kimo McVay. August 10, 1983.

———. Letter to Kimo McVay. September 23, 1983.

Kauffman, J. L., Commander, Philippine Sea Frontier. Letter to Chief of Naval Personnel supporting Lieutenant Stuart B. Gibson in the case of the sinking of the USS *Indianapolis*. October 26, 1945.

King, Fleet Admiral Ernest J. Memorandum to the Secretary of the Navy concerning Court of Inquiry's Inquiry into All the Circumstances Connected with the Sinking of the USS *Indianapolis* and with the Delay in Reporting the Loss of That Ship. September 25, 1945.

———. Order to Naval Inspector General to investigate the sinking of the USS *Indianapolis* and the delay in reporting the loss of that ship. October 18, 1945.

———. Recommendation to the Secretary of the Navy to delay court-martial of Captain McVay. November 10, 1945.

———. Memorandum to the Secretary of the Navy endorsing recommendation that Captain McVay's sentence be remitted. January 25, 1946.

Klappa, Ralph D. Letter to Senator Robert Kasten. November 16, 1984.

Langford, M. S., Air Combat Intelligence Officer. Report, Sighting of Survivors of USS *Indianapolis*; Participation in Air-Sea Rescue and Subsequent Search for Bodies and Debris. August 2–7, 1945.

Lockwood, Vice Admiral G. A. Letter to Chief of Naval Operations concerning reprimand of Commodore N. C. Gillette. April 10, 1946.

———. Letter to Chief of Naval Operations concerning reprimand of Captain Alfred H. Granum. April 22, 1946.

Marks, Adrian R. Statement to CINCPAC regarding rescue of survivors. August 5, 1945.

———. Address before the USS *Indianapolis* survivors' reunion. August 2, 1975.

———. Affidavit, to Some Bumbling Bureaucrat in the Veterans Administration (State of Indiana, County of Clinton) and to Anyone Else Who Gives a Damn. September 14, 1979.

———. Letter to author. November 3, 1988.

Matsunaga, Senator Spark. "Historical Note: Rectifying the Record to Honor Capt. Charles McVay III." *Congressional Record*, July 30, 1984.

———. Letter to Kimo McVay. July 31, 1984.

———. Letter to Kimo McVay. March 5, 1985.

McCormick, Rear Admiral Lynde D. Memorandum to CINCPAC. September 22, 1945.

McCoy, Giles. Letter to James W. Nance. August 6, 1975.

————. Letter to author. August 19, 1988.

————. Letter to author. January 17, 1989.

————. Letter to Secretary of the Navy Graham Claytor. N.d.

McKissick, Charles B. Letter to author. January 3, 1989.

————. Tape recording re USS *Indianapolis* tragedy.

McMorris, C. H., Chief of Staff, CINCPAC. Report to Pacific Fleet and Naval Shore Activities, Pacific Ocean Areas, Movements of Fleet Units, January 26, 1945.

McVay, Betsy (Mrs. Kimo McVay). Letter to author. September 28, 1988.

McVay, Charles B., II. Letter to his wife. September 5, 1898.

McVay, Charles B., III. Transcript of press conference. August 5, 1945.

————. Recommendations for Awards to Command Cruisers, Pacific Fleet. September 5, 1945.

————. Report to the Commander in Chief, U.S. Pacific Fleet and Pacific Ocean Areas, on the sinking of the USS *Indianapolis*, September 12, 1945.

————. Narrative, Sinking of USS *Indianapolis*. Recorded September 27, 1945.

————. Biography issued by Headquarters Eighth Naval District, New Orleans. N.d.

————. Military records (from National Personnel Records Center, St. Louis).

Moore, Katherine D. (Mrs. Kyle Campbell Moore). Letter to Senator Spark Matsunaga. September 28, 1984.

————. Letter to survivor Lindsey E. Wilcox. September 29, 1984.

Moore, Rosemond (Mrs. Alexander T. Moore). Letter to Senator Spark Matsunaga. September 24, 1984.

————. Letter to Secretary of the Navy John Lehman. September 26, 1984.

————. Letter to Kimo McVay. March 29, 1985.

Morgan, Armand. Letter to C. E. Coney, Office of the Chief of Naval Operations, providing information gathered in Japan about the sinking of the *Indianapolis*. December 10, 1945.

Mullen, M. D., Commanding Officer, USS *Tranquility*, to Commander in Chief, U.S. Fleet. Report of Medical Department activity, USS *Tranquility*, 22 July to 31 August 1945, 29 August 1945.

Murray, Robert J., Acting Secretary of the Navy. Letter to Giles McCoy. May 23, 1980.

Murrell, T. G. Letter to Secretary of the Navy James Forrestal pleading for clemency for Captain McVay. January 11, 1946.

Nance, James W. Letter to Giles McCoy. July 24, 1975.

Nash, Frank C. Memorandum to the Secretary of the Navy on the reprimands given to Commodore Gillette and Captain Granum. June 5, 1946.

Navy Department. Press release. Loss of the USS *Indianapolis*. August 14, 1945.

————. Press releases. December 3, 12, 1945.

————. Press release. Narrative of the Circumstances of the Loss of the USS *Indianapolis*. February 23, 1946.

Neupert, K. F., Commanding Officer, USS *Aylwin*. Report to Commander, Western Carolines Sub-Area. Search Operations for 4–5 August 1945.

Nienau, A. H., Commanding Officer, USS *Dufilho*. Report to Commander, Western Carolines Sub-Area. Rescue—Survivors Search, August 3–6, 1945.

Nimitz, Fleet Admiral Chester W. Memorandum to Judge Advocate General. Remarks on recommendations of the Court of Inquiry to Inquire into All the Circumstances Connected with the Sinking of the USS *Indianapolis* and the Delay in Reporting the Loss of That Ship. September 6, 1945.

———. Report to Chief of the Bureau of Ships on Abandon Ship Equipment in Connection with the Loss of USS *Indianapolis*. January 23, 1946.

———. Press conference. February 23, 1946.

———. Recommendation to Secretary of the Navy that letters of reprimand be issued to Commodore N. C. Gillette and Captain A. M. Granum. (Captain O. F. Naquin originally on list but his name deleted.) N.d.

Operational Intelligence Section, Guam. Intelligence brief for trip by USS *Indianapolis* from Guam to Leyte. July 27, 1945.

Philippine Sea Frontier, Headquarters. Organization Manual. August 28, 1945.

Record of Proceedings, Court of Inquiry, Guam, to Inquire into All the Circumstances Connected with the Sinking of the USS *Indianapolis*, and the Delay in Reporting the Loss of That Ship, August 13, 1945.

Record of Proceedings of a General Court-Martial Convened at the Navy Yard, Washington, D.C., by Order of the Secretary of the Navy. Case of Charles B. McVay, 3rd, Captain, U.S. Navy, December 3, 1945. 3 vols.

Robbins, R. C., Jr., Commanding Officer. Report to Commander, Western Carolines Sub-Area. Search for Bodies, Rafts and Debris from USS *Indianapolis*, August 9, 1945.

Rothwell, Robert M. Letter to Jim Borg. *Honolulu Advertiser*, August 4, 1983.

Ryan, Thomas J., Jr. Congressional Medal of Honor citation.

Sancho, J. C. Letter to CINCPAC concerning Court of Inquiry hearing on loss of USS *Indianapolis*. August 31, 1945.

Sanford, M. M., Commanding Officer, USS *Alvin C. Cockrell*. Report to Commander, Western Carolines Sub-Area. Rescue Operations USS *Alvin C. Cockrell*, August 3–6, 1945.

Sherman, Vice Admiral Forrest. Memorandum to Admiral Ramsey. Rough Draft of Narrative of the Circumstances of the Loss of the USS *Indianapolis*. February 20, 1946.

Snedeker, James, Chief, Military Law Division. Report to Judge Advocate General on competence of an alien enemy officer to testify at the court-martial of an American officer. N.d.

Snyder, C. P., Naval Inspector General. Request to CINCPAC for List of Ships That Left Guam for Leyte 26, 27, 28 July, 1945. November 5, 1945.

———. Report to Chief of Naval Operations on progress of *Indianapolis* case. November 10, 1945.

———. Report to Chief of Naval Operations on Progress on Further Investigation of the Sinking of the USS *Indianapolis* and the Delay in Reporting the Loss of That Ship. November 30, 1945.

———. Report to Commanding Officer, Naval Receiving Station, Camp Shumaker, Calif. Interrogation of Herbert J. Miner, December 5, 1945.

———. Message to Chief of Bureau of Ships Concerning Abandon-Ship Equipment Aboard the USS *Indianapolis*, by Order of the Chief of Naval Operations. December 6, 1945.

————. Message to Commander Clarke Withers, USS *Starr*, concerning rumor that distress signal from the *Indianapolis* was received by USS *Hyperion*. December 6, 1945.

————. Memorandum to Thomas E. Van Metro. Instructions for Further Investigation of the Sinking of the USS *Indianapolis* and the Delay in Reporting the Loss of That Ship. December 6, 1945.

————. Report to Commanding Officer, Uscoc Bibb, on distress message in connection with loss of USS *Indianapolis*. December 20, 1945.

————. Memorandum to the Secretary of the Navy concerning investigation of the sinking of the USS *Indianapolis*. January 2, 1946.

————. Report to Chief of Naval Operations on Investigation of the Sinking of the USS *Indianapolis* and the Delay in Reporting the Loss of That Ship. January 7, 1946.

————. Memorandum to the Secretary of the Navy concerning intercepted message from submarine *I-58*. February 27, 1946.

Stephenson, David C., Acting Pardon Attorney. Letter to Congressman Lawrence Coughlin. September 24, 1980.

Sullivan, John L., Acting Secretary of the Navy. Memorandum to Wilder D. Baker, Bureau of Naval Personnel. Precept for a General Court-Martial. November 21, 1945.

Todd, Donald W., Commanding Officer, USS *Madison*. Report to Commander, Western Carolines Sub-Area. Narrative of Search Operations, 2–5 August 1945. August 6, 1945.

Tucker, Forrest. Fitness report on Lieutenant Stuart B. Gibson. February 22, 1945.

Twible, Harlan M. Letter to author. March 25, 1988.

————. Résumé of the Life of Harlan M. Twible. N.d.

Van Metre, T. E., Memorandum to Naval Inspector General concerning intercepted message from submarine *I-58*. November 2, 1945.

————. Memorandum to the Naval Inspector General concerning investigation of the *Indianapolis* case. November 10, 1945.

Weddington, Harold R. Letter to Senator Mark O. Hatfield. September 16, 1984.

Wilcox, Lindsey Z. Letter to President Ronald Reagan. December 7, 1984.

Wilder, Kinau. Letter to author. August 4, 1988.

INDEX

321

Sir Thomas Malory

A BIOGRAPHY

LONDON : HUMPHREY MILFORD

OXFORD UNIVERSITY PRESS

In a north window of the Church,

Orate pro Iohe Malorey, et philippa vrore eius.

SIR THOMAS MALORY'S PARENTS.

(Dugdale's "Antiquities of Warwickshire": The stained glass window
formerly in Grendon Church.)

THE MALORY COAT-OF-ARMS.

(From Harleian MS. 1404, fo. 62.)

Sir Thomas Malory

HIS TURBULENT CAREER

A Biography by

EDWARD HICKS

Cambridge
HARVARD UNIVERSITY PRESS
1928

5811

10-28-42 ~

823.1

H

TO THE MEMORY OF

𝔐𝔶 𝔚𝔦𝔣𝔢

WHO, DESPITE HER ILL-HEALTH, WAS
KEENLY INTERESTED IN THE PROGRESS
OF MY MALORY RESEARCHES

Preface

En habes, lector benevole. — Here you may find, gentle reader, a multitude of exciting novelties about that Sir Thomas Malory of Newbold Revel and Winwick whom I had the good luck to identify, thirty odd years ago, with the author of *Le Morte d'Arthur*. Such a feast needs no proclaiming; but, since Mr. Hicks has done me the honour to request me to write a note of invitation, I must try to do what he asks as unobtrusively as I can.

To hard-headed and stout-hearted students of literary antiquities the important facts which our keen and indefatigable investigator has discovered will make instant appeal. Nor will they be shocked or disconcerted by the wildness of the actions recorded. To the sentimental reader we may leave the task of adjusting Sir Thomas's biography, as now revealed, to the notions he may have derived of him from his immortal romance. Everybody must admire the way in which Mr. Hicks has gathered such a wealth of pertinent information, historical and social, to set forth in a true light the extraordinary conditions which made Malory's career natural and normal in fifteenth-century England. As Pike, the historian of crime, remarked long ago: "The qualities of the knight errant and the gentleman have often been attributed to the highwayman and the brigand. Nor can it be disputed that the highwayman and the brigand have much in common with the knight errant."

Let us not be over-much concerned by the charges brought against Sir Thomas Malory in 1451, serious as

they may appear in the light of modern manners. "Possession by the strong arm had for so many centuries constituted the best title to land that the best legal claim to it was almost valueless until practically asserted by setting foot on the soil." The statute against forcible entry was not passed until the fifth year of Richard II, and the old custom long survived the enactment, yielding only to what we are prone to call the Tudor Despotism. A logical corollary to this rough-and-ready method of asserting title was the practice of seizing for one's self money or other personal property to which one laid claim. Such riots were of daily occurrence, and carried no stigma of social disgrace, whatever the law might have to say to them if they got into court, as most of them did not. Besides, an indictment is merely an accusation; it is not evidence: and the lawyers, as we know, had a way of including in such a document everything that the prosecution could think of, and far more than anybody expected to prove. Now Mr. Hicks, the discoverer of this extraordinarily interesting record and of other entries referring to the same case, has not succeeded in finding any account of a trial. For aught we know, then, Malory was acquitted on all the counts. Anyhow, there is no probability that he was convicted on all of them, or that, if convicted, he was punished by imprisonment. At worst, he had to make restitution and pay a substantial fine. The double charge of rape was manifestly absurd — a mere legal formula if the woman of the house was present and had been forcibly removed from her dwelling while it was ransacked. Nor is there any likelihood that Malory had lain in wait to kill Buckingham, though he may have been in Coombe woods while the duke was a guest at the

Abbey. What makes it clear that he was either not convicted, or not punished by imprisonment, is the fact
that on March 26, 1453, Duke Humphrey and others
were commissioned to arrest him again on what appear
to be new charges. Nor did this new prosecution, it
seems, result in the penalty of imprisonment. He had
the King's pardon for all offences committed before
July 9, 1455. Fresh offences, however, seem to have re-
sulted in Malory's continuous, or almost continuous,
imprisonment for three years, from 1457 to 1460. That
he was in confinement when he penned his valediction
in 9 Edward IV (at some time between March 4, 1469,
and March 3, 1470) may be regarded as certain. Perhaps he was still in prison when he died on the 14th of
the following March. But I see no evidence that he had
been confined for any considerable period between 1460
and 1469. His exclusion from the general pardon of
1468 was probably due to some political offence; for
almost all of the persons associated with him in this
exclusion were involved, or thought to be involved, in
recent Lancastrian plots.

But enough! I have yielded to the temptation to in-
terpret novel phenomena when my office is merely to
invite the reader to scan these for himself in Mr. Hicks's
vitally interesting presentation. If I have transgressed
the proprieties of my function, the stimulating nature
of his volume may suffice as an excuse.

G. L. KITTREDGE.

Contents

Illustrations

Sir Thomas Malory

Introduction

SHAKESPEARE'S genius, towering above that of all other Englishmen, has had one unfortunate effect on his native county; it has tended to focus all attention on the Swan of Avon to the almost complete neglect of other Warwickshire authors. Yet there is another name, standing high in the realm of letters, which Warwickshire folk are fully entitled to claim — that of Sir Thomas Malory, author of the *Morte d'Arthur*. Hitherto very little has been known about Malory; practically the only one to raise a corner of the thick curtain which has concealed the identity of the knight who in 1469 finished writing the immortal story of King Arthur and the Knights of the Round Table, has been Professor George Lyman Kittredge, of Harvard University.[1]

Professor Kittredge made it sufficiently clear that Sir Thomas Malory came from Newbold Revel, in the parish of Monks Kirby, Warwickshire — a point which will be found emphasised by additional matter in Chapter XV of the present work. Professor Kittredge's conjectural identification of the author of the *Morte* was put on record as long ago as March, 1894, when it was announced in Johnson's *Universal Cyclopædia*. This, however, did not attract notice in England; therefore, when Mr. T. W. Williams stated in the *Athenæum* of July 11, 1896, that he had discovered among Wells Cathedral MSS a document which excluded "Thomas Malorie, *miles*," from a general pardon in 1468, he did

"Who was Sir Thomas Malory?" An article contained in vol. V of *Studies and Notes in Philology and Literature*, Boston, Mass., 1897.

not connect the Warwickshire knight with the "Malorie" to whom he had found reference, although they were really one and the same person. Later — in January, 1920 — Mr. Edward F. Cobb brought to Professor Kittredge's notice an extract from the De Banco Rolls of Henry VI, 1443, showing that Thomas Malory, *miles*, and another were charged with assault with violence at Sprotton, Northants. This affair, whatever its rights or wrongs may have been, appears to have been settled out of court.

More serious was the trouble in which Sir Thomas Malory was involved in 1451 — reference to which was made by Sir E. K. Chambers in January, 1922, in a pamphlet published by the English Association. Sir E. K. Chambers quoted the Calendar of Patent Rolls to show that some dispute had occurred between Sir Thomas and the Carthusians at Monks Kirby, which brought about the intervention of Henry VI.

The present writer's researches at the Public Record Office have brought to light the proceedings against Sir Thomas Malory, who was accused not only of offences against the Carthusians, but of leading an assault on Coombe Abbey and setting an ambush in the Abbey Woods for one of the most powerful noblemen of the day, viz., Humphrey, Duke of Buckingham, uncle (by marriage) of the King-Maker. The indictment included several other counts — to all of which Sir Thomas pleaded not guilty; but their cumulative effect on the minds of the Warwickshire Jury who tried him must have been that he was, like Sir Corsabrin, "a passing felonious knight."

Malory's early career and his subsequent long confinement in Newgate Gaol are dealt with in the present

volume, which also indicates the conditions under which he wrote the *Morte*.

It is fair to assume that Professor Kittredge's interest in the subject of Malory was stimulated by the fact that America possesses the only perfect copy of the *Morte* printed by Caxton which is known to exist.[1] This was bought for £1,950 by Mrs. Norton Q. Pope at the sale of the Osterley Park Library in 1885, and taken to Brooklyn, New York. On the death of Mrs. Pope, it was purchased by Mr. Robert Hoe, of New York, and in 1911 acquired by the late Mr. J. Pierpont Morgan for $42,800. It is now in the Pierpont Morgan Library in New York City. Mr. Pierpont Morgan's son has recently made this Library a public institution (liberally endowed) under a special board of trustees. The volume is therefore at rest, and never will be sold again.

It was a recent pupil of Professor Kittredge at Harvard, Dr. J. Leslie Hotson, who in 1925 published the result of his researches at the Public Record Office concerning the death of Christopher Marlowe. Yet another American, Dr. J. Douglas Bruce (Professor of the English Language and Literature in the University of Tennessee) some years ago reëdited the metrical *Morte Arthur* for the Early English Text Society. To Englishmen, accustomed as they are to seeing the choicest MSS and books purchased by Dr. Rosenbach for shipment to the United States, it should be no small consolation to reflect that American scholars are justifying by their research work the avidity with which our literary treasures are being acquired for Transatlantic homes.

The Year Books covering the years 1455–1470 contain

[1] The only other Caxton copy, now in the Rylands Library at Manchester, has eleven leaves supplied in facsimile.

no references to Sir Thomas Malory; and to prevent the repetition of futile search, it may be well to state here that the Assize Rolls for Warwickshire and Leicestershire, the Close Rolls and the Patent Rolls for the period indicated have been searched in vain. The Coram Rege Roll for 1468, the year in which Malory was excluded from two pardons, has also been examined without result. Moreover, although it is certain that Sir Thomas's widow left a will, no trace of it is discoverable at Lichfield (where the records of the old Coventry and Lichfield diocese are kept) nor in the official archives in London.

Acknowledgment of the help given by Mr. Montague Giuseppi, Superintendent of the Legal Research Department at the Public Record Office, is made on page 19, but there are others whose assistance has been extremely valuable. Miss N. McNeill O'Farrell not only transcribed the record of the Inquisition at Nuneaton and the proceedings at Westminster, but discovered the document which bears the seal of Sir Thomas Malory's father. Mr. Philip B. Chatwin, F.S.A., F.R.I.B.A., has given the writer the benefit of his exceptional knowledge of Warwickshire archaeology, while Mr. F. J. Thacker of the Birmingham Reference Library, and Mr. W. E. Owen, the Leamington Borough Librarian, have done much to facilitate the compilation of this biography. Finally, I would acknowledge the help given by members of my family and especially by my daughter Phyllis, who not only prepared the map showing the Malory country but also compiled the index.

Chapter I

ANCESTRY AND MILITARY CAREER

Bale asserts that the author (of the *Morte d'Arthur*) was occupied with affairs of State, but practically no definite information is available respecting him outside his book. — *Dictionary of National Biography*, concerning Sir Thomas Malory.

PRIOR to the investigations of Professor G. Lyman Kittredge, the identity of Sir Thomas Malory had been a matter of speculation in many quarters. For example, Bishop Bale (1495–1563), after declaring "Thomas Mailorius" to be by race and country a Briton, recalled Leland's statement that "Mailoria" was a district within the Welsh borders, not far from the River Dee. But, to quote Professor Kittredge: "Bale's biographical statements are of the good old-fashioned sort, and convey no information. He admits that he does not even know under what king that 'Mailorius' flourished — something that he might have discovered from the closing words of the *Morte*." At one time, indeed, it was supposed that Sir Thomas was a Welsh priest — the "Sir" being regarded as the equivalent of "reverend" in translating *dominus*. Place-names are very apt to suggest wrong derivations, and a reader of the *Morte d'Arthur* who knew that in Denbighshire there was a little town named Maelor would be strongly tempted to jump to the conclusion that the author of this, the greatest of English prose romances, came from that place, especially if he were ignorant of the fact that Welshmen did not bear surnames till a good deal later

than Sir Thomas Malory's time — Henry VII's reign, to be precise.[1]

The writer of the *Morte*, it is now clear, belonged to a family whose ancestor [2] came over with the Conqueror, and established himself at Kirkby Malory, in Leicestershire. Sir Stephen Malory — great grandfather of Sir Thomas — acquired a footing in Warwickshire (*temp.* Edward III) by marrying Margaret Revell, heiress to the Fenny Newbold estates. The status of the family is shown by the fact that it furnished sheriffs of Warwickshire and Leicestershire in 15 Richard II, 4 Henry V, and 3 Henry VI.[3] Sir Thomas's own father, John Malory, *armiger*, was M.P. for Warwickshire in 1413, 1419, 1423, and 1427. An even more onerous duty was his in 1424, when he was appointed Escheator for Warwickshire and Leicestershire, and so became responsible to the Crown for estates the owners of which had died intestate. He married Philippa Chetwynd, of Grendon, in the County of Warwick — a marriage which, incidentally, seems to have made him a party, with Sir John Cockayne, Kt. and John Chetwynd, to the lawsuits which were carried on for years concerning land at Meriden (then known as Alspath). A nephew of Philippa Malory was "a person not a little eminent in his time" — we refer to Sir Philip Chetwynd, the fifth of that name. Born about 1400, he, like his cousin Thomas, was taken into the Earl of Warwick's service and in 1428 placed about the person of the little king, Henry VI.

---

[1] The object was to enable the authorities to keep better supervision of "undesirables."

[2] "Mallory" in Holinshed's *Roll of Battel Abbey*. "Malory" in Stow's *Chronicles*.

[3] Fuller's *Worthies*. It should be noted that the two counties were linked under one sheriff until 9 Eliz.

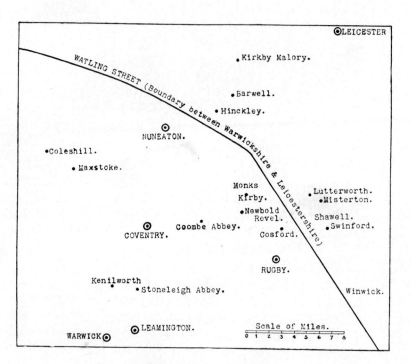

THE MALORY COUNTRY.

Subsequently Sir Philip was appointed Governor of Bayonne, — "where the wine of Beaume is," comments Malory appreciatively in the *Morte*, — and in the self-same year (1442) Sir Thomas [1] was one of the witnesses to a settlement of the Chetwynd estates in Warwickshire and Staffordshire on Sir Philip and Joan his wife.

Dugdale's *Antiquities of Warwickshire* contains several reproductions of what is described as the Malory coat-of-arms, together with the cognizance of the Revells; but Sir Thomas Malory's father, at all events, did not use the coat-of-arms assigned by Dugdale to his family, viz.: *Or, 3 Lyons Passant, Gardant Sa.*[2] This is proved by the wax seal attached to a deed of 12 Henry VI preserved at the Public Record Office.[3] By this document, dated shortly before his death, John Malory granted an annual rent of 12d. and three capons in respect of land at Wibtoft. The wax seal is identical with the coat-of-arms depicted in the pages of Papworth[4] as belonging to the Malory family, viz.,

Erm. a chev. between three 3-foils slipped arg. a bordure eng. sa.

It is interesting to compare this with the armorial bearings depicted on the cloak worn by Philippa, mother of Sir Thomas Malory, which are distinctly "Revell" in appearance (see Frontispiece). The dresses of ladies of that period were decorated with the arms of their families, so that when — as we read in the *Morte* — a knight wore a lady's sleeve in his helmet, it would have

---

[1] The Chetwynd Cartulary — which shows also that Malory had been knighted by this time.

[2] Fuller, in his *Worthies*, assigns this badge to the Leicestershire branch of the Malorys.

[3] Court of Wards (Deeds and Evidences), Box 1.

[4] J. W. Papworth, *Ordinary of British Armorals.*

been quickly identified, as no doubt it was intended to be.

As a member of the Retinue of Richard Beauchamp, Earl of Warwick, the author of the *Morte* saw military service in France at the period when Joan of Arc's inspiring presence had turned the tide against the English. Seeing that Richard Beauchamp furnished the special guard posted in Rouen market-place when Joan was burnt in 1431, it is highly probable that Malory was present on that occasion. One whom he was to face twenty years later in very different circumstances was also present — Humphrey, Earl of Stafford (afterwards Duke of Buckingham). As Constable of France for Henry VI, the latter had had more than one interview with Joan in her prison at Rouen. His ideas of knightly courtesy are illustrated by the following incidents. The Pucelle having declared that "Were there one hundred thousand *godons* more than at present, they would not conquer the kingdom," the Earl of Stafford (as he then was) unsheathed his sword, so that the Earl of Warwick had to restrain his hand. That the English Constable of France would have raised his sword against a woman in chains would be incredible did we not know that about this time the Earl of Stafford, hearing someone speak well of Joan, straightway wished to transfix him.[1]

Dugdale mentions, as an important item of Malory's war record, that he served in the garrison "at the siege of Caleys in King Henry V's time, being of the retinue of Richard Beauchamp, Earl of Warwick." As a matter of fact, however, there was no siege of Calais in this reign, although, early in 1414, when the Earl was appointed Deputy of the fortress, a French attack was

[1] Anatole France.

anticipated. Dugdale gives as his authority in this instance "Rot(ulus) in bibl. Hatton." Search for this Roll at the Bodleian Library and the British Museum has proved fruitless, and we are forced to conclude that it was among the valuable MSS, etc., destroyed in the great fire at the Birmingham Public Library in 1879. The same Roll, however, is cited by Dugdale as his authority for statements concerning other members of Richard Beauchamp's retinue, and it is by examining these references that we are able approximately to establish the date at which Malory served at Calais. To begin with, Dugdale is by no means always consistent on the point of there having been a *siege* of Calais in the reign of Henry V. For example, of Sir Ralph Bracebridge of Kingsbury he says that he was retained to serve the Earl "for the strengthening of Calais." Again, of Sir William de Bishopton we are told that he was retained by the Earl of Warwick "for the fortifying of Calais." On the other hand, Sir Ralph Arden of Curdworth and John de L'Isle of Moxhull are stated to have been two of the Earl's esquires "at the siege of Calais"; and if the categorical statement made regarding Sir William Mountford of Coleshill could really be accepted literally, it would follow that Malory was present at the brief siege of Calais in 1406. This, however, is incredible, for he must have been a mere lad at the time; and, moreover, Richard Beauchamp had not as yet been appointed Captain of Calais. We know that one member of the retinue, Sir Ralph Arden, died in 1421; consequently it must have been during a captaincy prior to that date that Malory served under the Earl at Calais. We know that the Earl was first appointed Captain of Calais on February 3, 1414; but a few days earlier he was ordered,

in that capacity, to proclaim a truce. On October 20, 1414, he was commissioned to go to the Council of Constance, and this caused an interruption in his captaincy. When he resumed the office, he did so under an indenture of June 19, 1415, by which he agreed "to serve the King as Captain of Calais until February 3, 1416. And to have with him in the time of Truce or Peace, for the safeguard thereof, Thirty Men at Arms, himself and three Knights accounted as part of that number; Thirty Archers on Horsback, Two Hundred Foot Soldiers, and Two hundred Archers, all of his own retinue. . . . And in time of War, he to have One hundred and forty Men on Horsbak," etc.[1] We may conclude, therefore, that the Roll which Dugdale cited as his authority bore date 1414 or 1415.

The point is important in another respect, for it helps us to estimate Malory's age. We read in the *Morte* that when Sir Bors desired to take his fifteen-year-old son with him on a knightly expedition, King Arthur objected. "Ye may well take him with you, but he is over tender of age." It is true that Malory makes Elaine say: "My lord Sir Launcelot, at this same feast of Pentecost shall your son and mine, Galahad, be made knight, for he is fully now fifteen winter old." This is one of the numerous passages which Malory has inserted "on his own," so to speak. But against this we must place Chaucer's description of

> A young squier
> A lover and a lusty bacheler;
>
> . . . .
>
> Of twenty yer of age he was I gesse.

---

[1] Dugdale's *Baronage*, i, 244.

The young man who in 1415 was accompanied by a lance and two archers when he joined the Earl of Warwick's retinue must have been something like 21 years of age. Hence when Sir Thomas Malory died in March, 1471, he must have been somewhere about 77 years old. If it be objected that this is scarcely credible, the reply must be that Malory was not the only septuagenarian of his day and county. John Rous, the Warwick antiquary, who was a lad when Richard Beauchamp founded the chantry at Guy's Cliffe in 1423, died in 1491 at the reputed age of 81. John Hardyng, a strictly contemporary writer, who was present at the battle of Agincourt, died somewhere about 1465 "at a great old age." [1]

As a member of the Retinue of Richard Beauchamp, the "Father of Courtesie," Sir Thomas Malory had full opportunity of studying one whom the world of chivalry, both in Europe and in the Holy Land, regarded as its *beau idéal*.

Whether or no Sir Thomas Malory, as a page, accompanied Richard Beauchamp on his world tour, it is certain that he benefited by the knowledge his lord had gained by travel. "The details (given in the *Morte*) of King Arthur's march to Rome are so accurate that I think that Malory may have had actual knowledge of the road," wrote the late Sir Edward Strachey, 3rd Baronet, in his preface to the very able edition published by him in 1868. Dr. Oskar Sommer, indeed, sug-

---

[1] Malory, when he died, must have been a mere lad compared with Johan Grauntpe, of Coventry, who, according to *Early Chancery Proceedings*, was 140 when he made complaint to the Chancellor of England that he and Agnes his wife had been unjustly deprived of a close called "Dudmounesfeld," worth 40s. a year. Certain feoffees, he alleged, would not let him enter therein because he is an old man aged 140, blind, decrepit, sick and bedridden, poor and feeble, ("a cause qil est veill homme dage de $\frac{xx}{vij}$ anz aveogls decrepit malade en sounz lite continuelment gisaunt povre et feble").

gests that geographical knowledge is not Malory's strong
point, this criticism being based on the mention of
"Sandwich" as the place where Arthur's armies gather
and set out to sea. "Considering that Arthur planned
to, and really did, cross over to Normandy," adds Dr.
Sommer, "it is more natural that Southampton should
be the port chosen than Sandwich in Kent." Against
this we have the actual record of troops having em-
barked at Sandwich in Henry V's reign.[1]

In many lands Richard Beauchamp displayed his
prowess, so that the Emperor Sigismund, when visiting
Henry V, was heard to declare "That no Christian
Prince hath such another Knight for Wisdom, Nurture
and Manhood, that if all Courtesie were lost, yet it
might be found again in him." And so, ever after, by the
Emperor's authority, he was called "the Fadre of Cur-
teisy." It is this nobleman whom Mr. George Bernard
Shaw has seen fit, in "St. Joan," to represent as the
cynic of his period! In the absence of information as to
the precise date of Sir Thomas Malory's birth, it is impossible to say whether he accompanied the Earl in his
Wanderjähre, which extended from 1408 to 1410; but we
know that the struggle with France, which entered on a
more violent phase when Henry V ascended the throne,
did not put a stop to those deeds of knight-errantry
which figure so prominently in the pages of the Morte.
When Richard Beauchamp was first appointed Captain
of Calais (in 1411) a French attack was anticipated, but
when the danger passed, the Earl "resolved to put in
practice some new point of chivalry." He therefore
caused three shields to be made, and in each of them a
lady painted, whose cause was to be championed respec-

---

[1] Exchequer Accounts, Q.R., 50/1, 9 Hen. V.

THE TOMB OF RICHARD BEAUCHAMP, EARL OF WARWICK, MALORY'S FEUDAL CHIEF.

tively by the Green Knight, the Chivalier Vert, and the Chivalier Attendant. In each of these guises the Earl was victorious, in so much that the Frenchmen alleged that he had bound himself to his saddle. Alighting in the presence of the assembly, he proved the baselessness of the accusation, and having feasted all the people and given handsome mementoes to his three opponents, he returned to Calais with great honour.[1]

Association with such a dashing and altogether attractive personality must have helped to colour Malory's whole outlook, of which we have striking evidence in the *Morte*. According to Dugdale, Malory served in the French Wars with one lance and two archers, receiving for his lance and one archer £20 per annum and their diet, and for the other archer 10 marks without diet. Exactly how to express these sums in terms of present-day currency is a difficult problem. As a writer on the history of Exchange has said: "Even now there are country districts in England where money will go half as far again as it would do in some of our great towns. But in old times the difference was infinitely greater, so that there is no possibility of gauging the difference between the old and the present values of money by any equational system." Dugdale, after recording that Richard Beauchamp left estate valued at 8306 marks 11s. 11d., attempts in his own way to arrive at the value of the sum. "At the time," he writes, "barley was sold for 4s. 2d. per quarter, oats at 2s. 1d., capons at 3d. apiece, and hens at 1d."

As the Earl of Warwick was not present at the battle of Agincourt, in October, 1415, it is to be inferred that Malory also was not there; but that Sir Thomas saw

---

[1] Dugdale's *Antiquities of Warwickshire*.

much military service in France is clear from the fact
that his name is absent from the lists of M.P.s and Sheriffs for Warwickshire while the war lasted, and that immediately the long struggle was over he represented his
county in Parliament. As a member of the retinue of
Richard Beauchamp he would accompany the Earl in
1436 to the relief of Calais, when the fortress was be-
sieged by the Burgundians. It is worthy of note that
the chief command of the relieving force was entrusted
to Humphrey, Duke of Gloucester, in his day the chief
patron of letters in this country, and the real founder of
the Bodleian Library. Richard Beauchamp's regard for
learning is also on record; he presented a copy of the
Decameron to Duke Humphrey, and it was at his instance that Lydgate, the poet, wrote his metrical account of the English claims to the French throne. Lydgate thus attested the fact:

> I moved was shortly in sentiment
> By precept first and commaundement
> Of the nobly prince and manly man,
> Which is so knyghtly and so moche can,
> My lord of Warrewyk, so prudent and wise.

Thus the circumstances of Malory's military service
were rather favourable than otherwise to the growth in
him of an interest in literature. The perpetual hand-to-
hand combats met with in the *Morte* can also be explained by Malory's experience in the French Wars. A
particular instance in point may be cited. In 1438 —
within twelve months after Paris had been recaptured
from the English — a near relative of the Earl of Warwick took advantage of a pause in hostilities to visit the
French capital and "maintain a duel on horseback
within the street called St. Antoine [adjacent to the

Bastille] against one Peter de Masse, a Frenchman, in the presence of Charles VII." The English champion was Sir John de Astley, of Patshull,[1] "who pierced the said Peter through the head and had his helmet to present unto his lady." This incident happened, not, as might be supposed, while the opposing armies were in winter-quarters, but in the month of August. Could a more telling example be quoted of the fifteenth-century passion for duelling, jousts, tournaments, which the *Morte* associates with a much earlier period? It should be added that so famous for valour did Sir John de Astley grow that early in the reign of Edward IV he was elected a Knight of the Garter. As has been well said, "the 14th and 15th centuries saw the Court of Chivalry at its best and strongest. The insight given by the Hundred Years War into the privileged position of the aristocracy in France doubtless contributed to a demand on the part of the quality in England for the maintenance of a Court that dealt with questions in which points of honour were concerned; with mere personal affronts."

[1] Dugdale's *Antiquities*. Sir John de Astley's sister Joan married Thomas Appelby. It seems probable that the latter was related to John Appelby, Sir Thomas Malory's aider and abetter in the outbreak of 1451.

Chapter II

PARLIAMENTARY SERVICE

WE NEXT catch sight of Sir Thomas Malory in 1445, when, the Hundred Years War having come to an inglorious end, he was free to return to Newbold Revel. There, "being a knight, he served for this shire in the Parliament then held at Westminster." [1] It is highly interesting to observe the two names associated with his in the Fine Roll of 23 Henry VI. One is that of Humphrey, Duke of Buckingham, the other is that of Sir William Mountford, of Coleshill. Six years later we shall see the latter arresting Malory and the Duke presiding at his trial.

The Parliament of 1445 in which Sir Thomas sat had some most important business to transact. We learn from Hansard that writs were issued on January 13 for the Parliament to meet at Westminster on February 25. In the presence of the King, sitting in person in his chair of state, and of the Lords and Commons, John Stafford, late Bishop of Bath and Wells, but now Archbishop and Chancellor of England, declared the cause of calling this Parliament, namely, to ratify the marriage treaty arranged between the King and Margaret, daughter of the King of Sicily. Parliament was then prorogued to April 19, when the Chancellor made protestation "that the peace which the King had made with the French king, or rather was about to make, was merely of his own mo-

[1] Dugdale's *Antiquities.*

tion and will and that he was not instigated thereto by himself or any of the lords whatsoever." Which protest was enrolled. Thereupon it was decided that the statute of Henry V "importing that no peace should be made with the French King that now is, and was then called Dauphin of France, without the assent of the three Estates of both realms should be utterly repealed and revoked, and that no person whatsoever should be impeached at any time to come for giving counsel to bring about this peace with France." Thus was indemnified the Earl of Suffolk, who had promoted the treaty. It availed little to save him five years later, when he was murdered on the way to banishment.

Another Act concerned the "wages" of Members of Parliament — the manner of their election — the remedy where one is chosen and another returned. Parliament also confirmed the King's letters patent for the erection and endowment of Eton College and King's College, Cambridge. (The endowment, by the way, was derived from the revenues of a large number of "alien" monasteries which had recently been dissolved.)

Sir Thomas Malory's name, although it appears in the Fine Roll already referred to, is not in the printed list compiled from the Writs of Summons to Parliament, and the fact that in the following year the name of Edmund Mountford, *armiger*, is so included "gives one furiously to think." For Sir Edmund (as he afterwards became) was a younger son, by a second marriage, of that Sir William Mountford who arrested Malory in 1451 (see page 30), and in view of what is known about him and the Duke of Buckingham, it appears extremely probable that he supplanted Malory in the Parliamentary representation of Warwickshire, just as he sup-

planted his brother, Sir Baldwin, in regard to the manor of Coleshill. Sir Edmund, it is to be noted, had been appointed an esquire to Henry VI in 1444, and was, "indeed, much in favour with that unfortunate prince."[1] All the weight of the Duke of Buckingham's influence would naturally be given to Edmund in view of the understanding that had been arrived at between them as to the possession of Coleshill. The "management of elections" had at this period become a scandal, although it was an obvious result of the restriction of the franchise which had just taken place. The complaint of the Kentish-men in Cade's revolt alleges that "the people of the shire are not allowed to have their free election in the choosing of knights for the shire, but letters have been sent from divers estates to the great rulers of all the county, the which enforceth their tenants and other people by force to choose other persons than the common will is."[2]

[1] Dugdale, *Antiquities*.
[2] J. R. Green, *History of the English People*.

Chapter III

A "RIGHT WILD" ENGLAND

FROM Sir Thomas Malory, Knight of the Shire representing his county in Parliament, to Sir Thomas Malory arraigned for armed assaults on monasteries in Warwickshire is a startling change. Without some knowledge of the period in question, the change would appear too violent to be credited. "The lawlessness of the country at this time," says Professor Ransome, "was such as had not been tolerated in England for many centuries." The loss of Normandy and the heavy load of taxation which had to be borne as a result of the struggle with France would in any case have made the task of government difficult; but matters were worsened by other evils, among which must be reckoned the removal of bishops from their dioceses in order to perform State duties in London. Thus, the Bishop of Coventry and Lichfield had been called from his proper sphere in order to act as chancellor to Queen Margaret of Anjou. It was the neglect of the bishops and clergy to do their several duties that led to Jack Cade's insurrection in 1450, wrote Dr. Gascoigne, an anti-Lollard. As the civil servants of the period, they no doubt could have retorted that they were fulfilling duties which no one else was then qualified to perform. In any case, the Bishop must have had an unenviable task in acting as chancellor to "England's dear-bought queen." So preoccupied was he with his duties at Court that his episcopal register contains

not a single reference to the stormy days of July, 1451, in his diocese.

The Patent Rolls record innumerable instances of the state of confusion and uneasiness that prevailed. In March of this same year (1451) the Bishop of Bath and Wells had been given permission to enclose the ecclesiastical buildings at Wells with a stone wall "and crenellate the same and make towers there for the greater security of the Bishop and Canons." One of the Pastons' correspondents warned his master that "the world is right wild." He was thinking more particularly of Norfolk. Documents now brought to light at the Public Record Office and set forth in Chapter VI prove that Warwickshire was also "wild." Coventry was one of the hot-beds of a militant Lollardy which in 1431 had made demonstration against the hierarchy. Their leader, "Jack Sharpe of Wygmoreland," had distributed pamphlets which took the form of a petition to the King and Lords in Parliament showing the waste which ensued from the possession of temporalities by bishops, abbots, and priors of the Church, and praying for their resumption by the Crown.[1] At that date, however, the central government was strong, with the result that no mercy was shown, all persons implicated being treated as guilty of high treason.

It is important to remember that, living at Newbold Revel, his principal manor, Sir Thomas Malory would be only six miles from Lutterworth, the fountain-head of Lollardy. Wycliffe himself, early in 1382, had urged the gradual confiscation of all clerical property by special taxation.[2] The grievance of paying tithe to a dis-

[1] K. H. Vickers, *Humphrey Duke of Gloucester.*
[2] Dr. James Gairdner.

tant religious house had, in the previous year, driven
men near Melton Mowbray to join Wat Tyler's rebellion, under the leadership of a curate from a neighbour-
ing village.[1] Similar cases occurred elsewhere. In bad
times, such as England experienced immediately after
the Hundred Years War, the strict demand for tithe
pressed hard on the poor, and the movement for refusal
of such dues was at this period a marked thing.[2]

The demand for payment of heriots when a monastic
tenant died was also a grievance at this time, as Warwickshire history proves. A great riot took place at
Shipston-on-Stour in the sixth year of Henry VI, with
reference to heriots, and the question was ultimately
referred to the Abbot of Winchcombe, who determined
that the prior and convent of Worcester had from early
times received at the death of every tenant the best
animal, while the parson of Tredington received the
second best.

"It was really not the theological doctrines half so
much as the external polity of the Church that Wycliffe
called in question," says Dr. Gairdner. But the Act of
Parliament passed against Lollardy twenty-two years
after Wycliffe's death shows the apprehension that the
movement had excited by this time in the breasts of the
ruling classes. "If the designs of these persons were not
resisted," it was declared, "they would in time succeed
in depriving the temporal lords likewise of their possessions, which they would treat as common property and
thus raise commotions which would be the complete
destruction of the Kingdom." How very modern it
sounds! The attitude of the House of Lancaster toward
Lollardy had not been made more friendly by what hap-

[1] André Reville.   [2] G. M. Trevelyan.

pened at the end of 1417 — only two years after Agincourt. While Henry V was spending his Christmas at Kenilworth, it is recorded, a squire of Sir John Oldcastle's laid an ambush for him.[1]

That discontent with the monastic system was not confined to Lollards, however, is clear. Richard Fox, Bishop of Winchester, was persuaded by Bishop Oldham of Exeter to found Corpus Christi College, Oxford, rather than "provide livelodes for a companie of bussing monks."[2] Even when the bishops insisted on a settled sum from impropriated livings being put on one side for the parish priest, the regular clergy (the monasteries) tried to cut this down as much as possible.[3] "The practice of impropriation has been regarded by most writers as a manifest abuse, and there is no call to attempt to defend it."[4] On the other hand, it is urged that "the churches and vicarages of places impropriated were the special care of the religious. An examination of these churches frequently reveals the fact that religious bodies did not hesitate to spend large sums of money upon the rebuilding and adornment of structures which belonged to them in this way."[5]

[1] Ramsay's *Lancaster and York*, i, 254.
[2] A. Abram, *English Life and Manners in the Later Middle Ages*.
[3] H. S. Bennett, *The Pastons and their England*.
[4] Cardinal Gasquet, *English Monastic Life*.
[5] *Ibid*.

Chapter IV

THE QUEST

SIR E. K. CHAMBERS, after noting Professor Kittredge's discovery of Sir Thomas Malory's identity, had observed that in July, 1451, the knight of Newbold Revel was ordered to find sureties for good behaviour towards the Priory of Axholme, Lincs., a Carthusian monastery to which the revenues of Monks Kirby had been granted. Further, that he was arrested in March, 1453, presumably because of some renewal of the dispute.[1] A search of the Warwickshire Assize Rolls for the period was suggested to the present writer as a likely method of gaining further information; but although a good deal of county interest was gleaned in the course of the search, nothing relating to Malory himself was encountered. There was, of course, always a doubt whether the trial — if any — was held in Warwickshire or in London. A survey of the Indictments from Middlesex was a task to baulk the most enthusiastic enquirer; but there remained one other section which might conceivably yield fruit. This was calendered as "Divers Counties." A few words of encouragement from Mr. Montague S. Giuseppi, I.S.O., Superintendent of the Legal Research Department, sped the writer to his task, and after a prolonged turning over of parchment strips — some long, some short, and all more or less faded — and noting how in the fifteenth century the counties of

[1] Patent Rolls.

"Myddx." and Essex appeared to be responsible for most of the crime of England, the welcome words "In Com. Warr." attracted attention. Warwickshire, then, was represented among the "Divers Counties" in this *dossier*. Closer examination of the parchment showed that it concerned some stabbing affray in the streets of Warwick; "glaives" were the weapons used.

Stimulated to a further search, the writer continued to turn over the strips of parchment, and after more time had been devoted to the task the words "In Com. Warr." once again jumped to the eye.

The document, of course, was in Latin, and a portion of the right-hand edge of it had been somewhat damaged; but, half-way down, the eye was caught and held by two words — "Thomas Malory" — written with almost copperplate clearness. The hunt was over, the quarry secured! One more proof had been found that the Public Record Office is a veritable treasure-house for those desiring to throw light on the mysteries of the past.

The Record of the Inquisition held regarding Sir Thomas Mallory's alleged misdeeds had been found.[1] But it was very surprising to read that it was held at Nuneaton, seeing that Coventry — a more important centre — was nearer the places concerned, and was in fact on the point of becoming an Assize town — by Royal Charter dated Nov. 26, 1451. Moreover, St. Mary's Hall in that city — which had been built a few years previously — would have been a most commodious place in which to hold the enquiry.

The probable explanation is that Coventry at this period was "a special nest of heresy," and therefore un-

[1] See Appendix.

suitable as the venue of a trial of persons charged with attacks on monastic houses.

Coventry's unsuitability for the purpose, indeed, was beyond question, as was proved by an incident which happened there a few years earlier. In 1423 the Lollard views of John Grace, an enthusiastic anchorite friar, "met with great favour from lower classes, and when the (Benedictine) Prior of Coventry and the Grey Friars opposed him, alleging that his preacher's licence had been withdrawn, they were nearly killed by the mob." [1]

On the other hand, Nuneaton, in the fifteenth century, comprised little besides "a goodly monasterie" belonging to Benedictine nuns — founded in connection with the parent house at Fontevrault in Normandy. Their Chapter House suggests itself as the place in which the Inquisition was held, and that it was big enough for the purpose is clear from the fact that at one time the nunnery had ninety inmates, although in 1450 there were only half that number. But quite possibly the Inquisition was held in the Abbey Church, or in the Parish Church of St. Nicholas. "Mediæval churches were put to strange uses. They served sometimes as a market place, sometimes as a granary, sometimes as a stage." [2]

[1] *Victoria County History of Warwickshire.*

[2] Eileen Power, *Mediæval Nunneries.* Some three months after the holding of the Inquisition, the Prioress, Maud Evryngham (daughter of Sir Henry Evryngham?), made complaint that the convent was impoverished, and was granted relief from the exactions of the King's purveyors. (Patent Roll.)

Chapter V

A POWERFUL ANTAGONIST

THE Inquisition was held on Monday, August 23, 1451, and was presided over by Humphrey, Duke of Buckingham, whom Malory would remember meeting in the old days at Rouen when Joan of Arc suffered martyrdom.[1] The Duke had just finished punishing Jack Cade's followers at Rochester, and he was now to act as judge upon an indictment in which he was personally concerned. Just as his grandfather had punished those concerned in Wat Tyler's rebellion, so Duke Humphrey, with relentless vigour, had quelled a Lollard rising in 1431 in the neighbourhood of Kenilworth and Coventry.[2] Ten years later he had been a member of the special Commission which tried Eleanor Cobham on a charge of witchcraft. Seeing that one of the charges to be preferred against Sir Thomas Malory was that of lying in ambush to attack the Duke, the latter — according to twentieth-century notions of legal procedure — would have done well to decline sitting on the Bench on this occasion. But the Duke was not one to be fastidious in a matter of this sort.

Parliament in Richard II's reign had indeed enacted that great lords were not to assert their powers by seating themselves with the King's Judges; but public opin-

[1] Grandson of Thomas of Woodstock, and great-grandson of Edward III, the Duke had just been appointed Captain of Calais and Warden of the Cinque Ports.
[2] Privy Council Ordinances.

ion no more prevented the Duke of Buckingham from
acting as judge in his own cause than it deterred "Mr
Justice Shallow" more than a century later from adjudi-
cating in a certain case of deer-stealing in his domain.
Less than a hundred years ago, indeed, — in 1830, — it
was possible at Wiltshire Quarter Sessions for the presiding magistrate to sentence to fourteen years' transportation a poor fellow charged with stealing a plank
ten feet long, the property of the aforesaid magnate.
The Duke of Buckingham might, at all events, have excused his action by saying that the Inquisition at Nuneaton was in reality a sort of Grand Jury proceeding,
and that the question of punishment was left to the
King's Bench at Westminster.

Duke Humphrey, who had married into the great
Neville family, — great in more senses than one, for
Ralph, Earl of Westmorland, had 23 children, of whom
all but one attained full age, — counted possessions in
seven and twenty counties. Some nineteen years before
the date of which we are speaking he had acquired, by
exchange with the Clintons, the castle of Maxsoke, in
Warwickshire. For this place he had "a very great liking," and in view of the probability that Sir Thomas
Malory was imprisoned there for a time before his trial
at Nuneaton, — after his escape from the Sheriff's custody at Coleshill, — Dugdale's reference to the castle
will be read with interest. "No sooner did he [the Duke]
obtain it, but that he plated the Gates all over with
Iron, and adorn'd them with his own Coat, impaled with
Neville (his Wife being the Daughter to Ralphe Neville,
Earl of Westmorland) and supported by two Antelopes,
in Respect that Anne, his Mother, was one of the Daughters and Co-heirs unto Thomas of Woodstoke, Duke of

Gloucester. And in further Memorie that these Gates were so strengthened and beautified, he caused the burning Nave and Knot (the antient Badges of his Ancestors) to be imbossed in the Iron-Work thwarting the Midst thereof, as are yet to be seen. This great Earl being created Duke of Buckingham (in 1445), constituted William Draicote his Constable of this Castle; for executing which Office he had the Fee of five Marks per annum."

We have said that Humphrey, Duke of Buckingham, was not one to be fastidious. An episode given in Dugdale's *Antiquities of Warwickshire* will serve to prove this, and also, it may be, to explain why Sir Thomas Malory should have lain in ambush for the Duke. A dispute over possession of the manor of Coleshill lay at the root of the matter. Since 1354 the Mountford family had been lords of Coleshill, and Sir William Mountford had served with Malory in the retinue of Richard Beauchamp, and been "Chief of the Councell unto the same Earl and Executor unto the Ladie Isabell his Countess." At the time the trouble with Sir Thomas Malory came to a head, Sir William was serving his third term of office as Sheriff of Warwickshire and Leicestershire, and when ordered to arrest the knight of Newbold Revel, his former comrade-in-arms, he decided to keep him in custody at Coleshill rather than place him in gaol at the recognised prison in Warwick or Kenilworth.[1]

High-handed action on the part of Sir William Mountford at a somewhat later date is indicated by *Early Chancery Proceedings*. Margerie Mariot, of Coventry, complains that her son William was arrested by the city

[1] Royal Commissions to hold General Gaol-deliveries at Warwick and Kenilworth are recorded at this period.

Humphery Duke of Buckingham.

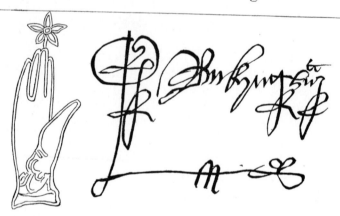

THE DUKE WHO PRESIDED AT MALORY'S TRIAL
AT NUNEATON.

officers because he intervened to protect his father from assault by John Couper, and was kept in prison "half a yere and more" by the Sheriff without any suit being brought against him. Those who would have gone bail for him were afraid to do so — "ther durste noe man for feir and drede of the seid Sir William him mainprise ne take to baill. . . . And the seid Sir William proposeth to holde him unto the tyme that he by duresse and longe emprisonment myght compelle the seid William Fader [*i. e.*, the father of the imprisoned man] to agree and satisfie the seid John Couper atte his own wille."

Coleshill Old Hall no longer exists, — it was demolished in 1810, — but there are still clear traces of the moat, which in the fifteenth century must have been both deep and wide. In winter-time it still fills with water from the river Cole flowing past the Mountford stronghold. Here it was that in 1575 Lettice, Countess of Essex, received clandestine visits from Robert Dudley, Earl of Leicester, a footbridge being specially constructed over the moat and pool at the back of the house leading into the park, to enable him to evade observation.

By the law of primogeniture, Sir William Mountford's son, Sir Baldwin (at this date 38 years of age), was heir to the manor of Coleshill; but, unhappily for him, he had a Breton step-mother, who conspired to gain the birthright for her own son, Edmund. Sir William, "being wrought upon by the Importunitie of Joane, his second wife, did endeavour the Disherison of his Children by the first; for the better bearing out whereof he enfeoft Humphrey, Duke of Buckingham (a potent Man in that Age) to the Use of the same Joane, and of Edmund, his son by her. Which Edmund, to make the said

Duke the more firm to his Interest, settled the Reversion, in Case he should have no Issue, upon him, and Humphrey, Earl Stafford, his son: So that when Sir Baldwin made his claim thereunto, the Duke, through his Greatness, so terrified him with Threats, that he forced him solemnly to disclaim the former Intail." Both Sir Thomas Malory and his lieutenant John Appelby would be well acquainted with the Mountford family, — Sir William Mountford's father had served with an Appelby in John of Gaunt's Spanish expedition, — and it is possible that, in the spirit of knight-errantry, Sir Thomas took the lead in an endeavour to prevent what he regarded as a gross injustice.[1] It was in such circumstances, therefore, that Malory faced his accusers at Nuneaton on the Monday preceding St. Bartholomew's Day, 1451.

[1] For further reference to Sir Baldwin Mountford, see p. 83.

Chapter VI

THE INQUISITION AT NUNEATON

SEATED on the Bench at Nuneaton with the Duke were Sir William Birmyngham (Sheriff-designate of the County) and two other Keepers of the Peace, Thomas Bate, Esq., of Arley, and Thomas Greswold, Esq., of Solihull. Greswold, it is important to note, was King's Sergeant as well as Coroner for the county of Warwick — an office which in the 15th century was somewhat equivalent to that of Public Prosecutor. For example, he was required by statute to go ". . . where houses are broken," and he was responsible for the attachment of criminals in cases of violence. Not long before this he had been acting in a judicial capacity against the Kentish rebels. Thomas Bate, the other member of the Commission, was at this time Escheator for Warwickshire. It will be seen, therefore, that the Commissioners were all men of exceptional prominence in the county — a proof of the importance which attached to the occasion.

Fifteen jurors, drawn from North Warwickshire, were empanelled and sworn, and after hearing the evidence they declared on oath:

(1) That Sir Thomas Malory, with his aider and abettor, John Appelby, gentleman, of Newbold Revel, had been arrested on Sunday, July 25, 1451, in pursuance of a royal warrant issued to the Duke of Bucking-

ham and Richard Neville, Earl of Warwick,[1] and at Coventry had been committed to the Sheriff's custody to await his trial before the King and Council on certain charges already preferred against him.[2]

(2) That on the Tuesday next ensuing, when in the custody of the Sheriff [Sir William Mountford] at Coleshill, the said Thomas broke out of prison during the night and swam across the moat there, thus evading the custody of the Sheriff. [As mediæval moats were tremendously deep and wide, and full of sewage, this was indeed an achievement.]

(3) That the said Thomas Malory and John Appelby, with half-a-score other yeomen, husbandmen, and grooms [mentioned by name], assembled on the following day "with many other malefactors and breakers of the King's peace in the manner of an insurrection," and unanimously rising, broke by night into the Abbey of Blessed Mary of Coombe — a Cistercian monastery midway between Newbold Revel and Coventry — and with great baulks of wood broke and entered divers gates and doors of the said monastery. Further, that they broke open two of the Abbot's chests and feloniously took and carried away a bag containing £21, another containing £25 gold and silver marks, and many other jewels and ornaments of the church of the said monastery, to the value of £40.

(4) That Thomas Malory, Knight, and 26 other [unknown] malefactors and breakers of the King's Peace, armed and arrayed in warlike manner, on January 4,

---

[1] The "King-Maker"; son-in-law of Malory's old chief in the French Wars.
[2] In respect of offences at Monks Kirby complained of by the Prior of the Carthusians.

FACSIMILE OF A PORTION OF THE MS. RECORDING THE INQUISITION AT NUNEATON.

1450, lay in ambush in Coombe Abbey Woods to kill and murder Humphrey, Duke of Buckingham. *Lancaster*

(5) That Thomas Malory, Knight, Richard Malory of Radclyff near Leicester, Esq., John Appelby, and some dozen others [all named], assembled in warlike manner with many other malefactors and breakers of the King's peace to the number of 100, on Thursday, July 29, 1451, and riotously broke 18 doors of Coombe Abbey, and insulted the Abbot,[1] his monks and servants. Further, that they broke open three iron chests, corded and sealed, and feloniously stole £40 4s. 4d. found in divers bags, three gold rings set with precious stones, two silver signets, a pair of psalters, two silver zones, three pairs of beads [of coral, "laumber," and "jete"], two bows and three sheaves of arrows, the goods and chattels of the aforesaid Abbot.

(6) That Thomas Malory, Knight, and John Appelby took 20s. extortionately by threats and oppression from John Mylner at Monks Kirby on August 31, 1450; and in the same manner 100s. from Margaret Kyng and William Hales on May 31, 1450, also at Monks Kirby.

(7) That Thomas Malory, Knight, on the Saturday before Pentecost, 1450, broke into the house of Hugh Smyth at Monks Kirby and feloniously raped Joan, the wife of the said Hugh.

(8) That Thomas Malory, knight, on Thursday, August 1, 1450, feloniously raped Joan, the wife of Hugh Smyth, at Coventry, and carried away to Barwell, co. Leicester, goods and chattels of the said Hugh, to the value of £40.

---

[1] Abbot Richard must have fully expected the same fate that befel his predecessor, Abbot Geoffrey, in 1345, viz., a violent death.

On another Inquisition, held at the same time and place, before the aforesaid Justices, a different panel of jurors — some drawn from more distant places in Warwickshire — testified:

(9) That Thomas Malory, Knight, and four others [named] on June 4, 1451, extortionately took seven cows, two calves, a cart worth £4, and 335 sheep worth £22, of the goods and chattels of William Rowe and William Dowde of Shawell, co. Leicester, and carried them off to Newbold Revel.

One cannot help speculating as to the reason why, when one jury at Nuneaton had returned its verdicts on counts 1–8 of the indictment against Sir Thomas Malory, it should have been necessary to empanel another jury to hear evidence on an additional count, that relating to the forcible removal of cows and sheep from Shawell, co. Leicester, to Newbold Revel.

"In those days," says Dr. S. R. Gardiner, — referring to the case of Lord Molynes and John Paston, — "a jury was not to be trusted to do justice. In the first place it was selected by the Sheriff, and the Sheriff took care to choose such men as would give a verdict pleasing to the great men whom he wished to serve; and in the second place, supposing that the Sheriff did not do this, a juryman who offended great men by giving a verdict according to his conscience, but contrary to their desire, ran the risk of being knocked on the head before he reached home."

Chapter VII

BEFORE THE KING'S BENCH

WE HAVE to go to the Coram Rege Roll to find what next happened. There it is recorded that the Sheriffs of London were ordered to bring Sir Thomas Malory before the King at Westminster. "And having been asked, in reference to what had gone before, if he desired to be acquitted of the premises, *he says that he is not in any wise guilty thereof, and for good or ill puts himself upon his country*, etc. And thereupon the said Thomas Malory was handed back to the said Sheriffs for safe custody until, together with the other causes," etc.

Had Sir Thomas refused to plead, it is worth remarking, he could not have been tried at all. According to mediæval law, a trial by jury could be held only with the consent of the accused; he must "*put himself* on the country." If he refused to plead, he could not be convicted, but the justices could keep him in prison and make life unbearable for him.

A curious point to be noted here — and one which seems highly significant — is that 24 jurors who were summoned at Westminster to try the case against Malory failed to answer their names. It is recorded that a levy was ordered to be made of their goods and chattels.

Another important fact to be observed is that when Sir Thomas died, in 1471, he was found to have no landed estate whatever, in spite of having inherited from

his father manors in three countries. But when his
widow died, nearly nine years later, she was credited
with his patrimony. We are forced to the conclusion,
therefore, that when Malory found himself prosecuted
by the authorities, he protected the interests of his family
by following the example of the monastic houses he had
been attacking. "From a very early period the bishops
and heads of religious houses, as one contrivance for
evading the laws prohibiting alienations in mortmain,
procured lands to be conveyed in fee simple to some
friendly hand, upon trust that they and their successors
should be permitted to enjoy the profits." [1] This contrivance, like others, was cut short by Parliament, and
effectually as regards its original purpose; but it was
quickly taken up by laymen, who perceived the extent
and usefulness of its application. Assuming the feoffees
to uses to be willing and faithful instruments of the bene-
ficial owner, his advantages were great. Though he were
involved in the civil strife of Lancaster and York, and
dealt with as a traitor by victorious enemies, the land
would be secured for his children; for it legally belonged
not to him but to the feoffees to uses, and therefore was
not forfeited by his attainder. [2]

A year elapses before we find the next reference.
Then, on March 26, 1453, the Patent Rolls record a
"Commission to Humphrey Duke of Buckingham,
Edward Grey of Groby, Knight, [3] and the Sheriff of
Warwick and Leicester, appointing them to arrest and
bring before the King and Council Thomas Malorre,

---

[1] Spence, *Equitable Jurisdiction of the Court of Chancery.*
[2] Sir Frederick Pollock, *The Land Laws.*
[3] Lord of the manor of Lutterworth, he also held the title of Lord Ferrers
of Groby. His son was the first husband of Elizabeth Woodville, afterwards
Queen of Edward IV.

Knight, to answer certain charges." In view of the fact that the second member of the Commission was lord of the manor of Lutterworth, it appears likely that the offence or offences charged against Sir Thomas on this occasion related to Leicestershire. No information on the subject, however, is contained either in the King's Bench Indictments or in the Leicestershire Assize Roll for the period. "Divers Counties" likewise yielded nothing on this occasion.

Turning again to the Coram Rege Roll, we find that in 34 Henry VI, Sir Thomas Malory — who by this time had had experience of imprisonment in the Tower of London — was "by special grace of the Court" admitted to bail on the sureties of Sir Roger Chamberleyn, of Queenborough, Kent; John Hathwyk, Esq., of Harbury, Warwickshire; and other gentlemen. But if he gained his liberty, it was for a very short period.

The Coram Rege Roll tells us that in Hilary term, 34 Henry VI, a writ of "habeas corpora juratorum" was issued to compel the attendance of jurors to enquire if Thomas Malory, late of Fenny Newbold, Knight, "be guilty of divers felonies, transgressions, insurrections and extortions whereof he is indicted and not placed in respite before the lord the King."

On Friday next after the Feast of St. Hilary, 34 Henry VI, — in other words, January 16, 1456, — Sir Thomas was committed by the King's Bench to the custody of the Marshal. He had proffered letters patent showing that the King had pardoned him for all felonies and transgressions committed before July 9, 1455; but although several friends, including Roger Malory, of Ryton, Warwickshire, gentleman, offered to go bail for him, "Thomas Malory remains in the custody of the Marshal until sufficient security be found."

It is highly significant that nearly all the sureties proffered on the second occasion were of considerably less social standing than those named as being accepted in 32 Henry VI. Whereas a knight and six gentlemen from divers counties were willing to go bail in the first instance, in the second a London saddler and two tailors constituted one-half of the sureties — whom the Court deemed insufficient. The change in the situation makes it clear: (1) That Malory had been unable to curb himself during a short period of liberty granted to him; and (2) that he had alienated the support of men of his own rank and could now obtain sympathy only from that class which supplied the chief support of Lollardy. The attitude of London tradesmen in this respect is attested by Dr. James Gairdner and other historians. It is not suggested, of course, that Malory himself endorsed all the 24 Propositions which John Wycliffe advanced; the Knight of Newbold Revel must be regarded as a political rather than a doctrinal Lollard.

The refusal of the King's Bench at Westminster to release Malory in spite of his producing a Royal pardon recalls a parallel incident recorded to the credit of Sir John Fortescue, the Chief Justice at this period. A certain Thomas Kerver had been imprisoned for some offence in Wallingford Castle, when the King pardoned him and wished him to be released. But Fortescue, to whom the King sent a command to issue a writ for the purpose, considered that he had no right or legal power to do so, and refused to comply.

Towards the end of Henry VI's reign the Controlment Rolls contain further references to Sir Thomas Malory. From these we gather that, although he appears to have been in Warwickshire for a short time, he was again in

prison in Hilary term, 38 Hen. VI. In Michaelmas term, 36 Hen. VI, it is recorded that Malory had been committed to the Marshalsea by the Chief Justice, Sir John Fortescue, "for divers causes pending before the King"; the Warwickshire Coroner, Thomas Greswold, is named also as a prosecutor of the Knight of Newbold Revel. Sir Thomas, meanwhile, was declared to be detained in prison by virtue of another writ of the King, of which the tenour was as follows:

Henry by the grace of God King of England & France & Lord of Ireland, to the Sheriffs of London Greeting. Because Thomas Malory, Knt., is detained in our prison of the Marshalsea for surety of the peace towards us & all our people, & especially towards the Abbot of Coombe & many others of our lieges, & for surety of good behaviour towards us & all our people, & for other causes specially moving us. We, for the greater surety of custody of the above-named Thomas, have committed the said Thomas to our prison of Newgate, to be kept safe & secure, Until we shall have ordered concerning him, & this under pain of 1,000 *li.* he shall not omit.

And now (continues the record), having learnt that the same Thomas is, for the reasons aforesaid, detained in our prison of Ludgate under your custody, we order & firmly enjoin you that you shall keep the aforesaid Thomas safe & secure for the causes aforesaid under the above-named penalty until you shall have order from us. Witnessed by J. Fortescu at Westminster on the 24th day of January in the 35th year of our reign.

Afterwards, on the Wednesday next after the 18th of Michaelmas this term, the aforesaid Thomas was delivered in bail to William Nevill Lord Fauconberge, William Briggeham of Briggeham in the county of York, Esq., & John Clerkson, of Arundel in the county of Sussex, Esq., until the morrow of St. John wheresoever etc, each of the pledges under pain of 20 *li.* & the aforesaid Thomas under pain of 400 *li.* under [?] etc. And for his good behaviour etc. On which day he appeared & was committed to the Marshalsea as well for

the surety of the peace aforesaid as for his good behaviour
etc. And also for the condemnation aforesaid etc. [*i. e.*, by
the Warwickshire Coroner].

Afterwards, namely in Easter term in the 37th year of the
said King's reign, the Court was informed by trustworthy
men of the county of Warwick that the said Thomas was out
of the custody of the said Marshal & had been at large in the
county of Warwick since the feast of Easter in the said term
of 37 (Hen. VI). Orders were thereupon given to the Marshal
to keep the above-named Thomas Malory in the King's
prison of the Marshalsea at Southwark in the County of
Surrey & not permit the said Thomas to be at large outside
the prison under pain of 100 *li*.

And afterwards, namely, in Hilary term in the 38th year of
the said King's reign, the aforesaid Thomas Malory was committed to the custody of the Sheriff of Middlesex for reasons
aforesaid, to be detained safe & secure in the King's prison of
Newgate until etc. Therefore the said Marshall is discharged
hereof etc.

Unfortunately the Controlment Roll for 39 Hen. VI
is missing; and, the Rolls from 1 to 9 Edward IV do not
mention Sir Thomas Malory so far as can be discovered.
He does not seem to have been indicted in the reign of
Edward IV, and the only further record to be discovered
is his exclusion from the general pardon of 8 Ed. IV;
but of course, as there are only two rolls for this period,
he may have been excepted any time between the years
1 and 8 Ed. IV. It is certainly worthy of note that seven
years after the attack on Coombe Abbey, it should be
placed on record that Sir Thomas "is detained in our
prison of the Marshalsea for surety of the peace towards
us & all our people *and especially towards the Abbot of
Coombe.*" This, too, after Malory had produced the
King's pardon for transgressions prior to 1455.

Chapter VIII

THE RAID ON COOMBE ABBEY

TWO things in particular are to be noted regarding the attacks on Coombe Abbey: that the first was made within twenty-four hours of Sir Thomas Malory's dramatic escape from the Sheriff's custody, and that the second attack came twenty-four hours later. That Malory should have renewed the assault in this way seems almost incredible; it may be that he was not personally concerned with the second attack, but was held responsible for it by the monastic authorities. Another theory, and probably the correct one, is that the two alleged attacks were one and the same affair. Once in possession of the Abbey during the Wednesday night, the rioters must have seized whatever Sir Thomas Malory claimed or they themselves fancied; there could have been no occasion to renew the attack on the following night. It would seem that we have here merely an instance of the regular legal fashion of describing the same offence, or parts of the same offences, in distinct counts. As Judge Parry humorously remarks of the old-style indictment: "How careful they were in the old days. One count of the Indictment would allege that the murderer was holding his knife in the right hand, another count thought it was his left, another alleged neither hand, and the last count always wound up by saying that the victim was murdered by means to the said jury unknown." [1]

[1] Judge Edward A. Parry, *What the Judge Thought*, p. 76.

But whatever may be the true explanation, the number and composition of Sir Thomas Malory's followers — yeomen, husbandmen, etc.[1] — prove that the Abbey was held in serious disfavour in the neighbourhood. Malory had only to apply the torch, in fact, to bring about an explosion. It is therefore well to see, if possible, what was the position of affairs at Coombe Abbey at this period. First of all, it has to be remembered that the time was one of stress for everybody, — "This was a-nother dere yere," commented a monastic chronicler in 1449, — and the strictness with which ecclesiastical corporations were accustomed to enforce their legal rights would naturally arouse resentment in some quarters. Serfdom in England, it is true, had received a mortal wound as the result of the Black Death and of Wat Tyler's Rebellion, but it lingered longest on ecclesiastical, and especially on monastic, estates. Evidence on this point is furnished by Sir Thomas Malory's own parish of Monks Kirby. Edward I had granted to the prior and convent of Kirkeby Monachorum "view of frankpledge with all that pertains to it . . . and infangtheof," and this grant was confirmed by Edward IV in 1469. "Infangtheof," it should be explained, was the right of doing justice to thieves apprehended on the lord's domain. What the manorial rights of Coombe Abbey were we may gather from the description Dugdale gives of those appertaining to another Cistercian monastery, that of Stoneleigh, a few miles distant. The custom was that "at the *Bederipe* in Harvest (*i. e.*, the general reap for the Lord's corn) the superior tenants (*sokemanni*) should all come upon request or notice with

---

[1] One of the raiders was a harpist, who came from Malory's own domain. The "bower" who also participated was evidently a maker of bows and arrows.

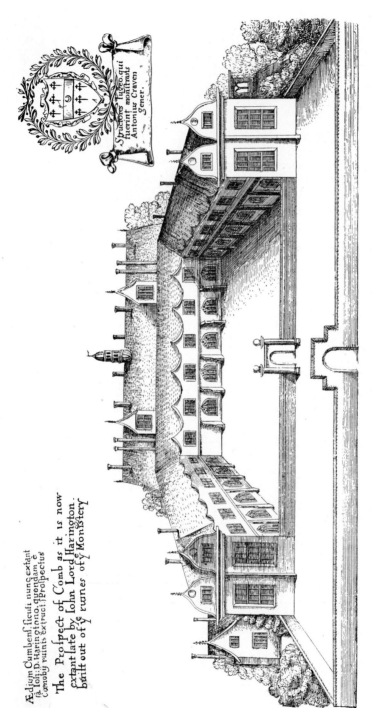

Ædium Cumbensisicuti nunc extant
(à Ioh:D.Haringtonno,quondam è
Cœnoby ruinis extructi)Prospectus

The Prospect of Comb as it is now
extant late by Iohn Lord Harington.
built out of y̌ ruines of y̌ Monistery

Structore Inigoqui
fuerint monstrabis
Antonius Craven
gener.

THE EARLIEST PICTURE EXTANT OF COOMBE ABBEY.

everyone of their tenants; the *sokemanni* to ride up and down on horseback, with wands, to see that they worked well, and to amerce those in the Court, then and there held, that made default or laboured idly. That they should be in the field at sunrising, and to work till sunset, not sitting down to breakfast, but each of them eating what he brought with him as they went up and down the lands to their work."

Passing from the general to the particular, we find in *Early Chancery Proceedings* the record of specific complaints made against the Abbot of Coombe at this time. To begin with, the tenants of "dame Katerine Reigne denglterre" at Brinklow complain that

Dan. Richard Atherston, Abbot of Coombe, would not allow the 15th granted to the King to be levied on his tenants. And when the complainants had taken distress the said Abbot strongly resisted, and they could not levy the 15th, to the great loss of the King. They ask for a writ of Appeal for the said Abbot to appear in Chancery, etc.

A curious complaint was that made by John Whalley of Coventry. He alleged that John Coton, "comoigne" to the Abbot of Coombe, had asked him to

take to farm of the said Abbot two messuages and two cottages in Bynley and a croft there called Dalby, for a term of years, paying yearly 38s. 4d., under certain conditions to be made in writing between the Abbot on one side and John Whalley on the other. By force of which John Coton gave the complainant a lease of the premises. The said John Whalley supposing the "licence of the said Comoigne had be lawfull and suffisaunt auctorite for hym to occupie," he entered the premises and for a year and more paid rent to the Abbot until the time that the Abbot and John Coton with one Richard Coventre, another of the monks, "ymagynyng to avoide the said suppliant of his said terme" and to deprive him of his goods and chattels, pretended that the complainant occupied

the premises without lawful lease. They "cam to the said grounde and with their servaunts, v oxen price of everych xxs and v kyne price of everych of xiijs iiijd" of the complainant's "for damage fesaunt in the soill of ther house dref away and yet withholden" to the great damage of the complainant. He asks for a writ of subpœna, &c.

The aforesaid Richard, Abbot of Coombe, is next sued for "deffamacion" by John Shawe of Coventry and Joan his wife. Their complaint is that, in the absence of the said John,

the Abbot took from Joan without reason or course of law two horses worth 46s. 8d., one pack of wool ... taffet cloth ... sangweyn colour, another part of grene cloth worth 5s., two saddles and two bridles worth 13s. 4d., for the which heinous offences a writ of subpœna was directed to the Abbot to appear at Coventry, but he did not come. And the Abbot cited Joan twice to appear, and in her absence he and his counsel "token sentence oute of thearches,[1] of which sentence youre seid Oratrice hadde at that tyme no knowleche." By which the said Joan was imprisoned for 16. ... Now the said Joan and her husband wish to sue the Abbot for "deffamacion."

"*Vi et armis*," it is quite clear, had become common form long before the phrase was employed to describe Sir Thomas Malory's conduct at Coombe Abbey on the night of July 23, 1451. But the Abbot's actions too could justify the use of the classic phrase, if we may judge by another petition addressed "to the Archbishop of Canterbury, Chancellor of England." In this

John Shawe of Coventry complains that Richard, Abbot of Coombe, with other persons unknown came with force and arms and at the same Abbey "on Wednesday before seint Gregorys day ... certen goodes that is to wyte two horses

---

[1] Court of Arches?

worth 4 marks, 2 packs of [wool] worth 20s., 5 yards of wollen cloth worth 4s., 1 cloak worth 8s. 6d., 1 saddle and bridle 10s."

The rest is illegible except for a word here and there which do not help with the meaning.

It is curious, perhaps even significant, that the *Register de Cumba*, preserved at the British Museum, makes no reference whatever to the attacks on the Abbey in 1451. The monastic chronicler alludes to storms and battles, even finds space for a mathematical treatise, but of the dramatic events already referred to there is not the slightest mention.

How intriguing are the silences of history!

In the previous year the Abbot of Ramsey, in the County of Huntingdon, — a Benedictine monastery some fifty miles distant from Coombe, — made complaint of an assault by ninety men on his property, and obtained the appointment of a Commission of Oyer and Terminer to deal with the matter. It is conceivable that the attack led by Sir Thomas Malory was inspired by what happened on the occasion of the Huntingdon outbreak. The Abbot complained that ninety men (at the head of whom were an esquire, a "gentilman," and a bailiff) broke his closes and houses at Fenny Stanton and St. Ives, and the gates, doors and windows thereof; they cut certain cups and vessels to pieces and threw them into the river, and then broke a fountain and filled it to the top with dung and other refuse. Next they threatened Robert, prior of St. Ives, and John Alconbury, — the Abbot's fellow monks, — and the Abbot's tenants and servants in St. Ives, so that the prior fled to the bell-tower of the priory, and John Alconbury to a secret corner, and the rest of the monks to the Abbey

of Ramsey. "And divers tenants dared not remain on
the Abbot's land there, and his servants dared not go
about his business." [1]

What the condition of affairs was at Ramsey Abbey
about this time may be learned from the record of
Bishop Alnwick's Visitation in 1439 (the last extant).
It fully deserved the severe injunction uttered against
Huntingdon Priory seven years previously by Bishop
Gray: — "In our Visitation some time ago, by our right
as Ordinary, of you and your priory, we found no good
thing in the same which might be likened to religion,
save only the outward sign. . . . The divine office, by
night and likewise by day, is neglected; obedience is
violated; the alms are wasted; hospitality is not kept.
There is nothing else here but drunkenness and surfeit,
disobedience and contempt, p^te aggrandise^t & apostasy,
drowsiness — we do not say incontinence — but sloth
& every other thing which is on the downward path to
evil & drags men to hell."

The practice of land inclosure, which caused so much
discontent in England, was just beginning at this time;
but the monks of Coombe Abbey are not among the
offenders named at the Parliamentary Inquiry of 1517.
Neither is Monks Kirby mentioned in this connection.
The Augustinian Priory of Kenilworth, on the other
hand, is declared to have taken part in the inclosures.

[1] Patent Rolls.

Chapter IX

MONKS KIRBY: A TROUBLED HISTORY

IT WILL be observed that in the long indictment drawn up against Sir Thomas no mention whatever is made of any attack on monastic property at Monks Kirby — an "alien" house at this period assigned to the Carthusian Order at Axholme, Lincs. Yet it was because of a complaint from this source that the King's warrant to arrest Sir Thomas was issued on July 13, 1451, at Westminster. The warrant was directed to Humphrey, Duke of Buckingham, and Richard Neville, Earl of Warwick, and was couched in the following terms:

Know that for a few certain and notable causes set forth in our presence and the presence of our Council we have assigned you to take and arrest Thomas Malory, knight, and John Appelby, servant of the same Thos. Malory, wherever they may be found — as well within liberties as without — and to find sufficient mainpernors [sureties] who will be willing to give mainprise for them under good and sufficient penalty, to be enforced by you according to your reasonable discretion, that they, nor either of them, shall cause no injury or evil to the Prior and convent of the Carthusian Order of the Isle of Axholme or to any of our people, nor shall burn their houses, nor shall procure or cause the same in any way, and that the same Thomas Malory, knight, and John Appelby in their persons shall appear in our presence and the presence of the Council aforesaid on the quinzaine of Michaelmas next to answer upon those charges which shall there and then be preferred against them.[1]

---

[1] Patent Rolls.

The probable explanation is that the acts of extortion alleged against Sir Thomas Malory (see Nos. 6 and 9 of summarised Indictment) were made by him to recover possession of property taken on behalf of the Priory of Monks Kirby. This monastery had had a similar experience in the previous reign (Henry V's), for it is on record that the prior of Axholme had complained:

That William Colman, William Bosevyll, and Robert Fox have forcibly entered the priory of Monks Kirby and have taken away from the said suppliant the profits arising therefrom, and hold them against the proclamation lately made to the contrary. Different goods and chattels of great value, together with written charters and other muniments and £25 12s. 1d. in money belonging to the said suppliant there found, they also have taken and carried away. That it may please your Majesty and wise Council to ordain a remedy, considering that the said priory is the sustenance of the said suppliant and his convent.

It was probably the William Bosevyll above-mentioned who in 1401 at Nuneaton was excommunicated for "manifest contumacy in not obeying certain canonical monitions addressed to him."

The career of Monks Kirby Priory had indeed been troublous. As an "alien" house, — it was an offshoot of the Carthusian monastery of St. Nicholas, Angiers (the principal city of Anjou), — its revenues had of course been sequestered on the outbreak of the Hundred Years War. Sir Thomas Malory's grandfather had, in 1389, been a member of a Commission appointed "to enquire concerning the lands of the alien priory of Kirkby Monachorum, in the County of Warwick." What the result of their deliberations was we do not know; but seven years later Papal Letters show that complaint had been made that only two monks, instead of seven,

resided at Kirby Priory (besides the prior); that the rule was not observed; and that on account of the dissolute life of the prior and French monks living there, and of their servants, who were at discord with the English, the buildings were partially falling. It was in consequence of this state of affairs that, at the instance of Thomas Mowbray, Duke of Norfolk, the priory was transferred to the Isle of Axholme, where he founded the important Carthusian monastery of Epworth. Scarcely had he done so when he was challenged to battle by the Earl of Hereford (afterwards Henry IV), and banished for life by Richard II. Claims for payment of tithe to a distant monastery were a fruitful source of discord at this period, and it seems likely that Sir Thomas Malory's "extortion" was in reality a form of reprisal.

Chapter X

THE MOST SERIOUS CHARGE AGAINST MALORY

TO MOST people, in our day, the gravest charge in the whole Indictment — and here Sir Thomas alone is concerned — is that in which he was accused of having twice violated the wife of Hugh Smyth of Monks Kirby, first at Monks Kirby, and then a couple of months later at Coventry. In one count, housebreaking and rape are alleged; in the next, rape and robbery — apparently from Smyth's house. Here again, however, Malory was probably merely seizing by violence goods and chattels to which he had (or said he had) some claim. The charge of *raptus* was doubtless merely incidental; it is very common in such cases, and often amounts to little more than a legal fiction, a formula used for good measure. Professor Kittredge thinks we may reconstruct events thus: "On May 23, 1450, Malory and his servants searched Smyth's house in vain. Smyth's wife, who objected to the search, may have been roughly treated; perhaps she was forcibly removed from the dwelling while it was ransacked. That would have been *raptus*. Then, on the first of August, the search was repeated with similar violence and with complete success, for goods and chattels valued (by Smyth!) at £40 were taken. On neither occasion is there any likelihood that Goodwife Smyth was actually ravished. The duplication of this particular charge is reason

enough for rejecting such an idea: it is ridiculous to suppose that Malory actually ravished the woman twice. Anything, to be sure, is possible in what Sir Peter Teazle calls this 'damned wicked world,' but we are in pursuit of what is reasonable — and we are reading an indictment, not a verdict or the sentence of a judge."

"In *Chancery Proceedings*," writes Mr. C. L. Kingsford, "we hear so often of trespass committed by a number of persons unknown to the complainant but armed with all manner of weapons of war, that we are moved to suspect that the language is no more than the legal formula. Similarly, if the offence is that of the forcible abduction of a woman, we shall probably be told that when she was lying in her bed in God's peace and the King's, divers persons broke into her house and carried her away, clad only in her kirtle and smock. In both instances it was necessary to show that an offence had occurred of so serious a character as to call for the intervention of the Court of Chancery. If, as is so often the case, only the Bill of Complaint is preserved, we have no means to check the accuracy of the statements. When we have the defendant's Answer, a different complexion may probably appear." [1]

"In no wise guilty" was Sir Thomas Malory's plea when brought before the King's Bench in London a few months later, as we shall see.

The mediæval lawyers' liking for "piling on the agony" is well illustrated by the curious record which has come down to us of an earlier episode in Sir Thomas's career — a reference "not, perhaps, very much to his credit but sufficiently illustrative of those unruly times." (We quote Professor Kittredge.) It embodies

[1] *Prejudice and Promise in the XVth Century* (1925).

a charge of assault with violence which had been brought
by Thomas Smythe, a parishioner of Sprotton, Northants, against Thomas Malory, *miles*, and another, in
1443; and the debased Latin of the De Banco Rolls is in
this instance so picturesque that it must be quoted in
all its legal verbosity:

(Northants). Thomas Smythe in propria persona sua
optulit se quarto die versus Thomam Malory de parochia
de Kirkeby monachorum in Comitatu Warw., militem, et
Eustachium Burneby de Watford in Comitatu predicto,
armigerum, de placito quare vi et armis in ipsum Thomam
Smythe apud Sprottone insultum fecerunt et ipsum verbera-
verunt, vulneraverunt, imprisonaverunt, et male tracta-
verunt, et bona et catalla sua ad valenciam quadraginta
librarum ibidem inventa ceperunt et asportaverunt, et alia
enormia ad grave dampnum et contra pacem etc fecerunt. Et
ipsi non venerunt, et preceptum fuit Vicecomiti quod attachiat
eos, et Vicecomes modo mandat quod attachiati sunt per
Richardum Gey et Johannem ffray.

It is worth recalling, in this connection, that the
Morte tells us how King Arthur himself got into trouble
on one occasion by paying a visit of inspection to La
Belle Isoud before Sir Tristam had invited him to do so.
Whereupon, Sir Launcelot (who accompanied the King)
offered as a very proper and sufficient defence, that "it
is every good knight's part to behold a fair lady."

Malory certainly affords no justification for the Ten-
nysonian tradition of a priggish and vacuous Arthur who
has nothing else to do but stalk about "wearing the
white flower of a blameless life."

Still more to the point is it to quote the celebrated
passage in which Malory likens true love to summer, his
words forming a prelude to the tragic situation in which
Launcelot is drawn this way by fidelity to his king, and

that way by fidelity to his mistress, whom he has to rescue from the stake.

Like as herbs and trees bring forth and flourish in May, in likewise every heart that is in any manner a lover, springeth and flourisheth in lusty deeds. For it giveth unto every lover courage, the lusty month of May, to constrain him to some manner of thing more in that month than any other. . . . Therefore like as May month flowereth and flourisheth in many gardens, so in like wise let every man of worship flourish his heart in this world, first unto God and next unto the Joy of her that he promised his faith unto; for there was never worshipful man nor worshipful woman, but they loved one better than another; but first reserve the honour to God, and secondly the quarrel must come of thy lady — and such love I call virtuous love.

Further evidence on this point is to be found in Book VI of the *Morte*, which tells how Sir Launcelot rode with a damsel mounted on a white palfrey and slew a knight that distressed all ladies.

Sir, said the damsel, here by this way haunteth a knight that distresseth all ladies and gentlewomen, and at the least he robbeth them or lyeth by them.

What, said Sir Launcelot, is he a thief and a knight and a ravyssher of women?

As Dr. Oskar Sommer has pointed out in his monumental work on the *Morte*, the words "ravyssher of women" do not occur in the prose *Launcelot*,— Malory's source-book for this particular section of his work, — and it seems incredible that the knight of Newbold Revel would have gone out of his way to mention this crime if he had himself been guilty of it. Nor does Malory confine himself to the words we have quoted. The following passage, which has no counterpart in the prose *Launcelot*, shows how deeply he detested conduct

that was dishonouring to women, and that was, moreover, expressly forbidden by the vows of knighthood. When Sir Launcelot is urged by the damsel to take a wife unto himself, he replies:

To be a wedded man I think it not, for then I must couch with her, and leave arms and tournaments, battles and adventures. And as for to say for to take my plesaunce with paramours, that will I refuse in principal for dread of God. For knights that be adulterous, or wanton, shall not be happy nor fortunate unto the wars, for either they shall be overcome with a simpler knight than they be themselves, or else they shall by mishap and their cursedness slay better men than they be themselves. And so who that useth paramours shall be unhappy, and all thing is unhappy that is about them.

An equally emphatic passage is to be found in Book XI — and here again it is peculiar to Malory's version of the *Morte*. Sir Percivale, after rescuing a comrade-in-arms from the castle where he had been imprisoned by "an uncourteous lady" whose advances he had rejected, reproaches the dame in the following words:

Ah, madam, said Sir Percivale, what use and custom is that in a lady to destroy good knights but if they will be your paramours? forsooth this is a shameful custom of a lady. And if I had not great matter in my hand, I should foredo your evil customs.

We do not know whom Sir Thomas Malory married except that her Christian name was Elizabeth and that she was evidently a woman of business capacity;[1] but after reading this we cannot help feeling that, whoever she was, she had a faithful husband, even if he was in the black books of the Cistercians and the Carthusians.

[1] The Reader MS. at Coventry contains the following (from the first Roll of the Pittancer, 1478–79): "To the servants of Lady Elizabeth Malory, bringing the Winwick rent, 1s. 8d." On the same page also appears: "To the Pittancer's servant riding to Winwick for the rent."

In this connection it is worth noting that Malory gives his wife's name to "king Mark's sister of Cornwall " — the mother of Sir Tristram. "She was called Elizabeth, that was called both good and fair . . . a full meek lady, and well she loved her lord" [king Meliodas]. Here Malory makes a definite alteration, for in the original Romance of Tristan the name of Meliodas's queen is "Isabelle." This is one of the few ladies in the *Morte* whose character is above reproach, — from a modern point of view, — and in bestowing on her the name of Elizabeth the knight of Newbold Revel was undoubtedly offering a compliment to his own spouse. Of both Elizabeths it could be said that they were deprived of the companionship of their husbands. The jealousy of another woman was responsible for the separation of Meliodas and his queen; whether Joan Smyth of Monks Kirby played the part of Potiphar's wife it is impossible to say.

Chapter XI

NOT AN ORDINARY FREEBOOTER

IT IS commonly supposed that in the Middle Ages the clergy — both Regular and Secular — were treated by the laity with profound respect, and that consecrated buildings in particular were kept inviolate. An examination of the facts does not bear out this supposition. We read in 1267 that the fine exacted for assaults on priests by men of knight's rank was £6 13s. 4d., — a substantial sum in those days, it is true, — but the fixing of a scale of fines for such offences tells its own tale. On one occasion alone the Papal nuncio received a faculty to absolve fifty persons who had laid violent hands on priests and clerks. Moreover, these assaults were sometimes perpetrated in sacred buildings, while services were being held.[1]

Warwickshire could furnish instances in point besides those already quoted. There were, in this county, two other Cistercian monasteries besides Coombe Abbey. In regard to Merevale Abbey we are told that, in 1292, John, son of John de Overton, brought a complaint against the abbot, four monks, and five brethren of the abbey, and others, for having caused the death of his brother Robert. Seven years later, John, probably in revenge, pulled down the abbot's house at Overton-by-Twycross, on the confines of the counties of Warwick

[1] A. Abram, *English Life and Manners in the Later Middle Ages.*

and Leicester, and carried away the timber by night.[1] Stoneleigh Abbey, the other Cistercian house, was in great trouble in the Spring of 1380, when malefactors seized the Abbey seal and used it to demise certain manors and granges and to grant certain pensions. They had also seized cattle, carried away books, chalices, vestments, jewels and other goods, and committed divers wastes.[2] It was, moreover, a descendant of the founder of Coombe Abbey who in 1418 was accused of leading an attack on the property of the Abbot of Evesham. Sir Thomas Burdett, of Arrow, was the Warwickshire knight against whom the complaint was made. It was asserted that, aided by his son Nicholas and other evil-doers, he broke into the Abbot's mill, put iron "pikkes" and "billes" between the mill-stones, and caused the mill to grind them — to the imminent peril of burning the mill-house. Not content with this, they hunted in the Abbot's warren and carried off 400 rabbits worth 10s. Nicholas Burdett had been a storm-centre five years earlier, when with 80 followers he had entered Shipston-on-Stour and wounded and ill-treated divers tenants of the Prior of Coventry, and killed certain tenants of the Prior of Worcester.[3] The number of assaults made on monasteries might surprise us, if we did not remember that these places, being corporate

---

[1] *Victorian County History of Warwickshire.*

[2] *Ibid.*

[3] When the two Burdetts finally appeared in Hilary Term, 1420, before the King's Bench, they were released on bail "pro eo quod ipsi profecturi sunt in partibus transmarinis in servitio dominis regis in Comitiva Johannis Ducis Bedeford." It seems clear that the King considered that men with the energy and courage to attack their fellow citizens could safely be employed in fighting the French. One is reminded of Pope Urban's plea: "Let those who for a long time have been robbers now become knights." — Miss B. H. Putnam, in *Early Treatises on the Practice of the Justices of the Peace in the 15th and 16th Centuries.*

bodies, had moved more slowly in the direction of emancipating their serfs than had the ordinary lord of the manor.[1]

We learn from the *Paston Letters* that in 1454 — shortly after Sir Thomas Malory was committed to prison — Robert Ledham's fellowship in Norfolk made an attack on two men while the latter were kneeling at Mass, and would have killed them had they not been prevented. The same year, two men beat the parson of Hashyngham, and "brake his hede in his own chauncell." Outrages like these were not the work of lawless brigands and recognised enemies of the whole community. They were merely the effect of party spirit. The men who did them were supported by noblemen and country gentlemen.[2]

What distinguishes Malory's case from that of a fomenter of disorder like Sir Thomas Todenham is that, whereas the latter is addressed by Richard Neville, Earl of Warwick (the King-Maker) as "our right trusty and well-beloved friend," [3] Malory incurs the displeasure of Red and White Rose supporters alike. Representatives of both factions are named on the Commission which arrests him; he is thrown into prison while the Lancastrians are in power; he is kept there when the Yorkists are in the ascendant. His views on the subject of civil war are expressed in Book X of the *Morte*, where, recounting how Sir Percivale delivered Sir Tristram out of prison, he interpolates the statement that King Mark had sworn

[1] G. M. Trevelyan.
[2] Dr. J. Gairdner's *Introduction to the Paston Letters*.
[3] In a letter written on All Souls' Day, 1449, "within our lodging in the Grey Friars within Newgate." The Earl was trying to negotiate a loan of money.

that he would go himself unto the Pope of Rome to war upon the miscreants. [Turks], and this is a fairer war than thus to raise the people against your king.[1]

Equally significant on this subject is another passage which Malory introduces in the account of Mordred's rebellion, when the people were "so new fangle" that for the most part they held with him

Lo ye all Englishmen, see ye not what a mischief here was, for he that was the most king and knight of the world, and most loved the fellowship of noble knights, and by him they were all upholden, now might not these Englishmen hold them content with him. Lo thus was the old custom and usage of this land. And also men say that we of this land have not yet lost ne forgotten that custom and usage. Alas this is a great default of us Englishmen; for there may no thing please us no term.

Moreover, Malory's "fellowship" included men of a higher social status than those who disturbed the peace in Norfolk. John Appelby, of Monks Kirby, who is given prominence as Malory's aider and abettor in the attacks on Coombe Abbey and Monks Kirby Priory, is described in the Indictment as "Esquire" and "gentilman." He appears to have belonged to a family which "fetched its name" from Great Appleby in Leicestershire,[2] and a member of which accompanied Wycliffe's protector, John of Gaunt, on his Spanish expedition.

Four yeomen and one husbandman, in addition to others of lower status, are named as having assembled with Malory "as rebels and breakers of the King's peace in the manner of an insurrection" and thereafter at-

---

[1] "On aperçoit ici une allusion aux événements politiques de l'époque, et notamment à la guerre des Deux Roses." — M. Eugène Vinaver, *Le Roman de Tristan et Iseut dans l'œuvre de Thomas Malory.*

[2] Fuller's *Worthies.*

tacked Coombe Abbey. The composition of Malory's "fellowship" recalls what a well-known historian has written about Jack Cade. "Cade was no leader of a second Peasant Rising. Among his followers were many yeomen, and not a few squires. Their grievances were not those of mere labourers, but of men of substance." [1]

It is very evident that Sir Thomas Malory, knowing he would be punished for what had happened at Monks Kirby, decided that he might as well "be hanged for a sheep as for a lamb." Nevertheless, he may have had no intention of going so far as he is declared by the Warwickshire jury's findings to have actually gone. But other popular leaders, before and since, have been carried off their feet by their followers; and particularly was this likely to be the case just after the close of the French Wars, when every county in England was disturbed by the presence of disbanded soldiery. We have it on record in Hardyng's Chronicle (1457) that:

> In every shire with jakkes [2] and salades [3] clene
> Myssereule doth ryse and maketh neyghbours werre.

Men of the type of Pistol were always ready to take advantage of any opportunity to commit robbery. Malory's effort to exact "wild justice" would give them the opportunity for which they were looking.

There is evidence, moreover, that men in a higher station of life brought home with them from France some of the manners they had acquired in the wars — manners more forcible than polite. A colleague of Sir Thomas Malory in the Retinue of the Earl of Warwick was Sir Thomas Lucy, of Charlecote. *Early Chancery*

---

[1] Sir J. H. Ramsay, *Lancaster and York.*
[2] Cuirasses.
[3] Open helmets.

Proceedings contain the "Complaint of Thomas Moston that Thomas Lucy of Charlecot in the county of Warwick, Gentleman, on the 25 of June last at Bishophampton with force and arms 'grevesly bette oon William Hewet' the complainant's servant 'thretyng hym to sle and to murder where he myght hym take where for he durst nought a byde to do shiche service' to the plaintiff 'as he hadde made his covenant to do atte his maner of Hontescote yn husbondrie and chargit other servauntes of your forsaid suppliant to voide froo his said maner and froo his service uppon the payne of deth' — which was greatly to the plaintiff's hurt because no one was there to look after 'suche good as God hath sende hym and may have noo servant a bydyng atte the said maner to gette ony frute beying upon the yerthe for drede of dethe.' He asks for a writ of subpœna to be issued to the aforesaid Thomas Lucy."

To regard the Knight of Newbold Revel as an ordinary freebooter is quite impossible in view of what we know about him. He had "a stake" not only in one county but in three. From his father and grandfather he had inherited his manors in Warwickshire, Leicestershire, and Northamptonshire. The right of presentation to the living of Shelton, Lincs., was also in his gift. When his widow died in September, 1479, leaving a 14-year-old grandson, Nicholas, as heir, it was placed on record that the property at Wynwyck which she held in chief was worth £10 per annum; the Newbold Revel manor, £6 13s. 4d.; the manor of Swynford, Leicestershire, four marks a year; and land at Stormefield, in the same county, 26s. 8d. yearly.

Sir Thomas Malory was not the only member of his family at loggerheads with the authorities. In 1454, a

near relative, John Poultney, lord of the manor of Misterton (adjoining Lutterworth), — "a member of a family usually conspicuous for loyalty to Church and State,"[1] — was accused before Bishop Chedworth "for refusing to pay tithes, withdrawing from confession and divine service, inciting others to do the like, and uttering divers speeches against the Christian faith." Poultney, however, recanted. It is significant, nevertheless, that when Sir William Peyto, Kt., of Chesterton,[2] co. Warwick, was in the Marshalsea prison, a year later, Poultney secured his release by giving surety for his good behaviour. The tendency for "birds of a feather" to flock together would seem to be further illustrated by the fact that Poultney's son married a daughter of the Lucys of Charlecote, where later (in 1545) Fox the Martyrologist was engaged as tutor.

It is to be hoped that during his long captivity Sir Thomas Malory derived some small share of benefit from the 53s. 4d. which John Poultney's great-grandfather, Sir John Poultney — five times Lord Mayor of London — had by his will left annually to the prisoners in Newgate. Malory, one imagines, must have been kept in touch with his native shire by the fact that the London residence, of the Earl of Warwick adjoined Newgate. The tables in the neighbourhood of Warwick's inn were full of meat which visitors were allowed to carry off from the Earl's hospitable abode.[3] Indirectly, therefore, the prisoners near by would stand to benefit.

[1] Leicestershire County Victoria History.
[2] It was at Chesterton that Sir John Oldcastle had lain concealed as a fugitive in Henry V's reign.
[3] Stow's *Chronicle*.

Chapter XII

NEWGATE GAOL. THE LONDON LIBRARY

NEWGATE GAOL, to which Sir Thomas Malory was finally committed, — after periods of confinement in the Tower of London, Ludgate Prison, and the Marshalsea, — was used at this period as a place of detention both for prisoners of State and for ordinary criminals. One offender of the same category as Sir Thomas had just been released from there, namely, William Wyghall, of Nottingham, yeoman, who "for certain offences against the cathedral Church of St. Peter, York, and John, cardinal and archbishop of that church," had been committed to Newgate. Wyghall, however, having "merited the benefit of absolution by the cardinal," had on February 20, 1452, received pardon "for all felonies, murders, escapes, and all other offences and any consequent outlawries." As the Bastille of the day, Newgate was an object of popular wrath during Wat Tyler's Rebellion, — it is recorded that "the mob brake up the prison of Newgate," — and it was rebuilt partly, if not wholly, at the expense of Lord Mayor Richard Whittington, a "Warwickshire lad," [1] who passed to his reward some 25 years before

[1] Long Compton, on the Gloucestershire border, claims to have been his birthplace. "Dick Whittington's cottage" is in the village. The superior claim of Pauntley, Glos., is based on an admittedly incorrect assumption. See Mr. F. Were's article in the Bristol and Gloucestershire Archæological Society's *Proceedings*, vol. xxxi, p. 286. This was published in 1908, but the makers of Gloucestershire guide-books still gaily repeat the error.

Sir Thomas Malory's arrival in London to await the King's pleasure. Not only had Whittington provided for the secure government of the city, however. He exemplified the new interest in literature by founding what was in fact the first city Library — this on the premises of the Grey Friars, just across the road. He laid the first foundation-stone on October 21, 1421 (the Feast of St. Hilary), and in three years the building — which was 129 feet long and 31 feet broad — was filled with books, costing £556 10s., "whereof Richard Whittington gave £400." [1]

It is unfortunate that the records of the London Grey Friars Library do not specify the volumes which it contained; but we know, from other sources, that monastic institutions were well provided with the literature Malory would find essential when compiling the *Morte*. Book V of his work, for example, is compiled from *La Morte Arthure*, an English metrical romance of which a copy has been found in the Thornton MS. in Lincoln Cathedral Library. [2] The Abbey Church of St. Augustine in Canterbury, in the 15th century, had a library that contained about 1,900 volumes, ". . . also the romances of *Guy of Warwick*, *The Knight of the Swan*, *Lancelot du Lac*, *The Story of the Graal*, and the *Four Sons of Aymon*." [3] The Dover Priory library contained 450 books, including *Le Romaunt de la Rose* and *Le Romaunt de Roy Charlemayne*. [4] "The Friers of All Orders, and chiefly the Franciscans, used so diligently to procure Monuments of Literature from all Parts, that wise Men looked upon it as an Injury to Lay Men,

[1] Dugdale's *Monasticon*.
[2] *Dictionary of National Biography*, Article on Malory.
[3] H. R. Plomer, *Wm. Caxton*.   [4] *Ibid*.

LONDON'S FIRST LIBRARY, NEAR NEWGATE GAOL.

who therefore found a difficulty to get any Books." [1]
To like effect, but in a different tone, is the testimony
of Richard of Bury: "When I happened to turn aside to
towns and places where the Mendicants had their con-
vents, I was not slack in visiting their Libraries. There,
amidst the deepest poverty, I found the most precious
riches treasured up." [2]

Sir Thomas Malory was neither the first nor the last
inmate of Newgate to indulge in literary activity there.
Eleven years before the Warwickshire knight's arrest,
Charles, Duke of Orleans, had been released from Newgate after a captivity in various English strongholds ex-
tending over a quarter of a century. [3] He had whiled
away the dreary hours writing ballads and rondels; but
besides confirming himself as an habitual maker of
verses, he was a celebrated bibliophile, and had vied
with his brother Angoulême in bringing back the library
of their grandfather Charles V, when the Duke of Bed-
ford put it up for sale in London. [4] It is impossible to
doubt that he, too, found the proximity of the Grey
Friars Library most useful. When released by the English Government, — who hoped that he would go home
and stir up discord at the French Court, — he retired to
his palace at Blois, which became famous as the centre
of one of the most literary and polite societies of his
time. [5]

The extent to which Newgate was used as a place of
detention for State prisoners, as well as those convicted

[1] *Monasticon.*
[2] *Philobiblon,* c. 8.
[3] Taken prisoner at Agincourt, he had since been held in close custody in
England.
[4] Champollion-Figeac.
[5] Kenneth H. Vickers, *Humphrey Duke of Gloucester.*

of felony, is further indicated by the fact that John, Duke of Bourbon, another captive of Agincourt, spent 18 years within its walls and died there, being afterwards buried in the church of the Grey Friars.

To Malory, as he reduced into English the many French MSS telling the story of King Arthur and the Knights of the Round Table, the existence of the Library so near at hand must have been a veritable godsend during his long detention. "Detention," indeed, expresses his situation much more accurately than incarceration: for had he been confined in the fetid dungeons which Newgate possessed, his life would have been as short as those of the Carthusians who, being imprisoned for refusing to acknowledge the supremacy of Henry VIII, succumbed in a few weeks to their loathsome surroundings.

Although unable to secure his freedom, Malory would be able through his wife and family to purchase various concessions from the Governor of Newgate Gaol — a recognised procedure in the Middle Ages and for centuries later. We find, for example, in December, 1448, a grant for life of the "appurtenances, wages, fees, and profits" of the County Gaol at Warwick to Thomas Trueblode as a reward for good services in France and Normandy.[1] Except in the worst cases, most prisoners were able to ameliorate their condition by money. The gaoler looked on his prisoners as a type of paying guest, and the more they paid, the less irksome became their confinement. "The sums paid to gaolers naturally varied very much according to the prisoner. The Earl of Surrey paid the great sum of 40s. per week for himself, and 2s. 6d. per week for each of his men."[2]

[1] Patent Rolls.   [2] W. G. Bell's *Great Fire of London.*

Malory's captivity, then, was not without alleviation. But when all is said, he must have known little liberty for nearly twenty years. "We may talk very wisely of alleviations; there is only one alleviation for which the man would thank you: he would thank you to open the door."[1] Years after, when Charles of Orleans was speaking at the trial of the Duke of Alençon, who began life so hopefully as the boyish favourite of Joan of Arc, he sought to prove that captivity was a harder punishment than death. "For I have had experience myself," he said, "and in my prison of England, for the weariness, danger, and displeasure in which I then lay, I have many a time wished I had been slain at the battle where they took me."[2]

What would Malory not have given to wet his boots once more with morning dew and join in the chase over those grassy expanses in Warwickshire and Leicestershire which still form the best hunting countries in England?

An event heralding the Wars of the Roses must have come under Malory's notice in 1457, for the monotony of life in prison was broken by the arrival of Lord Egremond, a member of the Northumbrian House of Percy, who had been involved in a miniature civil war at Stamford Bridge despite the royal warning to be "sad, a sober, and a well-rewl'd man." We may be sure that this year would stand out in Sir Thomas Malory's memory, for Lord Egremond, soon after his arrival at Newgate, "brake out of prison by night and had a horse ready and rode away and one of the jaylers with him." [Three years later he was slain with the Duke of Buckingham

---

[1] R. L. Stevenson, *Essay on Charles of Orleans.*
[2] Champollion-Figeac.

close to the King's tent at Northampton.] The other prisoners took to the leads of the gate and defended it a long while against the Sheriffs and all their officers, insomuch that they were forced to call more aid of the citizens, whereby they lastly subdued them and laid them in irons.[1]

Bearing in mind Sir Thomas's past record as a prison-breaker, it is highly probable that he too tried to escape on this occasion.

[1] Loftie.

NEWGATE:

MALORY'S LAST PLACE OF DETENTION.

Chapter XIII

AMONG THE UNPARDONABLES

THE year before he finished the *Morte*, "Thomas Malorie, miles," was with other gentlemen excluded from a pardon granted to a large number of Edward IV's subjects; [1] and four months later, when practically the same list was again promulgated, "Thomas Malarie, knight," was again one of those excluded from the amnesty, granted "tylle alle manere of men for all manere of insurrecyons and trespasses." [2] Much water had flowed under the bridges since the Inquisition presided over by Duke Humphrey was held at Nuneaton. The Duke himself had fallen in battle at Northampton (in 1460), fighting on the Lancastrian side, and any offence which Sir Thomas Malory had committed against him would not weigh with the Yorkists who were now in power. As a matter of fact, Duke Humphrey's overthrow was the signal for Malory's friend, Sir Baldwin Mountford, to press his claim to the manor of Coleshill, of which after his father's death in 1453 he had been unjustly deprived by the Duke. Emerging from the ecclesiastical sphere in which he had taken refuge, he now published "a particular Instrument, whereunto he set his Hand and Seal," in which he made manifest "what unjust and ill-dealing had been exercised by the before-specified Duke of Buckingham for

[1] Wells register (*Hist. MSS Comm. 10th Report*, App. iii, 184).
[2] *H. M. C. Wells MSS*, i, 407.

the utter disheriting of him and his Son. . . . 'For in trouth the seid Duke keped me in Coventre xiiii deyes, and after had me to the Castell of Maxstoke, and there kept me: And my son Sir Symond was put in the Castell of Gloucester, and we could never be delivered out, till we agreed to certain Articles written in a Bill anexid to this my writinge.'" [1]

How Sir Thomas Malory was regarded by the authorities in 1468 is seen by observing the names which preceded and followed his in the list of "unpardonables." The first-named offender, Sir Humphrey Nevyll, shared the Lancastrian sentiments of the elder branch of his house. After Towton he was captured and attainted; but later, breaking out of the Tower, he returned to Northumberland and "made a commotion of people against our sovereign lord the king." After sueing for pardon, he was knighted, but again took arms with the Lancastrians and lived the life of a freebooter for five years. His attainder was now revived, and when he was again captured he was executed at York (September, 1469) in the presence of King Edward IV.[1] After Sir Thomas Malory's name came that of "Robert Marshall, gentleman," who in 1465 had escaped from prison at Nottingham, thus causing the sheriff of the county to be liable to a penalty of 500 marks, from which he was excused by royal clemency.[2]

Further proof that Malory died under a cloud is found in the Record of *Inquisitiones post mortem*. He had, as we have seen, inherited from his father landed estates in Warwickshire, Leicestershire, and Northamptonshire; but after his death, in March, 1471 (1470, Old Style), the customary Inquisitions were not held in

[1] Dugdale.   [2] *Dictionary of National Biography*.

Warwickshire or Leicestershire; and that which was held in Northamptonshire — on November 6 — declared that he held neither lands nor tenements in that county. We learn from the Northampton Inquisition, however, that his son Robert — his heir — was 23 years of age at this time, a fact which may possibly help us to fix the date of Sir Thomas's marriage. (It does not at all follow, as we have suggested in a footnote on this page, that Robert was the only son of the marriage.) Robert's death, in 1479, caused a commission to be issued to Walter Mauntell, knight, and two others, "to enquire what lands Robert Malory, esquire, deceased, tenant-in-chief, held in Northamptonshire, Warwickshire and Leicestershire." [1] Soon afterwards Sir Thomas's widow passed away, — eight and a half years after her husband's death in Newgates, — and it is then that we find full record of the manors, etc., which were now recognised as being the property of Sir Thomas's grandson, Nicholas. The latter, it is worthy of note, lived to become High Sheriff of Warwickshire and Leicestershire in 18 Henry VII, thus retrieving the position in county life which Sir Thomas had forfeited.[2]

[1] Calendar of Patent Rolls, 1476–85, p. 183.

[2] Nicholas Malory was succeeded by two daughters, one of whose descendants is Lord Braye. Newbold Revel passed into other hands in 1640, and the site of the old manor house is now occupied by a mansion of the period of Queen Anne. It was from an uncle or brother of Nicholas Malory, probably, that "Master Melchisedech Mallerie" traced his descent. This Melchisedech — described as "of a good spryte, ready tonge, in audacitie forward" — came much into public notice in 1573, when with drawn sword he chased a certain Arthur Hall through the streets of London, and a short time afterwards was himself slain. In the legal proceedings which followed, mention is made of the fact that Melchisedech's personal friends were Edward Grevill[e] and Sir John Conway — both prominent Warwickshire names, — the latter at that period being connected with Monks Kirby. (*Miscellanea Antiqua Anglicana*, 1815.) "In audacitie forward": there can be little doubt whence Melchisedech Mallerie inherited this trait of his character.

Chapter XIV

MALORY'S BURIAL–PLACE

"WHEN I am dead, I pray you all pray for my soul," wrote Sir Thomas Malory as he laid down his pen on finishing the *Morte*. His great task was completed some time between March, 1469, and March, 1470, and just over a year later — in March,[1] 1471 — he died. His death was probably due to the plague, for Sir John Paston tells us that in 1471 there was a terrible outbreak, "the most unyversall dethe that evyr I wyst in Ingelonde." Less than a fortnight after Malory had passed away, Edward IV landed at Ravenspur and, marching *via* Leicester, Coombe Abbey, Coventry and Warwick, overthrew the King-Maker at Barnet. The King, however, had taken such fright that, before the danger from the Lancastrians was past, he swallowed ten pounds' worth of medicine, "contra pestem" (Issue Roll, 15 May).

Malory's body found sepulture in the Grey Friars' sanctuary. "In Capella Sancti Francisci" — so ran the record of the event — "sub 2ª parte fenestre 4ᵉ sub lapide jacet dominus Thomas Mallere, valens miles: qui obiit 14 die mensis Marcij Aᵒ dni 1470, de parochia de Monkenkyrkby in comitatu Warwici." [2]

The epithet "valens," inscribed on Sir Thomas Malory's tombstone of marble, may be translated "worthy"; but its value as evidence that the Grey Friars held him

---

[1] The inscription on his tombstone stated "Mch 14"; but according to the *Inq. pm* the date was March 12.   [2] Cotton MS., Vitellius.

in esteem is discounted by the fact that they applied
the same adjective to Nicholas Brembre, a Lord Mayor
of London, who was hanged at Tyburn in 1388 and whose
body was interred in the adjacent chapel of All Saints.
"Valens armiger," too, was said of Thomas Burdett,[1] of
Arrow, in the county of Warwick, who after his execution for high treason in 1477 was buried alongside
Brembre.

But the Grey Friars — "the Salvation Army of the
Middle Ages," as Miss Dormer Harris (the well-known
historian of Coventry) has termed them — could not
have maintained the splendour of their sanctuary merely
by interring those who had rendered themselves amen-
able to the law. "There were buried in this monastery
four queens, two daughters of kings, and almost innumerable earls, countesses, barons, bishops, and of the
better sort of citizens."[2] There was a reason for this
preference of a spot so close to "Stynkyng Lane."[3]
The Grey Friars' churchyard was thought to be pecul-
iarly free from evil spirits and flying demons of all sorts.[3]
As was to be expected, the Grey Friars utilised this idea
to enrich their establishment. After the manner of dogs,
declared Thomas de Walsingham, they greedily ate up
those who had become corpses. "You see he writes
somewhat passionately of the poor Friers: but consider
that he was himself a Monk, and the reason may easily
be discerned."[4]

To the Friars, who were very well aware of the light
in which the Monks regarded them, it must have been

[1] Enraged at Edward IV's action in killing a favourite white buck belonging to himself, Burdett passionately wished the horns in the King's belly.
For this he was convicted of high treason.
[2] *Monasticon.*
[3] W. Thornbury, *Old and New London.*   [4] *Monasticon.*

no small satisfaction to reflect that Sir Thomas Malory, *Malleus Monachorum*, had found a resting-place in their precincts; and probably — if the truth were known — had made a bequest, both of money and MSS, to those whose Library had been his help and solace during long years of captivity.

Malory's body reposed under a marble in the Grey Friars' Chapel until the Reformation (less than a century later), when Henry VIII ordered the sanctuary to be handed over to the Lord Mayor and burgesses of London for civic purposes. Malory's tombstone was one of "seven score all sold for £50 or thereabouts" by Sir Martin Bowes, Lord Mayor in 1545. "St. Bartholomew's Spittle (Hospital) in Smithfield, this Church of the Grey Friars, and two parish churches, the one of St. Nicholas in the Shambles, and the other St. Ewin's in Newgate Market, were all to be made into one parish in the said Friers Church . . . and called Christ's Church, founded by King Henry VIII. *A very odd Foundation to let two Churches of four stand, subverting the other two, and a good Hospital, and to call himself a Founder*. . . . Thus was a beautiful church defaced by sacrilegious hands." [1]

Scarcely had Sir Thomas Malory died when another Midland knight was also brought a prisoner to Newgate. This was Sir Walter Wrottesley, who, after being pardoned in 1471 for holding Calais against King Edward IV, was seized and imprisoned for debt. He died on April 10, 1473, and, like Malory, was buried in the church of the Grey Friars. "Miles strenuus in armis cum comite Warwici" was the epitaph granted to him — an epitaph defective in grammar and inaccurate in fact, seeing that really he belonged to Staffordshire.

[1] *Monasticon.*

Chapter XV

DID THE WARWICKSHIRE KNIGHT WRITE THE *MORTE?*

IT WILL be asked, How can it be proved that Sir Thomas Malory, Kt., of Newbold Revel, Warwickshire, was the author of the *Morte d'Arthur?* The answer is, He is the only one who fulfils the conditions, which are: (1) He must have been a knight; (2) he must have been alive in the ninth year of Edward IV — March 4, 1469, to March 3, 1470 (both included); (3) he must have been old enough in 9 Edward IV to make it possible that he should have written this work. Further, Caxton does not say that he received the "copy" directly from the author, and his language may be held to indicate that Malory was dead when the book was printed. In this case, he must have died before the last day of July, 1485, and we have a fourth condition to be complied with.

All these conditions (including the fourth, which can hardly be regarded as imperative) are satisfied by Sir Thomas Malory of Newbold Revel, and by none other. Professor Kittredge has dealt very exhaustively with this question, and his conclusion is as follows: "No one need hesitate to identify 'Thomas Malorie, miles,' of this (1468) pardon with the Warwickshire gentleman whom we are now considering. There appears to have been but one Sir Thomas Malory, Kt., living in England in 8 Edward IV. . . . This leaves, so far as appears at pres-

ent, the Warwickshire Sir Thomas in possession of the
field, for out of all the families examined in the present
investigation, he is the only person found who fulfils
the conditions of the problem."

The present writer, who has searched the *Inquisitiones
post mortem* of the period and made other genealogical
researches, can corroborate Professor Kittredge's testimony. It is a curious fact that in the very year in which
the writer of the *Morte* finished his great work (that is,
the ninth year of Edward IV's reign), the estate of
Thomas Malory, *armiger*, of Kent, came up for probate
— to use a well-understood phrase. But Caxton, in his
introduction to the *Morte*, quite definitely says that
this book was written by "Sir Thomas Maleore, knight."
In any case, Thomas Malory, *armiger*, must have died
prior to this, otherwise his name would not occur when
it does in the *Inquisitiones post mortem*.

Shortly after the appearance of Professor Kittredge's
essay (1897), Mr. A. T. Martin, F.S.A., read a paper
before the Society of Antiquaries in which he discussed
the claim of Thomas Malory of Papworth to be considered as the author of the *Morte d'Arthur*. This Malory
did not die till the autumn of 1469; hence he was alive
at the time when the *Morte* was finished, and possibly
for six months afterwards. In the Fine Roll of Edward
IV (1469, November 18) he is called "armiger," however, and this, combined with the fact that his will contains no designation of rank, makes it certain that he did
not write the *Morte*.

Another Thomas Malory of this period ought perhaps
to be mentioned before passing on to another point. In
the list of noblemen and gentlemen who accompanied
Edward IV in his northern expedition in 1462 appears

the name of "Thomas Malery," and as it is included among the *milites* there may seem strong reason for regarding this Thomas as fulfilling the conditions just enumerated. When the list is examined closely, however, it becomes quite certain that this warrior against the Scots was not the Malory with whom we are concerned. "Sir" is prefixed to the name of each individual knight in the list, and the "Thomas Malery" here mentioned has no such prefix.[1]

"We cannot tell when, or, very distinctly, where, Caxton set up the first English press; he was too busy" (to mention this), said Bishop Stubbs in his "Lectures on Mediæval and Modern History." A very different reason is assigned by a present-day writer, namely, that Caxton, in introducing printing, was running counter to a sort of trade-union interest — that of the men who earned their living by copying MSS.[2] We may be certain that Caxton, when he acquired what Malory had "drawn out into English," knew that the author had died in prison under a cloud; but in the interests of the book he was about to publish,[3] the Father of English printing would naturally refrain from saying anything as to the career of the man whose great work he was giving to the world.

Giving our attention now to the internal evidence, — that presented by the *Morte* itself, — we find at least three instances in which Malory contrived to introduce complimentary references to names possessing a special Warwickshire significance. In Book II, where he tells of the prowess of King Arthur against Nero and King Lot of Orkney, he says: "Sir Hervis *de Revel* did mar-

[1] *Three Fifteenth-Century Chronicles*, ed. Gairdner, p. 157.
[2] H. R. Plomer.
[3] Caxton finished printing the *Morte* on July 31, 1485.

vellous deeds with King Arthur." When the question
of filling vacancies amongst the knights of the Round
Table is being considered (Book IV), "Sir Hervise de
Revel, *a noble knight*," is suggested by King Pellinore
as one of the four senior candidates. "That is well devised, said King Arthur, and right so shall it be." In the
source from which Malory took Books I–IV, viz., Robert
de Borron's "Romance of Merlin," Sir Hervis indeed
has a surname — "de Rinel"; but whilst it is unsafe to
attach much importance to Malory's constant changing
of this to "Revel," it is certainly significant that he introduces complimentary references to Sir Hervis de
Revel which are not to be found in "the frensshe book."
The names of the other candidates, it should be observed, are recited by Malory as given in the "Merlin"
— without any complimentary addition of his own.
Tasso and Ariosto, among Malory's contemporaries,
furnish proof of the practice in which fifteenth-century
authors indulged of introducing bits of personal and
family history into their works; and when we consider
the high value which descendants of the Revells set upon
their connection with that family, it is natural that we
should attach importance to the piece of evidence just
cited. How prominent was the Revell name in fifteenth-
century Warwickshire is made clear by a number of
facts. First of all, the place of Sir Thomas Malory's
birth was tending to be known as Newbold Revel rather
than as Fenny Newbold. Secondly, the Revell coat-of-
arms is encountered in a considerable number of parish
churches — or rather, this was so when Sir William
Dugdale compiled his "Antiquities of Warwickshire."
For example, it was the Revell coat-of-arms which
adorned one of the windows at Grendon, where Sir

Thomas Malory's father, John Malory, *armiger*, had
married Philippa Chetwynd, daughter of a family which
held a leading position in North Warwickshire as well as
at Ingestre, in Staffordshire. Moreover, the Revell cog-
nisance appeared four times in the chancel windows at
Coleshill, — a place now, for us, always associated with
Sir Thomas Malory's prison-breaking, moat-swimming
achievement, — and it is still retained at Stanford-on-
Avon Church (near Winwick) in the central window of
the south aisle. Finally, we read that in 1408, Richard
Reynolds, of Emscote, co. Warwick., "affecting his
mother's name, called himself Revell."

Let us turn now to another and similar point. When
we remember that Malory's feudal chief, Richard Beauchamp, besides being Earl of Warwick, claimed the
barony of De Lisle in right of his wife, and that the title
was revived in 1443 in favour of the Earl's grandson,
John Talbot, Earl of Shrewsbury,[1] we cannot help recalling the important and highly honourable position
which a knight bearing that surname occupies in the
pages of the *Morte.* We read (Book XIII) how Galahad,
after meeting Joseph of Arimathea, was by a monk
brought to a tomb.

Anon, the squire [Melias de Lile] alight off his hackney,
and kneeled down at Galahad's feet, and prayed that he
might go with him till he had made him knight.
If I would not refuse you?
Then will ye make me knight, said the squire, and that
order, by the grace of God, shall be well set in me.
So Sir Galahad granted him, and turned again unto the

---

[1] Slain with his heroic sire at Chatillon in 1453. The Patent Roll of 1450
mentions the "appointment for life of John Talbot, lord of Lysle, as master
of the game of Fulbrooke Park, co. Warwick, together with the lordship and
manor of Fulbrooke."

abbey there they came from. . . . And upon the morn he made the squire knight, and asked him his name, and of what kindred he was come.

Sir, said he, men call me Melias de Lile, and I am the son of the king of Denmark.

Now, fair sir, said Galahad, sith ye be come of kings and queens, now look that knighthood be well set in you, for ye ought to be a mirror unto all chivalry.

Sir, said Melias, ye say sooth. But, sir, sithen ye have made me a knight, ye must of right grant me my first desire that is reasonable.

Ye say sooth, said Galahad.

Then Melias said, that ye will suffer me to ride with you in this quest of the Sancgreal till that some adventure depart us.

I grant you, sir.

Reference to the source from which Malory drew this particular portion of the *Morte*, viz., the French "Romance of Lancelot," shows that it contains no mention whatever of "de Lile." Melias there is pure "Melian" or "Meliane," with no surname. Nor indeed is the fanciful description of Melias as "the son of the King of Denmark" to be found in "the frensshe book." Instead we find this:

> *Et chil li dist qu'il auoit a non melian, "biaus amis," fait galaad, "puis ke vous estes chivalers,* ET DE SI HAUTE LIGNIE COMME DE ROY, *ore gardes bien que li hounours de chevalerie soit bien emploie en vous."*

The position of Deputy Captain of Calais was held for a time at this period by Sir William de Lisle. In the light of this fact it is interesting to note that Malory makes one of Sir Launcelot's knights, Nerovens de Lile, lieutenant of the Castle of Pendragon. Nothing whatever suggestive of this is to be found in the source-book which Sir Thomas Malory had before him when he wrote, so that it is reasonable to suppose he in this way

wove into the *Morte* a bit of the history of his own time. As in the case already cited, however, he half conceals while he half reveals. Here his method is fully in accord with that of earlier writers in the Arthurian Cycle.

Book XVIII furnishes us with a noteworthy example of Malory's habit of giving distinctive appellations to persons who in "the frensshe books" were nameless. When Sir Launcelot is dangerously wounded by accident at the hand of his friend Sir Bors, he pleads to be taken to the dwelling-place of "a gentle hermit, that sometime was a full noble knight and a great lord of possessions, ... and his name is Sir Baudewin of Bretayne." Malory knew a Sir Baldwin — son of the High Sheriff who had arrested him in 1451; he knew, too, that this Sir Baldwin when cheated out of his patrimony, "betook himself to a religious course of life ... styling himself *Knight and Priest*."

And then anon the hermit stanched Sir Launcelot's blood, and made him to drink good wine, so that he was well refreshed, and knew himself. For in those days it was not the guise of hermits as is nowadays. For there were none hermits in those days but that they had been men of Worship and of prowess, and those hermits held great household, and refreshed people that were in distress.

Nothing resembling this passage occurs in the source-books which Malory used. In the metrical *Morte Arthur* we are merely told that a leech healed Sir Launcelot's wounds, while the prose *Launcelot* says that an old knight of the neighbourhood, who knew much about surgery, was sent for. Malory's description of Sir Baudewin as "of Bretayne," [1] like his earlier statement that

---

[1] Sir E. Strachey's edition gives this as "Britanny" (meaning Brittany); but the spelling here adopted is that taken by Dr. Oskar Sommer from Caxton's copy.

Sir Melias de Lile was "son of the King of Denmark," must be regarded as proof of the large freedom he allowed himself. In this as in many other respects he shows how far he is from being merely a translator and collator of earlier contributions to the Arthurian Cycle.

That Sir Thomas Malory had in mind Guy's Cliffe, near Warwick, when he penned the following topographical details of Sir Baudewin's hermitage, is pretty certain. The passage occurs in Book XVIII of the *Morte*, and nothing corresponding to it is to be found in the prose *Launcelot* from which Malory derived the narrative.

Ever Sir Launcelot bled that it ran down to the earth. And so by fortune they came to that hermitage, which was under a wood, and a great cliff on the other side, and a fair water running under it.

This exactly describes the position of Guy's Cliffe, a place with which Malory would be well acquainted through his chief, Richard Beauchamp, Earl of Warwick. For it was here that, in 1423, the Earl founded a chantry, thus carrying into effect a wish expressed by Henry V on the occasion of a visit paid by the king to this hermitage, famous for its association with Guy of Warwick.

We come now to what is perhaps the most conclusive piece of *internal* evidence that Sir Thomas Malory, Knight, of Newbold Revel, wrote the *Morte d'Arthur*. If we think of the author as being detained in prison when a general amnesty is declared, we shall understand for the first time what he meant when he closed his work a year later with a request to all readers: "Pray for me, while I am on live that God send me good deliverance." And light will be cast on a passage concerning Sir Tristram, "who endured great pain" in captivity, "for

sickness had overtaken him, and that is the greatest
pain a prisoner may have. For all the while a prisoner
may have his health of body he may endure under the
mercy of God and in hope of good deliverance; but when
sickness touches a prisoner's body, then may a prisoner
say all wealth is him bereft, and then he hath cause to
wail and to weep."

Very seldom does Malory indulge in reflections not to
be found in the original romances from which he worked.
This is one of those rare passages; and it is natural to see
in it the impelling force of bitter personal experience.
We may take it, then, that — like certain of St. Paul's
Epistles, the *Pilgrim's Progress*, and Raleigh's *History
of the World* — the *Morte d'Arthur* was written in captivity.

The world is more indebted than is commonly supposed to prisons for outstanding works of Literature.
Boethius, Lovelace, Wilde, and Ernst Toller are some
of the names which may be noted in this connection.
English prisons of the present day are vastly superior to
old Newgate from a sanitary point of view, — although
it should be remembered that a water supply was provided for Newgate by Lord Mayor Richard Whittington, — but since the Bottomley episode it is very doubtful whether a gaol in this country is a favourable place
for literary endeavour.

Chapter XVI

MALORY'S PROSE STYLE

HAD Malory been permitted to pass his life on his manor of Newbold Revel, it is exceedingly unlikely that he would have had access to the manuscript books which were necessary to him in compiling the *Morte*. This, it must be remembered, was fused into its actual form out of crude materials ten times greater in bulk. When Malory began his task, the best of the Arthurian romances were still in French. But cultivated England was now following Chaucer's lead and ceasing to talk French; and Malory — with Wycliffe's example before him — would have no doubt as to what language would henceforth hold sway in England.

It should here be noted how prominently the Midlands were represented in this nationalist reaction. Layamon and Walter Langland are household words to us; and Lawrence Minot, who flourished exactly a century before Malory and whose dialect in his ballads proclaims him a Midlander, is the first to give literary expression to the protest against our native language falling to obscure rank and menial uses. It is worth noting, too, as a coincidence, that the fourteenth-century metrical *Morte Arthur* (one of the source-books used by Malory) has been definitely assigned to "the Northern border of the West Midland region" — precisely that part of England in which Sir Thomas spent his early days.

Warwickshire has always been noted for sport, and that Sir Thomas Malory was a sportsman through and through we may conclude from his original and carefully drawn picture of Sir Tristram.

Every day Sir Tristram would go ride on hunting, for Sir Tristram was, that time called the best chaser of the world, and the noblest blower of an horn of all manner of measures. For, as books report, of Sir Tristram came all the good terms of venery and hunting, and all the sizes and measures of blowing of an horn; and of him we had first all the terms of hawking, and which were beasts of chase, and beasts of venery, and which were vermins; and all the blasts that belong to all manner of games.

Sir Thomas Malory, too, had a genuine Warwickshire man's regard for horses. On the occasion of one of the innumerable tournaments spoken of in the *Morte* we are told:

Then was the cry huge and great when Sir Palamides the Saracen smote the neck of Sir Launcelot's horse that it died. For many knights held that it was unknightly done in tournament to kill a horse wilfully — except it were done in plain battle, life for life.

In spite of the bloodshed and the other features which Roger Ascham condemned in the *Morte*, we do get the vision of a really "Merrie England" when reading Malory's pages. On one occasion, we read, King Arthur and Launcelot "laughed that they might not sit"; and when Guinevere sees poor Sir Dinadan after a bout with Launcelot (he having been despoiled unto his shirt and a woman's garment put upon him) "then the Queen laughed that she fell down, and so did all that were there."

How picturesque, too, is the way in which Malory closes his account of a day's sport: "And then the King

let blow to lodging." How much more full of life than our phrases: "Hounds then returned to kennels," or "Home was then the order."

Sir Thomas Malory, surely, was a sportsman in another very different matter — his treatment of Guinevere's character. Some earlier writers on the theme of Launcelot and Guinevere had inferred that the origin of all the trouble was to be found on the Queen's side, — "The woman, she tempted me," — but Sir Thomas will not stoop to this. "While she lived," he contents himself with saying of Guinevere, "she was a true lover, and therefore she had a good end."

Take another example of Malory's prose, which should be prefaced by recalling that on one occasion the knights of the Round Table are subjected to a test — the curing of the wounds of Sir Urre of Hungary, who should never be made whole until the best knight in the world had probed his wounds. One after the other, King Arthur's paladins fail to achieve the miracle, until at last it is Launcelot's turn to try his hand. Conscious of his sin with Guinevere, he shrinks from the ordeal, but is ordered by the King to proceed:

Then Sir Launcelot kneeled down by the wounded knight, saying, My lord Arthur, I must do your commandment, the which is sore against my heart. And then he held up his hands, and looked into the east, saying secretly unto himself, Thou blessed Father, Son, and Holy Ghost, I beseech thee of thy mercy, that my simple worship and honesty be saved, and thou, blessed Trinity, thou mayest give power to heal this sick knight, by thy great virtue and grace of thee, but, good Lord, never of myself. And then Sir Launcelot prayed Sir Urre to let him see his head: and then, devoutly kneeling, he ransacked the three wounds, that they bled a little, and forth with all the wounds fair healed, and seemed as they had

been whole a seven year. And in likewise he searched his body of other three wounds, and they healed in likewise. And then the last of all he searched the which was in his hand, and, anon, it healed fair. Then King Arthur, and all the kings and knights, kneeled down, and gave thanks and lovings unto God, and to his blessed mother, and ever Sir Launcelot wept as he had been a child that had been beaten.

Judging from the *Morte*, it would seem that Malory accepted the doctrine of Transubstantiation as readily as did the average Lollard.[1] In Book XVII Malory says:

Then took he himself the holy vessel, and came to Galahad, and he kneeled down and there he received his Saviour, and after him so received all his fellows; and they thought it so sweet that it was marvellous to tell.

Let us quote Professor Saintsbury: "It is possible that Malory's art is mostly unconscious art — it is not much the worse for that. But it is nearly as infallible as it is either unconscious or thoroughly concealed. The pictorial power, the musical cadence of the phrase, the steady glow of chivalrous feeling throughout, the noble morality (for the condemnation of Ascham and others is partly mere Renaissance priggishness stupidly condemning things mediæval off-hand, and partly Puritan prudery throwing its baleful shadow before), the kindliness, the sense of honour, the melancholy and yet never either gloomy or puling sense of the inevitable end — all these are eminent in it." No effort in English prose on so large a scale had been made before Malory, and he did much to encourage a fluent and pliant English prose style in the century that succeeded him.

[1] "The Lollards never devised a new sacrament of their own, . . . and there is no suggestion in Lollard literature that they repudiated the obligation to hear Mass on Sunday and holy days." — M. Deanesley, *The Lollard Bible*.

We may agree with Professor Saintsbury that "The thing is important in Literature, not the man"; but in studying what is known of the knight of Newbold Revel we gain a better conception of a work which a competent critic has declared to be "not only the greatest of English prose romances, but also in a very real sense the pioneer of the English Novel." If, as Robert Louis Stevenson has so finely said, "a man would rather leave behind him the portrait of his spirit than the portrait of his face, — *figura animi magis quam corporis*," — then Sir Thomas Malory may rest well satisfied. "In audacitie forward," he is shaped after the pattern of Sir Launcelot de Lake, whose knightly exploits and human failings are depicted so faithfully in the *Morte*.

Four and a half centuries have passed since Caxton "enprised" to print Malory's "book of the noble histories of King Arthur," with its lesson so plainly written—

Do after the good and leave the evil, and it shall bring you to good fame and renommée.

Successive generations have approved the wisdom of Caxton's choice. If we regard Malory as in some measure typifying Sir Launcelot, we shall agree that, like him, he has received double for all his sins.

APPENDICES

APPENDIX I

THE TRIAL OF SIR THOMAS MALORY

INQUISITION AT NUNEATON.

King's Bench Indictments. File 265, Bundle 38. Supplemented from Coram Rege Roll 763 m 3 Crown Side. Hilary Term, 30 Hen. VI.

Inquisitio capta apud Nuneton coram Humfrido Duce Buk. Willelmo Birmyngeham milite, Thoma Bate & Thoma Greswold Custodibus pacis domini Regis Ac Justiciariis ipsius domini Regis ad diversas felonias, transgressiones, & malefactas in Comitatu Warr. audiendum & terminandum assignatis die lune proximo ante festum sancti Bartholome Apostoli Anno regni Regis Henrici sexti post conquestum vicesimo nono per sacramentum Ricardi Arblaster de Birmyngeham, Johannis Belle de eadem, Johannis Whatcroft de Solyhull, Rogeri More de eadem, — Corpeson de Bykenhull, Thome Dounton de Sheldon, Alani Gervys de Merston Culy, Ricardi Orme de eadem, Thome Mylner de Atherston, Ricardi Barbour de eadem, Henrici Blakenhale de Sheldon, Willelmi Parker de Atherston, Willelmi Vale de eadem, Willelmi Ludford de Austeley & Henrici Serche de Hurley qui dicunt super sacramentum suum quod cum Humfridus Dux Buk., virtute cuiusdem Commissionis domini Regis eidem Duci Ac Ricardo Comiti Warr. directi ad capiendum & arestandum Thomam Malory nuper de Fenny Newbold in Comitatu Warr. militem & Johannem Appelby servientem eiusdem Thome pretextu cuiusquidem commissionis Idem Dux die dominica in festa Sancti Jacobi Apostoli Anno regni Regis Henrici sexti post conquestum vicesimo nono apud Fenny Newbold dictum Thomam Malory capit [cepit?] & arrestavit & ipsum apud Coventre, Willelmo Mountfort militi vicecomiti Comitatus Warr. comisit ad ipsum Thomam salvo & secure custodien-

dum. Ita quod posset habere corpus eiusdem Thome coram
domino Rege & concilo suo in quindena sancti Michaelis
proxima future ubicumque tunc foret in Anglia ad respon-
dendum eidem domino Regi de & super diversis articulis in
eadem Commissione specificatis necnon faciendum & reci-
piendum que tunc de concilio predicto contingerit ordinari.
Super quo dictus Thomas die Martis extunc proximo sequente
in prisona sub custodia dicti vicecomitis apud Colshull in
manerio ibidem prisonam predictam in nocte dicte die Martis
noctanter fregit & ultra motam ibidem natavit sicque a custodia dicti vicecomitis evasit. Ac tunc dictus Thomas, Johannes Appleby nuper de Fenny Newbold in Comitatu Warr.
Gentilman, Johannes Sherd nuper de eisdem villa & Comitatu
yoman, ... Willelmus Halle nuper de Stonley in Comitatu predicto yoman, Johannes Masshot nuper de Fenny
Newbold in Comitatu predicto Grome, ... Rogerus Sherd
nuper de eisdem villa & Comitatu yoman, Thomas Sherd
nuper de eisdem villa & Comitatu yoman, Johannes Tynock
nuper de Wolvey in comitatu predicto husbondman, Gregorius Walshale de Brynkelow in Comitatu predicto yoman,
Ricardus Irysshman nuper de Fenny Newbold in Comitatu
predicto laborer & Thomas Maryot nuper de Kyrkeby Monachorum in Comitatu predicto yoman, aggregatis sibi quampluribus malefactoribus & pacis domini Regis perturbatoribus
ignotis ut rebelles ac pacis domini Regis perturbatores modo
nove insurrexionis unanimiterque insurrexerunt & die Mer-
curii ex tunc proximo sequente ad Monasterium & Abbatiam
beate Marie de Combe perrexerunt & diversas portas & ostia
eiusdem Monasterii cum magnis lignis noctanter fregerunt &
intraverunt & duas cistas Abbatis dicti Monasterii adtunc &
ibidem fregerunt & una bagam & viginti & una libras auri in
eadem contentas & una aliam bagam & viginti & quinque
marcas auri & argenti in eadem baga contentas de bonis &
catallis dicti Abbatis & Conventus ibidem ac quamplura alia
jocalia & ornamenta ecclesie dicti Monasterii et Abbatis ad
valenciam quadraginta librarum adtunc & ibidem inventa
felonice ceperunt & asportaverunt in magnam destructionem
& spoliacionem Monasterii & Abbatie predicte necnon contra
pacem coronam & dignitatem domini Regis.

Item dicunt quod Thomas Malory nuper de Fenny Newbold in Comitatu Warr. Miles ac quamplures alii malefactores
& pacis domini Regis perturbatores ignoti ad numerum viginti
& sex personarum armatarum & modo guerrino arraiatarim
videlicet gladiis, baculis, gleyves, arcubus, sagittis, Jakkes,
Salettes & crossebowes quarto die Januarii Anno regni Regis
Henrici sexti post conquestum vicesimo octavo apud Combe
in Silvis Abbatis beate Marie de Combe predicta jacuerunt
in insidiis ad interficiendum & murdrum Humfridum Ducem
Buk. & ad ipsum cum arcubus & sagittis predictis sagittan-
dum & interficiendum contra pacem dicti domini Regis.

Item dicunt quod Thomas Malory nuper de Fenneneubold
in Comitatu Warr. Miles, Ricardus Malory de Radclyff juxta
Leycestre in Comitatu Leyc. Armiger, Johannes Appulby de
Fenneneubold in Comitatu Warr. Gentilman, Johannes Sherd
nuper de Fenneneubold in Comitatu Warr yoman alias dictus
Johannes Shoo de Fenneneubold in Comitatu Warr. yoman,
Willelmus Podmore nuper de Fenneneubold in Comitatu
Warr. yoman, Willelmus Halle nuper de Stonley in Comitatu
Warr. Walker, Johannes Masshot nuper de Fenneneubold in
Comitatu Warr. Grome, Rogerus Sherd nuper de Fenneneu-
bold in Comitatu Warr. yoman, alias dictus Thomas Shoo
nuper de Fenneneubold in Comitatu Warr. yoman . . . . in
Comitatu Warr husbondman, Gregorius Walshale nuper de
Brynkelowe in Comitatu Warr . . . Brynkelow in Comitatu
Warr. husbondman, Ricardus Irysshman nuper de Fenneneu-
bold in . . . nuper de Kyrkeby Monachorum in Comitatu
Warr. Bower, Thomas Leghton nuper de . . . Robertus
Smyth nuper de Fenneneubold in Comitatu Warr. Smyth,
Johannes Warr . . . yoman, Johannes Harper nuper de
Fenneneubold in Comitatu Warr. harper, et Johannes . . .
Cook, die Jovis proximo post festum sancti Jacobi Apostoli
Anno regni Regis Henrici sexti post conquestum vicesimo
nono supradicto aggregatis sibi quampluribus malefactoribus
et pacis domini Regis perturbatoribus ignotis ad numerum
Centum personarum modo guerrino arraiatarum vi et armis
videlicet, gladiis, lanciis, lassinis, arcubus, & sagittis clausa &
domos Ricardi Abbatis Monasterii beate Marie de Comba

apud Combe in Comitatu Warr. modo riote intraverunt &
octodecim ostia monasterii predicti fregerunt & in predictum
Ricardum Abbatem, commonachos & servientes suos adtunc
& ibidem insultam fecerunt & tres citas ferro ligatas & ceratas
violenter fregerunt & quadraginta libras quatuor solidos &
quatuor denarios in pecunia munerata in diversis bagis contentas & tres annulos auri cum lapidibus preciosis precii
Centum solidorum & due signeta argenti precii sex solidorum
& octo denariorum unum parvum psalterum precii vjs viijd
duas zonas argenti precii xxxs tria paria preculum videlicet
"bedes" unum parum de Corall precii vs alterum de laumbir
precii vs tercium de Jete precii duorum solidorum duos arcus
precii vs & tres garbas de sagittis precii vjs de bonis & catallis
predicti Abbatis ibidem inventis felonice furati fuerunt.

Item dicunt quod Thomas Malory nuper de Fenny New-
bold in Comitatu Warr. Miles & Johannes . . . in eodem
Comitatu Gentilman ultimo die Augusti Anno regni Regis
Henrici Sexti post conquestum vicesimo octavo apud Mon-
keskirkeby per minas & oppressionem ceperunt extorciose de
Johanne Mylner viginti solidos. Iidem Thomas Malory &
Johannes Appelby ultimo die Maii Anno regni Regis Henrici
sexti . . . vicesimo octavo apud Monkeskyrkeby predictam
extorciose ceperunt per minas & oppressionem de Margareta
Kyng & Willelmo Hale Centum solidos.

Item dicunt quod Thomas Malory nuper de Fenny Newbold in Comitatu Warr. Miles die sabati proximo ante festum
Pentecostes Anno regni Regis Henrici sexti post conquestum vicesimo octavo apud Kirkeby Monachorum clausum &
domos Hugonis Smyth fregit & Johannam uxorem dicti Hugonis ibidem adtunc felonice rapuit & cum ea carnaliter
concubuit.

Item dicunt quod Thomas Malory nuper de Fenny Newbold in Comitatu Warr. Miles die Jovis proximo post festum
Sancti Petri Advincula Anno regni Regis Henrici sexti post
conquestum vicesimo octavo Johannam uxorem Hugonis
Smyth apud Coventre felonice rapuit & cum ea carnaliter
concubuit. Ac illam cum bonis & catallis dicto Hugonis ad

valenciam quadraginta librarum tunc & ibidem inventis usque Barwell in Comitatu Leyc. felonice furatis fuit cepit & abduxit contra pacem coronam & dignitatem domini Regis.

Item alias Inquisitio capta coram prefatis Justiciariis die loco & Anno supradictis per sacramentum Willelmi . . . Dunchurche, Ricardi Gebons de Ulfreton, Johannis Bynley de Rokeby, Willelmi . . . Thome Halle de Lalleford, Johannis Bemonde de Bromkote, Johannis Herdw . . . Saundres de Bedworth, Johannis Faukes de Radford Symly, Willelmi . . . Thomas Malory de Fenny Newbold in Comitatu Warr. Miles, Johannes Mas . . . , Willelmus Smyth de eisdem villa & Comitatu laborer, Galfridus Gryffyn de . . . Carleton in Comitatu Leycestr yoman & Johannes Arnesby de Ty . . . quarto die Junii Anno regni Regis Henrici sexti post conquestum vicesimo nono apud Cosford septem vaccas duos boviculos trescentas triginta & quinque oves precii xxijl*i* & una carecta cum ferro ligata precii iiijl*i* de bonis & catallis Willelmi Rowe & Willelmi Dowde de Shatewell in Comitatu Leyc. extorcione ceperunt & abinde usque Newbold abduxerunt contra pacem domini Regis etc.

BEFORE THE KING'S BENCH.

[Continued from Coram Rege Roll 763 Crown Side Membrane 3.]

Quequidem judicamenta dominus Rex nunc coram eo postea certis de causis venire fecit terminanda. Propter quod preceptum fuit vicecomiti quod non omittet ac quin caperet eos si &c. Et modo scilicet die Jovis in quindena Sancti Hillarii isto eodem termino coram domino Rege apud Westmonasterium venit predictus Thomas Malory per vicecomites London virtute brevis domini Regis eis inde directi ad baram hic ductus in propria persona sua et statim de premissis sibi superius impositus allocutus qualiter se velit inde acquietare dicit quod ipse in nullo est inde culpabilis. Et inde de bono & malo ponit se super patriam &c. Et super hoc idem Thomas Malory remittitur prefatis vicecomitibus predictis salvo custodiendis quousque &c. una cum causis &c.[1]

---

[1] In margin: "Remittitur London."

[Added later.]

Et in hac parte venit inde jurata coram domino Rege in octavo Purificationis beate Marie ubicumque &c. Et qui &c. ad recognoscendum &c. Quia &c. Idem dies datum est prefato Thome Malory &c. Ad quem diem coram domino Rege apud Westmonasterium venit predictus Thomas Malory sub custodia prefatorum Vicecomitum in propria persona. Et Vicecomites retornant nomina xxiiij Juratorum quorum nullas &c. Ita preceptum est Vicecomitibus quod non ommittant &c. quin distringant eos per mones terras &c. Et quod de exitibus &c. Et quod habeant corpora eorum coram domino Rege a die Pasche in xv dies ubicumque &c. ad faciendum Juratam predictam &c. Et quod apponant xx tales &c. Idem dies datum est prefato Thome Malory in custodia prefatorum Vicecomitum interim commissio &c. postea scilicet a die Pasche in xv dies Anno regni dicti Regis tricesimo secundo coram ipso Rege apud Westmonasterium venit predictus Thomas Malory in propria persona sua. Et Vicomites non nunc inde littere &c.

Preceptum est vicecomitibus quod non ommittant &c quin distringant juratores dicte jurate per omnes terras &c et quod de exitibus &c et quod habeant corpora eorum coram domino Rege a die sancti Michaelis in unum mensem ubicumque &c. Nisi dilectus & fidelis domini Regis Ricardus Byngham unius justicarius dicti Regis ad plactium &c prius die Jovis proximo ante festum sancti Matthei apostoli apud Warrewyk per formam statuti &c venerit ad faciendum juratam predictam. Idem dies datum est prefato Thome Malory. Et super hoc de gratia Curie speciali predictus Thomas Malory dimittitur per manucaptionem Rogeri Chamberleyn de Quynburgh in Comitatu Kanc. militis, Johannis Leventhorpe de London armigeris, Edwardi Fitz William de Framlyngham in Comitatu Suff. armigeris, Thome Ince de Comitatu Essex armigeris, Radulphi Worthyngton de Framlyngham in Comitatu Suff. Gentilman, Edwardi Wheteley de London Gentleman & Johannis Hathwyk de Herbury in Comitatu Warr. Gentilman qui eam inquisitionem habendi corporis eius coram domino Rege ad prefatum terminum &c. Postea scilicet die

Veneris proximo post xvam Sancti Hillarii Anno regni dicti
Regis tricesimo quarto coram ipso Rege apud Westmonasterium venit predictus Thomas Malory sub custodia Thome
Gower Armigeris locumtenentis Henrici Ducis Exonie Con-
stabularii domini Regis Turris sui London virtute brevis dicti
Regis eisdem Constabulario & locum tenenti inde directi in
propria persona sua. Qui comittitur Marescallo &c et cum
hoc idem Thomas Malory quod dominus Rex nunc de gratia
sua speciali & ex certa sciencia & mero motu suis post ultimam
contumacionem placiti predicti scilicet xvam sancti Michaelis
termino proximam precedentem per litteras suas patentes
pardonavit remisit & relaxavit eidem Thome quouscumque
nomine censedatur secta pacis sue que ad ipsum Regem versus
ipsum Thomam pertinet pro felonis, transgressionibus, insur-
rectionibus, extortionibus, oppressionibus & aliis offensis
predictis & pro omnibus aliis feloniis & transgressionibus per
ipsum Thomam ante novum diem Julii Anno regni dicti Regis
tricesimo tercio factis sive perpetratis et firmam pacem suam
ei inde concessit. Et profert hic in Curiam litteras patentes
predictas premissa testificantes quarum datum est apud
Westmonasterium vicesimo quarto die Novembris Anno regni
dicti Regis tricesimo quarto supradicto. Et super venit
Rogerus Malory de Ryton in Comitatu Warr. Gentilman,
Johannes Benford de London Gentilman, Willelmus Clyff
de London Gentilman, Walterus Boys de London Sadeler,
Thomas Pulton de London Taillour & David John de London
Taillour de manucaptione pro prefato Thoma Malory quod
ipse extunc se bene geret erga dominum Regem in & cunctum
populum suum juxta formam statuti in huiusmodo casu editi
& provisi. Quarum Litterarum domini Regis patencium ac
manucaptionis predicte predictus Thomas Malory petit quod
ipse de premissis per Curiam hic dimittatur &c Super quo visis
premissis Consideratum est quod idem Thomas Malory eat
inde sine die &c. et quod Juratores dicte Jurate in hac parte
exonerentur &c et predictus Thomas Malory remaneat in
custodia prefati Marescalli pro sufficienti securitati pacis erga
dominum Regem & cunctum populum suum inveniendo
quousque &c.

K.B. Coram Rege Roll 778 Rex m 34 Hil. 34 Hen. VI. Warr.

Juratores ad recognoscendum &c. Si Thomas Malory nuper de Fenny Newbolde in Comitatu predicto Miles alias dictus Thomas Malory de Fenny Newbold in Comitatu predicto Miles culpabilis sit de diversis feloniis, transgressionibus, insurreccionibus extortionibus unde indicatus est necne ponitur in respicium coram domino Rege usque a die Sancti Hillarie in xv dies ubicumque &c pro defectu Juratorum &c. Ideo Vicecomes habeat corpora &c. Idem dies datus prefato Thome &c. Et sciendum est quod littere inde deliberantur hic in curia Willelmo Coton deputato Willelmi Hastynges Armirgei Vicecomitis Comitatus predicti die Sabati proximo post xviija Scancti Martini isto eodem termino ad exequendas &c.

K.B. Controlment Roll 87 Michs. 36 Hen. VI m 17. London.

Thomas Malory nuper de Fenny Newbold in Comitatu Warr. Miles per Willelmum Edward & Thomam Reyner Vicomites Londonie virtute brevis domini Regis de habeas corpus eis directi coram Rege ductus cum causa videlicet, quod idem Thomas commissis fuit prisone domini Regis in Civitate Londonie per Johannem Fortescu Militem Capitalem Justiciarum domini Regis pro diversis causis coram domino Rege pendentibus & pro eo similiter quod ipse cuidem Thome Greswold condempnatus existit. Et idem Thomas Malory detentus est interim in prisona predicta pretextu cuiusdam alterius brevis domini Regis cuius tenor sequitur in hec verba — Henricus Dei gratia Rex Anglie, Francie & dominus Hibernie Vicomitibus Londonie Salutem. Quia Thomas Malory Miles in prisona nostra Marescalcie nostre coram nobis pro securitate pacis nostre erga nos & cunctum populum nostrum & percipue erga Abbatem de Combe & plures alios de ligeis nostris ac pro securitate de se bene gerendo erga nos & cunctum populum nostrum invenienda & aliis certis de causis nos specialiter moventibus detentus exitit. Nos pro maiore securitate custodie prefati Thome ipsum Thomam nuper vicecomiti nostro Middlesex com-

miserimus in prisona nostra de Neugate sub custodia ipsius
nuper vicecomitis salvo & secure excausis predictis custo-
diendum quousque aliud de eo ordinaverimus & hoc sub pena
milla librarum nullatenus omitteret. Jamque pro eo quod
predictus in Curia nostra coram nobis acceperimis quod predictus Thomas in prisona nostra de Ludgate sub custodia
vostra ex causis predictis modo existit detentus vobis preci-
pimus firmiter injungentes quod predictum Thomam in
prisona nostra salvo & secure ex causis predictis custodiatis
sub pena supradicta quousque aliud a nobis inde habuertis
in mandatis. Teste J Fortescu apud Westmonasterium xxiiij
die Januarie Anno regni nostri tricesimo quinto. Qui com-
mitatur Marescalcie &c.

[*Added later.*]

Postea die mercurie proximo post xviiia Sancti Michaelis
isto termino predictus Thomas Malory traditur in ballivum
Willelmo Nevyle domino de Fauconberge, Willelmo Briggeham de Briggeham in Comitatu Eboracie Armigero & Jo-
hanni Clerkson de Arundell in Comitatu Sussex armigero
usque crastina [Sancti] Johannis ubicumque &c. quilibet
plegiarius sub pena xxl*i* & predictus Thomas Malory sub pena
ccccl*i* sub r [?] &c. Ac de bono gestu suo &c. Ad quem diem
comparuit & commititur Marescallo tam pro securitate pacis
predicte quam de bono gestu suo &c. Aceciam pro condemp-
natione predicte &'c.

[*Added later.*]

Postea scilicet termino pasche anno regni dicti Regis trice-
simo septimo pro eo quod informatur curia hic per fidedignos
Comitatus Warr. quod dictus Thomas extra custodiam dicti
Marescalli fuit in dicto comitatu Warr. ad largum post festum
Pasche dicto termino tricesimo septimo dictum [?] est hic per
curiam prefato Marescallo quod idem Marescallus prefatum
Thomam Malory in prisona domini Regis Marescallcie domini
Regis apud Suthwerk in Comitatu Surrie custodire faceret &
non ad largum . . . permittit ipsum Thomam extra pri-
sonam [decetero ire] & hoc sub penam centum librarum &c.

[Added later.]

Et postea scilicet termino Sancti Hillari Anno regni dicti
Regis tricesimo octavo predictus Thomas Malory comittitur
custodie vicomitis Middlesex pro causis predictis in prisona
domini Regis de Nugate salvo & secure moraturi quousque
&c. Ideo dictus Marescallus de eo hic exoneratur &c.

[TRANSLATION.]

Inquisition taken at Noneton [Nuneaton] before Humfrey,
Duke of Buckingham, William Birmyngham Knt., Thomas
Bate and Thomas Greswold, Keepers of the Peace (Custodibus Pacis) of the lord the King and Justices of the same lord
the King, assigned to hear and determine divers felonies,
transgressions and misdeeds in the County of Warwick on
Monday next before the feast of St. Bartholomew the Apostle
in the twenty-ninth year of the reign of King Henry the sixth
since the Conquest, by the oaths of Richard Ablaster of
Birmyngham, John Belle of the same, John Whatcroft of
Solyhull, Roger More of the same, —— Corpeson of Bykenhull, Thomas Dounton of Seldon, Alan Gervys of Mers-
ton-Culy, Richard Orme of the same, Thomas Mylner of
Atherston, Richard Barbour of the same, Henry Blakenhale
of Sheldon, William Parker of Ath[ers]ton, William Vale of
of the same, William Ludford of Austerley, and Henry Serche
of Hurley, who say on their oath that Humfrey Duke of
Buckingham by virtue of certain commissions of our lord the
King directed to the same Duke and Richard, Earl of Warwick, to take and arrest Thomas Malory late of Fenny Newbold in County Warwick, Knight, and John Appelby, servant
of the same Thomas, by authority of such commissions, on
Sunday in the feast of St. James the Apostle in the twenty-
ninth year of King Henry the sixth after the Conquest, at
Fenny Newbold took and arrested the said Thomas Malory,
and at Coventry committed the same to William Mountford
Knt. Sheriff of the County of Warwick to keep the same
Thomas safe and secure, so that he might have the body of
the same Thomas before the lord the King and his Councell
in the quinden [fifteen days] of St. Michael next ensuing

wheresoever he might then be in England. To answer to the same lord the King of and upon divers articles in the same commission specified as well as to do and receive what shall then be ordered by the Councell aforesaid.

Upon which the said Thomas on Tuesday then next following under the custody of the said Sheriff in prison in the manor of Colshull [Coleshill], broke out of the aforesaid prison in the night of the aforesaid Tuesday and swam across the moat there thus evading the custody of the said Sheriff. And then the said Thomas Malory and John Appelby late of Fenny Newbold in the County of Warwick, Gentleman, John Sherd late of the same town and county yoman, . . . William Halle late of Stonley in the aforesaid county, yoman, John Masshot late of Fenny Newbold in the same county, grome, Roger Sherd late of the same town and county, yoman, Thomas Sherd late of the same town and county, yoman, John Tyncok late of Wolvey in the county aforesaid, husbondman, Gregory Walshal of Brynkelowe in the county aforesaid, yoman, Richard Irysshman late of the said Fenny Newbold in the aforesaid county, laborer, and Thomas Maryot late of Monks Kyrkeby in the county aforesaid, assembled with many other malefactors and breakers of the King's peace unknown, as rebels and breakers of the King's peace in the manner of an insurrection, unanimously rose, and on Wednesday then next following broke into the Monastery and Abbey of Blessed Mary of Combe and with great baulks of wood by night broke and entered divers gates and doors of the same monastery and there and then broke into two chests of the Abbot of the same monastery and one bag containing twenty-one pounds of gold and another bag containing twenty-five gold and silver marks of the goods and chattels of the said Abbot and Convent and many other jewels and ornaments of the church of the said monastery and abbey to the value of forty pounds then and there feloniously took and carried away in great destruction and spoiliation of the monastery and abbey aforesaid as well as against the peace of our lord the King, his crown and dignity.

Item, they say that Thomas Malory late of Fenny Newbold in the county of Warwick, Knight, and many other male-

factors and breakers of the King's peace unknown, to the number of twenty-six persons, armed and arrayed in warlike manner, namely, with swords, staves, glaives, bows, arrows, Jakkes, Salettes, crossebowes, on the fourth day of January in the twenty-eighth year of the reign of King Henry the sixth after the Conquest at Combe, in the woods of the Abbey of Blessed Mary of Combe aforesaid, lay in ambush to kill and murder Humfrey, Duke of Buckingham, and the same with the bows and arrows aforesaid to shoot and kill, against the peace of the said lord the King.

Item, they say that Thomas Malory, late of Fenny New-bold in the county of Warwick, Knt., Richard Malory, of Radclyff-next-Leycestre, in county Leicester, Esq., John Appulby late of Fenneneubold in county Warwick, Gentilman, John Sherd late of Fenenewbold &c., yoman, otherwise John Shoo . . . Fenenneubold, &c., William Podmore late of Fenneubold &c. yoman, William Hall, late of Stonley in county Warwick, walker [fuller], John Masshot late of Fenneneubold in county Warwick, grome, Roger Sherd late of Fenneneubold in county Warwick, yoman, otherwise Roger Shoo late of, &c., Thomas Sherd late of Fenneneubold in county Warwick, yoman, otherwise Thomas Shoo, late of &c. . . . county of Warwick, husbondman, Gregery Walshale, late of Brinkelowe in county Warwick . . . Brynkelowe in the county of Warwick, husbondman, Richard Irysshman late of Fenneneubold in . . . late of Monks Kyrkeby in the county of Warwick, bower, Thomas Leghton late of . . . Robert Smyth late of Fenneneubold in the county of Warwick, smyth, John Warr . . . Warwick, yoman, John Harper late of Fenneneubold in the county of Warwick, harper, John . . . , cook, on Thursday next after the feast of St. James the Apostle in the abovesaid twenty-ninth year of the reign of King Henry the sixth after the Conquest assembled with many other malefactors and breakers of the King's peace unknown to the number of a hundred persons arrayed in war-like manner with force and arms, namely with swords, lances, ropes, bows and arrows, entered the close and house of Rich-ard, Abbott of the monastery of Blessed Mary of Combe at

Combe in the county of Warwick in a riotous manner and broke eighteen doors of the aforesaid monastery, and then and there insulted the aforesaid Richard, the Abbot, his monks and servants and violently broke open three iron chests corded and sealed and forty pounds four shillings and fourpence in money found in divers bags and three gold rings with precious stones worth a hundred shillings and two silver signets worth six shillings and eightpence and one pair of psalters worth six shillings and eightpence two silver zones worth thirty shillings, three pairs of "preculum" — namely "bedes," one pair coral worth five shillings, another of "laumber" worth five shillings, and the third of "Jete" worth two shillings — two bows worth five shillings and three sheaves of arrowes worth six shillings of the goods and chattels of the aforesaid Abbot there found were feloniously stolen.

Item, they say that Thomas Malory late of Fenny Newbold in the county of Warwick, Knight, and John [Appelby] in the same county, gentilman, on the last day of August in the said twenty-eighth year of the reign of King Henry the sixth after the Conquest at Monkeskirkeby by threats and oppression took extortionately from John Mylner twenty shillings; and that the same Thomas Malory and John Appelby on the last day of May in the aforesaid twenty-eighth year &c. at Monkeskyrkeby aforesaid extortionately took by threats and oppression, a hundred shillings from Margaret Kyng and William Hales.

Item, they say that Thomas Malory late of Fenny Newbold in the county of Warwick, Knight, on Saturday next before the feast of Pentecost in the twenty-eighth year of the reign of King Henry the sixth after the Conquest, at Monks Kirkby broke into the close and house of Hugh Smyth, and Joan the wife of the said Hugh feloniously raped and lived carnally with.

Item, they say that Thomas Malory late of Fenny Newbold in the county of Warwick, Knight, on Thursday next after the feast of St. Peter-in-Chains in the twenty-eighth

year of the reign of King Henry the sixth &c. feloniously raped Joan the wife of Hugh Smyth at Coventry and lived carnally with the same. And that the goods and chattels of the same Hugh to the value of forty pounds then and there found he feloniously stole, took, and carried away to Barwell in the county of Leycester against the peace of our lord the King, his crown and dignity.

Item, another inquisition taken before the aforesaid Justices, the day, place, and year aforesaid, by the oath of William . . . of Dunchurch, Richard Gebons of Ulfreton, John Bynley of Rokeby [Rugby], William . . . . Thomas Halle of Lalleford, John Bemonde of Bromkote, John Herd . . . . Saunders of Bedworth, John Faukes of Radford Symly, and William . . . that Thomas Malory of Fenny Newbold in the county of Warwick, Knight, John Mas[shot], William Smyth of the same town and county, labourer, Geoffrey, Gryffyn of . . . , . . . of Carleton in the county of Leycester, yoman, and John Arnesley of Ty[?Twycross] on the 4th day of June in the said twenty-ninth year of the reign of King Henry the sixth after the Conquest at Cosford in the county of [Warwick] extortionately took seven cows, two calves, a cart worth four pounds, and three hundred and thirty-five sheep worth twenty-two pounds of the goods and chattels of William Rowe and William Dowde of Shatwell in the county of Leceyster and from thence carried them off to Newbold, against the King's peace.

BEFORE THE KING'S BENCH.

The Indictment came before our lord the King to determine after certain other causes. Wherefore it was ordered that the Sheriff should not omit, etc., and that he should take the same, etc. And now on Wednesday the 15th day of St. Hilary's Term the said Thomas Malory came before our lord the King at Westminster, brought by the Sheriffs of London by virtue of a writ of our lord the King directed to them that he should be led to the bar there in his own person (*in propria persona sua*). And having forthwith been asked, in reference

to what had gone before, if he desired to be acquitted of the premisses, he says that he is in no wise guilty thereof, and for good or ill puts himself upon his country, etc. And thereupon the said Thomas Malory was handed back to the Sheriffs for safe custody until, together with the other causes, etc. [A marginal note appears here: "Remittitur London." (Sent back to London).]

[Later notes added on the Coram Rege Roll.]

Ordered that Thomas Malory be distrained of all his goods. 2nd Feb. 30 Hen. VI.

32 Henry VI. By special grace of the Court, Thomas Malory was dismissed by the bail of Roger Chamberleynn of Quynburgh in the county of Kent, Knight, John Leventhorp of London Esq., Edward FitzWilliam of Framlyngham in the county of Suffolk Esq., Thomas Juce of the county of Essex Esq., Ralph Worthyngton of Franlyngham in the county of Suffolk Gentleman, Edward Whetely of London Gent., and John Hathwyk of Herbury in the county of Warwick Gent., who have mainprision of his body.

On Friday next after the 18th of St. Hilary, 34 Henry VI, Thomas Malory was in the Court committed to the custody of the Marshal. And there Thomas Malory proffered Letters Patent bearing date at Westminster the 24th of November 34 Henry VI by which the King had pardoned the said Thomas for all felonies and transgressions committed by him before the 9th July 33 Henry VI. And Roger Malory of Ryton, Warwickshire Gent., John Besford of London Gent., William Clyffe of London Gent., Walter Boys of London Sadler, Thomas Pulton of London Taillour and David John of London Taillour went bail for Thomas Malory that he would bear himself well towards the King and all people. And Thomas Malory remains in the custody of the Marshal until sufficient security be found.

[Here a marginal note (in Latin) appears: "Letters Patent allowed. *Sine die.*"]

APPENDIX II

Chanc. Inq. P.M. Edw. IV, File 75, No. 46.

Inquisition taken at Northampton in the county of Northampton on Tuesday in the Feast of St. James the Apostle in
the 20th year of the reign of King Edward the Fourth after
the Conquest before Thomas Haselwode Escheator of the
said lord the King in the county aforesaid, by virtue of a writ
of the lord the King to the same escheator directed and by
this inquisition made, by the oaths of John Fosbroke, Gentyl-
man, John Alyn of Grendon, John Sma . . . of Earles Barton,
Edward Berwyk of Whissheton, John Adam of Chadeston,
William Nell of Dodington Parva, Richard Ketull of Earles
Baton, John Smythe of Wollaston, Richard Julyan of Wen-
dlyngburgh, John Hayne of the same, Thomas North of the
same, Thomas Fysher of Dodyngton Magna, Thomas Bar-
nard of the same, William Chery of Tukone and William
Wythinale of the same. Who say on their oath that Elizabeth Malory, late the wife of Thomas Malory Knight in
the said writ named, was seized in her demesne as of free
hold for term of her life, the day on which she died, of one
messuage, one virgate of land with appurtenances in Wynwyke in the county aforesaid. Which certain messuage and
virgate of land with appurtenances is held of the King in chief
by Knight Service namely, in the fourth part of one knights
fee, as of the said King's Honour of Peverell. And they say
that the said messuage and land are worth yearly besides
deductions, xxs. And further the aforesaid Jurors say that
the reversion of the said messuage and lands discends to
Nicholas Malory as kinsman and heir of Thomas Malory late
husband of the said Elizabeth, namely, son of Robert, son of
the aforesaid Thomas and Elizabeth. And the aforesaid
Jurors say that the aforesaid Elizabeth died on the first day
of October last past. And that the aforesaid Nicholas Malory
is kinsman and next heir of the said Elizabeth, namely, son of
Robert, son of the aforesaid Thomas and Elizabeth. And the

aforesaid Jurors say that the aforesaid Nicholas Malory is aged fourtenn years and more. And besides the aforsaid Jurors say that the said Elizabeth was seized in her demesne as of free hold for term of her life, on the day she died, of the manner of Wynwyke with appurtenances in the county aforesaid the reversion of the said manor descends to the abovenamed Nicholas Malory as kinsman and heir of the aforesaid Thomas, namely, son of Robert son of the aforesaid Thomas. And they say of whom the aforesaid manor with appurtenances is held and by what service they do not know. And the said Jurors say that the aforesaid manor with appurtenances is worth x*li*. a year besides deductions and the said Elizabeth did not hold any more lands &c. in the county aforesaid of the said lord the King or of any other on the day she died. On testimony of which things the abovenamed escheator and aforesaid Jurors have alternatively placed their seals the day and year abovesaid.

Inquisition taken at Ruyton upon Dunnesmore in the county of Warwick on Thursday after the feast of St. James the Apostle in the 20th year of the reign of King Edward IV before William Bristowe Escheator of the said Lord the King in the county aforesaid, by virtue of a writ of the said lord the King of "diem clausit extremum" to the said Escheator directed, by this inquisition made, by the oaths of William Durant Gentilman Thomas Desert Gentilman, Nicholas Croke of Stokton, William Westley of Eythorp, Richard Gode of Stretton, John Thurkyll of the same, John Bynley of the same, Thomas Robyns of Brokhurst, John Smart of the same, Henry Carpenter, William Howet of Rokeby, John Bykley of the same, John Newcombe of Brynkelowe, John . . . of Palyington, Jurors. Who say on their oath that Elizabeth who was the wife of Thomas Malory Knight in the said writ named was seized, the day she died, in her demesne as of free hold for term of her life of the manor of Newbold Fenne otherwise called Newbold Ryvell with all its appurtenances in the county aforesaid with reversion therof, after the death of the said Elizabeth, to Nicholas Malory, kinsman and heir of the aforesaid Thomas Malory, namely, son of

Robert Malory, son of the aforesaid Thomas Malory Knight and his heir. And they say that the said manor is held of Richard, Duke of York and Norfolk and Anne his wife as of right of the said Anne, daughter and heir of John late Duke of Norfolk deceased, by the service of one knights fee. Which Anne is under age and in the guardianship of the aforenamed lord the King, and holds the said manor of the said lord the King in chief by service of one knight's fee. The same Jurors say that the said manor with appurtenances . . . besides deductions, vj*li*. xiij*s*. viij*d*. And further the aforesaid Jurors say that the said Elizabeth in the said writ named died on the last day of September last past. And that the aforesaid Nicholas Malory is . . . and heir of the aforesaid Elizabeth namely a son of Robert, son of the aforesaid Thomas Malory and Elizabeth and is aged xiij years and more. And that the aforesaid Elizabeth in the said writ named did not hold any more lands or tenements in the county . . . of the lord the King nor of any other on the said day on which she died. In witness of which things to this indented inquisition as well the said Escheator as the aforesaid Jurors have placed their seals. Given the day and . . . abovesaid.

Inquisition taken at Lutterworth in the county of Leicester on Tuesday next after the feast of St. Anne in the 20th year of the reign of King Edward the IV, before William Bristowe Escheator of the said lord the King in the county aforesaid, by virtue of a writ of the said lord the King of "diem clausit extremum" to the same Escheator directed and by this inquisition made, by the oaths of William Wolman of Lutterworth, Robert Welyams of the same, Ralph Brakley of the same, William Thorpe of Misterton, John Tebot of the same, John Smyth of the same, Richard Hellowes of Walcott, Thomas Chapman of the same, William Lastell of the same, Thomas Wale of the same, John Campyon of the same, John Carter, Thomas Hande of Shawell, William Tidman of Lutterworth, Robert Roberdes of Swynford, Thomas Mariot of the same, John Gibbe of Swynford and Henry Sharpe of the same, Jurors. Who say on their oath that Elizabeth who was the wife of Thomas Malory Knight in the writ named was seized, the day she died, in her demesne as of free hold for

term of her life of the manor of Swynnerford with appurtenances in the county aforesaid. And of one messuage and two virgates of land with appurtenances in Stormefeld in the same county, with reversion thereof . . . Elizabeth . . . Malory kinsman and heir of the said Thomas Malory namely, son of Robert Malory son of the aforesaid Thomas Malory Knight and his heir. And they say that the manor aforesaid is worth in all issues besides deductions iiij marks a year. And the said messuage and lands in Stormefield are worth in all issues besides deductions xxvj*s.* viij*d.* yearly. But of whom or by what service the manor, messuages and lands aforesaid are held or any part of them is held the Jurors do not know. And moreover the same Jurors say on their oaths that the aforesaid Elizabeth in the said writ named died on the last day of September last past. And that the aforesaid Nicholas Malory is kinsman and heir of the aforesaid Elizabeth namely, son of Robert son of the aforesaid Thomas Malory and Elizabeth and is aged xiij years and more. And that the aforenamed Elizabeth in the said writ named did not hold any more lands or tenements in the county aforesaid of the lord the King, or any other on the day she died, in the county aforesaid. In witness of which things to this indented inquisition as well the abovenamed Escheator as the aforesaid Jurors have placed their seals. Given the day and year abovesaid.

INDEX

INDEX

DAN KURZMAN, a former foreign correspondent for *The Washington Post*, is the author of ten previous books and the winner of five major literary and journalistic awards. He won the Overseas Press Club's Cornelius Ryan Award for the best book on foreign affairs for *Miracle of November: Madrid's Epic Stand 1936* and for *Subversion of the Innocents*; the George Polk Memorial Award for articles that formed the basis for his book *Santo Domingo: Revolt of the Damned*; the National Jewish Book Award for *Ben-Gurion: Prophet of Fire*; and the Newspaper Guild's Front Page Award for dispatches he wrote from Cuba.

Mr. Kurzman has written or broadcast from almost every country in Europe, Asia, Africa, the Middle East, and Latin America. Before joining *The Washington Post*, he served as Paris correspondent for the International News Service, as Jerusalem correspondent for NBC News, and as Tokyo bureau chief of the McGraw-Hill News Service.